Echoes From Gettysburg:

South Carolina's Memories and Images

To Larry,

Hope you enjoy
these soldiers' stories!

All the best,

J. Keith Ra~~

Books by J. Keith Jones

In Due Time (2010)

The Boys of Diamond Hill:
The Lives and Civil War Letters of the Boyd Family of Abbeville County,
South Carolina (2011)

Georgia Remembers Gettysburg (2013)

Echoes From Gettysburg:

South Carolina's Memories and Images

J. Keith Jones

FOX RUN
PUBLISHING
QUALITY PUBLISHING ONE BOOK AT A TIME

Publisher's Cataloging-in-Publication
(Provided by Quality Books, Inc.)
   Jones, J. Keith, 1964- author.
      Echoes from Gettysburg : South Carolina's memories
   and images / J. Keith Jones.
      pages cm
      Includes bibliographical references and index.
      LCCN 2016910214
      ISBN-13: 978-1-945602-00-9 (hard cover)
      ISBN-10: 1-945602-00-7 (hard cover)
      ISBN-13: 978-1-945602-01-6 (trade paperback)
      ISBN-10: 1-945602-01-5 (trade paperback)

      1. Gettysburg, Battle of, Gettysburg, Pa., 1863.
   2. United States--History--Civil War, 1861-1865--Personal
   narratives, Confederate. 3. South Carolina--History--
   Civil War, 1861-1865. 4. Soldiers--South Carolina--
   History--19th century. 5. Confederate States of
   America. Army.   I. Title.

      E475.53.J665 2016   973.7'349
                                 QBI16-1214

Maps by Philip Laino are from his Gettysburg Campaign Atlas courtesy of Gettysburg Publishing.

Cover design by OctagonLab - http://octagonlab.com/
Cover images courtesy of the Library of Congress

Published by
Fox Run Publishing LLC
2966 South Church Street, #305
Burlington, NC 27215
http://www.foxrunpub.com/

For Melissa

Also dedicated to the memory of Thomas Curtwright Jones, my 3x great uncle and a Gettysburg veteran of the 2nd South Carolina. Another is a man I am not related to, but feel like I knew, Daniel Boyd of the 7th South Carolina, a man from Diamond Hill in Abbeville County. He was wounded on the Rose Farm and later paroled from DeCamp General Hospital on David's Island in New York.

Thomas Curtwright Jones was part of a family that had three generations of soldiers at the front. Along with all of his brothers, his father and eldest nephew had been soldiers in the Confederate army earlier in the war. Jones was included in the surrender of Johnston's army in North Carolina.

(the author's collection)

Acknowledgements

There are a number of people, as with any book, that played a part in bringing this work into print. First of all, I want to thank my wife. Without her, my efforts would be much less effective. The same goes to my daughter and other members of my family, particularly my brother Mike. His lifelong support is appreciated. Lauren and Moe Dunn, thank you for your friendship and occasional place of refuge. Steven Campbell, I learn so much each time we speak. My writer friends, Michael Hardy, Lynn Salsi, Joe Owen, Richard McCaslin and Eric Wittenberg, I would like to thank for their friendship, encouragement and knowledge. Eric Wittenberg was particularly helpful with proof reading and fact checking of this work.

I want to thank Bill Smedlund for providing and pointing out additional sources included in this book. Family members of some of the soldiers represented here also contributed information and photographs. The Davis and Wilson Libraries at the University of North Carolina, the Cooper and South Caroliniana Libraries at the University of South Carolina, the Rubenstein Rare Book and Manuscript Library at Duke University and the Museum and Library of Confederate History in Greenville, South Carolina all helped with sources and facilities. Michael Couch and Jack Marlar of the Museum in Greenville deserve particular thanks for all their support.

One person who always deserves thanks for her help is Sharon Strout. Her tireless efforts at transcribing and interpreting faded and smudged newsprint makes my life and work much easier. I hope I never forget to thank her for all the help and friendship.

There are always more people that deserve thanks than are remembered, so to anyone I may have overlooked, I send a hearty thanks for helping make this work come to life.

Table of Contents

Sketch of Kershaw's Brigade attacking the line of the federal 3rd Corps' 1st Division 2nd Brigade commanded by Col. John Henry Hobart Ward of New York on July 2. London born artist Alfred R. Waud drew this for Harper's Magazine.

~ *Section 1* ~

Kershaw's Brigade

General Joseph Brevard Kershaw
(Library of Congress)

Introduction:
Kershaw's Brigade

The brigade of Brig. Gen. Joseph Kershaw marched into Pennsylvania with 2,183 fighting men organized into five regiments and one battalion. Considered one of the most stable brigades in the Confederate army, Brig. Gen. Milledge Luke Bonham was its original commander, beginning with the First Battle of Manassas. Bonham resigned his commission on January 27, 1862 to accept a seat in the Confederate House of Representatives from South Carolina's Fourth District, which was the same district he had represented in the United States Congress from 1857 until the state seceded in 1860. After Bonham's resignation, brigade command passed to Joseph Kershaw, commander of the 2nd South Carolina Infantry.[1]

The brigade was a mixture of men cutting across the social strata of South Carolina and of all occupations. They forged a great reputation by participating in the many hard fights in Lee's Army of Northern Virginia. They cleared Maryland Heights, which over-looked Harper's Ferry, during the Maryland Campaign and held the position behind the stone wall on Mayre's Heights which withstood charge after charge from Gen. Ambrose Burnside's forces at the Battle of Fredericksburg.[2]

General Joseph Brevard Kershaw had much in common with his predecessor Bonham: both were lawyers, politicians and veterans of the

1. Gottfried, Bradley M. Brigades of Gettysburg: The Union and Confederate Brigades at the Battle of Gettysburg. Cambridge, MA: Da Capo, 2002. 403-04. Print; "BONHAM, Milledge Luke - Biographical Information." BONHAM, Milledge Luke. U.S. House of Representatives, n.d. Web. 20 June 2015.
2. Gottfried, 404; Wyckoff, Mac. "Kershaw's Brigade at Gettysburg." Gettysburg Magazine 5 (1991): 35. Print.

Mexican War. Kershaw came from solid patriot stock, growing up in Camden, South Carolina. Kershaw's early years were not easy. Despite being from a prominent family, he was orphaned at the age of seven. He rose above this, studied law, and then set up a legal practice with James Pope Dickinson. Both partners volunteered for service in the Mexican War and Kershaw became 1st Lieutenant in the local company, which was known as the DeKalb Rifle Guards. Dickinson was killed during the Battle of Churubusco. Kershaw became deathly ill with a fever while in Mexico and was sent home. Later, Kershaw was part of the Secession Convention, which voted to withdraw from the Union in 1860. He helped form the 2nd South Carolina Infantry and was elected its original colonel.[3]

The forty-one-year-old Kershaw was a popular officer. His division commander, Maj. Gen. Lafayette McLaws described him as "a very cool, judicious and gallant gentleman."[4]   The rest of the brigade's regiments were commanded by a complement of solid and respected officers. Col. John Doby Kennedy, a fellow Camden lawyer and friend of Kershaw, commanded the 2nd South Carolina. Col. James Drayton Nance, commander of the 3rd South Carolina, was recovering from a wound he received on Mayre's Heights at the Battle of Fredericksburg and did not rejoin the regiment until the last day of the battle. For the first two days of the battle, Maj. Robert Clayton Maffett commanded the 3rd. Col. David Wyatt Aiken, an educator, newspaper editor and leading authority on agriculture, commanded the 7th South Carolina. Col. John Williford Henagan, long-time sheriff of Marlboro, commanded the 8th South Carolina. Col. William Davie DeSaussure, the officer with the most military experience of any man in the brigade, commanded the 15th South Carolina. DeSaussure was a veteran of the Mexican War and was serving as a captain on the western frontier at the outbreak of the war. Lt. Col. William George Rice of Laurens District commanded the 3rd South Carolina Battalion.[5] Capt. D. Augustus Dickert described Kershaw's staff as "young men of unequalled [sic] ability, tireless, watchful, and brave to a fault."[6]

3. Gottfried 404; Dickert, D. Augustus. History of Kershaw's Brigade. Newberry, SC: Elbert H. Aull, 1899. 87. Print.
4. Wyckoff, 35.
5. Wyckoff, 35-36.
6. Dickert, 223.

Kershaw's men were impressed with the landscape of Pennsylvania, but less impressed with the women. One soldier wrote that Pennsylvania "has [some] of the finest land in it in the world and some of the ugliest women that I ever saw." Corporal Tally Simpson of the 3rd South Carolina wrote, "I saw a great many young ladies, but none very pretty." In fairness, they may have been put off by the coolness with which they were met. Lieutenant Colonel Franklin Gaillard of the 2nd South Carolina noted that many of the women wore U.S. flags on their smocks and "held their noses and made faces" at the soldiers.[7]

The brigade crossed the Potomac River on June 26, 1863 after marching through a morning thunderstorm. The band played "Maryland, My Maryland" and the men sang "All Quiet On The Potomac Tonight." Spirits were high and the men were awarded extra whiskey in Williamsport from a large quantity confiscated by the Confederate army earlier. They proceeded through Hagerstown, Middleburg and Greencastle before camping five miles from Chambersburg the evening of June 27.[8]

They stayed there until June 30, when they broke camp and marched east to Fayetteville, about twenty miles west of Gettysburg. On July 1, they were placed behind Anderson's and Johnson's divisions as well as the 2nd Corps' wagon trains, so they did not begin their march toward the battlefield until 4:00 p.m. At midnight they halted within two miles of Gettysburg. During the march, Captain Robert Pulliam of the 2nd South Carolina remarked on the sound of cannon fire, "Boys, that sounds familiar." They rested that night – after halting about 2:00 a.m. near a large house sheltering the wounded from Hill's 3rd Corps.[9]

McLaws' column was to depart about 4:00 a.m. on July 2, with Kershaw's brigade in the lead. The South Carolinians waited and did not march until sunrise. The column turned right at the eastern edge of Herr Ridge and marched through open woods after a two-hour rest. They arrived at a hill that overlooked the town, and then halted until noon.[10]

They then proceeded to Bream's Hill just beyond the Black Horse Tavern and halted again. After McLaws and Longstreet personally

7. Gottfried, 404.
8. Wyckoff, 38.
9. Gottfried, 405; Wyckoff, 40.
10. Gottfried, 405; Wyckoff, 40.

reconnoitered the situation, the Confederates turned around and countermarched to the previous hill. They then continued on to a road along Willoughby Run to the schoolhouse beyond Pitzer's Woods and then turned left toward the Emmitsburg Road and the Peach Orchard. The South Carolinians halted in the woods shy of the Peach Orchard and deployed behind a stone wall. Many of the troops rested or slept, but Augustus Dickert recounted how several of them walked approximately one hundred yards to an opening in the woods. They had no idea how famous the ordinary looking Peach Orchard and the two picturesque round hills lying out before them would soon become. They quickly returned to their unit when they were "sharply called back" for exposing themselves to the enemy.[11]

William Wallace began the war as Captain of Co. C, 2nd S.C. Infantry. Brig. Gen. Joseph Kershaw promoted him to major on June 3, 1863. At the time of the surrender he was the Colonel of the regiment.

(History of Kershaw's Brigade)

Kershaw provided great detail about what he saw from the woods in his report of the battle. He said that he "found [the enemy] to be in superior force in the orchard, supported by artillery, with a main line of battle intrenched in the rear and extending to and upon the rocky mountain to his left far beyond the point at which his flank had supposed to rest." He requested a modification to his orders, telling McLaws that carrying out his orders as issued "would have been, if successful in driving him from the orchard, to present my own right and rear to a large portion of his line of battle." McLaws and Longstreet sent several messages back adjusting the orders based on Kershaw's observations.[12]

11. Report of Brig. Gen. J. B. Kershaw, O.R.-- SERIES I--VOLUME XXVII/2 [S# 44] ; Wyckoff, 40.
12. OR Kershaw.

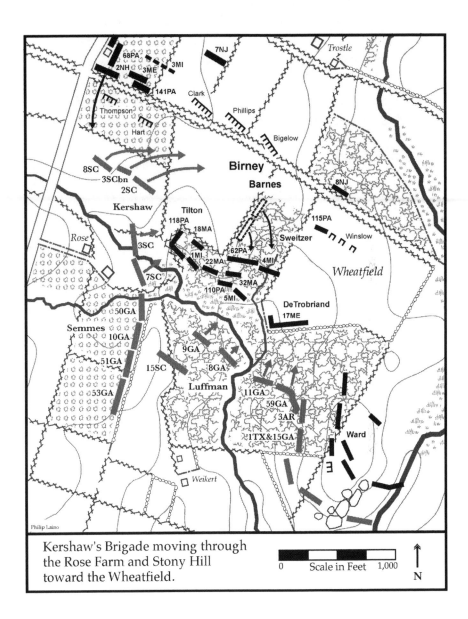

Kershaw's Brigade moving through
the Rose Farm and Stony Hill
toward the Wheatfield.

0   Scale in Feet   1,000

N

Kershaw formed his men behind the stone wall. A battery of artillery took position along the Millerstown Road parallel to Kershaw's projected attack trajectory to support his attack. Skirmishers under Maj. William Wallace of the 2nd S. C. engaged the Federals near the Emmitsburg Road. Kershaw laid out his line with the 8th S. C. on the far left beside Alexander's Artillery Battalion. Then came the 3rd Battalion, 2nd, 3rd, 7th then Cabell's Artillery Battalion with the 15th S. C. on the far right of the line.[13]

Kershaw ordered his brigade to advance across the Rose Farm and wheel left to assault the Stony Hill. As he did this, Hood's Division would attack the Federals on his right and Barksdale's Brigade would attack on his left. The Georgia brigade of Brig. Gen. Paul Jones Semmes was positioned behind Kershaw in support. They were to commence the attack after a signal of three individual guns firing in sequence from Cabell's Battalion, which indicated that Hood's men were engaging the enemy. The signal was to take place at 4:00 p.m., but it did not come until about 5:00 p.m.[14]

As the men rose up to prepare to attack just before the signal guns boomed, the color sergeant of the 7th S. C. – Sgt. A. D. Clark – prematurely unfurled the flag, drawing artillery fire directed at the color guard. Two of the 7th's color guard were killed and three wounded. Once the signal guns boomed, Kershaw called out the order, "for-ward." According to Dickert, the men "sprang to their work with a will and determination and spread their steps to the right and left as they advanced. Kershaw was on foot, prepared to follow the line of battle immediately in rear, looking cool, composed and grand, his steel-gray eyes flashing the fire he felt in his soul." As they moved out, a shell exploded amongst two companies of the 8th S. C. wounding sixteen men as well as taking off the right leg of Capt. Thomas E. Powe of Company C. The line hesitated until Powe shouted "forward boys – forward." A comrade wrote of the highly esteemed officer, "No one, perhaps in his regiment possessed so completely the respect and love, both of his superiors and inferiors, as did Captain Powe." The South Carolina College graduate and lawyer later died in Gettysburg of his wound on July 22.[15]

13. Wyckoff, 40; Gottfried, 405.
14. Gottfried, 405-406.
15. Wyckoff, 41; Dickert, 238.

Kershaw and his staff proceeded on foot because of the obstructions and rough terrain. As they advanced, Longstreet accompanied Kershaw, jointly leading the charge until they reached the Emmitsburg Road. At that point, Longstreet wished them well and headed back toward Seminary Ridge. Kershaw understood that Barksdale was to step off at the same time, but heard his drums signaling their movement, meaning that they did not coordinate their attacks as planned, Kershaw was stunned, realizing that his left, the 8th S. C., was completely unsupported and vulnerable to attack. Kershaw knew his original plan had to be altered or the artillery batteries on his flank would destroy his line. Kershaw shifted his left wing away from the original target, the Stony Hill, and instead sent them against the Federal batteries shelling them from the Peach Orchard. The brave South Carolinians advanced under a costly heavy fire of canister and spherical case. Lieutenant Alex McNeill of the 2nd S. C. said it was "the most terrible fire to which they ever were exposed."[16]

The right wing continued toward the Stony Hill, as the left wing advanced to within one hundred yards without firing a shot. John Coxe of the 2nd S. C. wrote that they moved "in perfect order and with the precision of a brigade drill," and that on each side of him his comrades "were stricken down by grape and canister." He believed "that none could escape." On the right, the 3rd S. C. advanced between the Rose barn and Rose farmhouse on its left flank while the 7th marched to the right side of the house, causing the 7th to surge ahead of the 3rd. Kershaw ordered the 3rd to move by the right flank. It was later speculated that this same order was mistakenly relayed to the 2nd S. C. on the left flank, as it also advanced upon the Federal artillery. This shift slowed the Palmetto men down, causing many casualties.[17]

Lt. Col. Gaillard wrote that because of that movement, "we were in ten minutes or less, terribly butchered... I saw half a dozen at a time knocked up and flung to the ground like trifles..." He graphically continued, "parts of their heads shot away, legs shattered, arms torn off, etc." Surviving members of the 2nd took shelter in a depression that a Federal cannon was already sighted in on, making matters worse for them. Others simply lay down and fired on the artillerymen with great effect.[18]

16. Gottfried, 406; Wyckoff, 41.
17. Gottfried, 406; Wyckoff, 42.
18. Gottfried, 407.

The right wing of the brigade, meanwhile, had more success. After driving the Federals back and reaching the Stony Hill between the Peach Orchard and the Wheatfield, they opened fire on the Union batteries in the Peach Orchard. To cover a gap exposing his right flank, Kershaw ordered the right flank of the 7th to curl its right back, which took advantage of the cover offered by the Rose Woods. At this time, Brig. Gen. George T. Anderson's Georgia Brigade pushed through to help protect this area because the troops on the Stony Hill faced a new threat from the division of Federal Brig. Gen. John C. Caldwell, which had marched south into the Wheatfield.[19]

Brig. Gen. Samuel K. Zook's federals attacked the left wing on the Stony Hill, Anderson's Georgians were being threatened by Col. John R Brooke's Brigade and the Irish Brigade under Col. Patrick Kelly, who were moving toward a ravine that could place them in Kershaw's right rear. Kershaw sought reinforcements, riding across the field to beseech Brig. Gen. Paul J. Semmes to hurry forward with his Georgians. The 15th South Carolina had gotten separated from the rest of Kershaw's Brigade and was now with Semmes. The 15th now advanced on Semmes' right, and Kershaw watched as his most experienced regimental commander, Col. DeSaussure fell, shot through the breast after passing a mock-orange hedge and was at a point about forty yards west of the stone wall. Kershaw personally oversaw the transfer of command to Maj. William M. Gist., the younger brother of Brig. Gen. States Rights Gist and the son of a former governor of South Carolina. Once this was accomplished, Kershaw returned to the Stony Hill.[20]

Kershaw gladly received other help. Barksdale's Mississippians had appeared on his left, connecting with the 8th South Carolina and the 3rd South Carolina Battalion, which were then moving against the Federals in the Peach Orchard. The Mississippians attacked Graham's Brigade from the west while the South Carolinians hit them from the south, crumbling the enemy's line. Kershaw made no attempt to mask his anger toward Gen. Barksdale in his after-action report, declaring, "this brigade [Barksdale's] then moved so far to the left as no longer to afford me any assistance."[21]

19. Wyckoff, 42.
20. Wyckoff, 42, 44.
21. Gottfried, 407; O.R, Kershaw.

Zook's brigade and the Irish Brigade, a force more than double the size of the 7th and 3rd, now assaulted Kershaw's right wing on the Stony Hill. Zook engaged them to the front while the Irish Brigade assaulted the right flank of the 7th. As this attack commenced, Kershaw was returning to the Stony Hill. He commented that he "may never have been in a hotter place" and refused his right flank, bending it back further to give it greater strength. A gap between the 7th South Carolina on Kershaw's right and Anderson's Georgians still existed, allowing this enemy movement. Lt. Col. Elbert Bland, a popular officer, former surgeon, and Mexican War veteran, commanded the right of the 7th. Bland fell with a wound to his thigh, but refused to leave the field. The Carolinians hung onto their position despite paying a high price.[22]

During this fighting, the color guard for the 7th and the 3rd regiments were particularly hard hit. All members of the color guard for the 7th were wiped out, with Cpl. Thomas Harling being the last to fall, shot in the head. After four different color bearers were shot down, someone called out for them to lower the colors. Responding, Sgt. William Lamb grabbed the flag and waved it more fervently, proclaiming, "This flag never goes down until I am down."[23]

Kershaw rode back to urge Semmes to bring his men forward. Before he could reach the Georgians, Kershaw saw Semmes fall from his horse with a mortal wound. Although desperately wounded, Semmes was aware enough to transfer command and order that the brigade advance to support the South Carolinians.[24]

The 7th traded volleys with the Irish Brigade, which kept pouring into the hundred-yard gap between Kershaw's right and the left of the 50th Georgia. Kershaw said that the enemy continued closing until the troops of the 7th were only thirty paces away. In response, the 7th continued to refuse the line until the two flanks of Kershaw's men on the Stony Hill were nearly touching. The 15th South Carolina arrived, but Semmes' men separated them from the rest of Kershaw's men.[25]

22. Wyckoff, 44; Gottfried, 407; Jones, J. Keith. "The Boys of Diamond Hill: The Lives and Civil War Letters of the Boyd Family of Abbeville County, South Carolina". Jefferson, NC: McFarland, 2011. 107. Print.
23. Dickert, 241.
24. Gottfried, 407.
25. Gottfried, 408.

In the Peach Orchard, to the left, the 8th South Carolina and the 3rd Battalion had silenced the Federal artillery, bringing much needed relief to the 2nd South Carolina. With the 2nd no longer pinned down, Kershaw ordered it to support his right flank. Unfortunately, they did't arrive in time, as the pressure on the 7th became so severe, with the Union troops having "swung around and lapped" the whole line of the 7th. Responding, Kershaw ordered Col. Aiken to withdraw his men to the stone wall and reform there, in the rear of the Rose Farm, two hundred yards to the right of their current position.[26]

The 2nd attempted to come to the relief of the 3rd, which was moving into the woods east of the Peach Orchard. The 2nd planned to move to the left of the 3rd. They were near, but were unable to connect with the 3rd, which was now in danger of being cut off. Kershaw ordered them back to the Rose Farm with the 7th. If the 3rd had held out a few moments longer, it might not have had to retreat, as Brig. William Wofford's Georgia Brigade advanced through the Peach Orchard to their aid. Wofford rode up the Wheatfield Road and urged the 2nd South Carolina to fall in with his men and renew the attack. Kershaw's left wing joined Wofford's Georgians, and the combined commands forced Caldwell's Second Corps division from the Stony Hill and back across the Wheatfield. Semmes' men and the 15th South Carolina fell in behind Wofford along the way. The Georgians and South Carolinians flooded into the Wheatfield, crushing Sweitzer's Brigade near the southern end of the Wheatfield. They then poured into the remaining two small brigades of Romeyn Ayres' Fifth Corps division, quickly turning Ayres' flank and driving his men out of the Wheatfield as well. The victorious Confederates now controlled the Wheatfield from Plum Run to the east to the Wheatfield Road to the north.[27]

The Yankees retreated and rallied on Little Round Top. Sweitzer's Brigade moved back into the Wheatfield to counter the Confederate movement, but was nearly destroyed as a result. Kershaw's men captured two Union flags in the process of again crushing the federals. Col. Harrison Jeffords of the 4th Michigan used his sword on the South Carolinians while

26. Gottfried, 408; Wyckoff, 44.
27. Wyckoff, 45.

trying to protect his flag, only to have it wrenched from his hands and his body bayoneted. Burbank's Regular brigade also ventured into the fray and met a similar fate as Sweitzer's. The Confederates of Kershaw, Wofford and Anderson were exhausted, but pressed on toward Little Round Top.[28]

Only darkness finally halted the Confederate attack. Col. Gaillard noted that the bullets "literally came down upon us as thick as hailstones" from the doubled lines of Federals above them. Kershaw's men rallied back at the stone wall on the Rose Farm again, where their fighting on the second day ended.[29]

Later that night, they moved to the left of the Peach Orchard, where they remained until noon on July 3, when he reoccupied his previous position near the Rose Farm. That afternoon, they moved to connect with the right wing of Hood's Division, which was being attacked by Brig. Gen. Elon J. Farnsworth's Federal cavalry brigade.[30]

The brigade lost 649 soldiers in the battle plus 28 surgeons, nurses and cooks who were left behind to tend to the wounded after the Army of Northern Virginia began its retreat after the battle. The brigade's officer corps sustained particularly heavy casualties, including two colonels, one lieutenant colonel, two acting lieutenant colonels, one major, one acting major, two adjutants, thirteen captains, and fifty-one lieutenants. The 2nd South Carolina was hardest hit of all. Unofficial sources list its losses as 181, or about 52 percent of its strength. Its colonel, major and adjutant numbered among the wounded. Company E, from Gen. Kershaw's hometown of Camden, brought forty men to the fight and left with only four standing.[31]

28. Gottfried, 409.
29. Gottfried, 409; Wyckoff, 45.
30. Gottfried, 409.
31. Wyckoff, 46.

Chapter 1
2nd South Carolina Infantry

THE SUMTER WATCHMAN AND SOUTHRON
SUMTER, SOUTH CAROLINA
JULY 4, 1882

THE SECOND REGIMENT

A Chapter in the History of Kershaw's Brigade—The Flag Furled

----

Maj. C[harles] Kerrison, Jr., in Charleston Weekly News

THE CHARGE AT GETTYSBURG

As the order to forward is issued to the line, the artillery ceases, a calm comes, only to be banished by the carnage to follow. With rifles at the 'right shoulder shift,' the march common time, the infantry advances in steady column. The storm breaks. Shrieking, crushing, tearing, comes the artillery fire. Grape, canister, shell and minnies from the Federals heap their destruction upon the devoted Confederates. Yet steady, onward, without firing a gun till the charge. Many a brave fellow bit the dust long before the regiment opened. The bravery and courage exhibited were almost superhuman. Color-bearers were shot down one after another. In one instance, which may have been the case of many others, the color-bearer, a gallant youthful looking boy, when the order was given rally on the colors, in anticipation of his death, pushed his staff in the ground, and when struck by the death-dealing Minnie, his colors were there on which his battalion rallied and dressed. Charge after charge, but impossible. Two

John Doby Kennedy began the war as the 21-year-old Captain of Co. E of the 2nd S. C. Infantry. At the time of Gettysburg, Kennedy was the Colonel of the 2nd S.C. By the end of the war, he was promoted to brigadier general.

(History of Kershaw's Brigade)

captured guns were rolled off by two members of the Second, but of no avail, for the devastating fire soon leaves them intact. The very dust around the feet, from the grape and canister, rises as if from a Sirocco.

Pictures of battlefields may be vivid, but what is the reality? Many a gallant command swept forward only to destruction. When the pall of night came to close the bloody scene the army thought unsuccessful, was not defeated. The heroic spirit, the confidence was still unimpaired. One company of the Second South Carolina entered the fight with twenty-three men, at night but five remained; and that is the history of many.

After Gettysburg and the re-crossing of the Potomac, the command fell back at Culpeper, remaining nearly all summer. In the fall, under its corps commander, was ordered to join Bragg's army, participating in the battle of Chickamauga, after which, with the detached command of Gen. Longstreet in the fight at Knoxville and Beans' Station; after this going into winter quarters till the movements of Gen. Lee command our return to the mother Army of Northern Virginia.

* * *

FAIRFIELD NEWS HERALD
WINNSBORO, SOUTH CAROLINA
JUNE 30, 1897

Some Valuable Relics

A short time ago Mr. Severs, of Charlotte, sent to Mrs. L. C. Gaillard a portfolio prayer book and pocket dictionary which he has had in his possession for over thirty years. These books were the property of Corporal T. Edmund Gaillard [Company I, 2nd S. C.] and were picked up on the field by Mr. Severs after the battle of Gettysburg; Corporal Gaillard received in this battle the wound from which he died three months after. After this battle Mr. Severs and Mr. Gaillard were both taken prisoners and Mr. Severs was detailed by the Federal surgeon to take charge of some of the wounded, and Corporal Gaillard was one of the men under his care. After Mr. Gaillard's death, which occurred in October, Mr. Severs took the books, hoping to deliver them to the family of the dead soldier. During the rest of the war these books were carried by Mr. Severs, and ever since the close of the war he had tried to find the rightful owner but succeeded only a short time ago. These sad relics of her dead son were of course gladly received by the mother of Corporal Gaillard and she feels grateful to Mr. Severs for keeping them for so many long years.

* * *

ATLANTA JOURNAL
ATLANTA, GEORGIA
JULY 27, 1901

The Battle of Gettysburg
July 2, 1863
By William A. Johnson
[Private to Lieutenant Company F, Second South Carolina Infantry]

I went into the Confederate Army at the age of 21 years, and I was a brimful of hatred for the Yanks that I ran away from college, and this, too, against the wishes of my teachers and my father. My mother did not object, as she was a real Southern woman when it came to fighting Yankees. My father was more conservative and had his heart set on my education. He was the best man I ever knew, but I was so full of fight and fire that it even led me to disregard the wishes of those I loved, and I went. To my youthful mind war came first and love of all kinds came second in my estimation, I was full of impulse, and that often passes muster for "sense." So in that day and time I got lots of credit for sense when I ran away and went to war; and I am glad I went, as I feel that it is always right to stand by the best people around one in every emergency. It is better to serve the best under all circumstances. In the Civil (?) War all of the best people in the South were engaged, and the Confederate Army was made up of the best material, rank and file that ever fought for the "right."

I pictured war to be the rattle of musketry, the booming of cannon, the charging and shouting of men, bursting shell, prostrate forms; in fact, just such a scene as is shown in the Cyclorama in Grant Park. [Atlanta, Georgia]

I never dreamed that war was anything but fight. I never thought of starvation, hunger and thirst, freezing and burning up. I thought a soldier was a gentleman who carried a gun and ammunition and had any easy time generally. But this was a dream born of youthful impulse and want of thought. I found a soldier to be a regular "pack mule," or camel. He had to carry his wardrobe, kitchen and dining room and his house in the bargain. I found him to be a tourist without knowing it. When I count up the days one is a soldier in battle, and the days he is simply a touring pack mule, I find that a soldier is one part hero and thirty parts pack horse. But really both parts are heroic with the preponderance in favor of the pack mule part, as it takes more heroism to resist the cravings of hunger, and the pinchings of cold than it does to die in battle. In other words, it is easier to die in battle than it is to die from want of food.

I am thus glad I went to war, for I learned all about the patriot business, and it were well if all our people would consider the sacrifice one must make to serve their country as a soldier, especially the Confederate soldier, as his country furnished fighting in plenty, while the soldier fed and clothed himself; and licked the Yanks to get guns and ammunition. Besides all this he lost the opportunity of four of the best years of his life to get a start in life. I got from Jeff Davis' Government one pair of shoes, $33 in Confederate money and $1.15 in silver at the surrender at Greensboro, N. C. My folks furnished the rest. The Confederate soldier was a patriot pure and simple. What has all this got to do with the battle of Gettysburg? A whole lot, for I want to tell you what a pack mule-soldier-tourist-patriot saw on that occasion. You must first know the functions of a soldier, before you can understand his narrative.

The field of Gettysburg is called by [missing line] Glory, in his history a battlefield. I saw much of its awful scenes, and I can't for the life of me make it out as all glory. I see it thus:

> Behold him now.
> Olympian Jove, so white his brow!
> No truant hand against him turned.
> Nor warning hosts his power hath spurned;
> No trust the Gods hath him betrayed.
> That him hath angered or dismayed
> To wrath divine his pity yields.
> -Mid broken spears and battered shields
> Where palid forms forms bedeck the main.
> And love had struggled all in vain;
> Where battered, bruised the flowers lie
> And ghouls enhance the scenery,
> Where angels passing in the sky,
> Shun the scene with sudden cry:
> Where shouts exultant, and the cries
> Of him who fights and him who flies;
> "Glory" sits in grand estate,
> And views the ruin with mind elate.

Gettysburg was simply Malvern Hill No.2. McLaws division, of which my regiment and brigade was an humble part, was in line so that its right was about opposite "Devil's Den."

It was formed into two lines, and on the left of Hood's division.

The front line was: Kershaw's South Carolinians on the right and Barksdale's Mississippians on the left. The two Georgia brigades ["Tige" Anderson's and Benning's] were in the second line. As we marched up the slope to take position, I noticed Generals Lee and Longstreet standing in the shade of a tree looking at a map which was spread on the ground. Not far from this point our brigade was formed in line of battle. My regiment was posted in a clearing between two bodies of woods, and on the edge of the wheat field. The field was enclosed with a stone fence, and we sat on the ground so that the field would shield us from the enemy's skirmishers, who were thickly posted on our right. We were near the woods on our right. And in the angle nearest us of these woods, one of our batteries was unlimbered and went into action.

As soon as they began firing, the Federals returned the fire from a number of batteries, and in a few minutes the air was full of fluttering, bursting shells. I noticed the Georgians in the woods behind the battery, dodging the falling limbs. The Federals had too many guns playing on our guns, and our folks were forced to retire. After a while General Lee rode along the line, and then after a while Hood's division advanced to the attack. Between us and the Federals was an open field without any sort of protection to an advancing force, and the distance across was about one mile and a quarter. As soon as Hood started, the music began. I was sitting behind the stone fence talking to Captain George McDowell of my company, and Captain [Robert C.] Pulliam of the Butler Guards [Co. B] of my regiment. I made the observation to these two that we would fall unless our division was moved forward with Hood.

Both of these men were killed, and I think they had that presentment from the way they looked and talked.

Hood went ahead and reached Round Top. The Yankees moved troops from our front and attacked Hood's left flank. This compelled that flank to give way. At this juncture we started in. We jumped the wall and the Yankees at once began to fire on us. We had orders not to fire, yell or charge, but to take things "cool" and keep a stiff upper lip at a common time gait. Under pressure, I forgot about all about my pack, although it had been reinforced with sixty rounds of fresh ammunition. To make room for this in my haversack I had unloaded my "grub," some beef tallow biscuit, fit more for cannon balls than food. We were forbidden to fire, consequently I was simply a pack mule sight-seer. Yes, and I saw a sight and heard a sight and thought a sight. Shells were cutting off the arms, legs and heads of our men, cutting them in two and exploding in their bodies, tearing them into mincemeat. Then there was the solemn thud of the minnie balls, men crying for water, groaning, praying and so much that was harrowing that my speech fails to describe it all. I am not writing as a soldier now, but simply as a tourist. This thing went on until we got to within about four or five hundred yards of the batteries, then we began to get grapeshot fired into us. More horrors. But horrors or no horror, we made straight for the batteries, and I did long for the order to fire and charge, so that we could raise the "yell!" But no, we were simply on exhibition. On we went, leaving the field behind us covered with heads, arms, legs, tangled bodies and the like. About 300 yards from the guns now, when we got the order to move by the right flank. Guess they thought we had had enough sightseeing from the front, and now we were to have a side view. Moving by the flank, there was a depression through which the men passed. In this depression the men were out of the fire of the grapeshot. But the depression ran right up to a Yankee battery, and they quickly placed a gun so as to rake it. I noticed that about every other squad which got in it was decimated, and I saw that the men about me would be the unfortunate ones. We got in it, and while crossing it I kept my eye on the gun. As I saw the man about to pull the lanyard, I stopped still and turned my thin edge to the fire. Bang! Went the gun, and then the grape reaped the harvest of souls. I was the only man left unhurt. Poor John Fooshe of my company, fell behind me, his leg broken by a grape. Poor "Whig" Chaney of my company fell on my right. He got a grape, which frazzled my jacket behind. Fooshe looked up at me with such a pleading look and asked for water. I gave him my canteen. I can see him now just as he looked then. He died. Then there was Jimmy Casson of my regiment, one of my schoolmates. He was on his hands and knees with a portion of his skull shot away above one eye. He was out of his mind instantly. He died. Then my bosom friend, George McKenzie, of my company, had his gun knocked across his chest, which almost finished him. Then William Lomax of my company, who with me sat up as pickets all night at Fredericksburg on the dead bodies of Yankee soldiers, was killed. But I had to go, and go quickly.

After a little we got orders to lie down. Up to this time I had acted tourist to perfection and according to orders. But I had come to the point that I intended to play soldier and general on my own account.

I turned towards the Yanks and standing there alone I opened fire on them at the battery that had graped us so heavily. I had a rifle which I got out of a dead Yanks hands at Fredericksburg. This Yank was one of Meagher's Irish brigade. The Inspector General of our army informed me in an inspection near Fredericksburg that I had the finest gun in the army. It was a beauty.

With this gun I took aim at a Yankee officer, who was riding a white horse. He was riding back and forth behind the infantry which was supporting the battery afore mentioned. The distance was about three hundred yards. I guessed I could not miss the whole crowd. I fired 12 rounds as fast as I could load the gun, the men lying down calling on me to desist, as I was drawing fire of the enemy. They were doing their level best in that line before I fired a shot. As I was loading my gun the Yankees charged us and came out of a piece of woods to our right. They got up pretty close before I could load, and one fellow, who was in advance of the rest, stopped about 30 yards from us and pulled down on me as I was capping my gun. I thought my occupation as a tourist was gone. He missed the mark. About this time the men lying down arose. We raised a yell and fired into them. We downed the most of them, and of the others, a great many threw down their arms and ran into our lines. We followed those who fled, and it resembled a rabbit hunt.

We about cleaned this line up. We soon encountered another. We got a volley and returned it and the carnage in their line was heavy. Great numbers of the unhurt threw down their guns and fell flat on the ground. When we passed over them they arose and ran into our lines. We ran afoul of the third line, and it shared the fate of the first two. Then over and past the batteries, up to the Round Top. Here, we encountered several lines of battle posted on the hillside so that they could shoot over the heads of the men in front.

We got close up and kept the men who were attempting to fire some guns which were posted there thinned out so that they could not do much. But the lines of battle fired into us and many of our men fell. Colonel J[ohn] D. Kennedy, of my regiment, who was by my side got hit and had his hat knocked off. He turned to leave the field and told me that he was wounded, and instructed me to go and tell Lieutenant Colonel [Franklin] Gaillard to take command of the regiment. I started on a run down the line to find him. When I got about the center of the regiment the men began to fall back, and of course I did too. I was then in a road which wound its way behind the Round tops. We retreated in good order, loading and firing on the Yanks. We reached the edge of a woods and here we made a stand,

and Colonel D. Wyatt Aiken of the Seventh South Carolina, as he jumped over a log, called to his regiment to rally on us. Here while in the act of capping my gun, I was knocked senseless. This put an end to my participation in the battle.

I have often thought of that flank movement in the open field, and it made right up to their guns. This stumps me yet. It was war, I reckon, but I fail to see the science in it. In this battle McLaws' division inflicted greater loss on the Yanks than any division engaged in the three days battle.

The Yanks lay so thick that it was almost a repetition of the stone wall at Fredericksburg, December 13, 1862. I think that, in addition to this, the division took five thousand prisoners. This battle is remarkable for the fact that each division fought almost alone, and had about double its numbers in front and four or five times as many on the flanks. Each division which was engaged had one or the other of its flanks turned because of want of support.

One mile is a good wide gap to be left between divisions, and this was the case with Hood's and McLaws' divisions.

I think McLaws' division did the best and most effective fighting done at Gettysburg, and it surely inflicted greater loss on the Yanks than any other. It routed Sickles' corps and more besides. The name or fame, or something else which the head of a division has, has a whole lot to do with its place in history.

General McLaws was not a "catchy" personage, but his division never failed to fill the bill in an emergency.

I see very little about McLaws' division, but I know that it was composed of good and true men and whose fame and valor deserve as high a place in the annals of fame as any division in the army.

If McLaws' division had advanced along with Hood's division, the Yanks could not have flanked Hood and we would not have had to make the flank movement we did. The time taken in making the flank movement cost us lots of men, and if we had consumed that time right on to the guns we would have lost less men and would have routed the Yanks before they could have formed the lines which we last encountered. But then I suppose the best was done that could be thought of by our officers. We had an army of eighty thousand men and with the prestige they should have won the battle. The want of concert all along the line was the cause for failure. On that battlefield I prayed for "Stonewall" Jackson, and not only then, but ever thereafter.

* * *

ATLANTA JOURNAL
ATLANTA, GEORGIA
SEPT. 21, 1901

"Ze Var Ought To Be Stopt"
By William A. Johnson

[Private to Lieutenant Co. F, Second South Carolina Infantry]

Editor Journal:

On the march preceding the battle of Gettysburg, and about the time our army crossed the Potomac river, considerable rain had fallen, and in some places the road was heavy.

After we got into Pennsylvania, and while on the march, our column came to a creek, and a road had been cut through a small hill, so that the creek could be reached and crossed by wagons. In this cut the mud was very bad, and a cannon was fast in the mud. We could not go through the mud very well, and the column was ordered to go through the wheat field on the right of the cut. We marched up the little hill and commenced to upset the fence which enclosed the wheat. The wheat was headed out and was fine. On the left of the cut from us was the residence of the owner of the wheat, as it turned out pretty soon.

While tearing down the fence I noticed a man coming toward us in a hurry from the direction of the house aforesaid. Excitement was plainly marked on his features. He was in his shirt sleeves and held his hat in one hand and a handkerchief in the other. Stopping on the opposite side of the cut and fanning with the hat in one hand and wiping the perspiration from his brow with the other, he violently exclaimed: "Vat you's doing dere?"

Some one answered it was none of his business. In the meantime the fence was being rapidly demolished. He exclaimed again loudly: "Vat you's doing dere, I shay?" He got the same answer as before, except it was fringed all around with jest and laughter. By this time the men had entered the field and were marching through the wheat and treading it down. Throwing up both hands, he exclaimed: "Mine gotte, mine gotte, if dat's de vay de var's to be carried on, me vants it stopt."

By the time the army got through the wheat field and across the creek he was undoubtedly sick of "de var."

W. A. Johnson, Co. F, 2d S. C. V. Atlanta, Ga.

* * *

MANNING TIMES
MANNING, SOUTH CAROLINA
JULY 13, 1904

A Prisoner of War Forty-One Years Ago

Reader, I write this sketch of my prison life of nine months. One month at Gettysburg and Baltimore jail, and eight months at Point Look Out, Maryland, entirely from memory. If you were ever a prisoner of war, I have your sympathy. If otherwise I ask your sympathy. Perhaps it would not be out of place to preface this article with a brief account of the second day's fight at Gettysburg, Pa., in which the writer took part. Reader, this may be stale stuff to you, but it is truth, "and truth is stranger than fiction." On the first day of July 1863, our brigade "Kershaw's" the oldest brigade in Lee's army, was marching rapidly through the town of Chambersburg, Pa. We heard the booming of the cannon in the distance. The advance column of Lee's army and the advance of the Federal army, were fighting at Gettysburg. The citizens of Chambersburg took great pleasure in guying us, as we passed through their town, that their troops was getting the best of the fight. In reply we told them that they were very much mistaken that our boys was thrashing the Federals. As the red sun was setting behind the western hills, (I remember the sun was unusually red; could it have been indicative of blood?) we halted on Marsh creek a small stream four miles from Gettysburg. Why we halted there, I do not know, history does not explain the reason. We could easily have made the balance of the distance in a short time to Gettysburg. We soon had our supper. Yes readers we ate, sometimes. We were soon resting our tired limbs on the soil of Pennsylvania. By six o'clock on the morning of the second day of July, we reached Gettysburg. (Oh, fateful battlefield). Although we whipped those people, in the first day's fight, we did not profit by the advantage. Reader do you know why? If not, I will tell you. "Stonewall" Jackson was dead. Oh! cruel bullets that took away "Stonewall Jackson, the "blue light" of the army of Northern Virginia, who fell at Chancellorsville of the eve of the great victory, had he lived to have shared with us in the battle of Gettysburg, we would have won a decisive victory which would have staggered the Government at Washington, and the end would have been in sight. (Lee's army wept when Stonewall Jackson died.) Reader, perhaps you might ask the question, why so, I would hesitatingly answer. His lightning like perception, and his impelling force of action, his great soul would not have allowed his wearied body to have rested on Pennsylvania soil, the night of the first day of July, 1863, until he had occupied the vacant heights afterwards held by the Federals. He thought not of impossibilities. But would have said. It must be done. He had to get up and get about him as the soldier puts it. Some one has said that Gen. Forrest was questioned, as to his success in war, replied that "to get there first with the biggest crowd." Jackson never got there first with the biggest crowd, but always got there first with the winning crowd. Gen. Meade hurried his troops from Pipe creek to Gettysburg all night of the first day of July, and therefore got the advantage position. At Fredericksburg, Va., in December, 1862, we had the position on the Federals, and repulsed them with all ease. Position counts for much in war. Gen. Lee did not realize the loss of the great Jackson, until after the battle of Gettysburg. But his magnanimous spirit would not allow him to criticize or censure any one, he took the responsibility of the result of his failure, to drive the enemy from the heights of Gettysburg. "His like we will never see again until the end of time." Pardon me for digressing. Now for the second days fight at Gettysburg. As I have already mentioned, that we reached the ground that was to be the field of carnage. We discovered quickly, that the Federals had it on us, as to ridges and heights. However it was our destiny to fight at Gettysburg. We marched and counter marched for some length of time before we got into position. In the meanwhile skirmishers were taken from our Brigade, by companies: my company was taken which was Co. "D" of the second regiment which was the color company, I was one of the color guard, I was placed there by the lamented Captain Leonard W. Bartlette of

Co. "D" who fell in front of his company leading them in a charge in the seven days fight around Richmond in 1862. I was ninth color corporal at that time. At Gettysburg I was first color corporal. You see at once that there was a considerable gap between first and ninth, brought about by the enemies bullets, it was not a desirable position. As my company was placed on the skirmish line, I had to remain with the regiment.

The skirmishers were deployed in the front of our division, which was "McLaws." Hoods division was on our right, fronting Big Round Top, our division was in front of Little Round Top and through a peach orchard. While we were waiting for the command forward, I had a change of clothing in my knapsack. I said to some of the boys nearby, if they thought I would have time to change my clothing. Some one answered that they thought it was a very risky undertaking. I decided not to make the attempt for we were listening for orders to advance every moment. I had a plug of fine Virginia in my knapsack, I took it out, and placed it in the bosom of my shirt, and threw the knapsack away, clothes and all. Perhaps I did wrong, in throwing away everything I had, but it was my custom not to hamper myself with a superfluous load when going into battle. Gen. Kershaw was near his brigade, grand soldier he was. At four o'clock the command was given, forward. We had been waiting behind a rock fence, as we crossed over this fence, we entered a large wheat field. As we marched forward, I discovered just in front of me, one of my company stiff in death, killed on the skirmish line. Thoughts flew through my mind, thick and fast. Isolated from me, was my dear company, though in command of one of the best Captains of the Confederate Army, (generous and brave he was) others may be dead, and if I am spared through this fiery ordeal of strife, I will not know, until the battle ends, who is killed and who survives. All at once we heard the order, by the right flank. What did this mean? We soon found out that there was a gap between the left of Hood's division and the right of our division McLaws. We soon moved up quickly our right on Hood's left. We then fronted and moved forward. While we were making this movement, the enemies cannon opened on us with grape canister; men fell in great numbers. The heights and ridges occupied by the federals, were crowned with bristling artillery, grape and canister made great swaths in our division, you could see as many as a score fall at once. "Dixie" "Land of the orange and cotton bloom" thy sons were dying for thy cause, which they loved so well. We soon got near enough to use our rifles and the fight was on. In the midst of the battle our color bearer fell by my side. The brave Col. John D. Kennedy of the 2nd regiment was also wounded. Eleven times he was wounded during the war. Gallant soldier has gone to his reward. The guns planted on "Little Round Top," the shells from them, exploded in every direction, the shelling was terrific. The batteries on the ridges were making terrible gaps in our line. Our brigade (Kershaw's) advanced against Little Round Top.

It was considered the impregnable part of the federal line, and defended by Regulars, who were the best fighters in the federal army. Men were falling in every direction, gap after gap was made in our line by shells from the hills and grape and canister from the ridges. The fighting was furious. The enemy were reinforcing this point of their line, Little Round Top was completely parked with cannon. Kershaw's brigade pushed forward, during the enemy upon their strongholds, when night with her sable curtain put an end to the bloody struggle. The ground was covered with dead, dying and wounded Confederates and Federals alike. The red earth of Pa., was made crimson, pouring from the veins of several thousand soldiers. The earth truly drank blood. Thus ended the second days fight at Gettysburg. Reader, I was spared, I was thankful to my Heavenly Father, who has protected me, through these sixty-six years of my life. We drove those people on the second days fight as we did on the first, but they still held their strongholds. "So near and yet so far." Sometime after dark my company came to the 2nd regiment. In command of our good captain who was also wounded he reported three killed and six wounded on the skirmish line. We had not eaten anything since seven o'clock in the morning; about 10 o'clock we had our rations cooked and we are them. Reader, what would you have called that meal? Dinner or supper. I thought of my plug of tobacco, not a chew in six hours, I took it from the bosom of my shirt and I could almost squeeze the perspiration out of it, I took a chew and put it by to dry.

We were soon asleep, waiting for the coming day. The sun rose clear and bright over the field of blood. This was the day that Gen. Picket made his forlorn charge upon the centre of the enemies lines. Gen. Lee parked his cannon, one hundred and forty-five in number. At one o'clock these cannon opened their fiery mouths, sending their shrieking missiles of death, across the valley. Eighty pieces replied to ours from the heights. For two hours, these two hundred and twenty-five cannon poured their iron hail through the heated air. Language cannot express the intensity of this blood curdling, sullen thunder, of these war dogs of destruction. Reader, I did not see Picket's charge. Our division was still occupying the right of our line, we were not near enough to see the awful charge. It was soon over. And at a frightful cost of the effusion of blood. Fate was against us.

The battles around Gettysburg had ended. Later on in the war it was said by some one, that Picket's division had given way on a certain portion of the line of battle. A soldier who had been in the battles of Gettysburg spoke and said, how could that be, for it was a certain fact that Picket's division was buried at Gettysburg July, 1863. Some years after the war ended, Gen. Picket disinterred the skeletons of these braves, perhaps forty wagon-loads were borne to Richmond, Va., and buried in her historic soil.

The bones of these, her gallant sons, are now mingling with her blood drenched soil. The fourth day of July came, nothing eventful occurred on that day, with us. We were still fronting the enemy. We had failed to drive them from their strong positions, and we thought per-adventure, they might attempt to assail our lines. But no such thought entered their brain, from Gen. Meade down to the privates in his army. We waited patiently, but those people did not move. Everything was quiet not a gun was fired during the day. Men were detailed to bury the dead, which was of great importance, to give our dead comrades a decent burial as far as circumstances admitted. Poor fellows, they were wrapped in their blankets and laid away at rest, awaiting the resurrection morn. About dark it began raining. I was taken quite sick. I reported my condition to the Captain, he advised me to go at once to the hospital, where the wounded of our company was, I did so. About nine o'clock, I heard my Captain and several of the boys, one being the tallest man in Co. "D" who always stood at the head of the company. I got up from my bed of straw and inquired of the Captain what was up. He replied that Lee's army was retreating. I said to him, if that be the case, I won't stay here. Oh, no said the Captain, you are in no condition to go, you may get worse on the retreat, and be left in the mud. You stay here, and when you get better, you can see after these wounded boys of ours. With this the poor fellows entreated me to stay with them. Reader, I wilted and staid wilted nine months. The Captain reasoned in this way. It will be unwise for you to undertake to keep up with the army. In a short while you will be paroled or exchanged. I then consented to stay, thinking that discretion better be used. The Captain gave us "greenbacks" federal money, and so did the private who always stood at the head of the company. They bid us good bye, and we were left within the lines of the enemy. Both of these men, Captain and the private are dead now. And if good deeds count for anything in the great beyond, the spirit of my noble Captain is in that "beautiful land of rest," I hope that the soul of the private who always stood at the head of Co. "D" is there also. On the next morning, the fifth day of July the Army of Northern Virginia wended its way southward. Looking from the hospital door, I discovered Gen. R. E. Lee sitting on his horse, Traveler, he was the last Confederate soldier that I saw that morning. About thirty minutes afterwards, Hancock's corps of Meade's army, passed in front of the hospital. I took medicine and in a short while I was feeling much better. As soon as I was sufficiently able to assist in caring or our wounded boys, I did so. I made myself generally useful the short time I staid there. Three of my comrades was badly wounded. Two lost a leg each and one was shot through the lungs, the others were not so badly wounded. Our brigade lost dreadfully in killed and wounded. Right hear, I will say something about Gen. J. B. Kershaw. He was the first Colonel the second regiment had. He also was our second Brigadier, and lastly our Major Gen. of McLaw's old division. A superb soldier he was. I will mention and incident. A soldier of his brigade, was severely wounded, in the campaign of 1864. The Gen. rode up hastily in the rear of his old regiment. Shells were flying thick and fast, tearing the earth in every direction. Addressing this soldier, said to him I am sorry you are so badly wounded, I hope you will soon get well. Speaking to the officer in command of the company, See that he is taken out of this place at once, and rode away. I merely mention this occurrence to show what manner of man he was. Some years ago his noble spirit took its flight across the mystic river. He is now resting "under the shade of the trees" with Jackson and Lee. Reader I have digressed again. Some ladies came over from Baltimore, for the purpose of administering to the wants of the Confederate wounded, (Noble women). They brought with them everything that was nice and savory, for the poor fellows. It was sad privilege of mine, to share in the burial of three soldiers of the second regiment, who died in a few days after the battles. We buried them in one grave, wrapped in their blankets. There was some sad sights that I witnessed. One poor fellow who had his lower jaw torn from its socket, he did not live long. Another with a leg amputated, arteries broke in some way, and could not be taken up. Poor young soldier, he bled his life away. Reader, I will not weary you, mentioning any more of these sad sights. I was strolling over the ensanguine battle field, viewing those formidable heights. I met a wounded Mississippian, belonging to our division. I said to him, friend and comrade, I see that you are wounded in the arm, left arm it was. Yes, said he. But let me show something that saved my life. He took from his left breast pocket a bible, no doubt given him, by his dear mother. I did not ask him, who was the donor of this precious gift. He handed it to me. I opened it and followed the course of a Minnie ball, that pierced it, page after page, fully half way through the book. I did remember at that time how far into the book that ball went, but have forgotten now. It glanced outward and entered his arm. That book divine had been a providential shield to that good soldier. After being at the hospital about ten days, a wounded comrade from Company "I" of the second regiment and myself were ordered to report at the town of Gettysburg; strange order. I thought that prisoners generally were always conducted to prison by a guard. But in this instance, there was no guard, to hurry us onward. It was right laughable, to see a great grandson of General Moultrie, of revolutionary fame, and your humble servant going alone to prison. If we had known then what we knew later, we would have skipped, but alas, we did not know. On the road, we met those good ladies again on their kind mission, to the hospital, with good things for our wounded. They inquired where we were going. We told them. They gave us some delicacies which they had with them, and informed us, if we were detained as prisoners any length of time, to inform them by letter, and if we needed any thing, to just let them know and, and our wants should be supplied. We thanked them, for their kind consideration of us, bade them farewell, and went on our way. We soon reached the old, apparently sleepy town, I say sleepy, for there was not any signs of three battles having been fought so near. My comrades and I entered a shoe store, and I purchased a pair of shoes. We went on and reported at the town jail. We were ushered into the yard of the jail, with many other prisoners. Next morning we boarded the train for Baltimore. On reaching this city, where a great many sympathizers of our cause abided, marching through the streets, we cut from our Jackets, palmetto buttons, and threw them along the pavements, pretty maidens and girls would pick them up as fast as chickens eating corn. I do not meant to infer, that they ate the buttons, but picked them up as quick as chickens would corn.

We were incarcerated in a building inconceivable almost in its construction. An expansive rotunda, with two large wings. We prisoners of war, occupied one wing. This was Baltimore jail. We remained there the balance of the month of July. The water we drank was warm. We were fairly fed. The time was monotonous. There was a young soldier, who was a fine singer, and in the lonely midnight hours, he would sing some of his pretty songs. "It was just twenty years ago" and "home sweet home" were among the number that he sang. It made me think of my Dixie home far away. The month of August came. We were marched out one afternoon to the river edge, and got aboard a Steamed bound for Point Look Out. At day light next morning we arrived at our destination. We were marched into an old field, grown up in weeds, our abode for eight months. We were on a point of land between the Chesapeak bay and the Potomac river. Sentinels were thrown around us. In a short time they had erected a substantial prison, enclosing us from the outside world. Tents were furnished us, and they were soon dotting the prison camp. Wells were dug and pumps were placed in them. The water was horridly bad, it was impregnated with copperas. We had one pump of water out of a dozen or more, of which, the water was much better. Cook houses were built, with mess halls perhaps a hundred feet in length, nine of these buildings were erected, each fronting a street, containing a division of prisoners. The number of prisoners kept augmenting. In a short time there must have been at least nine thousand. The weather was quite warm at that time. However we got a breeze from the bay, as the gates were opened in the day, but closed at night. There were no trees with their umbrageous branches, to shield us from the heated rays of the burning sun, no birds to sing their sweet songs, to be wafted by the gentle winds, toward the beautiful skies. Everything around us, made the sunlight sad. My good friend and comrade of Co. "I" fell in with some Virginians, fine fellows they were too, he tented with them. It was my fortune to be thrown with a Georgian two Lousianians and a soldier from Texas. My bed fellow was the soldier from Georgia. As cool weather came on we were looking about to see if we could increase our covering, we had only a blanket; my Georgia comrade came up with a piece of an old tent, we sewed the blanket and piece of tent together. We were then prepared for the coming winter, but we had nothing to lie on, but some sand, which we obtained from the beach of the bay.

Later on when winter was in full blast. Yes, winter came in double force, with its piercing, bitter cold, which filled our prison home, with intensified gloom. We thought we would try and increase our comfort, substituted some sea-weed for the sand. We tried for one night, the next day we carried it back and placed it upon the briny waters of the bay. Reader, it was something that would never dry. I had written to one of those ladies I met with at Gettysburg, and elderly lady she was, stating that I was very much in need of some clothes, and some tobacco, which was a scarce article in prison. The dear old woman, promptly, sent me what I desired, and several dollars in federal money. She was my friend, peace to her sacred dust. We were guarded by a brigade of New Yorkers, and reasonable men they were, we suffered no harm at their hands. It was said by some of the prisoners, that others looking through the cracks of the fence at a pile of coffins, one spoke to another standing aside, addressing him as "Johnnie Reb" come here and let me show you your "wooden overcoat," yes, a good many of the poor fellows got their wooden overcoats there. We were given only two meals each day, breakfast and dinner, no supper, a cup of coffee quite thin, and five small crackers or a half loaf of bread for breakfast. For dinner, a cup of bean soup and five crackers with a slice of pickle pork alternating with a cup of carrot soup with a slice of fresh beef. We did not complain of the quality of the food we had reader, but, oh, my, the quantity. For supper we drank a double portion of copperas water, retired to our humble couches dreaming of our breakfast the coming morning. Tobacco was hard to get, and sometimes we had to exchange a cracker for a chew of tobacco. They were at par. The only thing that cheered me in my seclusion from the world outside, was "Dixie" and her glorious cause. My friend of Co. "I" came around sometimes to see me. I reciprocated his visits, he was always a gentleman, in war and in peace, in prison, and out of prison, he still lives. An unseen hand has protected him all these years. There was a young soldier from Maryland, who had been taken quite sick, he was taken out of the prison camp, and carried to the hospital. Before leaving, however, he told my comrade of Co. "I", that he expected a valuable box of provisions from Baltimore, that he, my friend, could appropriate it, he and his messmates. I think the Marylander died. The box came filled with eatibles of every variety, ham, turkey, light pickles and a intermixture of other good things, too tedious to mention. My good friend ever thoughtful, invited me to partake with him, of the luxuries. We ate carefully and left no scraps for the cats, but fortunately, reader, the cats were conspicuously absent, had they been there, they would not have held any hand in the game. For several months thousands of boxes were shipped from Baltimore. What a blessing it was, to have such friends, among strangers. Some bad fellows one night made a charge upon one of the cook houses carried off boxes of crackers, meat and other things. The entire camp of prisoners, had to suffer for the wrong doing of those unthoughtful fellows. We had no meat to eat for some considerable time. That was the privation we had to endure without complaint. The month of March came 1864. I said to my friend of Co. "I" see here, our old uniforms are getting right old and thin. Won't you write to Mrs. H and see if you can get her to send us a suit each. He answered me in this way. I would cheerfully write the letter for the much needed clothing, but the trouble is this, they won't let letters be mailed now going from prison camp. I replied, you write the letter and leave the matter to me. I unfolded my plan to him. He saw the point at once. I will explain the trick. Here it is.

One of the Louisianians who tented with me, was acquainted with some of the New Yorkers, who guarded the prison camp. I asked him, if he would do me a favor. Yes, he said, certainly I will. The letter was already written. Friend take this letter said I, and have it mailed out at the Point, by one of your New York friends, and you will confer a kindness, which I certainly will appreciate. He did so. Within a week, my friend and comrade of Co. "I" and myself, received, each a nice grey suit: "It is better to be born fortunate than rich." Sometime after the war ended, my friend went to Baltimore on Mercantile business, he called on Mrs. H. If living may God bless her. If otherwise, may she be numbered with the blessed in that everlasting home beyond the skies. Some of the prisoners undertook to tunnel themselves out of prison, they made a failure of their attempt. One morning the latter month of March, I had just eaten breakfast, when I stood in the presence of my honored comrade and friend of Co. "I" of the old second regiment of South Carolina volunteers. Good news, good news for you my friend. Oh, what is it? said I. We are bound for "Dixie" in the morning. Reader, I was completely overwhelmed with joy. Reader, did you ever know how to appreciate gladness. The clouds of despair rolled away, which had so saddened the sunshine of my prison life. Am I to go away from this place and be where beautiful roses bloom, and view again the meadows green? Could it be a reality? I will anxiously await and see. Sure enough we were to be paroled, that is our division of prisoners. Welcome morning I said within my heart. Oh, may time hasten its speed, that I may leave this place forever. The next morning we were marched to the steamer New York, she was loosened from her moorings, and the good steamship moved blithely down the bay laden with eight hundred or a thousand rejoicing hearts. The next morning we cast anchor off Fortress Monroe, for what purpose I know not. Some mischievous fellow aboard, circulated a report, that we were to be conveyed back to Point Look Out. His ruse was so monstrously absurd, I did not for a moment give it credence, but some of the boys took the rumor seriously. We lay at anchor that day and night. The next morning we hoisted anchor, and steamed up the James to City Point, where the two steam boats were in readiness to bear us on the Capital of the then young nation. About midday we reached Richmond. The inhabitants of the war shakened city, were on the banks of the river awaiting to welcome us back to Dixie land. Old men and Matrons, Maidens, boys and girls, with their well filled baskets, greeted us on every side. Some one has said that the most tender thing they have ever heard, was the bleat of a young lamb. Reader, that person had never been shut up in prison for a long time, and denied the privilege of hearing a woman's voice. And, if he had, and to be suddenly turned loose from confinement, and hearing all around him, Mr. have something from my basket, wont you, wont you. Think of those sweet voices around, entreating you to have something, holding it in their pretty hands, food prepared no doubt by themselves expressly for you. Reader, the bleat of that fellows young sheep would not have been in it. We were escorted to the Capitol square, by several regiments, with bands playing "Dixie." When we reached the Capitol we fronted. Reader, then came one of the most imposing scenes that was ever witnessed. The president of "the storm cradled nation" leaning upon the arm of Gen. William Smith, Ex-Gov. of Virginia, who escorted him down the line of soldiers, as he passed along, you could hear the cheering greeting, soldiers I welcome you home, soldiers, I welcome you home. What joy swept through our hearts. It was indeed an impressive sight, long to be remembered. After a short respite of twenty-one days, we were declared exchanged. We promptly reported to our commands, and ready to fight Grant's ponderous army in the wilderness. The confederate yells are heard no more. "Dixie" flag guides no more the charging lines, it is furled forever. No camp fires are made now. No roll call of companies are heard now. "But may we all be there when the roll is called up yonder."

OLD ROCK

* * *

CONFEDERATE VETERAN MAGAZINE
SEPT. 1913

THE BATTLE OF GETTYSBURG.
BY JOHN COXE, GROVELAND, CAL.

At Gettysburg I was a private in Company B, 2d South Carolina Volunteers, Kershaw's Brigade. McLaws's Division, Longstreet's Corps. On the 29th of June, 1863, we marched from Chambersburg and bivouacked at a little town called Longwood, near the Caledonia Iron Works and also near the foot of South Mountain, on the west side. The iron works had been burned by the Confederates a few days before on the night of the 30th there was a heavy rain, and we passed the forenoon of the 1st of July in cooking, eating, and drying our wet blankets. The little town was built on both sides of the pike and was very long, therefore we changed its name and called it "Longstreet."

So far we had heard of no enemy, but knew that Ewell was ahead of us somewhere. About 2 p.m. the sun came out vigorously, and almost immediately the order to swing knapsacks and "fall in" was given with sharp emphasis, and in less than twenty minutes the command was marching rapidly north along the pike. Just after passing old Thad Stevens's ruined iron works the pike turned sharply to the right, and soon afterwards we reached the foot of South Mountain at the entrance of a low gap. We went along in quick time, and quite frequently our officers would say "Hurry up, men!" The slope up the mountain was gradual, but not very steep at any point. Near the summit we came to a watering place called Graffenburg's Springs, halted, and were told to rest.

Hot and tired after a two hours' rapid march, we down on the ground and rested; but while enjoying the cool and inspiring appearance of the white cottages of the springs, hark! all of a sudden the distant sound of cannon coming through the gap from the east side of the mountain struck our ears and threw us into extreme alertness. Officers looked at one another, and so did we privates. Then Captain [Robert C.] Pulliam said: "Boys, that sounds familiar." Then Private [John H.] Pickett said: "That explains why we've been racing." And still others, looking at the sun, remarked: "It isn't likely that we'll get into it before to-morrow."

Although we didn't know it then, that was the sound of A. P. Hill's and Ewell's battle of the first of July at Gettysburg. Soon after this our rest was cut short, and up and onward we rushed. Just before reaching the summit and above the din of our tramping feet and rattling canteens we heard the crash of small arms, and at a clearing just east of the top we saw clouds of smoke hanging like a pall over the valley beyond; but by this time, which was after sunset, the firing had ceased and we heard no more noise of battle. Still we rushed on down the east side of the mountain, unencumbered either by artillery or wagons, and didn't stop again till we readied level ground, after nine o'clock,

It was quite dark when my company baited directly in front of a large house about fifty feet back on the left of the pike. Many wounded, mostly Confederates, were in the front yard, and these were being tenderly cared for by three women, ladies of the house, while surgeons were attending the wounded both in and outside of the house. The lights, being candles, were rather dim, and occasionally we heard groans of the wounded.

Lieutenant [William R.] Powell respectfully approached one of the women and inquired how far it was to the battle field. "Why, you are right now on the edge of the battle field," she replied: and then, turning around, she pointed forward a little to the right of the pike and continued: "The big fight was right over there in those woods" "Which side got the better of it?" continued Powell. "O," she said, "I think the Lincoln men got whipped, because we saw them running over the hill toward town and the Rebels running after and shooting at them." "Where is the town?" inquired Powell. "About a mile over there," and she pointed forward again. "Was there any more fighting after that?" asked Powell. "Yes, we heard more fighting over in town, but it didn't last long." answered the woman.

Soon after this we were edged over to the right side of the pike, stacked arms, and ordered to pass the night as best we could. As we had nothing to cook, no fires were lighted, and so we lay down and slept. I was up at dawn the next morning and walked a little forward on the pike. There was no noise. Some distance forward I saw on the left a large bivouac, but it was as quiet as death. Going farther, I saw straight ahead a large building on a low hill partly surrounded by trees. I didn't know it then, but that was the famous seminary where Lee stood and watched most of the fighting at Gettysburg. I was at the edge of the McPherson wood. The town was on the left, obscured by hills and woods. In a small clearing I saw about a dozen dead Federals. Returning to our bivouac. I was surprised to find nearly everybody there still asleep, although the sun was nearly up. Few had anything in their haversacks, and so there was precious little breakfast for us that morning.

Soon after sunrise we were called into ranks and marched slowly forward on the pike. Still no noise. Just before reaching the seminary we passed a brigade cooking breakfast on the left of the pike, and some of the men told us that they were in the fight on the day before. Coming to the foot of the seminary hill, we debouched to the right down a slight declivity and soon afterwards reached Willoughby Run, in the woods, directly west of the seminary. Here we halted and lay around for at least two hours, during which Gen. A. P. Hill and staff rode over from the west of the Run and then slowly on up through the woods toward the seminary. General Hill was an interesting person-ality. A slight but very pleasant smile seemed to light up his face all the time, while his eagle eyes took in everything about him. His flowing whiskers were red, but his hair was a little darker.

Shortly after General Hill passed, a Confederate field gun was fired from the wooded hill to the right of the seminary. We heard the shell explode in the distance and adjusted our ears for the next shot. But it didn't come, and we never knew why that single shot broke the quietness all around us.

At last we were brought to attention and marched in column through open woods down the east side of the Run. Proceeding about half a mile, another halt was called and we lay around another hour. Meanwhile we heard desultory picket firing in the distance our left. With several others I walked to the left about one hundred yards to an opening in the woods. We looked across a field and road and saw the famous peach orchard beyond. To the right of the orchard and farther away we saw two cone-shaped hills partly covered with scrubby timber. These were the now celebrated Round Tops, the smaller of the two being on the left. The field to the right of the peach orchard extended as far as we could see from that point. The light skirmishing was going on in the peach orchard, which was so densely green that we couldn't see the men of either party. We were sharply called back to ranks and cautioned not to expose ourselves to the view of the enemy.

Soon after this, hearing a noise in the rear, we looked and saw General Hood at the head of his splendid division riding forward parallel to us about fifty yards to the left. This explained our last halt. Hood, who had marched to Gettysburg in the rear of McLaws, was to take position on our right and therefore on the extreme Confederate right. Why this great loss of time at that important juncture to get Hood and his artillery on the extreme right and thus delay the battle of the 2d of July could never be understood by us private soldiers, but General Longstreet was responsible for it, doubtless believing that it would be better to have the great fighter Hood on his right. But, in fact, it was a very bad error for two reasons—namely, it allowed the Federals time to bring up tremendous forces of all arms to meet us, and as it happened, Hood was wounded and disabled right at the beginning of his fight on the extreme right.

It seemed to take an age for Hood's men and train of artillery to pass us; and when finally it did get by, our division followed, Semmes's Brigade leading. But it didn't take us long to reach the open near the Emmetsburg Pike and in plain view of both Round Tops and the peach orchard. I looked and saw a Yankee flag waving signals from the apex of little Round Top. Indeed, we were so much exposed to view that the enemy had no trouble counting the exact numbers under Hood and McLaws. However, we were placed behind a stone fence along the west side of the pike and ordered to lie down. Immediately in our front and to the left, extending to the peach orchard, was an open field, then mostly in buckwheat. At the farther side of this field and in front of Round Tops was a thick woods, mostly of heavy oaks. About fifteen field guns under Cabell were brought up and unlimbered on the pike in front of an oak grove a little to our right, and a little later a Federal battalion of many guns galloped from the woods into the field near the peach orchard and somewhat to the left of our front, followed by a heavy Federal line of battle; but the latter soon after about-faced and returned to the woods. The Federal batteries quickly deployed and unlimbered guns, but didn't open fire. By this time the sun was observed to be getting down toward the top of South Mountain to the west and in our rear. Then suddenly we heard Hood's cannon under Lattimer open on the right and the furious reply of the Federal guns. Then pretty soon a few sharp bugle notes were heard and then boom! boom! boom! Blazed away Cabell's[32] guns at the Federal batteries near the peach orchard.

The Yankees were ready and replied with spirit, and in less time than it takes to tell it our ears were deafened by the noise of the guns and exploding shells. A little to the right I saw General Longstreet and staff dismounted behind the stone fence watching the effects of our shots through their field glasses. I don't know how long this awful cannonade lasted (probably twenty minutes), but as it began to slacken we were ordered to scale the stone fence behind which we were standing. This was quickly done, and then we were on the Emmetsburg Pike. On the other side of the pike was another stone fence to cross; and this done, there was no other important obstacle between us and the enemy.

The cannonade suddenly ceased, and then we could hear Hood's small arms fighting on the right in terrible crashes and roars. Our line, formed in perfect of battle, faced a little to the left so as to sweep the Federal batteries near the peach orchard. Just before the order, "Forward march!" was given I saw General Kershaw and staff immediately in our rear dismounted. About halfway from our start at the pike to the Federal batteries was a little down grade to a small depression. We went along in perfect order, the 15th South Carolina Regiment being on the right. As yet we could see no Federal infantry, because it was covered by the woods in the rear of the batteries; but we saw plainly that their artillerists were loading their guns to meet our assault, while their mounted officers were dashing wildly from gun to gun, apparently to be sure that all were ready.

Just before reaching the depression already mentioned a Confederate battery on the pike somewhat to our left opened fire, and I heard one of our men say, "That will help us out," believing as we all did that its fire was against the Federal guns in our front. But, alas! the next moment we saw that its fire was directed to a point farther to the left in the peach orchard.

32. Cabell's Artillery Battalion

Well, just as our left struck the depression in the ground every Federal cannon let fly at us with grape. O the awful deathly surging sounds of those little black balls as they flew by us, through us, between our legs, and over us! Many, of course, were struck down, including Captain Pulliam, who was instantly killed. Then the order was given to double-quick, and we were mad and fully determined to take and silence those batteries at once.

We had gotten onto the level land of the Federal guns when the next fusillade of grape met us. One of the little black balls passed between my legs. We were now so close to the Federal gunners that they seemed bewildered and were apparently trying to get their guns to the rear. But just then—and, ah me! To think of it makes my blood curdle even now, nearly fifty years afterwards—the insane order was given to "right flank." Of course no one ever knew who gave the order or any reason why it was given. General Kershaw denied being responsible for it, but somebody must have been. Why, in a few moments the whole brigade was jumbled up in a space less than a regiment behind a rocky, heavily wooded bluff with the right flank in the air, close to that historic scarecrow the Devil's Den and also little Round Top, quite near, with our left flank disconnected and wholly unsupported for a mile or more. We were truly "in a box," liable to be captured or annihilated at any moment.

It was some time until the Federals who had partly charged turned loose all their guns upon the woods over our heads. My! how the trees trembled and split under the incessant shower of shot and shell! But we were well protected from the front of the rocky bluff, and only a few men were injured by falling limbs. However, it wasn't long till the Federal infantry in great force advanced to the rim of the bluff and begun to pour lead down upon us; but they soon found out that bullets could go uphill with death in their songs as well as downhill so they dared not rush down upon us. It soon became evident, though, that they were taking steps to flank us at both ends. About that time Charley Markley, of my company, was killed, a ball piercing his forehead. Many others fell; but our "spunk" was up to white heat, and we didn't care, but made up our minds to die right there to the last man if necessary.

We fought in that position for nearly half an hour, when to our surprise the thunder and roar of the Federal cannon and musketry in our front suddenly stopped, and the next moment we heard a tremendous

Rebel cheer, followed by an awful crash of small arms, coming through the woods on our left front and from the direction of the peach orchard. Then one of our officers shouted and said: "That's help for us! Spring up the bluff, boys!" And we did so. Meanwhile the crashes of small arms and Rebel yells on the left increased. As we reached open ground over the bluff we saw the Federal artillery we had charged deserted and an almost perfect Confederate line of battle just entering the woods, hotly engaging and driving the Federal infantry.

"Who is that?" shouted an officer. But before we had time to think of getting an answer an officer galloped from the right of the advancing line and ordered us to join his right and go forward. And that officer was Brig. Gen. William T. Wofford. Until that moment we didn't know that when the division advanced from the Emmetsburg Pike Wofford's Brigade had been held in reserve on the pike near the peach orchard. Both Longstreet and McLaws knew Wofford well, and that in a "tight pinch" he could be relied on for succor. Hence on that day they decided to hold his splendid brigade in reserve for a probable emergency. And, indeed, the trying emergency had come. Semmes had fallen on the right and Barksdale had fallen on the left, while the predicament of Kershaw in the center has already been described. From his position in reserve on the pike Wofford plainly saw the death struggle of Kershaw's men, cut off as they were and fighting against such frightful odds, and it was said at the time that he asked McLaws for permission to go to our relief as many as three times before it was granted.

But to return to the fight. When Wofford ordered us to join his right and rush forward, a tremendous Rebel yell went up from our powder-choked throats. Wofford took off his hat and. waving it at us, turned back and charged along his line to the left. And here was seen how the right sort of officer can inspire his men to accomplish next to superhuman results. Always Wofford rode right along with his men during a fight, continually furnishing examples and cheering them with such words as, "Charge them, boys." The wonder was that he wasn't killed, he had many "close calls." but survived the war many years. Those who saw it said they never such a fine military display as Wofford's line of battle as it advanced from the pike. He went right for those Federal cannons that were firing at us. Nor did it take him long to reach those batteries and smash them even before the gunners had time to turn their guns upon him. Rushing over the artillery, he kept right on and tackled the Yankee infantry in the woods beyond. And his assault was so sudden and quickly executed that the Federal lines of infantry were smashed and gave way at every point in Wofford's way; and as the remnant of Kershaw's Brigade, combined with Wofford's splendid body of men, rushed along through the woods, all the Federal supports met the same fate of their first line. It became a regular rout; and while the panic-stricken enemy fell by the scores and hundreds. Wofford lost only a few men.

Emerging from the woods on the other side, we drove the enemy across a wheat field and on to the western slopes of little Round Top, up which they scampered in great disorder. While crossing the wheat field I looked along our line both ways, but saw no other troops. At that time, and while putting on a cap for another shot, a bullet from little Round Top tore open my right coat sleeve from wrist to elbow, but I wasn't hurt much. At the farther edge of the wheat field we were met by shots from Federal cannon on the apex of little Round Top, but all went high over us. Of course every one of us expected to go right on and capture that famous hill, which at that time seemed easy to do; but Wofford, seeing that night was near and that there were no supports on right or left or in the rear, ordered a halt, and after surveying the hill through his field glasses ordered us to about-face and fall back across, the wheat field and into the woods from which we had so recently driven the enemy. And, strange to say, when we ceased firing not another gun was heard on that part of the field during the remainder of that 2d of July. The wheat field and woods were blue with dead and wounded Federals. At the edge of the woods we met McLaws and cheered him, and he seemed well pleased with the evidences of our victory lying around him.

I felt sorry for the wounded enemy, but we could do little to help them. Just before dark I passed a Federal officer sitting on the ground with his back resting against a large oak tree. He called me to him, and when I went he politely asked me to give him some water. There was precious little in my canteen, but I let him empty it. His left leg was crushed just above the ankle, the foot lying on the ground sidewise. He asked me to straighten it up in a natural position and prop it with rocks, and as I did so I asked him if the movement hurt him. "There isn't much feeling in it just now," replied he quietly. Then before leaving him I said: "Isn't this war awful?" "Yes, yes," said he, "and all of us should be in better business." He wore long red whiskers and was large and fine-looking. I shall never forget his profuse thanks for the little service I was able to render him.

Our lines were established at the west rim of the woods leading to the wheat field. There we built fires, and from haversacks of the dead enemy all about us got something to eat. About 9 P.M. our cooks from the rear brought camp kettles of fine boiled beef, but without either salt or bread. After eating heartily we passed most of the remaining part of the night picking up and helping our wounded that lay between the peach orchard and Devil's Den. Poor First Sergeant Pool, of my company! He was brought into our ranks suffering horribly from the grapeshot in his stomach. The surgeons could do nothing for him. Death relieved him, however, at four o'clock the next morning. Let the reader understand that Longstreet's Corps, the Confederate right, held the battle field all that night and till late the next day. During the forenoon of the 3d we buried our dead and sent the wounded to the rear. For a while we heard firing on the left beyond the peach orchard, but otherwise the field was quiet, A little before noon we noticed that much of our artillery was being posted across the field in our rear, with spaces of about one hundred and fifty yards between guns.

About 1 P.M. General Pendleton, of Lee's staff, attended by a single orderly, rode rapidly from the right along the line of cannon as if inspecting them. At about 2 P.M. we were called to attention and told to be prepared for any emergency in our front. Some time after this we heard two cannon shots in quick succession on the left, and immediately our artillerists jumped up and manned their guns. And then, O then it really seemed that every cannon in both armies had turned loose its hail of iron. The echoes coming back from South Mountain, in our rear, had the effect of combining the noise into one continuous, solid, tremendous roar.

I lay there and watched the workings of the Confederate gun immediately in our rear, and the coolness of the officers and men was wonderful. The opposing Federal gun on the opposite heights fired solid shot, the first three of which went high over our gun. All the others struck the ground in front of our gun and then safely ricocheted over our gunners, but at the same time covering them with dirt and dust. I think that this furious cannonade must have gone on for fully half an hour. Then the fire on both sides slackened and soon ceased altogether. And then it was that for just a few moments we heard crashes of small arms and cannon at one point on the left.

The woods and peach orchard obscured our view, but we heard it very well, and that was the news of Pickett's famous charge and repulse to which, by both books and pictures, most of the Federal historians have ever tried their best to confine and limit the three days' battle of Gettysburg. The thing is not only misleading, but stupid, as witness the great losses on both sides and the ground taken and held by the Confederates during the first and second days. At the point of actual contact there were less than 6,000 under Pickett. Old soldiers knew about such things. Moving reports and official guesses of "present and effective" do not "pan out" in actual fighting. And even the repulse of Pickett's worse than foolish charge was not followed up a single inch by Meade, which proved that he didn't want to fight Lee any more on that field. Shortly after Pickett's charge a squadron of Federal cavalry had the foolish temerity to charge our right; but it was annihilated in short order, including the death of its commander, and this was the single attack made by the Federals at Gettysburg.

After that there was no more fighting, and absolute quietness prevailed on our part of the field till about 6 P.M., when the heavens were suddenly darkened by an angry black cloud. Soon the thunder and lightning became terrific, and I heard a cool-looking officer say. "Now for heaven's thunder and lightning," tacitly including in the reference the late "thunder and lightning" of men. Just before the storm broke, our lines were slowly drawn back to the line of the Emmetsburg Pike. The Federals on the opposite heights, seeing our movement, advanced slowly but in great confusion down to the battle field in the woods, where they found their dead and wounded. The storm broke and, great Jupiter Pluvius, how the rain did pour down upon us! Soon all the streams were out of their banks and the low places covered with sheets of water. Before dark, however, it was all over, and so we built fires and under the circumstances passed the night comfortably. About 11 P.M. we saw General Ewell and staff go by to the rear, and then it became apparent that our army was slowly retiring to the gaps in South Mountain. We didn't leave our position till nearly dawn, and the following night camped in Monterey Gap.

Meade made no attempt to follow us in force, but instead marched south and crossed at the lower gaps. Lee stopped at Hagerstown and took up a line of battle along the west bank of Antietam, partly on the old battle field of Sharpsburg, and there he waited nearly a week for Meade to attack; but fortunately for the Federal army, Meade knew better.

Many believe that in deciding to attack the Federal army at Gettysburg Lee was at his worst. He seems not to have had any clear plans. All the important attacks were dilatory, disjointed, and noncooperative. The only chance of winning a profitable victory on Lee's part was on the first day. When early on the 1st of July A. P. Hill struck the enemy west of Gettysburg, there was no sufficient reason why Longstreet should not have been in easy supporting distance east of South Mountain. Instead he lay west of the mountain till late in the day, and didn't get into fighting position till late on the 2d, but even as it was, many thought that if we had only had Stonewall Jackson, Meade would have been maneuvered out of all his strong positions about Gettysburg not later than 2 A.M. on July 2. And many also thought that the only other officer in Lee's army who could have fitted into Jackson's shoes was Wofford, who had been a captain of cavalry in the Mexican War. Longstreet and McLaws and Hood knew his ability and dash from what happened at Second Manassas, where Wofford was only a colonel, and many other fields. Yet Wofford never rose above a brigadier, and was trusted with independent command in Northern Georgia only after Sherman had passed through to the sea and where there was no fighting and little else to do. But notwithstanding civilians and some military men strongly urged his promotion, the authorities at Richmond and also General Lee thought that because Wofford hadn't been educated at West Point he was not competent for higher command.

Finally, the very most that can with truth be said in favor of the Federals at Gettysburg is that it was a drawn battle. With its unlimited men and means and backed by the world, the Federal government could stand "drawn battles"; but it was the reverse with the Confederates, without either.

* * *

CONFEDERATE VETERAN MAGAZINE
SEPTEMBER, 1917

GETTYSBURG AND THE BATTLE.
BY W. A. JOHNSON, LIEUTENANT
COMPANY D, 2D S. C. V.

Nazareth of old, an out-of the-way place, with no hope of immortality as esteemed by the great of that day, became as widely known and the most highly cherished of its contemporaries. Here was born a Man, or, better, a revelation, which is accepted as the light of our present civilization. In the case of Nazareth we find that which was least esteemed raised to the height of great importance. In this case we find that there is no such thing as insignificance. The revelation is that all great things are simply misses of small things, so called, working together and that greatness and glory are the result of the combined effort of the multitude, for without the multitude there would be no city, no nation, no "Sermon on the Mount."

The village of Gettysburg, hidden in a range of little hills, was about as obscure as Nazareth once was. It was scarcely noted above a whisper in the great concert of human activity; but divinity makes no distinction in its creation, for on its annual visitation it seeks out all things and bestows its bounties upon all alike and according to their needs. To Gettysburg it came in the spring and the summer time of 1863 and spread a carpet of living green thickly set with colors of many hues. It reared the grain of golden crowns and tinted the fruit with red, purple, yellow, black, and green, and peace and prosperity reveled on the hillsides and in the valleys.

Close by, on Cemetery Ridge, was the city of the silent ones, where a day is as a thousand years and a thousand years as one day, where tears have watered the soil and dewdrops, like diamonds, cluster on grass and shrub, and the One of Nazareth keeps the gate. Rising above all is Round Top, the silent watcher over the surrounding hills and valleys.

This was the condition at Gettysburg when, on the first day of July. 1863, the armies of the blue and the gray met there. There was no halting and waiting, no studied line of action taken as a preliminary, but an instant clash between the advanced ranks of the two armies. This sudden shock of arms, booming of cannon, and shouts of men banished peace, and the ruthless god of war became master of the scenery. For three days the din of battle raged with its ebb and flow, and on the third day, when Pickett's men retired from the charge, the hope of the gray army was shaken, but their determination and courage not a bit; they had baptized Gettysburg with the crown of immortality.

Here the selected ones from its ranks rest from their labors, where no shifting seasons or human migration can deny them a habitation or change the place of their abode. They went to sleep with their hopes and aspirations at the flood tide, and they are divinely anchored beyond the silent river, "beneath the shade of the trees," as the great Stonewall expressed himself at the crossing.

This battle was different from all other great battles, as it was not of race against race nor of nation against nation. It was a world's battle, for men from about every nation or race on the globe were the participants, and all civilized nations were equally interested in the kind of man or revelation that would be born there. It was a world battle over the vital axiom laid down by the fathers in the Declaration of Independence, that "all men are created free and equal and are endowed with certain inalienable rights, among which are the right to life, liberty, and the pursuit of happiness."

This battle was a parody of principle, for each army looked upon the axiom from different viewpoints; still they fought for the same thing—equal rights. Man has been a parody in this matter since the beginning, and all wars have been waged over this axiom. Being paradoxical, no peaceful interpretation can be placed upon it that will be universally accepted; hence war is a necessity. But, however this may be, we have a work to do of a cooperative nature, and that is to protect the battle field of Gettysburg from the despoiling hand of hate, malice, and all uncharitableness. If hate and malice were the inspiration of this battle, then its glory must dim with the passing years, for the future is destined to be ruled by a new and a better conscience. Such was not the case, however, for the battle was not out of the brain of any one individual, but was the work of a multitude of people. A cause championed by large masses of people is divine and consequently great and eternal. No individual could build the Panama Canal, for it took a world to do it. The canal, then, is a divine work. Divinity works by massing or through masses of people, and the individual, unless one of the mass, is a useless piece of junk.

In welding two pieces of iron the hammering and the sparks are the battle, the two pieces of iron the armies, the anvil the battle field, and the arm wielding the hammer and directing the blows is the architect, the divinity. The crowd, the mass, is divinity made visible to the individuals of the mass. However, there are those who attempt to suppress the work of the mass, individuals suppressing divinity, and that without apology. There is nothing strange about volcanoes except the people who live within the range of their overflow. The positive and the negative poles of the electric current meet, have a battle on a piece of carbon, a bright light appears, and we behold divinity. This is analogous to all activity and is just what happened or took place at Gettysburg. What seemed to be discord there was accord to the divinity of the occasion.

In the friction between the electric currents and the friction between the masses of mankind divinity is manifested and with a flaming torch lights up the world. This nation is of pilgrims from all the nations, and in this mass we find the positive and the negative currents of life. Their friction must of necessity develop a world light or a world battle.

Thus it is that no individual can overthrow the cooperative work of the many at Gettysburg.

In the erection of a statue of Gen. Robert E. Lee at Gettysburg we note a concession, if but partial, to the principle we have enunciated. This is, as far as it goes, satisfactory, but we feel that it is not a full and free-hand likeness of General Lee as a Confederate general. Somehow we cannot look upon him as a Confederate general except at the head of his army. To make this token effective, there should be also a statue of a Confederate soldier by his side, with the Stars and Bars unfurled over both. General Lee will be quite lonely at Gettysburg without his army and his flag.

A statue simply stands for a person; and as much as we love and honor General Lee, we know that it is based upon the fact that he was a soldier with us and not as a man whom we had taken along to worship or to make an idol of. If this was not the case, then we loved our flag and home folks least. No one soldier was the custodian of the people. The mass, the army, was the custodian, and we find it impossible to separate ourselves from the mass and our responsibility to it. Hence we appeal for the mass, the divinity which was commander in chief at Gettysburg. Divinity had planned and fought the battle before the armies got there, and the result was what neither army expected. As divinity was the author and finisher of this battle, it follows that the Confederate soldiers were as loyal to the divinity as were the Federal soldiers and consequently could not be traitors to any cause and are entitled to equal recognition at Gettysburg, flag and all, as the Federals. General Lee could not be a general without an army and a flag; then his presence on this field alone would not be a good likeness of him. This does not necessitate hoisting the Stars and Bars anywhere except upon the battle fields where it waved over the boys in gray.

The visitors to the battle field would like to see every possible thing connected with it; therefore we wish to see the Confederate soldier and his flag placed on ibis battle field. We honor our fathers, the past, and we are equally bound to honor our children, the future Youth earned the glory, and it is the duty of age to preserve it. This we wish to do, not upon the basis of the savage and his scalps, but as civilized human beings. Since this battle has been selected as the culminating work and the corner stone of the war, everything pertaining to it should be placed there.

No one has ever yet invented a way to furl a battle flag.

Richard R. Kirkland was perhaps the most famous member of the 2nd S.C. Infantry. Seven months before Gettysburg, at the Battle of Fredericksburg, he climbed over the stone wall at night loaded with canteens to bring water to the suffering wounded Union soldiers. For that he is known as the Angel of Mayre's Heights. At Gettysburg, he was first sergeant of Co. G. He was later killed at the Battle of Chicamauga and is buried in the Quaker Cemetery in Camden, S.C.

Richard R. Kirkland
(Confederate Veteran Magazine)

Dr. Thomas W. Salmond was the chief surgeon of the 2nd S.C. Infantry. At the time of Gettysburg, he was the Brigade Surgeon of Kershaw's Brigade. Dr. Salmond distinguished himself on the second day by riding into the midst of the battle to retrieve his friend Capt. William Z. Leitner – Col. John D. Kennedy's law partner – who had been seriously wounded. Leitner, believing his wound to be mortal, had refused to allow his men to expose themselves by removing him from the field. Salmond immediately left the hospital and "went to the field where Captain Leitner lay, amid the storm of lead and iron" and placed the dying man upon his horse and brought him off the field. Thanks to Salmond's efforts, William Leitner survived his wound.

Dr. Thomas W. Salmond
(History of Kershaw's Brigade)

Chapter 2

3rd South Carolina Battalion of Infantry

SUMTER WATCHMAN AND SOUTHRON
DECEMBER 2, 1884

A Gettysburg Bullet

A rifle bullet fired at Gettysburg just made its appearance in a rather remarkable way. Henry Southern[33], of this county, who lives a short distance from the city, was an active participant in the memorable conflict. He received a severe wound in the neck. He finally recovered but failed to secure the bullet which inflicted the injury. Recently Mr. Southern has been annoyed by a pain in his neck near the collar bone. Suspecting that the ball was the cause of the trouble, he determined to secure the services of a physician in order that the missile might be extracted if possible. He sent for Dr. Wallace, who soon saw that the long imprisoned lead could be released successfully with a little care. The other day, Dr. Wallace in company with Dr. Wright called upon Mr. Southern, and after considerable effort extracted a large sized rifle ball from beneath the collar bone. The operation is quite an extraordinary one, and relieves Mr. Southern of a very unpleasant companion. The bullet is not at all disfigured and looks as new as it was on the day it was discharged in the decisive struggle.

----Greenville News----

* * *

33. Henry Southern served in the Third (Palmetto Battalion) South Carolina Light Artillery and First S. C. Artillery in 1864, but no service records indicate where he served at the time of Gettysburg.

CONFEDERATE VETERAN MAGAZINE
MARCH, 1910

Simon Baruch, 51 W. Seventieth Street, New York City, who was assistant surgeon of the 3d South Carolina Battalion, desires to obtain the address of the surgeons who after the battles of Boonsboro (South Mountain), Md., and Sharpsburg, Va. were sent to be exchanged on the Steamer Louisiana from Baltimore to Fortress Monroe, and thence to Acker's Landing in September, 1862; also the addresses of any of the one hundred and six surgeons and fifteen chaplains who were "detained" at Fort McHenry after the battle of Gettysburg. Dr. Baruch was among those ordered by General Lee to "remain until further orders" in charge of the wounded after these battles.

* * *

NEWBERRY HERALD AND NEWS
MAY 12, 1911

Capt. R[obert] H. Jennings' Address

[3rd South Carolina Battalion, Co. G]

Memorial Day, May 10, 1911, in Newberry.

[Excerpt of a longer account]

Mrs. President of the Drayton Rutherford Chapter, U. D. C., Comrades, Ladies and Gentlemen: I am called on for, to me, a unique service; that is, to make a public address. But as my motto is. "Do your best when duty calls," I beg that you will not "view me with a critic's eye, but pass my imperfections by."

To tell of my experiences in the late unpleasantness would take more time than I have to spare and tax your patience beyond endurance. I will, therefore, have to confine myself to a few incidents in my soldier life.

...

From Chancellorsville we took up our march to Pennsylvania, skirmishing almost daily with the enemy till we crossed the Shenandoah river near Williamsport. On this march our company lost Lieut. Gladney, at

Gaines Cross Roads, from fever, and Private Charles Broom, at Front Royal. We reached Gettysburg, Penn., and on the third and fourth of July was fought the decisive battle of the war when Gen. Lee received his first heavy backset. It was a terrible fight, in which both sides lost heavily in killed and wounded. Gen. Lee retreated in good order, the enemy were so badly worsted they did not press him. Among the killed I recall Gen. Barksdale, of Mississippi, Capt. Warren and Col. Dessaussure, of the 15th S. C. regiment; Sergt. Stokes. the color bearer of our battalion. Wounded, Lieut. Blair, of our company, R. H. Jennings struck in the breast with a schrapnel shot, not seriously hurt.

* * *

Confederate Veteran Magazine
February 1915

ON THE BATTLE FIELD OF SOUTH MOUNTAIN

Frank P. Firey, postmaster at Pomona, Cal., writes of having seen a copy of the VETERAN which aroused his recollection of some incidents connected with the battle of South Mountain. He says:

"I was born and grew up on the battle field of Antietam, in Maryland, and have a vivid recollection of those stirring times. I witnessed the battle of South Mountain, which was fought a day or so before Antietam, in September, 1862. In visiting the field of South Mountain the morning after the battle my father came upon the body of a magnificent specimen of manhood, which proved to be [Lt.] Colonel [George Sholter] James[34] [3rd South Carolina Battalion], of a South Carolina regiment. Before having him buried, my father cut out several buttons from Colonel James's uniform, and my sister had a jeweler arrange one of the large ones for a breastpin and two smaller ones for ear bobs.

---

34. As a captain of artillery, George S. James fired the first shot on Fort Sumter. Although popular legend often attributes this to secessionist Edmund Ruffin, the man commanding the gun that fired the actual first shot of the war, according to Lt. Gen. Stephen D. Lee, was Capt. George S. James. The distinction can be drawn that James fired the signal shot rather than the first ballistic shot. Wright, John D. The Routledge Encyclopedia of Civil War Era Biographies. New York: Routledge, 2013. 308. Print.

"In the latter part of June, 1863, as Lee's army was marching to Gettysburg, passing by our farm in Maryland, my father chanced to talk with several Confederate soldiers of a South Carolina Regiment who had asked for a drink of water, and he told them of having buried a South Carolina colonel who fell in the battle of South Mountain—a Colonel James, With one voice they exclaimed: 'Colonel James! My God! He was the colonel of our regiment, and his brother is the captain of our company.' They immediately ran for the ranks and in a few moments returned with their captain, a tall, muscular man with blue eyes and wearing a handsome gray uniform. As he talked with my father about his brother the tears rolled down his checks, and his tall frame shook with emotion. My father chanced to mention having cut the buttons from Colonel James's uniform, when Captain [Benjamin Sampson] James [3rd South Carolina Battalion, Co. D] said: 'Mr. Firey, do you think your daughter would let me have those buttons?' My father replied: 'Why, certainly. Captain James; she would be more than pleased to let you have them.' My sister brought the buttons and placed them in his hand, and he gazed on them tenderly, weeping like a child. He then folded them in his handkerchief and placed them in his inside breast pocket. Captain James wished to take up the remains of his brother and send them home for burial, but at the time the battle field of South Mountain was in the Union lines. So Captain James said: 'When we return from Pennsylvania or when the war is over, I will, with your kind assistance, secure the remains of my brother and take them home for burial.' With a courteous farewell, for he was a polished gentleman, he resumed his position at the head of his company and moved on with the marching army.

"On its return from Gettysburg Lee's army marched diagonally through our farm in Maryland. Captain James was not among the hosts that passed by, and the poor fellow never returned for the remains of his brother; so I suppose he may have fallen in Pickett's charge at Gettysburg.

"I remember seeing General Longstreet, Gen. Fitzhugh Lee, and others. General Longstreet wore his hair long and had a full wavy beard of chestnut brown. Gen. Fitzhugh Lee was a slim young fellow about twenty-five or twenty-seven years old with a black mustache, and he rode a fine dapple-gray horse. He must have been partial to dapple-grays, for I was told by one who served under him in Cuba that he rode a dapple-gray there.

"At the time above referred to, on the battle field of South Mountain, my father found the body of a fair-haired, beardless boy, about eighteen years old. A Minie ball had struck him in the center of his forehead. In the breast pocket of his coat there was a letter from his sister in Georgia, in which she urged him to 'Hurry up and whip the Yankees and come home.' That poor girl, I presume, never knew just how her brother met his death."

George S. James was a captain of artillery at the seige of Fort Sumter. He was given the honor by then Capt. Stephen D. Lee of commanding the gun that fired the signal shot which launched the bombardment of the fort. He was killed at the Battle of South Mountain as Lt. Col. of the 3rd S. C. Infantry Battalion and was buried on a nearby farm. His soldiers – along with his brother – were shown his grave as they passed through on their way to Gettysburg.

(National Park Service)

Chapter 3

3rd South Carolina Infantry Regiment

CONFEDERATE VETERAN MAGAZINE
NOVEMBER 1901

Charles J. Beck, Columbia, S. C, writes:

I was wounded at the battle of Gettysburg in 1863, and captured by the Federals, but made my escape from the hospital with Thomas C. Paysinter, Company E, Third South Carolina Regiment, Kershaw's Brigade, A. N. V., about the first of September. On our way homeward through Maryland we stopped at a house where we were very kindly treated by the ladies, to whom we gave our names, regiments, etc., and they in turn gave their names, with request that we notify them if we arrived home safely. They were burned out in 1865, and we have made repeated efforts to find them. These ladies lived on the Monocacy River, about a mile from the Potomac. We should be glad indeed to hear from them again.

* * *

Colonel James D. Nance commanded the 3rd S. C. Infantry at Gettysburg. During the retreat from Gettysburg, while in Maryland, Nance placed nine out his ten company commanders under arrest. During the night before, a number of the men of the 3rd had stolen rails from a fence for either shelter or firewood in disobedience of General Robert E. Lee's orders against disturbing private property. Captain R. E. Richardson had stated that his men removed rails, but had replaced them, so he was exempted from arrest. The rest were forced to march at the rear of the regiment and endure the jeers of all the troops who passed. A black cook undertook the task of calling out orders handed down the line, in effect commanding this group of officers. The soldiers and black cooks took great sport seeing a "company of officers" commanded by a cook. Their arrest was lifted that night during a clash with the enemy.

(History of Kershaw's Brigade)

LAURENS ADVERTISER
MAY 13, 1903

JUDGE ALLEN BARKSDALE
[3rd South Carolina Infantry, Co. G]
WRITES OF GETTYSBURG

Experiences of the Briars Retreating between Parallel Lines of Federal Troops—Col. [James D.] Nance's Regard for His Men

----

April 7th, 1903

Hon. O[liver] G. Thompson, Laurens, S. C.

Dear O': Yours of February 27th we received long ago, but I have neglected to answer. You and all the "Briars" are dear to me and the older I get the oftener I think of Laurens,--of its men and women whom I knew so long ago and especially do I think of the "boys" with whom I went to Virginia and marched over the Blue Ridge Mountains, waded the Shenandoah, Rappahannock and Chickahominy and with whom I fought at several close places. Think of Fredericksburg. The "Briars" carried in 26 rifles at about one o'clock P. M. At sundown there were four, and no commissioned officer with them. Seven killed—among them Bob Hellams,--"Wheat", as we called him, Tom Starnes, Jim and Don Dorrah and J[ames] A. Hobby. Fourteen were wounded besides Capt. [Richard P.] Todd and Lieutenant [B. W.] Lanford.

O', as we ran into line and Col. Nance ordered us forward at the double quick, without waiting for the four right companies to form I was scared that evening. For several days I have been thinking of some things connected with our last night at Gettysburg. Some of the "Briars" may not know of these and few, if any, outside of the "Briars" know of them and I will write out my recollections of that night and enclose you the paper. If you think it worthy read it at the meeting Saturday next.

I was once fearfully wicked. Now don't think me a hypocrite when I say that I pray that God will bless every "Briar" and all the "Briars'" children.

Your comrade,

ALLEN BARKSDALE

April 7th, 1903

P. S. I hope to see some of you at New Orleans in May.

GETTYSBURG MEMORIES

To the officers and members of Co. "G" 3rd S. C. Regiment, known as the "Briars" who may be at the reunion of our Company on Saturday next:

MY DEAR COMRADES—A conversation with a citizen of this place, has made me think continuously of our latest night at Gettysburg. I happen to know of some circumstances, connected with that last night, which some of you may not know. And it is certain that not many besides the "Briars" ever did know anything about these things. To tell this tale may be old to some of you and tiresome. That night is a part of history of the "Briars." We were in a fearful position. I feel that I ought to tell it as I know it—as I saw it—as I felt it—as I know others felt it, and to some extent preserve this one bit of "Briars" history. So here goes:

ON THE MARCH

July 1st 1863—nearly 40 years ago—our Division, Kershaw's Brigade in front, marched from within seven miles of Chambersburg to Willoughby Creek, after 5 P. M. We camped on the ground where part of Gen. A. P. Hill's Corps had fought on the 1st. Early on the morning of the 2nd we were marching, but by some mishap we were marched five or more miles out of our way and had to march back over the same ground, losing twice the distance. We were finally in line. Our brigade and Gen. Barksdale's brigade went on the first line, Gen. Semmes supporting us, and Gen. Wofford supporting Gen. Barksdale's brigade. Just here, I would like to know if in the history of the world any Division of our four brigades had such Brigadiers as these—Kershaw, (our own—our beloved) Barksdale, Semmes, Wofford. You remember how we fought that day. John Fairbairn was killed that evening from a suppurating wound on him, which he had received at Fredericksburg. Before the sun went down on those bloody hills, Semmes and Barksdale had found out what there is "over the river."

READY TO GO IN

The next day if you remember we were ready to go in. You remember that Col. [Elbert] Bland of the 7th came limping by us and told us that certain signals were to be given—that all the cannon on Lee's lines would open—that under cover of this cannonade Pickett's Division would advance and when that Division had reached a certain point that our Division would go in. The signals were given, Pickett advanced, he passed the given point—still we had no orders—to this day I know not why. Probably it was not a private's business to know. Late that afternoon we marched back to the ridge from which we had charged the enemy on the 2nd.

My memory is at fault. I cannot say positively whether we left the ridge on the night of the 3rd or 4th, but I believe it was the 4th. Capt. Todd was not with us—had not recovered from the wound he received at Fredericksburg, or if he was with us he was acting as a field officer. I remember that John Watts commanded the "Briars" at Gettysburg—that Ben Lanford was with the Company and that Hugh ___ley was on Gen. Kershaw's staff at that battle or he was at regimental headquarters.

At dark of the night our division retreated from the ridge—the 4th as I recollect it, the "Briars" were ordered to "fall in" and we were marched out some 400 yards or more beyond the stone fence behind which our regiment was "holding the fort." Those of you who were in ranks that night will remember how lonesome it was away out there behind nothing but the weeds which had grown there that last year and under nothing but the stars. Then too there was that stone wall in front of us 100 to 150 yards, and as the Yankees had been behind that during the afternoon, this wall did not tend to enliven the lonesomeness.

AS SKIRMISHERS

We were deployed as skirmishers, only the space between the men was greater than the rules said it should be. Capt. Watts arranged that each third man was to watch so long, then the next be waked, and so on through the night. He was to watch one-third the night, Ben Lanford one-third and I was to watch one-third. I was not a commissioned officer, I was orderly sergeant and was only put to watch like Watts and Lanford because officers were scarce. After making these arrangements Watts and Lanford took a notion that we must go further forward and take charge of the stone fence. I was called up and given a message to Col. J. D. Nance, who had come with us that day. You remember he was seriously wounded at Fredericksburg. My instructions were to go to Col. Nance to tell how close we were to that terrible fence, that there was nothing to cover us where we were, that the weeds would not even hide us, and if he would cause a detail of about 25 or 30 men to be made from the other companies and let me carry them back with me to Capt. Watts he would at once attack the Yankees behind the stone fence—though he thought they had retired; but we would take that fence at all hazards and the next day we would hold that fence, no matter who should come against us.

NEEDED THAT FENCE

The fact is comrades, we needed that stone fence in our business that night and I was to be certain that Col. Nance should know that we needed it and that the possession of that fence was a most pressing military necessity. I am not trying to repeat the exact language—I can only give the substance. It was dark but as I now remember, not cloudy, so I went and went cheerfully, for to me the stone fence was as great a military necessity as it was to Watts and Lanford. Once there was a young man, who felt that the happiness of his whole life depended on its success in gaining the love and the hand of a young lady. So one day he talked to her about the matter. He talked. He had never in his life talked as he did that day. He was terribly in earnest. After exhausting himself he stopped. The young lady calmly answered "No." And then he ramblingly asked her if she would tell him where he had put his hat. This closed the case. Well, I went to Col. Nance's tent, where there were several officers, and like the young man aforesaid I most earnestly tried to make Col. Nance see the situation—the necessity—the military necessity of our taking that fence, and how the last one of us would be shot from that fence if we did not ourselves take it.

NO MORE MEN

Col. Nance said for me to return and tell John Watts that he could not send him the additional men. I failed as completely as my young friend did in his courting. I saluted, about-faced and marched out of the tent and had gone about ten or fifteen steps when I heard Col. Nance's voice, calling my name. I answered and he ordered me to stand till he came up to me. Then, my comrades, Col. Nance exhibited a love for the men in his regiment, which I did not dream that he felt. He took me by the hand and said, that possibly he ought to let me go on to our company, without any further being said, but that he could not do so. He told me to tell Watts that the Division would retreat that night; that it was the "Briars," (and he used that name) turn to go on to the skirmish line; that as the army retreated it would be the duty of the skirmishers to hold the enemy, back at all hazards; that he seriously doubted if we would be able to do what was required of us; that we would probably be cut to pieces and what remained be captured. He spoke of us so feelingly; said how sorry he was that we were so placed; declared that he would not have told me if he had not believed that we would stand the trial. I had never seen Col. Nance so moved. He said that he was much grieved that we were so placed but that he would not be justified in sending any more men into such a danger unless it was a necessity; and bidding me good bye most feelingly he turned and walked towards his tent.

MADE HIS REPORT

When I got back to the company I told Watts, and I think Lanford, what Col. Nance said; do not remember whether he told the men who were deployed or not. John Watts was excited for a while. Ben Lanford, as usual with him, did not seem to pay much attention to this news. As for me, I was very nearly "stampeded," I was scared. Not a wink did I sleep that night. Watt and Lanford slept their turns as soundly as if no Yankees were down at the fence—that military necessity. I walked up and down the line trying to keep all the "Briars" awake. We had marched and fought three days, been kept awake a great portion of the nights and it was hard to watch. It was not hard for me. Amid all the watching I heard no noise on our side, I heard rumbling wagons going down the hill-side on the Yankee side. About sunrise the morning of the 5th we heard a clear distinct voice calling "Attention skirmishers Kershaw's Brigade" and we at once sprang to our feet, faced to the front with our guns at the shoulder. We were ordered to march in retreat and when we got nearly to the place where we had left the regiment the night before the comrades were rallied. We at once struck into the road our Division had gone back on. We marched in perfect order as though we were on drill.

ALL IN LINE

Not a man missed the step. All the time I expected that we would be attacked. When we had gone several miles, someone called out "look over yonder" and looking I saw a line of federal cavalry half a mile to our left, about even with us and going the same way. Directly another man said "look over yonder" and looking to the right I saw a column of federal infantry, a little further off than the cavalry but even with us and going in the same direction. I did not think I would see the 3rd regiment soon and I had visions of being shut up in Yankee prisons. Capt. John Nance commanded the skirmishers and about the only command I remember hearing him give was "close up" and "quick step." We swung along lively; there was no straggling. About twelve or one o'clock we began to come up with the main body of Lee's army and finally we caught up with Kershaw's Brigade. Then they began to shout and when the "Briars" marched into their place—the right color company—all hands of us were glad.

Excuse me for writing such a long story of this. Remember me always kindly. Come as many of you as possible to New Orleans in May. "God be with you till we meet again."

Your comrade,

ALLEN BARKSDALE

D. Augustus Dickert was a nineteen-year-old 1st Lt. commanding Co. H, 3rd S.C. Infantry at Gettysburg. He was later promoted to captain and became the adjutant of Kershaw's Brigade. He wrote the definative history of Kershaw's Brigade at the insistance of his surviving comrades in 1899.

(History of Kershaw's Brigade)

Chesley W. Herbert was the captain of Co. C in the 3rd S.C. Infantry at Gettysburg where he was wounded on July 2. He was furloughed for 60 days from General Hospital 10 in Richmond on July 20, 1863 where he had been admitted for "injuring his tibia."

(History of Kershaw's Brigade)

(History of Kershaw's Brigade)

John W. Wofford of Spartanburg was a 21-year-old private in Co. K at Gettysburg. A month later on Aug. 1, 1863, he was promoted to Bvt. 2nd Lt. from ranks. He assumed command of the company following the Battle of Chickamauga. Wofford was in command of the rear-guard on one of the main roads during the retreat from Bentonville, the last battle before the surrender of Johnston's army. He was active in the election of Wade Hampton as governor which ended carpet-bag rule in S.C. and later served in the state senate.

Dr. James Evans was surgeon of the 3rd S.C. Infantry and a brother of Brig. Gen. Nathan G. Evans. Dr. Evans was described as "kind and considerate to his patients, punctual and faithful in his duties, and withal a dignified, refined gentleman." It was said "that none felt uneasy when their lives or limbs were left to his careful handling."

(History of Kershaw's Brigade)

Richard Alexander Leavell of Newberry, S.C. Was a member of Co. E, 3rd S.C. Infantry at Gettysburg. The twenty-year-old 3rd Corporal was promoted to 2nd Corporal on July 2, 1863 during the battle.

(Confederate Museum and Library, Greenville, SC)

David Mason Henry "Mase" Langston was the captain of Co. I, 3rd S.C. Infantry. He was killed at Gettysburg. He had been severly wounded in the neck, thigh and lower leg at Savage Station on June 29, 1862. Despite expectations, Capt. Langston survived and was acting Lt. Col. at the time of his death at Gettysburg on July 2, 1863.

(Confederate Museum and Library, Greenville, SC)

Chapter 4

7th South Carolina Infantry Regiment

Edgefield Advertiser
July 29, 1863

Casualties in the 7th Regt. S. C. V.

FIELD OFFICERS.

Wounded—Lieut. Colonel [Elbert] Bland, slightly

CO. A, LIEUT. [Augustus W.] BURT, COMMANDING.

Killed—Sergeant [Robert L.] Mims; Privates James Johnson and Charles Hammond.

CO. B, CAPT. [Thomas A.] HUDGINS.

Killed—Lieutenant W[illiam] C. C Hodges and Private [William C.] Barmore.

Wounded—Lieut. [S. W.] Callahan, seriously; Sergt. Agnew, severely; Corp'l [A. C.] McGee, severely; Privates E. B. Bowie, slight; J. M. Graham, severely

Missing—J. N. [James V.] Young. [Captured on July 2. Sent to Ft. McHenry then Ft. Delaware.]

David Wyatt Aiken was colonel of the 7th S. C. Infantry at Gettysburg. He had been severely wounded at the Battle of Sharpsburg. His wound was believed to be mortal, but Aiken recovered in time to lead the 7th at Gettysburg. Soon after Gettysburg he was reassigned as commandant of troops and defenses in Macon, Georgia due to lingering effects of his earlier wounds. Aiken, South Carolina was named for his uncle, William Aiken.

(History of Kershaw's Brigade)

CO. C, LIEUT. [Albert T.] TRAYLOR, COMMANDING.

Killed—Corporal [Thomas W.] Willis.

Wounded—Lieut. [Albert T.] Traylor, seriously, in breast; Sergt. [Samuel F.] Edmonds, slight; Corp'l. Cohen, seriously; Privates T[homas] W. Barksdale, J. [G. M.] Banks, W. Banks, all slight; J[ohn] C. Martin, Reagan W. Willis, Bordell [Socratees A. Bosdel], all seriously.

Missing—Lieut. [Nicholas Hodges] Palmer and Private Posey Davis.

CO. D, LIEUT. M'GEE [M. McDuffie McGehee], COMMANDING.

Killed—Sergeant [William L.] McCurry.

Wounded—Lieutenant [Bob] Davis; Sergeants [Alfred D.] Clark and [John Bannister] Allen, Privates [Hiram F.] Cowan and [Samuel Pingen] Haddon, all slight; Sergeant [J. Thompson] Kennedy, Corporal [Daniel] Boyd and Private [Benjamin F.] Hutchinson, all severely.

Missing—E[lijah] H. Spear.

CO. E, CAPTAIN [James] MITCHELL.

Killed—Corporal [U. G.] McGee and Private [Paul] Mitchell

Wounded—Sergeant J. M. Daniel [2nd Lt. James M. Daniel], mortally, since dead; Lieutenant [William A.] Rutland, Privates J[ames] A. Corley, J[ames O.] Denny, W. Crouch [actually was Milledge Crouch, not Willis Crouch] and [John R.] Pinson, all severely; [Alfred] Maroney, very slight; W[illiam A.] Mitchell, slightly; [James P.] Salter and S Smith, slightly.

Missing—J [H] Smith.

CO. F, LIEUT. [Warren D.] BROOKS, COMMANDING

Killed—none

Wounded—Corporal [Mark] Maddox, leg amputated; Privates [James M.] Kadle and Friday, slightly.

CO. G, CAPT. [John W.] KEMP.

Killed—Corporal [Thomas L.] Aiton.

Wounded—Privates [either H. P. or Jesse W. both wounded at Gettysburg] Duffie and A C Griffith, seriously; M Griffith, Ira Turner and [Larkin] Edson, all slightly.

Missing—J[ohn] R Sentell.

CO. H, CAPT. ADDISON.

Killed—Thos J Smith

Wounded—Sergeant ____, leg amputated; Sergeant [Carly M.] Gray, Privates [George W.] Elrod and Laborne [Most likely Van L. Laboon], all slight.

CO. I, CAPT. [Benjamin] ROPER.

Killed—Corporals [Thomas] Harling, [Thomas N.] Pressly, W[illiam] H Mathis and Private [S. C.] Ridgeway.

Wounded—Sergeant [W. H.] Bussey, Privates [William G.] Berry, [F. M.] Brown, M. [N.] Floyd, Petter [most likely J. M. Pettis], all severely; J [either Jeptha or James, neither service record indicates a wound] Floyd, [Drury] Sparks and [James H.] Whitcomb, slightly.

Missing—Lieutenant [Benjamin F.] Sharpton.

CO. K, LIEUT. [Jiles M.] BERRY, COMMANDING.

Killed—M B Gentry.

Wounded—Sergeant L M Lanier, severely; Corporal [W. L.] Talbert, severely; Privates [J. H.] Rampey, W. J. Holmes, severely; [John T.] Henderson, leg amputated.

CO. L, CAPT. [George T.] LITCHFIELD.

Killed-Privt [James] L Faulk.

Wounded--Lieutenant [Kenneth M.] Newton, severely;

Privates [W. D.] Lilly and [A. D.] Parker, severely; [W. B.] Jones, severely; [J. B.] Graddy and [M. C.] Cook, slightly.

Missing-Private [James C.] Jenkins.

CO. M, CAPT. [Jerry E.] GOGANS

Killed—Benj. R. Smith

Wounded—Lieutenant [A. P.] Bouknight, slightly; Sergeants [J. J.] McDaniel and [G. W.] Jennings, severely; W. Edison, W. Harris, severely; Sergeant Wise, slightly; Private [T. A.] Merchant, severely; Joel Miller, J D Rushton and James Bedenbaugh, seriously; [Joseph P.] Henson, leg amputated.

Recapitulation—Killed, 18; Wounded, 85; Missing, 7; Aggregate, 110.

JOHN R. CARWILE, Adjutant.

* * *

EDGEFIELD ADVERTISER
JULY 29, 1863

OBITUARY

Another brave and gallant spirit has fallen! THOMAS LOWNDES BUTLER died in the great battle at Gettysburg, Pennsylvania. Struck by a Minnie ball, he fell lifeless from his horse without speaking a word or uttering a groan. He was the son of Dr. WILLIAM BUTLER, formerly a Representative in the old United States Congress from Greenville District, and a younger brother of that preux chevalier, Col. CALBRAITH M. BUTLER, of the 2nd Regiment of South Carolina Cavalry, Hampton's Brigade, who recently lost his leg in the battle of Brandy Station. The deceased was only twenty-one years old.

At the commencement of this terrible revolution, he volunteered his services as a private in a troop of cavalry raised by his brother in Edgefield District, and has constantly and faithfully served his country ever since in most of the cavalry fights in Virginia. He was modest and unassuming, always ready for duty, however arduous or hazardous, and possessed all the other characteristics of true courage. In battle, no one was more cool and self-possessed. With manly courage he united, in an eminent degree, a woman's kindness and gentleness, which greatly endeared his to his fellow soldiers. He declined a Lieutenantcy in the regular army, because it was not his purpose to make arms his profession after the war was over. His loss is a sad bereavement to his family and friends. It has wrung a widowed mother's heart with anguish which none but a mother can feel so deeply—a mother who, has, still, five other sons now in the service of her country.

THOMAS HARLING, a son of Mr. JOHN HARLING, Sr., was killed at the battle of Gettysburg, Pa., on the 2nd instant. Capt. BEN ROPER, of the 7th S. C. V., in a letter to the father of the deceased, dated Hagerstown, Md., July 7th, speaks thus of this gallant young soldier:

MR. JOHN HARLING, --Dear Sir: It is with grief and pain of heart to you that I seat myself to communicate to you the sad intelligence of the death of your son THOS. HARLING, who fell in battle near Gettysburg, Penn., whilst gallantly bearing the colors of the Regiment. It fell to his lot, after the Color sergeant was wounded, to bear the colors, and it was nobly done by him until he was pierced through the bead by a Minnie ball and fell dead upon the field.

He was a noble and gallant soldier, ever ready and willing to go forward in the discharge of his whole duty. His conduct was such as to gain the love and esteem of the entire Company, both officers and men.

His loss to the Company is irreparable, and has cast a gloom over the hearts of us all. It should be some consolation to you to know that your son offered himself a sacrifice for all that is dear to man in this life—Liberty and Independence.

After the battle was over I had his remains put away as well as circumstances would admit, but the spot marked so it can be pointed out in after days. May God comfort you in this, your sad bereavement, is the prayer of

Your sympathizing friend,
BENJ. ROPER,
Capt. Co. I, 7th S. C. Reg't.

* * *

EDGEFIELD ADVERTISER
AUGUST 5, 1863

Capt. W[illiam] E. MCCASLAN[35], of Abbeville, a noble and a gallant spirit, fell at the battle of Gettysburg. He was well known and esteemed in this vicinity, having taught school in the Village for several years.

* * *

35. This appears to be Captain William E. McCaslan of Company E, 2nd Florida Infantry. He had been the principal of the Brookstown Academy in Brookstown in Hernando County, Florida. He had gone there in 1857. Other educators such as Thomas Coogler had been recruited from South Carolina to the southern frontier of Florida. EARLY HERNANDO COUNTY HISTORY (http://www.fivay.org/hernando1.html, captured March 23, 2014)

EDGEFIELD ADVERTISER
AUGUST 26, 1863

Rutland, Daniel, McGee, Mitchell

We are proud and happy to grace our paper to-day with the following simple, but noble tribute from Co. E, 7th Regt., to the memory of four gallant and departed spirits whose forever-to-be-hon-ored names stand above:

CAMP 7th S. C. Regt., August 12th, 1863

MR. EDITOR: Allow Co. E. 7th Regt., a space in your columns to announce, to relatives and friends at home, and in the army, the death of four of its members, viz; Lieut. W[illiam] A. RUTLAND, who fell mortally wounded at the battle of Gettysburg, Penn., on the [no day listed] of July, and died at Williamsport, Md., on the 8th of the same month. Lieut. J[ames] M. DANIEL was also mortally wounded in the same battle, and died on the 3rd, near the battle-field. Corp'l M. G. MCGEE and PAUL MITCHELL were both killed dead on the field.

The former two fell while urging their men to victory or death; while the latter showed by the place they laid on the field, that they intended to carry out these orders. The names of other men may be written high in the temple of fame, while the names of these heroes may lie still with their honored remains in a distant land; yet the Company has the proud consociation to feel that no Officers or Soldiers ever discharged their duties more faithfully, more gallantly, more devotedly, than they. Ever ready to discharge any duty that involved upon themselves as officers and soldiers, they had gained for themselves the love and esteem of the entire command.

To their relatives and friends, we would say: You have suffered an irreparable loss, for never can their places be filled in your heart. No more will their loved and cheerful faces illumine your firesides, and assist in making your homes abodes of brightness and peace. They are gone never to return! Yet while we know that their places can never be filled, either at home or in the field, let us remember that the Lord "doeth all things well," and it is He that hath taken them from us. Trusting in the goodness and mercy of an Allwise God we hope one day to meet our departed comrades in a better land, among those "green pastures" and by those "still water brooks," where there will be no more wars nor rumors of war, but eternal peace and rest.

That God may help all the bereaved to bear their trials and crosses, and at last take them home to rest, in those heavenly realms, where we hope our brave heroes are only gone before, is the prayer of COMPANY E.

* * *

EDGEFIELD ADVERTISER
AUGUST 26, 1863

DEPARTED this life on the 30th July, Mr. LUKE DEVORE SHIBLY [7th S.C. Infantry, Co. K], in the 22nd year of his age.

The deceased, when a small boy, was left an orphan, but was taken under the care of that devoted and upright man, LUKE DEVORE, to raise as one of his family; yet that kind man was not spared to see him grown, and hence his raising devolved on his affectionate aunt CATHARINE DEVORE, and well did she discharge her duty. By precept and example she early instilled into his youthful mind the principles of piety and holiness. We find him at a tender age uniting himself to the Baptist Church at Gligal. This profession he held sacred to the last. His education was not neglected, as he received the benefit of the instruction of qualified teachers. But when the war broke out books were laid aside, and he volunteered in the 7th S. C. Regiment. As a soldier he acted his part faithfully. His officers spoke highly in his favor, assuring his aged aunt that she need feel no uneasiness about his moral deportment nor heroism. He was in the battles through which his Regiment passed, and was wounded in the battle of Sharpsburg, and came home, but soon returned to his Regiment and remained with it until stricken down by disease, and sent to the Hospital, where a kind sister visited him and found him quite prostrated. Thinking that a return home might restore his health she accompanied him there. But it was all in vain. He lingered until the 30th of July, when he sweetly fell asleep in Jesus. He continued rational to the last, and so lucid and happy were his last moments that we must allude to them. Just before he died, after having been quiet for some time, he mentioned the disposition he wanted carried out about his pecuniary affairs. He then took his aged aunt by the hand and said to her, "You have been better to me than a mother; don't grieve after me; I am going to glory and we won't be long apart." Several of his relations were present, all of whom he exhorted to meet him in heaven, and gave each his hand for the last farewell. He then turned to the colored boy, who had attended him both in camp service and at the bedside, and calling him by name, gave him his hand and said, "I do wish that you could go with me to glory." Thus ended the life of this pious young man. Who would not wish to die the death of the righteous?

J. A.

*＊＊

EDGEFIELD ADVERTISER
SEPTEMBER 9, 1863

General News Items

The following members of the 7th and 14th S. C. Regt's., were received at the South Carolina Hospital, Richmond, by flag of truce boat on the 28th August, viz: Messrs. A. E. McGee, Hezekiah Burnett, Daniel Boyd, Socrates Bordell, J[ames] A. Corley, 7th Regt., and Spencer Word, Thomas Whittle, Elisha B. Biggers, David Etheridge and Joel Minnick, 14th Regiment.

*＊＊

EDGEFIELD ADVERTISER
SEPTEMBER 9, 1863

WHILE it is a mournful duty, it is intermixed with emotions of pleasure, to present to public view the character of one who fell a victim to Death, nobly defending his country's rights. The subject of this tribute, Corporal THOMAS HARLING, volunteered at an early period of the war in Co. I, 7th S. C. Regiment, under Capt. Wm. F. Prescott, and served in much credit to himself through the many difficulties attending a soldier's life; never making any complaint whatever; always ready and willing to go forth in discharge of any and every duty assigned him. He fought bravely in every battle in which his Regiment was engaged, and came out triumphant until the memorable 2nd day of July at Gettysburg. Being a member of the Color-Guard of his Regiment, when all of its members were disabled but himself, it became his duty to bear the Colors, which duty he performed most gallantly until he was pierced through the head by a ball, which terminated in his immediate death.

He was the son of that firm and patriotic citizen of Edgefield, JOHN HARLING, who freely gave five sons to struggle in our con-flict for Southern Independence and common Rights.

This gallant young man, by his manly and approved course of conduct, achieved for himself the kind feeling of his company, both Officers and men; and while his remains will moulder and mingle with Pennsylvania dust, (and we trust his Spirit is at rest,) his memory will be cherished by his relatives and many friends, who sadly mourn their loss.

* * *

EDGEFIELD ADVERTISER
NOVEMBER 4, 1863

OBITUARY

FIRST LT. ALBERT THOMAS TRAYLOR, of company C, 7th S. C. V., was mortally wounded on the bloody field of Gettysburg on the 2nd, and, after intense suffering, died at Cashtown, Penn., on the 8th of July last, aged 24 years, 11 months and 8 days.

Lieut. T, entered the above command when it was ordered to Charleston in April 1861, and with it went to Virginia in June following, after which he never had an opportunity of visiting home or beholding the faces of his fond mother and loving sister. Though unaccustomed to hardships, and not naturally of a strong constitution, his steady devotion to duty made him a prompt and faithful soldier, while his modesty, bravery and generosity won friends on every hand.

Upon the reorganization of the Regiment in May 1862, his comrades expressed their high appreciation of him as a soldier and gentleman by selecting him as their 1st Lieutenant, and not one time did they regret the choice. In this capacity he passed through the battle before Richmond and Maryland Heights. From that time he was in command of his Company, and heroically led it in the battles of Sharpsburg, Fredericksburg, Chancellorsville, and finally at Gettysburg, upon whose blood-stained field none better or braver fell in defense of Southern freedom. After six days of the most intense suffering, in a land far from his home, which he bore with a fortitude and resignation at once becoming the Christian, the soldier, the man, that he was, his noble spirit winged its flight to its bright reward.

His erect manly form and bright handsome face, which we shall see no more, prepossessed all at first sight, while those who knew him well loved and respected him for his warm, generous, honest heart—his dignity, modesty, and spotless character. He ever discountenanced skulkers and cowards, and in all the battles, marches and attendant sufferings through which he was called to pass, he set an example of true bravery, unwavering fortitude and faithful devotion to duty. The future truly opened a brilliant career to one possessed of so many noble qualities. His comrades in arms loved him as a brother and feel their loss is irreparable.

He leaves a devoted mother, a sister, and brothers, to mourn his untimely death. But they should be comforted with the reassurance that their loss is his eternal gain. He was a member of the Baptist Church, and we humbly believe his pure spirit now rests in that bright abode where suffering and death are no more forever.

---C---

* * *

AIKEN STANDARD
JULY 22, 1896

THE BATTLE OF GETTYSBURG
An Old Reb Visits the Scene and Recounts the Deeds Performed

GETTYSBURG, PA. July 6, 1896

In my last letter of the 4th July, I told you of running over the battlefield on the electric cars. I saw at once the field could not be seen and studied in that way, so I hired a horse and buggy and secured the services of a competent guide for the next day. At 8 a. m. we got off to the field. We first went to where the first day's battle began (July 1st), on the road between Gettysburg and Chambersburg, and then followed the line of battle from point to point. The three day's fighting around Gettysburg is divided into eight distinct engagements.

First day, first engagement on the 1st of July, Hill's corps first struck the enemy six miles from Gettysburg. At night after hard fighting the Confederates had driven the enemy back and occupied the town; the Federals occupying Cemetery Ridge.

Second day, second engagement, 2nd July. On the morning of July 2nd the Union army occupied Cemetery Ridge and extended from Round Top northward and then eastward to and around the crest of Culp's Hill. The Confederates along Seminary ridge, through the town and extending to the foot of Culp's Hill. The Confederate lines at this time were about six miles long and in just about the shape of a mammoth fish hook. The Federal lines were about four miles long. On this day the greatest amount of fighting took place, and (Longstreet's) corps attacked the enemy on the Emmettsburg road, drove them back from the peach orchard, through the wheat field, from "Devil's Den," through the "Valley of Death," and well up Little Round Top Mountain, taking the first line of breastwork, but failed to fully drive them off the mountain. The task was too great; they had there three lines of breastwork on Little Round Top. The ground on this field was thickly strewn with dead and dying men that awful night.

Third engagement was Ewell's attack on Culp's Hill in which he drove the enemy from a large portion of his breastworks and held them.

Fourth engagement. Early and Rhode's charge on Cemetery Hill, driving the enemy from their rifle pits and taking their cannon at the top of the hill; but reinforcements came to the assistance of the enemy and our men lost the hill.

Third day, fifth engagement, 3rd July. As the morning wore away, the Confederates were getting their artillery in position on Seminary Ridge; by 2 p.m. we had 150 guns in position; the enemy a larger number, and then for two hours the awful artillery duel went on with heavy slaughter on both sides. The like had never been heard before or since by this old Reb. When the artillery ceased, then Pickett's division made their grand charge of over one mile under fire of cannon and musketry through open fields and up the ridge to the enemy breastworks and then drove them out of the bloody angle and held it until the enemy brought up a new division and took it back.

In the few minutes during which this encounter lasted the greater part of Pickett's division disappeared from the lines—death and wounds had done its awful work. Of the fifteen field officers and four generals leading that charge, only Gen. Pickett and one lieutenant-colonel remained to tell the awful story. During this charge Gen. Hancock was wounded. Thus ended the greatest charge of modern times without giving us what we wanted.

Third day continued. Seventh engagement. On our extreme right the Federal cavalry under Gen. Kilpatrick charged our right flank. Gen. Law's Alabama brigade soon drove them from the field with great loss.

Eighth engagement, 3rd day. Gen. Lee ordered Gen. J. E. B. Stuart with his cavalry around the Union's right flank intending to divert Gen. Meade's attention while Pickett made his charge, and in the event of Pickett's success have him fall upon the retreating forces of Meade. Three miles east of Gettysburg he encountered the Federal cavalry and a sharp engagement was the result. Gen. Hampton was wounded in this engagement. Thus ended this three day's bloody drama. At night on the third day we held the whole battlefield, had driven the enemy back for miles into their breastworks on the ridges, hills and mountains, and had driven them from large portions of their breastworks on those high elevations. Yet we cannot claim the battle of Gettysburg as ours. It had cost so much up to this time we could not press on. Our ranks thinned by death, wounds and prisoners, rations out and ammunition nearly exhausted. The enemy stuck to the hills and breastworks, would not come out of them. We had to move into Maryland and the strangest thing of all is the Union forces claimed it as their battle.

I did not find it difficult to locate our (Kershaw's) position, where we formed the line of battle on Willoughby Run and then up through the roads to the stone fence where [Cpl.] Mark Maddox [Company F, 7th S. C.] lost his leg, then across the Emmetsburg road where the friend of my boyhood days, James Kadle [Company F, 7th S. C.], was killed; then on through the fields by the Rose farm house into the "Valley of Death" and the wheat field until night closed the bloody strife.

Thus we come to the close of a most imperfect sketch of the pivotal battle of the war, and the greatest of modern times. Over forty thousand men were killed, wounded and missing in three days. We only needed Stonewall Jackson to have given us a complete victory at Gettysburg.

Judging by the hotel registers there is no large number of Confederates

Caloway K. Henderson of Edgefield County, S.C. was a 1st Corp. at the time of Gettysburg in Co. F, 7th S.C. Infantry. He volunteered at the beginning of the war at the age of sixteen. He was later captured at the Battle of the North Anna River and sent to Point Lookout, Maryland. He was later a trustee of Furman University and on the commission from South Carolina arranging the gathering of veterans at the 50th Gettysburg Reunion.

(Confederate Veteran Magazine)

who visited this battlefield. It should not be so, com-rades, you should visit it; you will never regret it; the people there will treat you well. You need not believe all you hear about the battle.

> "Months have passed, thirty-three long years
> gone by,
> As side by side these heroes lie;
> Yet still we come as years roll by
> To view the place where heroes lie;
> And learn the tales these tablets tell,
> How brave men fought, how brave men fell.
> Though many tears have fallen here,
> For loving friends, or brothers dear,
> May gentle words from all arise
> To bind our hearts with strongest ties,
> And over each grave a requiem say
> For him who wore the blue or gray."

Our trip is ended. We retrace our steps back to Baltimore, Washington, Fredericksburg, Richmond, Petersburg, Rocky Mount, Florence, Den___ ___ Aiken. Goodbye.

[Sgt.] C[aloway] K. HENDERSON [Company F, 7th S. C.]

* * *

CONFEDERATE VETERAN MAGAZINE
MARCH 1901

[Sgt.] George W. Lott [7th S.C. Infantry, Company H], of Johnston, S. C.: "Any information you can give me of my brother, John Lott [7th S.C. Infantry, Company H], will be appreciated. We have had no information of him since the battle of Gettysburg. My eldest brother thinks John heard that I was wounded in that battle, and tried to find me, and that he must have met the Federal army. We have long and anxiously wished for any knowledge of his fate."

* * *

THE ATLANTA JOURNAL
MARCH 30, 1901

PICKETT DID NOT DO IT ALL

Statement of Interest About the Fighting at Gettysburg

Editors Atlanta Journal:

I have been much interested in the stories of the war between the States written by men who served in your ranks and lately appearing in your columns. I served in the infantry from First Manassas to Appomattox. At First Manassas I was a private in the Seventh South Carolina Volunteers and especially detailed as orderly for General M[illedge] L[uke] Bonham, who held Mitchell's Ford or the center of our line. In 1862 I was transferred from Kershaw's brigade and the Seventh South Carolina Volunteers to the First South Carolina Rifles of Gregg's (afterwards McGowan's) brigade, which was under Jackson until his death, and then under A. P. Hill until the surrender. This statement will introduce me to the Georgia survivors of the Army of Northern Virginia.

One of your correspondents from Wright's brigade, speaking of Pickett's charge at Gettysburg, says: "It certainly was a most hazardous affair. They suffered heavily, and yet I have never been convinced the battle of the second day previous should stand in history as the bloodiest fought of the two."

Another correspondent, a survivor of [Paul Jones] Semmes' brigade, says: "The subsequent sacrifice of Pickett's gallant division was simply murder."

I believe in giving honor to whom honor is due. Pickett's loss has been greatly exaggerated, and for nearly 38 years the fancy story of this "sacrifice" has been written up in glowing words until many persons believe that Pickett did all the fighting at Gettysburg, and that Georgia, North Carolina and the other States were "not in it."

Let us see what the figures prove as to Pickett's command at Gettysburg before the battle and after it.

From July 1, 1862, to June 30, 1863, 13 battles were fought by parts or the whole of the Army of Northern Virginia. In these, Pickett's division, consisting of Garnett's, Armistead's and Kemper's brigades, lost in killed and wounded 772 men, while the brigades of Archer, Lane and Scales lost in killed and wounded 3,610 men.

At Gettysburg Pickett's division lost in killed 232 men; Hood's division 343; Early's division, 156; Johnson's division, 329; Rhodes' division, 421; McLaw's division, 313; Anderson's division, 147; Heth's division, 411; Pender's division, 262, and the cavalry lost 36.

At Gettysburg the loss in wounded by divisions was as follows: Pickett, 1,157; McLaw's, 1,538; Hood, 1,504; Early, 806; Johnson, 1,269; Rodes, 1,728; Anderson, 1,128; Heth, 1,905; Pender, 1,312, and the cavalry 140.

In the captured or missing the losses by divisions were: Pickett, 1,499; McLaw's, 327; Hood, 442; Early, 226; Rodes, 103; Anderson, 840; Heth, 534; Pender, 116 and the cavalry 64.

From the above it will be seen that Hood, Rodes, McLaws, Heth and Pender each had more men killed than Pickett. Early, Anderson and Johnson each lost fewer men killed.

In wounded, McLaws, Hood, Johnson, Rodes, Heth and Pender each lost more than Pickett. Early and Anderson lost fewer men.

Pickett lost in captured 1,499, nearly three times as many as Heth, whose men went as far in the charge and stayed as long as Pickett's did.

Pickett's division was composed of 15 regiments and his loss in killed averaged a little more than 15 men to the regiment. This certain-ly was not much of a slaughter or sacrifice.

Georgia lost in killed at Gettysburg 421, while Virginia lost 388. This does not include the cavalry and artillery.

North Carolina lost in killed 686 or 198 more than Virginia.

This destruction wrought by the artillery at Gettysburg has been described as appalling, but the loss in killed of the Confederate artill-ery was only 78. While the loss was so small the moral effects were somewhat like at the cannonade at Valmy, where the invading army under the Duke of Brunswick was defeated by the French Republicans in 1792.

Most of these figures are taken from "Official Records of the War of the Rebellion," Series 1, volume 27, part 11, page 338, etc. They are published so that justice may be done and that the present generation may know who bore the brunt of the battle at Gettysburg.

On March 1, 1865, Pickett had 388 officers and 6,151 enlisted men effective and present for duty, but at Appomattox only 120 officers and 911 men were paroled.

ROBERT R. HEMPHILL

Abbeville, S. C., March 22, 1901

James Hillary Masters served throughout the war in Co. D, 7th S. C. Infantry. After the war he returned to his occupations as a master mason and farmer.

(Masters Family)

Chapter 5
8th South Carolina
Infantry Regiment

John Williford Henagan commanded the 8th S.C. Infantry at Gettysburg. He was the former sheriff of Marlboro County, S.C. and was a member of the S.C. legislature. Col. Henagan was captured near Winchester, Va. the next year and died April 22, 1865 as a prisoner of war on Johnson's Island, Ohio. His remains lie buried there. His comrades said that he was a quiet man who "expressed his views firmly and candidly when called upon."

(History of Kershaw's Brigade)

Eli Thomas Stackhouse was captain of Co. L, 8th S.C. Infantry at Gettysburg. He was promoted to major on July 5, 1863 and ended the war as colonel of the 8th S.C. It was said that Stackhouse "had that peculiar faculty of endowing his soldiers with confidence and a willingness to follow where he led." He was "instrumental in the establishment of Clemson College, and became one of its first trustees." He died in Washington, D.C. while representing his district in the U.S. Congress.

(History of Kershaw's Brigade)

Andrew T. Harllee of Marion, S.C. was the captain of Co. I, 8th S.C. Infantry at Gettysburg. He was a member of the commission appointed to negotiate South Carolina's secession terms with President James Buchanan. Harllee was wounded at Gettysburg.

(History of Kershaw's Brigade)

Duncan McIntyre of Marion, S.C. was the captain of Co. H, 8th S.C. Infantry. He was wounded in the chest at Fredericksburg, but was counted as present in his records by the time of Gettysburg.

(History of Kershaw's Brigade)

Theodore F. Malloy of Cheraw, S.C. was a 1st Lieutenant of Co. C, 8th S.C. Infantry at Gettysburg.

(History of Kershaw's Brigade)

Richard J. Tatum served in the 8th S.C. Infantry, Co. G. He had been serving as wagon master for the regiment leading up to Gettysburg and was captured on July 13, 1863 by Brig. Gen. Benjamin F. Kelley's forces at New Creek, Va. He was sent to Camp Chase, Ohio and later sent to Fort Delaware where he spent the balance of the war.

(Men of Mark in South Carolina Volume 3)

Chapter 6

15th South Carolina Volunteer Infantry

NATIONAL TRIBUNE
WASHINGTON, DC
AUGUST 27, 1908

Gen. Kershaw's Account

Gen. Kershaw, whose brigade led in these assaults, gives a graphic picture of the closeness and determination of the fighting in his official report:

"In a few minutes after my line halted the enemy advanced across the Wheat Field in two lines of battle, with a very small interval between the lines, in such a manner as to take the 7th S. C. in flank. I changed the direction of the right wing of the regiment, under Lieut.-Col. Elbert Bland, to meet the attack, and hurried back to Gen. [Paul Jones] Semmes, then some 150 yards in my right rear, to bring him up to meet the attack on my right, and also to bring forward my right regiment (15th S. C., Col. [William D.] DeSaussure), which, separated from the command by the artillery at the time of the advance, was now cut off by Semmes Brigade. Its gallant and accomplished commander had just fallen when I reached it, and it was under the command of Maj. Wm. M. Gist. Gen. Semmes promptly responded to my call, and put his brigade in motion toward the right, preparatory to moving to the front. I hastened back to the 7th S. C., and reached it just as the enemy, having arrived at a point about 200 yards from us, poured in a volley and advanced to the charge. The 7th received him handsomely, and long kept him in check in their front. There was still an interval of 100 yards between this regiment and the right of the 7th, and into this the enemy was forcing his way, causing the 7th to swing back more and more, still fighting at a distance not exceeding 30 paces, until the two wings were doubled on each other or nearly so.

"Finding that the battery on my left had been silenced, I sent for the 2nd S. C. to come to the right, but by this time the enemy had swung around and lapped my whole line at close quarters, and the fighting was general and desperate. At length the 7th S. C. gave away, and I directed Col. [David Wyatt] Aiken to re-form them at the stone wall, some 200 yards in my right rear. I fell back to the 3rd regiment, then hotly engaged on the crest of the stony hill, and gradually swung around its right as the enemy made progress around our flank. Semmes's advanced regiment mingled with the 3rd, and among the rocks and trees, within a few feet of each other, a desperate conflict ensued. The enemy could make no progress in front, but slowly extended around my right. Separated from view of my left wing by the hill and wood, all my staff being with that wing, the position of the 15th being unknown and the 7th being in the rear, I feared the brave men around me would be surrounded by the large force pressing around them, and ordered the 3rd and the 15th Ga. with them to fall back to the stone house, whither I followed them.

"On emerging from the wood I saw [Brig. Gen. William T.] Wofford coming in, in splendid style.

"My left wing had held the enemy in check along their front and lost no ground. The enemy gave way at Wofford's advance, and with him the whole of my left wing advanced to the charge, sweeping the enemy before them, without a moment's stand, across the stone wall, beyond the Wheat Field, up to the foot of the mountain. At the same time my 15th regiment and part of Semmes's Brigade pressed forward on the right to the same point. Going back to the stone wall near my rear, I found Col. Aiken in position, and at the stone building found the 3rd S. C. and the regiment of Semmes's Brigade. I moved them up to the stone wall, and, finding that Wofford's men were coming out, I retained them at that point to check any attempt of the enemy to advance."

D. J. Griffith was a 19-year-old 3rd Lieutenant in Co. C, 15th S.C. Infantry at Gettysburg. At consolidation of the 15th during the last month of the war into the "New 7th" S.C. Infantry, Griffith became Captain of Co. H.

(History of Kershaw's Brigade)

Francis Marion Farr was wounded in the right shoulder on July 2, 1863 at Gettysburg as a member of Co. F, 15th S.C. Infantry. He was taken prisoner and sent to DeCamp General Hospital on David's Island in Long Island Sound in New York. He was exchanged on Sept. 27, 1863 at City Point, Virginia. Farr was a newcomer to the regiment having enlisted June 1, 1863 after graduating the South Carolina Military Academy. At Gettysburg, he was a private, but was appointed 2nd Lieutenant on July 3, 1863. It appears that this promotion did not take effect until January 1864 when he was transferred to Co. H. Farr ended the war as Captain to which he ascended directly when 1st Lt. John L. Bailey declined promotion to allow Farr to take the post.

(Men of Mark in South Carolina Volume 2)

~ *Section 2* ~

McGowan's / Perrin's Brigade

Col. (Later General) Abner Perrin
(Library of Congress)

Introduction:

McGowan's (Perrin's) Brigade

The brigade of Brig. Gen. Samuel McGowan marched into Pennsylvania with a new commander. Its original commander, Brig. Gen. Maxcy Gregg, had formed the brigade in June of 1862. After Gen. Gregg was killed at Fredericksburg, the Colonel of the 14th South Carolina, Samuel McGowan, replaced him. Under McGowan's capable command, the brigade thenceforth became known as McGowan's Brigade. However, when a serious wound suffered at the Battle of Chancellorsville sidelined McGowan, brigade command devolved upon the brigade's senior officer, Col. Abner Perrin of the 14th South Carolina.[36]

This brigade served in Maj. Gen. William Dorsey Pender's division in the newly created Third Corps of Lt. Gen. A. P. Hill. On July 1, Col. Perrin received orders to march at 8:00 A.M., leading the division's advance toward Gettysburg. The 1st South Carolina Rifles (Orr's Rifles) was the exception, having been left to guard the divisional wagon train. Pender's division followed Maj. Gen. Henry Heth's lead division east along the Chambersburg Pike. After marching about three or four miles, the Palmetto men heard the sounds of battle drifting from the direction of

36. Caldwell, J. F. J. The History of a Brigade of South Carolinians, Known First as "Gregg's" and Subsequently as "McGowan's Brigade." King & Baird, Printers, 1866. Marietta, GA: Continental Book, 1951. 7, 80. Print.

Gettysburg. Couriers brought orders for them to fill their canteens with water and hurry up.[37]

Ahead, Heth's Division clashed with dismounted Federal cavalry and rapidly arriving infantry troops from the Federal First Corps on McPherson's Ridge outside Gettysburg. Perrin's men double-quicked into position and were resting along the road. They stopped there for about an hour of the mid-morning until receiving orders to march again. After covering two miles, they filed to the right of the road. Pender ordered Perrin to form a line of battle there beside the Chambersburg Pike, "leaving sufficient room between my left and the [road] for General [Alfred] Scales brigade, and to throw out skirmishers to cover my right flank." Perrin laid out his line with the 14th on the left and the 1st, 12th and then the 13th on the right.[38]

Perrin was then ordered to advance, following and supporting Heth's renewed attack on McPherson's Ridge. He carefully preserved his alignment with the brigade of Brig. Gen. Alfred M. Scales on the left. Brig. Gen. James H. Lane's North Carolina Brigade soon formed on Perrin's right as the South Carolinians pressed forward to face Brig. Gen. John Buford's cavalry division. At 3:00 P.M., they were ordered to advance another half mile, which exposed them to artillery fire, which, fortunately, was aimed high. The grapeshot intended for Perrin's men sailed over their heads. A visibly relieved Corporal Thomas Littlejohn of the 12th South Carolina observed, "Had they been a little lower, I don't see how any of us could have escaped."[39]

Lane closed on Scales' Brigade along the Chambersburg Pike while Brig. Gen. Edward L. Thomas' Georgia brigade closed the gap that this created on Perrin's right. Pender's Division pressed forward to support Heth's attack, driving the Federals from McPherson's Ridge and back onto Seminary Ridge, the last bastion for the Yankee forces protecting the town from the west. Heth's battered troops could not muster sufficient to

---

37. Gottfried, Bradley M. McGowan's Brigade." "Brigades of Gettysburg: The Union and Confederate Brigades at the Battle of Gettysburg". Cambridge, MA: Da Capo, 2002. 642. Print; Miller, J. Michael. "Perrin's Brigade on July 1, 1863." Gettysburg Magazine 13 (1995): 22. Print.
38. Gottfried, 642; Miller, 22, 24.
39. Gottfried, 642.

assault this line, so Heth called for Pender's Division to join in this task.[40]

At 4:00 P.M. Perrin was ordered to move his men in advance of Heth's line, marching through Brig. Gen. James J. Pettigrew's North Carolina brigade, exposing Perrin's men to enemy artillery fire. The South Carolinians advanced in line of battle to the banks of Willoughby Run, where Perrin paused to reform his men. He then ordered his regimental commanders to advance to the crest of the hill and told them that "If Heth does not need you, lie down and protect yourselves as well as you can; if he needs you, go to his assistance at once." He further ordered them not to fire their guns and to use the bayonet instead. They were not to stop for any reason until they drove the Federals from Seminary Ridge. Perrin feared that his troops would halt to reload and become pinned down by trading volleys with the Yankees, thereby stalling the attack.[41]

Col. Joseph Brown of the 14th South Carolina recalled that as they rushed forward, Pettigrew's fatigued North Carolinians yelled out, "Go in, South Carolina! Go in, South Carolina!" Captain Washington Shooter of the 12th South Carolina recalled that his regiment passed over Heth's men and pressed the "enemy rapidly before us without firing a gun..." The federals retreated "in wild disorder and everything went as merry as a marriage bell until we ascended a hill where we saw their batteries and their last line of entrenchment – a stone wall." They now faced the remainder of Col. Chapman Biddle's brigade of Pennsylvanians.[42]

Col. Perrin rode at the head of his advancing troops, waved his sword and shouted, "Three Cheers for Gregg's Brigade," recalling the brigade's original name under Maxcy Gregg. Despite the heavy artillery and musket fire, they advanced smartly. Their valor and perfect order left an impression on all who witnessed it. Lt. Col. Rufus Dawes of the 6th Wisconsin called their bearing "magnificent." He noted "They maintained their alignment with great precision. In many cases the colors of the regiments were advanced several paces in front of the line."[43]

Lane's and Scales' Brigades took heavy enemy fire. Gen. Scales fell to a

40. Miller, 24; Caldwell, 97.
41. Gottfried, 643; Miller, 25; Perrin to Bonham, "Mississippi Valley Historical Review, 522.
42. Brown, B. F., "Some Recollections of Gettysburg", Confederate Veteran Magazine, (1923), Vol. 31, 53; Gottfried, 643; Shooter, Washington, Captain Shooter letter, Drumbeat, newsletter of the Charleston Civil War Round Table, June 1989.
43. Miller, 25; Dawes, "Service with the Sixth Wisconsin Volunteers", (Marietta, Ohio: E. R. Alderman and Sons, 1890; reprint, Dayton, Ohio: Morningside, 1991), 175.

wound and every officer in his five regiments but one was either killed or wounded. Both brigades were soon out of the fight, leaving Pender's hopes pinned solely on Perrin's 1,500 South Carolinians, who had advanced to within 100 yards of the enemy line. Daniel Tompkins of the 14th South Carolina reported hearing the Federal commanders ordering their men to hold their fire until the Palmetto men came closer and the order was given. He reported that the enemy "rose to their feet and took as deliberate aim as if they were on dress parade." Company K took thirty-nine men into the action and lost thirty-four on this slope.[44]

Despite the losses, the South Carolinians pressed on. Many of the men threw away their knapsacks and blankets to lighten their load. Perrin rode amongst the men and repeated the order to close in on the enemy line without firing. Each of the four regiments lost their initial color-bearers. Union fire ripped great holes in the line, but the undaunted South Carolinians pressed forward toward the Seminary building fifty yards ahead. Repeated blasts of canister tore holes and slowed the advance. However, under the circumstances, retreat would have been as deadly as attack. Col. Brown said, "to stop was destruction. To retreat was disaster. To go forward was 'orders.' ... Not a foot of ground presented a place of safety."[45] Left with no alternative, the attack continued despite the severe Union fire.

Perrin ordered a masterful move. Confronted by a breastwork of rails, and likely looking to exploit a gap between Biddle's infantry brigade and Col. William Gamble's cavalry brigade, Perrin ordered the 1st South Carolina to oblique to the right to avoid the breastwork, where they found the enemy positioned behind the rails. Perrin then changed front to the left and attacked the Federal flank. Buoyed by the courage of their commander, the 1st and 14th "threw themselves desperately on the line of Federals and swept them from the field," Caldwell wrote in his history.[46]

With their flank exposed to the fire of South Carolinians, the 121st Pennsylvania scampered to the rear, and the Union line crumbled. Col. Biddle was wounded in this attack, forcing him to turn command over to

---

44. Miller, 27; Gottfried, 644.
45. Miller, 28; Gottfried, 644; Caldwell, 97-98.
46. Gottfried, 644; Caldwell, 98; Miller, 28.

Col. Theodore B. Gates of the 80th New York before ordering a retreat. Perrin later claimed that if he had had any support, he could have captured all of the enemy artillery as well. The lack of support permitted the Federals to extract most of their cannons from the field. As it was, the South Carolinians captured four Federal battle flags, including the colors of the Federal First Corps.[47]

At this same time Perrin simultaneously ordered the regiments on his right flank—the 12th and 13th—to oblique to the right to face Gamble's dismounted cavalry, which was positioned behind a stone wall. Perrin wrote that the 12th gained the stone fence and poured "an enfilading fire upon the enemy's right flank. The 13th came up and made it an easy task to drive the enemy down the opposite slope and across the open field west of Gettysburg."[48]

The 1st and 14th chased the fleeing Yankees into the town of Gettysburg, capturing many along the way. The 1st marched up the Chambersburg Pike while the 14th turned left onto North Boundary Street before stopping at Main Street. Union troops still occupied streets all around the two South Carolina regiments. The two South Carolina regiments then moved to the center of town, where the 1st South Carolina had planted its flag in the town "diamond." The Palmetto men thus claimed the honor of being the first regiment to do so during the three day battle.[49]

Perrin's Brigade was less heavily engaged during the remainder of the battle. On July 2, it was resting on Cemetery Hill when orders came through to throw out skirmishers to engage a mass of the enemy in control of a road to their front at about 6:00 P.M. They did some heavy skirmishing on Cemetery Hill on July 3, drawing enemy fire during the artillery duel preceding the Pettigrew-Pickett-Trimble charge. Once the firing died down, they watched Pettigrew's portion of the charge from a prime vantage point. Perrin's brigade occupied Cemetery Hill until the retreat to Virginia began on July 5.[50]

---

47. Gottfried, 644.
48. Gottfried, 644-645.
49. Miller, 31; Gottfried, 645.
50. Gottfried, 646.

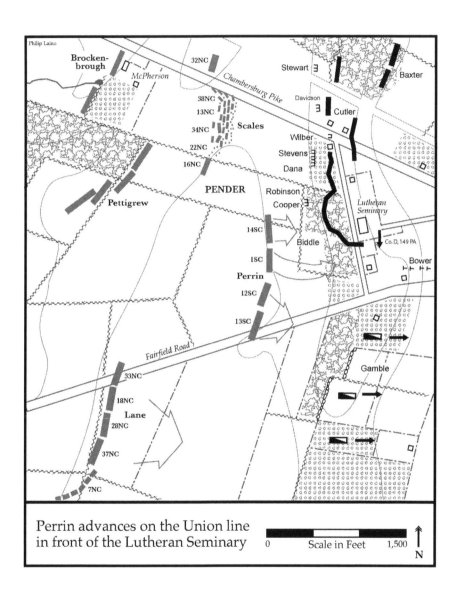

Perrin advances on the Union line
in front of the Lutheran Seminary

Chapter 1

1st South Carolina Volunteer Infantry

(Gregg's / McCreary's Regiment)

EDGEFIELD ADVERTISER
JULY 29, 1863

List of Casualties in Co. G, 1st S. C. V.
CAPT A P BUTLER COMMANDING

Killed: Sergt John C Mays, J C Shafer, C H Wate. Wounded: Sergt P O Ransom, left ankle, slight fracture; Sergt T C Tomkins, right thigh, contusion; Sergt W T Scott, right buttock; Corpl J F Harling, left knee, slight fracture; _____ Attaway, right thigh, amputated; J L Turner, right leg, amputated at knee joint; W H Holloway, right thigh; R P Holloway, left calf, contusion; W A Sales, left arm fracture; John Carpenter, left shoulder, contusion; Thos Weeks, left leg amputated; L P Andrews, contused; Wm McGill, left forearm, contusion.

* * *

EDGEFIELD ADVERTISER
JULY 29, 1863

[Excerpt from original article]

The Advertiser

JAMES T. BACON, EDITOR

Wednesday, July 29, 1863

Edgefield Officers

"Personan" at the close if a piece in the Courier, describing the fight at Battery Wagner on the night of the 18th, says:

"None among our dead is more lamented than Lieut. Col. [John C.] Simkins, of the First S. C. Infantry. No officer stood higher in personal worth, or was more beloved by his comrades and men, and none have left behind a brighter or purer memory. He fell in the front cheering on the troops—a noble type living and dying, of a true friend, a perfect gentleman and a brave soldier."

A gentleman writing us an account of the action of the 14th Regiment in the battle of Gettysburg, says: "Col. [Abner Monroe] PERRIN conducted himself most gallantly in command of the Brigade, and gained the applause of Gen. [William Dorsey] PENDER, Division Commander."

* * *

EDGEFIELD ADVERTISER
AUGUST 12, 1863

OBITUARY

Fell in the battle of Gettysburg, Pa., on the 3rd July last, JOHN C. MAYS, of Co. G, 1st Reg't., S. C. V., only son of Mr. GEO. R. MAYS, of this District, in the 26th year of his age.

No braver man has fallen in this cruel war than the esteemed and worthy young MAYS. In the walks of social life he was ever the true gentleman, honorable in all his dealings, modest, affable, generous and noble. Around the hearthstone of his now grief-stricken home he was the joy and hope, and pride of a kind father, a fond mother and loving sisters. Alas! What a sad void now exists in that once happy household. With them we mingle the sympathies of an admiring friend of the departed loved ones, and hope that God, in his mercy, will soothe their sorrows and prepare them the meet their loved and lost in Heaven.

JOHN MAYS was not only noted for his social qualities and gentlemanly deportment in civil life, but imbued with the spirit and actuated with the principles of the true hero and patriot, when his country required his services, we find him ready and willing to lay down his life, if necessary, in her defense. Right nobly has he offered himself a sacrifice in the name of Southern honor and independence. The gallant Capt. A. P. BUTLER, in a letter to the father of the deceased speaks in flattering terms of the conduct of young MAYS in the camp and on the battlefield. From this letter we are allowed the privilege of making the following extract:

"No one sympathizes with you and your family more than I in the great loss you have sustained in the death of your noble and gallant son, as he was one of the few left with whom I had been intimately associated since the 7th of Jan. 1861. While his death is a source of such exceeding great grief to you, it will be gratifying to know that he fell far in advance urging his fellow-soldiers forward. He not only distinguished himself on that occasion, but was highly complimented by a number of Officers, not only in his own Regiment, but by those of other Regiments, for his gallant conduct in the battle on the 1st July, being the first at the battery we captured on that day. I sincerely hope he has gone from a world of war to one of eternal peace."

And with Capt. B, we earnestly trust that so dear a friend, so brave a soldier, is at rest forever.

* * *

NEWS AND COURIER

ANDERSON, SOUTH CAROLINA

JULY 27, 1882

M'GOWAN'S BRIGADE AND THE PART IT PLAYED AT GETTYSBURG

The Confederate Victory July 1, 1863—Advancing Mid a Storm of Shot and Shell—The Losses Immense—Incidents of Personal Daring—importance of the Engagement

ANDERSON, S. C., July 12

To the Editor of the News and Courier: Under the Act of Congress approved June 9, 1880, entitled "An Act to complete the survey of the Gettysburg battlefield, and to provide for the compilation and preservation of data, showing the various positions and movements of troops at that battle illustrated by diagrams," I was requested by Col. D. Wyatt Aiken, M. C., to meet Col. John B. Batchelder, the historian and a landscape painter, to whom the work was committed under said Act, and to point out the positions and movements of McGowan's Brigade in order to preserve our Confederate success on that hard-fought battlefield. Col. Batchelder also wrote me to meet him and the Union officers commanding the opposing forces on the first day of the battle, and fixed June 14th for the day of the meeting.

We met, as requested, and spent two days in the work, one of which was taken chiefly with the battle of the first day. There was not the least difficulty in establishing every position and movement of the brigade, in all of which the Union officers concurred with me. We had stakes driven into the ground at all proper points and Col. Batchelder assured me that he would take pleasure in giving us a correct showing in his illustration of the battle.

The Union officers frankly admit their defeat, and the retreat through the town, qualifying it with their weary condition from long forced marches. As heavy were our losses, theirs were much greater.

In May last you requested me to write up one of the battles of McGowan's Brigade for the Weekly News, which was also urged on me by officers of the brigade, and I have taken Gettysburg.

Very truly yours,

JOSEPH N. BROWN

McGowan's South Carolina Brigade at Gettysburg

[By Lieut.-Col. Joseph N. Brown, 17th S.C.V.]

Gen. [Samuel] McGowan and Capt. A[lexander] C. Haskell, were both severely wounded at Chancellorsville, May 3, 1863, and Col. Abner Perrin, of the Fourteenth South Carolina, commanded the Brigade on the Pennsylvania campaign, with Lieut. J[ohn] G. Barnwell, of the First, as his A. A. G. The field officers of the several regiments were: Major C. W. McCreary, First; Major W[illiam] M. Haddon, Orr's Rifles; Col. J[ohn] L. Miller, Lieut. Col. H[enry] C. Davis, and Major E[dwin] F. Bookter, Twelfth; Col. B[enjamin] T. Brockman and Lieut. Col. I[saac] F. Hunt, Thirteenth; Lieut. Col. Joseph N. Brown and Major Edward Croft, Fourteenth, and Capt. W[illiam] T. Haskell, of the First, commanded the Battalion of Sharpshooters.

On the thirtieth day of June, 1863, the armies of Gens. Lee and Meade were in Pennsylvania. The long march from the Rappahannock had relieved both armies of all their weak and faint-hearted, and none but brave and strong men had marched there to battle. They went there prepared in their minds for hard fighting, and the make-up of the mind has much to do in making the fight of the soldier. The Union soldier had now been recalled from Virginia to defend his own soil.

On the morning of the 30th day of June A. P. Hill's corps moved from the Cumberland Valley and, crossing the mountains to the eastern side, encamped near their base. Pender's light division of this corps comprised the four brigades of Gen. E[dward] L[loyd] Thomas, of Georgia, Gen. James H. Lane, of North Carolina, Gen. A[lfred] M[oore] Scales, of North Carolina, and Gen. Samuel McGowan, of South Carolina.

THE LINE OF BATTLE

On the morning of the first day of July an early conflict appeared imminent. McGowan's brigade was called to arms. Artillery and infantry were passing towards Gettysburg, six miles distant. Artillery firing opened in front. Maj. Haddon, with Orr's regiment, was detached from the brigade for guard duty. The remainder of the brigade, with the field and staff officers already mentioned, moved towards the town. A line of battle was formed, with Gen. Lane's brigade on the right, McGowan's in the centre, and Gen. Scales on the left. The left rested on the Chambersburg turnpike. Gen. Thomas' brigade was not in line. Gen. Perrin gave orders to the field and staff, and then communicated to the rank and file, that they were to move forward without firing. That they were not to stop under any circumstances, but to close in, press the enemy close, and rout it from its position. The firing of artillery increased and that of small arms began. This continued for several hours, during which time the brigade approached nearer the scene of action, resting at intervals in the shaded woods. Rumors of disaster and success alternately passed along the lines, derived from the wounded and prisoners. Gen. Reynolds, commanding the Union army, had been killed. Gen. Archer, of our army, had been wounded, and he, with most if his brigade of Gen. Heth's Division, had been captured. But upon the whole the advantage was on our side, and by 4 o'clock p.m. the Union army had fallen back to a line of hastily constructed breastworks of earth, rails and the like on the slope fronting and west of the Lutheran Seminary, one-fourth of a mile west of the town. This line was continued by a strong stone fence beginning some two hundred yards south of the Seminary near a brick house, and running southwardly along the crest of Seminary Ridge, and a little further back, or east, than the breastworks. On the turnpike, and near the Seminary, the Union artillery was strongly posted, being on our left. As thus presented Gen. Scales on our left had on his left flank all this artillery and in his front the rail and earthworks above described full on Union soldiers pressed back, but not defeated, and replenished with fresh troops from the rear.

In front of McGowan's brigade were the breastworks, defended by the same line continuing southward. In front of Gen. Lane was the strong stone fence, behind which was posted a strong line of dismounted cavalry with repeating rifles, which outflanked him. The ground from which these works and the stone fence presented a gradually declining slope to the valley westward; then on a level of about two hundred yards, then a like gradual ascent up to the crest of the ridge, making perhaps half a mile from crest to crest, and presenting the fairest field and finest front for destruction on an advancing foe that could well be conceived.

THE ASSAULT

If, in this position of affairs the brigades of Gens. Scales and Lane should fail to keep pace with McGowan's in the assault to be made, it would be no disparagement of their gallant officers and men.   It was an impossibility. The centre must be broken.

The order to advance was now given.   The order to hold fire until ordered forward and close in on the enemy was repeated.   The Thirteenth Regiment was on the right, next to it the Fourteenth, next Twelfth, and next the First.   Passing a burning house on our right and crossing a small run, the brigade mounted the hill beyond and passed over the crippled lines of Gen. Pettigrew's brigade, which, after hours of gallant fighting, had been withdrawn and were resting from their toils.

In front and in view amid the grove of trees was the Seminary, now changed from the halls of learning to a scene of bloodshed and carnage. Beyond was a beautiful town partly concealed from view by the shade trees surrounding the Seminary.   Its 3,000 inhabitants were a thrifty, industrious and moral people.   Crests of ridges in successive ranges stretched southwardly with the richest valleys between.   Beyond and to the south of the town rising still higher was Cemetery Heights, so soon to become historical ground.   It was but the glance of the eye for a moment, and then its grandeur was lost in the tumult of battle.

STORM OF SHOT AND SHELL

The advancing columns now moved on and encountered the storm of shot and shell from the batteries on the turnpike fronting Gen. Scales, and pressed on as ordered, without firing until the line of breastworks in front became a sheet of fire and smoke, sending its leaden missiles of death in the faces of the men who had often, but never so terribly, met it before.

William Thomson Haskell, the captain of Co. H was killed on July 2 at Gettysburg. In 1863, in preparation for the invasion of Penn., the sharpshooters of the division were organized into a battalion, and he was selected to command it. On the 3rd day of July following, at Gettysburg, he fell dead at its head.

(Belles, Beaux And Brains of the 60s)

Alexander Cheves Haskell was a brother of Capt. W. T. Haskell and John Cheves Haskell. He was wounded at Chancellorsville while serving on Gen. Samuel McGowan's staff. Haskell missed Gettysburg due to his wounds, but recovered and played a pivotal role in S.C. politics later in life.

(Alexander Cheves Haskell: The Portrait of a Man)

The impenetrable masses of artillery and infantry in front and on the flank of Gen. Scales impeded his progress, enfilading and sweeping his whole front. He was wounded, and every field officer of his brigade, save one, had fallen. In like manner, on our right, Gen. Lane was held in check by the stone wall in his front, and the cavalry on his flank, threatening certain destruction if his advance continued. The valley had nearly been reached. The want of support on the right and left exposed the brigade to a raking enfilade fire from both right and left without abatement in front.

STILL FORWARD

To stop was destruction. To retreat was disaster. To go forward was "orders." Then Gen. Perrin on horseback dashing through the lines of the brigade, and with his flashing sword in the evening sunshine and his voice above the din of battle, directed and led the charge. Three hundred yards yet intervened between the advancing column and the breastwork in front, and the assailing forces with quickened pace pushed forward amid the Minnie balls sweeping the earth in front and flank. The dead, the wounded and the dying were falling at every step. Our firing had begun in earnest, and was pouring in on the enemy thick and fast.

THE CREST OF THE RIDGE

The enemy in front of the Seminary were closely massed, and strongly supported at the building as well as from the rear and on its flanks. The lines from this point curved slightly back on either side near to the crest of the Ridge, and this made the Seminary the salient or point of attack, and to break the line and take the breastworks here the brigade threw itself against it with all its fury. Here the opposing forces grappled with each other, one determined to hold its position, and the other determined to take it. The close quarters at which they were now engaged made the losses on both sides heavy. By this time the brigade had attained a point which exposed it to a raking fire from the cavalry with repeating rifles behind the stone fence on our right. Its greatest force was spent on the Thirteenth and Fourteenth with deadly effect. But they maintained their unbroken front, closing in, and replying in all directions whence the missiles of destruction came. The ever solid Twelfth with unbroken front pressed on and was dealing deadly blows in its front, carrying terror before it. The First on our left, outflanked and enfiladed, pressed on in the usual contest, drawing closer to the breastworks, approached firmly and steadily along at equal pace with its comrades, though confronting such fearful odds against it, both in front and on the flank.

THE FIELD WON

The desired point was at last reached. The brigade carried the works, and the centre was thus broken and the field was ours. The whole line then gave way, and the Union soldiers, Pennsylvanians they were, after making such heroic resistance were pressed back, closely followed, with fearful loss.

While the contending forces were thus grappling at close quarters at the breastworks, the artillery limbered up and was making for the rear. This timely prudence alone saved it. The stone wall on our right was carried, and the whole field was ours. The Thirteenth and Fourteenth had suffered most from those repeating rifles. The Union columns were broken, pressed back, at first rapidly and disorderly, with our men close to them, still pouring into their ranks a deadly fire. As they neared the town they became more massed, and moved more slowly and stubbornly, with lines still broken. As they were entering the town they looked backwards, as if half minded to turn on the pursuing foe and renew the conflict. But doubtless their movements were obstructed by the crowded streets in their front. Gen. Abner Doubleday, who commanded the Union forces, in his official report of the battle says: "I remained at the Seminary superintending the final movement until thousands of hostile bayonets made their appearance around the sides of the building. I then rode back and rejoined my command, nearly all of whom were filing through the town. As we passed through the streets our frightened people gave us food and drink."

ON TO THE TOWN

The Union forces had been pressed out of their breastworks, and our weary soldiers had entered them, and passed on to the town. The Fourteenth passed on both sides of the Seminary, Col. Croft, with a portion, passing to the right, and pushing forward for the possession of a desirable piece of artillery. Others were pushing for the same point. Major Croft probably reached it first, as he with an eye for the immediately useful secured the only injured horse, which he mounted with the harness still on, presented a captured sword to his lieutenant colonel, and soon afterwards loaned the horse to the gallant Capt. T. P. Alston, of the First, to ride into town in command of the skirmishers.

The brigade had now reached the town, which Gen. Perrin ordered the First and Fourteenth to enter. This they did simultaneously with flags unfurled, the First by the Chambersburg turnpike, and the Fourteenth passing to the left, or rather directly along and between North Boundary street and the old railroad embankment or bed, until it reached the Main street running south through the town, and marching up that street was passed by Gen. Pender, at the shade trees on the right, who extended a compliment in passing. A few paces further on Major McCreary with the First had reached the same street by the Chambersburg turnpike where Gen. Pender complimented the regiment for its gallant conduct. In like manner he complimented each regiment through its commander for its glorious day's work. The fourteenth having the shortest cut reached the Main street first, but Major McCreary reached it further on and first held the more central or advanced position, where the Fourteenth again joined it. The streets and fencing look now as they did then. Only a hedge has been allowed to grow up and spread on the north side of Boundary street by which the Fourteenth passed into town.

Gen. Rode's Division of Gen. Ewell's Corps now coming up, the First and Fourteenth were ordered back and joined the Twelfth and Thirteenth between the town and Seminary, where we rested.

GEN. LEE AND THE CAROLINIANS

Gen. Pender was at the Ridge were we first entered the battle and saw the close fighting throughout. He saw the Brigade as it appeared from his point to almost mingle with the Union soldiers, and passing the Seminary and the Ridge almost together, and out of sight and the firing ceasing he supposed that the Brigade was captured. Riding forward however, he met Lieut. Simmons, of the Twelfth, who was wounded, and of whom he made the inquiry if the Brigade was captured, to which the Lieutenant answered, "No, it's over the hill yonder." (The large body of the enemy known to be there well justified his fears.) The General then rode forward with speed, and ordered the Twelfth and Thirteenth back to a point between the town and the Seminary to protect the right flank, and then into town where he overtook the Fourteenth and First, as above stated. Gen. Lee then came up, and all honor was given to "the South Carolina Brigade that captured Gettysburg."

THE LOSSES

The points of greatest danger were held by the regiments on the right and left, the Thirteenth on the right and the First on the left. The Thirteenth was nearest the cavalry with repeating rifles at the stone fence, and lost more in killed than any other. Col. Bruckman, although too sick for duty, was at his post, but the movements for that reason were largely conducted by Lt. Col. I. F. Hunt. It added to the regiment's already high reputation acquired under its former gallant commander, Col. O[liver] E. Edwards, who fell commanding the brigade, after the wounding of Gen. McGowan at Chancellorsville.

The First, being on the left, had to encounter a long line of infantry overlapping its left, and was nearest the artillery.

The centre, comprising the Twelfth and Fourteenth, was swept by the same enfilading fire that enfiladed our flanking regiments, and the losses in men were nearly equal in all the regiments in proportion to the numbers engaged. The Twelfth sustained heavy loss from the artillery fire directed towards the centre.

It would seem impossible for any of the regiments to have sustained more than it had to meet or to have borne more than it had to encounter. There would have been enough glory in any one of them to have carried its own front. All of them had more than this to do.

NO ESCAPE FOR THE WOUNDED

The losses were immense. The Fourteenth, which was the largest regiment, lost over 200 killed and wounded out of 475 carried into action. The Thirteenth had sixty-four killed or to die of their wounds. All the regiments lost one-third. There was no loss of prisoners. They were all killed or wounded. Over six hundred had fallen in front of the breastworks. The thousand of hostile bayonets that appeared and passed around the sides of the Seminary building comprised what remained of fifteen hundred carried into action. The nature of the ground was such and the contest so brief that the wounded could not be moved, and were wounded twice, thrice and as many as four times, after being stricken down. Large numbers died of their wounds. A few who, with shattered arms or wounded bodies, ran back in safety to the surgeons, have not ceased to admire their legs for the good service rendered. It was the only battlefield in which all avenues of escape for our wounded were closed. There was nothing that the ambulance corps could do. The ground was swept at every point by the deadly Minnie balls. The artillery fire is terrible, but the almost silent whirl of the Minnie ball is the death-dealing missile in battle. Not a foot of ground presented a place of safety. The Union troops fired low, and their balls swept close to the ground in the dish-like field in their front. The terrible strife was over in a few minutes—fifteen, say maybe twenty at most. Men never fell faster in this brigade, and perhaps never equaled, except in Orr's regiment at Gaines's Mill. On our side the firing was not slack nor wild. The trees in the Seminary grounds where the Union lines ran are still thickly covered with scars, from the ground to the height of a man, made with the bullets of our unerring rifles. They are well marked on their western sides. And the ground strewn with their dead and wounded well attested the accuracy of the deadly aim.

THE GALLANT ENEMY

It was no ordinary soldier that we had met. The prisoners captured were more intelligent than on other fields. They were mostly Pennsylvanians fighting for everything they held dear. The celebrated Iron Brigade was in our front. The 121st Pennsylvania, 143rd Pennsylvania, 149th Pennsylvania, 151st Pennsylvania, and others not remembered. Maine troops were there, who stated that they came in not more than fifteen minutes before the action began, then the artillery on our right, cavalry behind the stone wall, all holding to the death. But there was no crossing of swords and bayonets, for this is seldom done except on paper. It was no time for a thousand hair-breadth escapes with nobody hurt. It was not the clipping off of clothing, but the bodies of men that were struck. While the losses in line officers and men were great it was remarkable that not a single field officer was disabled for duty, though they did not escape un-struck.

INCIDENTS OF PERSONAL DARING

The Rev. W[illiam] B. Carson, chaplain of the Fourteenth Regiment, remained with the wounded, of whom ninety of his own regiment were too badly wounded to be removed in ambulances south of the Potomac. He went into the heavily shelled woods for blankets for his wounded men and remained to administer to their wants until death freed many from their sufferings.

Dr. Louis V. Hunt, the eminent surgeon of the Fourteenth, performed many skillful operations, drawing praise from Union surgeons. He returned with us on the final retreat.

A soldier boy of the Fourteenth captured the large flag of the 149th Pennsylvania in the works, where all its guard were slain. Another captured a smaller one, and folding it in his bosom, fell two days afterwards advancing in the picket line if front of Cemetery Heights.

[T.] R. Owens, color bearer, son of Capt. R[obert] S. Owens, of the Fourteenth, who had fallen at Frazier's farm, was shot dead while carrying the flag of his regiment, and all his color guard but one was slain.

In the Twelfth Regiment one color bearer after another was shot dead until four were killed and two others wounded. And a scarcely less fatality attended the colors of the other regiments. The land of the Shamrock, as in other fields, contributed its quota on the strongly contested ground.

IMPORTANCE OF THE ENGAGEMENT

The importance and magnitude of this sanguinary engagement and glorious victory was lost sight of by the public eye in the grand movement which culminated in the great events immediately succeeding. But it was not lost sight of nor forgotten by the great Lee. He promoted Col. Perrin to Brigadier-General, who on the 12th of May, 1864, while leading his Alabama Brigade to the charge at Spottsylvania, as he did McGowan's Brigade at Gettysburg, fell in the front of battle and his great spirit ceased from war.

We rested on the field of battle and the next day held Seminary Ridge along the stone fence which covered Gen. Lane's front the first day. We supported the artillery, and the only fighting by the brigade, except by the Sharpshooters, was done by Capt. T. F[rank] Clyburn (afterwards Colonel) who with two companies of the Twelfth drove back a line of battle and restored our pickets who had been driven from their posts. Our line passed by a farm-house surrounded by a fine orchard, and owned by a gentleman named McMillan, who canned his fruit, and who abandoned all on the morning of the 1st. Abandoned property is lawful prize in war, and our weary soldiers enjoyed those fruits, on the volunteer system, in the intervals of quiet. The old gentleman and his wife still live, and although nineteen years have passed he still laments the loss of his earthly store. Every building and tree now looks as it did then, and the same well of water again quenched the wayfarer's thirst. During the night of the 2nd the brigade was moved forward to the dirt road on the slope fronting Cemetery Ridge and was joined by Orr's Regiment, but was not engaged in the great battle of the 3rd.

The pickets were driven in at one time, and the Fourteenth ordered forward to restart the line, which was quickly done. But it drew a heavy fire from the heights in front, inflicting some loss, in which both the field officers were wounded. The wounds of Major Croft were severe, and his valuable services lost to his regiment for more than a year. Then returning with an unhealed wound in the side and his arm in a sling, he continued at his post until the close of war.

KILLED IN ACTION

As before stated, our losses were immense. But the greatest individual loss to the brigade was that of Capt. William T. Haskell, of the First Regiment, commanding the Battalion of Sharpshooters. He was killed in front of Cemetery Ridge on the second day, and the gravity of his loss can scarcely be estimated. It was only known to those who knew him best. Gen. Pender also fell mortally wounded on the second day while reconnoitering, and our army lost in him another of our great generals.

And then the long list of line officers who fell, leaving whole companies without a commissioned officer. Among them the First Regiment, besides Capt. Haskell, Killed, Lieut. A. W. Pogue. Wounded, Capt. J[ames] S. McMahon, Lieuts. J[osiah] Cox, James Armstrong, W[illiam] M. Murray, J. F. J. Caldwell.

Twelfth Regiment—Killed, Capt. J. Hunnicutt. Wounded, Capt. J[ohn] M. Moody, Lieuts. J[ames] A. Watson, M[ike] T. Sharpe, A[lexander] W. Black, W[illiam] J. Stover, J. M. Jenkins, [Richard L.] Simmons.

Thirteenth Regiment—Killed, Capt. [W. P.] Cromer, Lieuts. [William C.] McNinch and [David M.] Leitsey. Wounded, Capt. [John] Dewberry, Lieuts. Leitsey, [Joseph W.] Hill, A[ndrew] M. Bowers, John Dabney, J[ohn] F. Banks.

Fourteenth Regiment—Killed, Sidney Carter and N[athaniel] Austin. Wounded, Adjutant W[illiam] J. Ready; Capts. H[arrison] P. Griffith, W[illiam] M. Jordan and G[eorge] W. Culbertson; Lieuts. Robert B. Watson, John M. Bell, H. J. Roach, William H. Bronson, J. F. Jordan, A[ndrew] F. Jordan, W[illiam] R. White, J[ames] H. Williams, S[imeon] Cogburn, James P. Sloan and Jesse Gwin.

And the hundreds of brave men, most of them young, and on the threshold of life, whose names were not recorded in the official reports of the battle. But they still live in the memories of the loved ones at home, and years afterwards their bodies were removed to Southern cemeteries by patriotic and loving hands. Here let them rest until the morning of the general resurrection.

In the afternoon of the 3rd the great world-renowned assaults were made on the iron-crested and rock-bound heights in front, resulting in disaster, and then the star of the Southern Confederacy began first to wane.

Of the regimental commanders in this campaign, Col. J[ohn] L. Miller, of the Twelfth, was killed at the Wilderness, May 5, 1864; Col. B[enjamin] T. Brockman [13th Regiment], at Spottsylvania, May 12, 1864; Major W[illiam] Haddon, of Orr's Rifles, at Deep Bottom, July 28, 1864, and Col. C. W. McCreary, of the First, at Gravelly Run, March 31, 1865. It was distressingly sad that Col. McCreary, after so long and brilliant service, should fall in almost the last battle, even as the fabric of the Confederate power was tottering and being broken to pieces and the last blow being struck. The smile that always lit up his pleasant face paled in death near the enemy. Of these and the long list who stood shoulder to shoulder with us at Gettysburg and who fell on these and other battlefields, and those who have survived the sad and closing scene at Appomattox—a brigade which the writer as senior colonel at times had the honor to command—he would say, with feelings akin to Scotland's bard—

> "The bridegroom may forget the bride
> Was made his wedded wife yestreen;
> The monarch may forget the crown
> That on his head an hour has been;
> The mother may forget the child
> That smiles so sweetly on her knee,
> But I'll remember thee, Glencairn."

REGIMENTAL COMMANDERS

The promotion of Gen. [Abner] Perrin and his death has already been stated. He was a martinet in discipline and every inch a soldier. His accomplished wife, a daughter of Col. P[ierce] M. Butler of the Palmetto Regiment, preceded him a short time to the grave, and two children survived them. He was the last colonel but one of the Fourteenth Regiment. He was captain of company "D," from Edgefield, at the organization in 1861. The former colonels were field officers at the organization—Col. James Jones in the camp of instruction, and Cols. Samuel McGowan and W[illiam] D. Simpson, who so often led it to battle. The First boasted of its Maxey Gregg, a name so inseparably connected with it and the Brigade. Orr's Rifles had its Col. James L. Orr in the camp of instruction and J. Foster Marshall, D[aniel] A[lexander] Ledbetter, who had fallen at Second Manassas. The Twelfth with Col. R. G. M. Dunovant, of honorable service before, who was succeeded by the gallant Col. Dixon Barnes, who distinguished himself and regiment on many fields and so much at second Manassas, and who fell at Sharpsburg, regretted by all. Col. O[liver] E[vans] Edwards of the Thirteenth, so brave, and so efficient in all departments of the service and especially in battle has already been mentioned. These officers left with their regiments the impress of their own gallant spirits, which was preserved unimpaired on many battlefields, and on one of which they submit was never excelled.

GETTYSBURG IN 1882

An inspection of the field at Gettysburg on the 14th and 15th of June, 1882, presented precisely the view it did nineteen years ago. It looked as if seen but yesterday. Time seemed to have made scarcely a change. The impressions on the mind had been so strong that the hills, valleys, parcels of woods, Seminary, slopes, houses, streets, fencing, then thrown down, and roads, were all of them fresh in the memory. When it looked a little too far from McMillan's house to the woods on the south, and inspection disclosed a small clearing from that side of it. The existence of the dirt road was denied by some, but a search at once located it. The field only lacked the surging masses of men and arms to complete it. The portion if the stone fence nearest our right, on the first day, had been removed.

On the other side the view from Cemetery Ridge, Culp's Hill, Little Round Top and other points held by the Union forces, disclosed positions which the "Rebel soldier" would have regarded as havens of safety. No wonder Gen. Pickett failed in his charge.

In peace, the men who had met there before the war now met again. On the Southern side were Gen. Trimble, accompanied by his niece, Miss Trimble. The General, though hale and hearty, still carries with him the evidence of the hard-fought battle. Gen. A[lfred] M[oore] Scales, M. C., of North Carolina, Col. [William C.] Oates, M. C., of Alabama, with only one arm, Capt. ____, of Pegram's Artillery, and the representative of McGowan's Brigade and his school-girl daughter, who took a lively interest in the incidents of battle as related by both Union and Confederate officers, and with them inspected all the fields.

On the Northern side were many officers assembled for their reunion. Several of them inquired specially for that gallant officer of ours who rode through the lines of his brigade and led the charge. They stated that it was the grandest sight they ever saw in battle. Among them were Gen. Richard Coulter, of Pennsylvania, with his wife and daughter; Gen. Edward L. Dana, Col. Of 143rd Pennsylvania Volunteers, commanding second brigade at Gettysburg; Lt. Col. Geo. F. McFarland, 151st Pennsylvania Volunteers, accompanied by his amiable wife. We thought that Col. McFarland had been killed by us nineteen years before. We had shot him and his horse near the Seminary, wounding him severely, from which he lost a leg, but his cheerful disposition well supplies the loss. Major E. P. Halstead, A. A. G. of the First Corps; Capt. M. L. Blair, of 143rd Pennsylvania; Capt. J. M. Clapp, of 121st Pennsylvania; Capt. Beaver, son of Gen. Beaver, of Pennsylvania, and others whose name and rank are not remembered. These officers were all in our front on the first of July, 1863, and gave a most hearty welcome to the Southerners. And the citizens were alike courteous. All points of the battlefield are accessible and in two days all the important and strategic points can easily be taken in by the tourist.

With many thanks to Col. John B. Batchelder, the historian, for the aid rendered, to his amiable wife for courtesies in the brief time allowed, to the officers we had the pleasure to meet, and to the citizens of the town of Gettysburg, we bid an affectionate adieu. And now, as to the senior officer in rank of McGowan's Brigade now living who participated in the battle, the duty requested of him has been performed. The points of the battlefield, the positions of the several regiments, their movements and the movements of the Brigade have been carefully and correctly pointed out to Col. Batchelder, the historian, and the Brigade will now have its place in the picture.

The record thus given of one battle will show that defeat did not everywhere confront the Confederate forces at Gettysburg, and at least one gem will be preserved from that ill-fated field.

* * *

LAURENS COUNTY ADVERTISER
MARCH 1, 1898

[Excerpt of longer article]

GREGGS' BRIGADE OF SOUTH CAROLINIANS

BLOODY RECORDS OF FEDERALS AND CONFEDERATES

Orr's First Regiment of Rifles Headed the List on Our Side—The Eighty-Third Pennsylvania Led Federal Hosts.

Charleston Sunday News

The bloody records of the civil war show some interesting parallels between the records of regiments on the opposite sides, as shown by George L. Rumer, writing in the New York Sunday Advertiser.

...

The Carolina brigade marched to the field of Gettysburg in July with well filled ranks. Gen. A. P. Hill was their corps leader in place of the dead "Stonewall." With him they assaulted Reynold's corps, in McPherson's Woods on July 1. As at Gaines's Mill, a battery confronted their advance, and rained shell and canister into ranks, chiefly upon the 1st regiment. The battery was doomed. One place was the prize of the 1st, and they dashed forward without a halt until their banner was floating in the town, the first Confederate flag in Gettysburg.

One day later, almost to the hour, at the other flank of the same field, the 83rd Pennsylvania fought gallantly to defend Round Top, with success equal to that of the Carolinians in their charge. The 1st lost one officer (Capt. William J. Haskell) and nineteen men killed; six officers (Capts. J[ames] S. McMahon, Josiah Cox, [James] Armstrong as lieutenant, W[illiam] M. Murray and J. F. J. Caldwell) and ninety-four men wounded—one hundred and twenty in all, which was more than half its membership.

...

(Gregg's "Old First," as it was called, was composed of three companies from Charleston—the Irish Volunteers, the Carolina Light Infantry and the Richardson Guards—one from Columbia—the Richland Volunteers—one from Barnwell, one from Newberry, one from Marion, one from Horry, one from Edgefield, and one partly from Beaufort and partly from Charleston. The original regiment was the first regimental organization in Virginia, and it may be said that the whole Army of Northern Virginia was gathered around its colors, which were planted in the town of Gettysburg, and which are now in the library in the State House at Columbia. By special orders the regiment was allowed to carry on its battle flag "Fort Sumter," as its first engagement, every company of which it was composed on its reorganization in July, 1861, having been present at the bombardment of that fort on the 12th and 13th of April, 1861. The regiment thus went from Fort Sumter to Appomattox, where it surrendered under the command of Lieut. Col. A[ndrew] P. Butler.

Editor—The Sunday News

* * *

NEWBERRY HERALD AND NEWS
MAY 27, 1904

WAR'S BLOODIEST RECORDS.
Made by South Carolina and Pennsylvania Troops.

By J. Colton Lyne.. Company "I."

1st S. C. Vol.. Maxey Gregg's Regiment.

The bloody records of the civil war show some interesting parallels between the records of regiments on the opposing sides. Pennsylvania championed the north in the contest for first place on the roll of honor and a trifle over 7 per cent of her quota of soldiers met, death on the battle-fields. South Carolina led the southern states and sacrificed over 23 per cent of her military population as it stood in 1861.

South Carolina furnished the regiment that lost the highest number killed in battle during the war--"Orr's S. C. Rifles*--which piled up a death roll of 334. Maxcy Gregg's 1st S. C. Vol. scores 281, thus taking the second place. Orr's Rifles was, however, a much larger organization at the start.

The first place on the Union side was taken by the 5th New Hampshire with a score of 295 and the second place fell to the 83d Pennsylvania regiment, which has a score of 282. The 83d Pennsylvania score or killed and wounded was 971. While the first S. C. Vol. had rolled up a score of 90 killed and wounded.

The 83d Pennsylvania came into being as a reorganization of a regiment composed of volunteers and militia companies that responded to President Lincoln's first call and served three months.

The colonel. John W. McLane, had served as a volunteer officer in the, Mexican war and distinguished himself as a master in organization and drill.

The 1st South Carolina Volunteers had a similar history, for it was formed out of the disbanded 1st South Carolina, of the provisional army called into being by the Convention when the state seceded. That regiment was made up of the old militia companies and volunteers enlisted to serve the state six months.

This provisional regiment and the one formed out of it were both created and led by the same colonel, Maxcy Gregg, who had been a volunteer officer in the war with Mexico, and had acquitted himself as an able disciplinarian and master of military tactics. And it happened that at the very time, to the month, and almost to a day, when Col. Gregg was getting his Palmetto men out of the old harness into the new and touching them up with his Mexican war reminiscences, Col. McLane was doing the same thing with his Keystone boys. The 83d was ready for orders in the fall of 1861 and the 1st South Carolina also.

...

Its Flag the First in Gettysburg.

The Carolina brigade marched to the field of Gettysburg in July, with well filled ranks. Gen. A. P. Hill was their corps leader in place of the dead but immortal Jackson. With him they assaulted Reynold's corps, in McPherson's Wood on July 1. As at Gaines' Mill, a battery confronted their advance, and rained shell and canister into the brigade, chiefly upon the 1st regiment. The battery was doomed. One piece was the prize of the 1st and they dashed forward without a halt until their banner was floating in the town, the first Confederate flag in Gettysburg.

One day later, almost to an hour, at the other flank of the same field the 83d Pennsylvania fought gallantly to defend Round Top with a success equal to the Carolinians in their charge. The 1st lost one officer and nineteen men killed, six officers and 94 men wounded--one hundred and twenty in all, which was more than one-half its membership.

In the Wilderness battle on May 5, 1864, the 1st led its brigade and division in an attack on the Confederate left along the Orange turnpike, a couple of miles distant. Both regiments suffered in the ensuing three days, the 1st with a loss of sixteen killed and fourteen wounded, besides six officers killed.

* * *

EDGEFIELD ADVERTISER
FEBRUARY 27, 1907

[Excerpt from longer article]

RECOLLECTIONS OF A CONFEDERATE SOLDIER

BY CAPT. GEO. B. LAKE

...

In the first days fight at Gettysburg he [William Henry Brunson, 1st South Carolina (Gregg's), Co. C] was shot through both legs. He fell on a Federal captain who was shot through one leg. After getting himself off the Federal officer he said, "Captain, you are bleeding profusely, I have some whiskey in my canteen that I thought I might need if badly wounded. Drink it," handing him the canteen; the other taking the canteen and seeing it was light said, "There is not more than a drink here. Have you had any?" When Brunson said he had not he for a time refused to take it, until he was convinced that he would soon faint if he did not. Two heroes had met. They both recovered. After Brunson was again well enough for duty, he was assigned to the command of the 2nd Company of the S. C. Battalion of Sharpshooters commanded by Maj. W[illiam] S. Dunlop [12th South Carolina, Co. B], McGowan's Brigade.

. . .

Capt. Brunson is the post master at Edgefield, S. C., now.

No man ever had a truer friend, no community a courtlier gentleman, no country a better soldier.

* * *

AIKEN STANDARD
MAY 22, 1929

[Excerpt of longer obituary]

DEATH OF A PROMINENT CITIZEN
Capt. Wm. W. Williams Died Early Sunday Morning

Capt. William White Williams, one of Aiken's best known citizens, died at the home of his daughter, Mrs. A. R. Roman, of South-boundary avenue, early Sunday morning, after a short illness. He was 84 years old.

...

At the outbreak of the Confederate War he entered the army, being a member of the famous First South Carolina Infantry. He served throughout the war until about nine months before the surrender of Lee, when he was captured and was sent to Elmira, N. Y., where he was held as a prisoner until the war was over. At the battle of Gettysburg he carried the battle flag of his regiment. His company was shot to pieces, but he carried the flag throughout the fight. Only four men of his company came out of this fight.

Nathaniel I. Hasell was a 3rd Sgt. In Co. L at the time of Gettysburg. Hasell was called "the boy hero" by his captain, W. T. Haskell. He was wounded during the charge up Seminary Ridge, but stayed with his unit. Hasell ended the war at Appomattox as a 1st Lt. Post war, he returned to Charleston where he served as a police sergeant then for 28 years with the postal service.

(Confederate Veteran Magazine)

Eli Franklin of Newberry, S.C. joined Co B of the 1st S.C. on July 27, 1861 and served throughout the war.

(Library of Congress)

Chapter 2

1st South Carolina (Orr's) Rifles

THE ANDERSON INTELLIGENCER
OCTOBER 14, 1903

Orr's Rifles at Gettysburg

The Anderson Intelligencer published a communication from "An Old Reb," in which he gives some reminiscences of the march of Orr's Regiment to Gettysburg. He admits that he may have made some mistakes in the names of places but according to our recollections he has made no serious errors in that respect. Butler's Ford as he has it, should be spelled "Boteler's," and the proper way to spell other names is: Hagerstown, Leitersburg, Funkstown, Waynesborough.

These errors are immaterial but further on he says: "So you see Orr's Regiment was not engaged in the great battle of Gettysburg, but the other four regiments certainly left their mark upon the battlefield on the first day's fight." In this "An Old Reb" is mistaken. During the first day's fight the regiment came from its post on the mountain, was halted at Willoughby Run and put in charge of a lot of prisoners taken from the enemy. The next day the regiment remained on this duty but afterwards the prisoners were sent back and the regiment ordered forward. The distance was about three miles from the town of Gettysburg. The regiment was halted near the Female Seminary and rested along a line of stone fence during the big cannonading. After Pickett's failure the regiment was ordered forward. It marched down a gentle slope, crossed a small branch and ascended a rising ground, deployed as skirmishers and went on until halted within fifty yards of the Yankee skirmishers, which was deployed beyond a wheat field. This position was held by the regiment until the field was abandoned about ten o'clock at night. The loss of the regiment was not so great as that of other regiments in the brigade which had been actively engaged on the first day. Orr's Rifles did all that was required of them in the battle of Gettysburg and was entitled to place the name of that battle on her flag.

In Caldwell's History of McGowan's Brigade the author states: "I should not omit to mention that Orr's regiment of Rifles was brought up and joined with the other four regiments of the brigade on the third day of the battle, July 3rd. It was required to take no further part in the operations of the day than the remainder of the brigade; and therefore its casualties were very few, all of us being, for that time, comparatively unmolested by the enemy."

This shows that the author, who was on the staff of Gen. [Samuel] McGowan, looked upon Orr's Rifles as having been at the battle of Gettysburg.

We also have before us the original book kept by Gen. McGowan, in which were entered the casualties in the brigade in every battle they fought under him and on page thirty he puts down, "Casualties in Orr's Rifles, S.C.V., Capt. [William M.] Hadden, Com'nd'g at Gettysburg. In Co. "A," E. A. Nickobraw[51] was killed, Joseph Chapman wounded. In Co. "G," Henry D. Gray was killed. In Co. "C," Lt. J[ames] H. Robins, T[homas] T. Hopkins and W[illiam] J. Hughes were wounded. In Co. "F," J. B. Cully was wounded.

This report was made on July 17th, 1863, at camp near Bunker Hill, Va., by Abner Perrin, Colonel commanding brigade at Gettysburg and signed by J. G. Barnwell, Jr., A.A.A.G.(Acting Assistant Adj-Gen.)

So it seems that Capt. Hadden and Col. Abner Perrin looked upon Orr's regiment as having been in the battle of Gettysburg.—Abbeville Medium--

---

51. Elijah A. Nicholson

* * *

KEOWEE COURIER

JULY 26, 1911

THIRTY-NINTH ANNUAL REUNION, ORR'S REGIMENT

Record of Proceedings—Sixty-Six Survivors of Orr's Regiment and Many Veterans of Other Commands Were Present—Addresses, Etc.

[Excerpt of a longer article]

The 39th annual reunion of Orr's Regiment of Rifles was held at Walhalla last Thursday and Friday, July 20 and 21, and was largely attended by the survivors of this famous regiment and other commands. The proceedings were brought to a close Friday evening by an automobile excursion to Westminster, where the survivors and visiting veterans were welcomed and entertained in the park.

…

The next feature was a recitation by Mrs. S. Bleckley, entitled "Old Mose." It was a pathetic story of the faithful service of an old-time darkey for his master, and his constant care and watch over him in camp and on the field of battle. The story runs that this faithful bodyguard, true to his natural impulse, inspired by love for his master, often disobeyed orders in breaking through the line of battle and following his master into the very jaws of death. The master falls, mortally wounded, on the battlefield of Gettysburg. He was found among the dead and dying by "Mose" and carried from the field, and Old Mose, faithful to his trust, carried him home. He kept watch by his side until the tide of life ebbed away, and he follows his body to the grave, and only when the sod has covered the face and form of his master forever from his view, does "Mose" shed his first tears and turn his feet away to tread unknown paths as he goes forth alone in the world. This true story was written by C. T. Merrill, of Texas, and dedicated to the late Henry W. Grady of Georgia. It sets forth in vivid language the faithfulness and fortitude of the old-time darkey who loved his young master as his own life. It is pathetic in the extreme and pays a deserved tribute where it is justly due.

* * *

CONFEDERATE VETERAN MAGAZINE
MARCH, 1922

WHEN BUT SIX ARE LEFT.

BY W. E. DOYLE, TEAGUE, TEX.

In "Some Incidents of Army Life," published in the VETERAN for February, comrade Theodore Hartman, referring to the Veteran, says: "I find so many good things in it I do not want to die." By this I am reminded of a statement made by George W. Abbott, of Company F, Orr's South Carolina Rifles, who said:

"During the war I was not sick, not wounded, did not miss roll call, and was in all the battles in Virginia and Maryland from Gaines's Mill to the last night in the trenches at Petersburg—save one—and yet I never saw but one battle—the Battle of Gettysburg. There our regiment was detailed to guard prisoners, and, therefore, I saw that battle. In all the other battles I saw nothing but what was immediately in front of me.

"I want to live to be one of six of the last surviving soldiers of the Confederate armies, and then I want to make a fortune in exhibiting them throughout America and Europe as the remnant of the best soldiers of which the world's annals give an account."

Think of it. When but six soldiers of the Confederate armies are left, and they should be exhibited as suggested, should not the lovers of truthful history and of real soldier life pay liberally to see them?

The night that Petersburg was evacuated a few soldiers had to be left in the trenches to keep up an occasional firing that the enemy might not be apprised of the evacuation, Comrade Abbott was one of those, and he was captured next morning. It was sad that fate decreed that such a soldier as he should not end his service at Appomattox.

George W. Abbott was reared in the same neighborhood as myself in South Carolina. He came to Texas in the fall of 65, and made as good a citizen as he was a soldier, but did not live to realize his fond wish. He died in Parker County, Tex., about two years ago.

It is said that a Virginia soldier was wounded in the head at Second

Manassas, a piece of bone pressing on his brain, and he remembered nothing till about twenty years later, when an operation was performed, the bone raised from the brain, and he immediately exclaimed: "The army was at Manassas yesterday; where is it to-day?" How appropriate is that question now. Where is the army to-day? Soon but six will be left, but the story of the Confederate armies will make the brightest pages of history as long as history is read.

Of all who write for the Veteran, Dr. McNeilly's articles are more interesting to me. May the Lord spare him to write for many years.

Samuel Amaziah Purdy was a member of Co. G of Orr's Rifles at Gettysburg. He was captured at Falling Waters during the retreat from Gettysburg on July 14, 1863. He was held first at Point Lookout, Maryland then later at Elmira, New York.

(photo courtesy of Billy L. G. Purdy)

James N. LeRoy was a member of Co. A, Orr's Rifles. He was 43 years old at the time of Gettysburg.

(Confederate Museum and Library, Greenville, SC)

John LeRoy was a 3rd Corporal in Co. E, Orr's Rifles at the time of Gettysburg. His records indicate he was serving on the Division Ordinance Reserve Train as the acting Div. Ordinance Sgt. He was captured April 3, 1865 at Petersburg and sent to Hart's Island POW Camp where he signed the Oath of Allegiance June 16, 1865.

(Confederate Museum and Library, Greenville, SC)

Chapter 3

12th South Carolina Infantry

WINNSBORO NEWS AND HERALD
AUGUST 12, 1879

THE TWELFTH REGIMENT

Meeting of the York companies—Arrangements Made for the Formation of a Permanent Association

[Condensed from the Enquirer]

In pursuance to previous notice, on Monday last the survivors of Companies A, B and H, of the Twelfth South Carolina Regiment, met in the Court House for the purpose of effecting a permanent organization of the survivors, to be known as the Survivors' Association.

Col. W[illiam] H. McCorkle [Company A] called the meeting to order, and on his motion [Sergeant] J[ames] C. Chambers [Company A], Esq., was called to preside as temporary chairman, and Mr. James A. Watson [1st Lt. Company A] was requested to act as temporary secretary.

On taking the chair, Mr. Chambers briefly explained the object of the meeting, heartily approving the object for which it was called, and then declared the meeting organized and ready for the transaction of business.

Mr. W[illiam] J. Kimbrell [Company H] moved that a committee of nine, consisting of three from each company, be appointed for the purpose of reporting a constitution for the permanent organization of the Association.

The motion was carried, and the chairman appointed the following committee:

Company A.—James A. Watson, S[amuel] M. Scott, Daniel A. James

Company B.—[1st Lt.] M[artin] V. Darwin, [1st Sgt.] R[obert] W. Whitesides, [Sgt.] R[ufus] G. Whitesides

Company H.—[2nd Lt.] A[lexander] M. Black, W[illiam] J. Kim-brell, W[illiam] J. Miller

During the absence of the committee, Major James F. Hart brought to the attention of the meeting the destitute condition of the family of the late Gen. R[ichard] H[eron] Anderson, and suggested some action.

Resolved, That it is due to the eminent services of Lieut.-General Anderson that his comrades in arms should assist the widow and daughters, who, we are informed, are without means of support, and that a committee of three be appointed by the chairman for the purpose if receiving a contribution.

In conformity with the resolution, the chairman appointed the following committee: Col. Cad[wallader] Jones [Sr.], Col. I. D. Witherspoon and Mr. R. G. Whitesides.

The committee on permanent organization submitted a constitution, which was unanimously adopted. The constitution is substantially the same as that adopted by the Fairfield committee.

Mr. J. A. Watson moved that a committee of three—one from each company—be appointed to nominate permanent officers for the Association.

The motion was carried, and the chair appointed the following committee: W. J. Kimbrell, R[ichard] L. Simmons, R[obert] M. Plexico.

The committee then retired, and in their absence, on motion of Col. W. H. McCorkle, the members present were requested to enroll their names, which was done.

After the enrollment of names the committee on permanent officers of the Association reported the following:

President—Col. Cad. Jones

First Vice-President—Col. W. H. McCorkle

Second Vice-President—J. A. Watson

Third Vice-President—R. L. Simmons

Secretary—J. C. Chambers

Treasurer—Capt. Lewis M. Grist

Corresponding Secretary—Capt. A. Jones

The report of the committee, recommending the above officers, was unanimously adopted.

On taking the chair, Colonel Jones addressed the Association briefly, expressing the honor he felt on being selected to preside over any portion of the illustrious Twelfth Regiment—a regiment that had made itself famous—and with which he was proud to say he had served. In 1861, said he, we were the "Boys in Gray;" to-day I address you as veterans of forty battles—soldiers who have made a proud record from Hilton Head, in the lower part of the State, through North Carolina and Virginia, and even into the confines of Pennsylvania, on the bloody field of Gettysburg. I address men who composed a regiment that has never been known to turn its back upon an enemy—a regiment, it is true, of which not much has been said in history, but which has a bright record in the Army of Northern Virginia. The President then alluded to the battle-worn flag of the regiment, which had been tattered in many hard-fought battles. At Gettysburg it was pierced by thirty balls; four ensigns fell beneath it; and at the bloody angle of Spottsylvania, a massive oak cut down by rifle balls of the enemy, fell upon the ensign. This flag, after being riddled with bullets, was carefully folded and sent to the Soldiers' Home in Richmond, where it was burnt. But its representative, which the regiment afterwards carried, though not mentioned among the flags in the procession at Columbia of the 13th of May, was entitled to all the honors of the first.

He next alluded to the object of the meeting, and the praiseworthy motives of the survivors in organizing a permanent Association, in which all the members should take active part, and closed by urging upon all who could do so to attend the reunion of the regiment at Winnsboro on the 20th instant.

When the President concluded his address, Mr. Chambers moved that all who do could so, be requested to attend the reunion at Winnsboro.

The question was put, and all who proposed to attend the reunion were requested to rise to their feet, whereupon nearly all who were present rose. The meeting then adjourned.

John Alexander Rosborough was the 1st sergeant of Co. L of the 12th S. C. Infantry at Gettysburg. After the war he moved to Windsor, Florida and later served as the commander of the Florida division of the United Confederate Veterans.

(Confederate Veteran Magazine)

James R. Harvey of Co. F, 12th S.C. Infantry was shot in the right hip on the first day at Gettysburg and left behind as a prisoner. He was sent to DeCamp General Hosp. on David's Island in New York. He was later held at Ft. Wood and Ft. Delaware. He was paroled Sept. 14, 1864 and discharged due to disability Feb. 18, 1865.

(The News and Herald, Winnsboro, SC)

Chapter 4

13th South Carolina Infantry

Excerpt from "A Confederate Surgeon's Letters to his Wife" by Spencer Glasgow Welch, Surgeon, Thirteenth South Carolina Volunteers, McGowan's Brigade

---

Franklin County, Pa.,

June 28, 1863.

We are in Yankeedom this time, for certain, and a beautiful and magnificent country it is too. Since we started we have traveled about fifteen miles a day, resting at night and drawing rations plentifully and regularly. We are about fifteen miles over the Pennsylvania and Maryland line and within seven miles of Chambersburg. We are resting to-day (Sunday) and will get to Harrisburg in three more days if we go there.

We hear nothing of Hooker's army at all, but General Lee knows what he is about. This is certainly a grand move of his, and if any man can carry it out successfully he can, for he is cautious as well as bold.

We are taking everything we need horses, cattle, sheep, flour, groceries and goods of all kinds, and making as clean a sweep as possible. The people seem frightened almost out of their senses. They are nearly all agricultural people and have everything in abundance that administers to comfort. I have never yet seen any country in such a high state of cultivation. Such wheat I never dreamed of, and so much of it! I noticed yesterday that scarcely a horse or cow was to be seen. The free negroes are all gone, as well as thousands of the white people. My servant, Wilson, says he "don't like Pennsylvania at all," because he "sees no black folks."

I have never seen our army so healthy and in such gay spirits. How can they be whipped? Troops have so much better health when on the march. I must say that I have enjoyed this tramp. The idea of invading the Yankees has buoyed me up all the time. Last year when invading Maryland we were almost starved, and of course anyone would become disheartened. My health was never better than it is now, and I feel gay and jovial every way.

My brother Billie [William E. Welch, Co. D, 13th South Carolina Infantry] is out to-day guarding a man's premises. He was also out last night, and he told me this morning that they fed him splendidly. The reason houses are guarded is to prevent our troops plundering and robbing, which would demoralize them, thereby rendering them unfit for soldiers. Soldiers must have a strict and severe rein held over them; if not, they are worthless.

I have George's picture with me, and I look at it frequently.

RETREAT FROM GETTYSBURG.

Near Bunker Hill, Jefferson County, Va.,

July 17, 1863.

You will see by this letter that we have gotten back into "Old Virginia" again. It seems that our invasion of the North did not prove successful. We fought a dreadful battle at Gettysburg, Pa. It was the greatest battle of the war. We drove the Yankees three miles from the battlefield to a long range of high hills, from which it was impossible to dislodge them. General Lee had to fall back to keep them from getting the advantage. My brother was not hurt in the battle. Milton Bossard, Captain [W. P.] Cromer [Co. D, 13th, S.C.], Buford Wallace, Mr. Daniel's two sons and many others from Newberry were killed; but it is better for us all to be killed than conquered.

We have had some very disagreeable marching, as it has rained so much, but I have gotten hold of an old horse, which helps me along very much.

We have plenty of beef and bread to eat. We gathered up thou-sands of beeves in Pennsylvania enough to feed our army until cold weather. This is a great consideration.

My servant got lost in Maryland. I do not think it was his intention to leave, but he was negligent about keeping up and got in rear of the army and found it too late to cross the river.

One of your letters came to me in Pennsylvania, and three since we left there.

We hear that Vicksburg has fallen. That is unfortunate, but I do not feel at all discouraged. Countries have been overrun, and then not conquered.

When we get settled down in camp again I will try to write you a longer and better arranged letter. We don t know what minute we may move, and under such circumstances I never can write with any satisfaction. I have George's picture yet. It is a wonder I did not lose it.

THE BATTLE OF GETTYSBURG

Camp near Orange Court House, Va.,

August 2, 1863.

In a recent letter I promised to write you more about our campaign in Pennsylvania.

On the night of the 29th of June we camped on the west side of the Blue Ridge Mountains, where they extend into Pennsylvania. On the morning of the next day (30th) we renewed our march. Shortly after starting it began raining, but the road was hard and well macadamized and the rain made the march rather agreeable than otherwise. On this same morning we passed where a splendid iron factory had been burned by General Early, of Ewell's Corps. It belonged to a very celebrated lawyer and politician of Pennsylvania by the name of Thaddeus Stevens, who is noted for his extreme abolition views and his intense hatred for slave-holders. The works are said to have been worth more than one hundred thousand dollars. The burning had thrown a great many operatives out of employment, and they seemed to be much distressed.

During the day we wended our way up the mountains. The scene around us was very different from what we had just passed through. Instead of the enticing field and lovely landscape, we had now around us that which was rugged, grand and towering. In the afternoon about one or two o clock we halted and bivouacked among the mountains. Our stopping-place was in a basin of the mountains, which was very fertile and contained a few very excellent and highly cultivated farms. Awhile after we stopped I started off to one of these farmhouses for the purpose of getting my dinner, as I was quite hungry, and wanted something different from what I had been accustomed to most of the time on the march. On going to the house a very nice, smiling young girl met me at the door, and, upon my making known my wishes, she very pleasantly said she "guessed" so; but said they already had agreed to accommodate a good many, and that they would do the best they could by us all if I would return at four o'clock.

This I did, and found Adjutant Reedy of the Fourteenth Regiment and several others of my acquaintance. Reedy, being quite a young man, talked a good deal to the girl. I was hungry as a wolf, but when I came to the table and viewed what was upon it my hunger was aggravated more than ever. It seemed that there was no end to everything that was good. We had nice fried ham, stewed chicken, excellent biscuit, lightbread, butter, buckwheat cakes that were most delicious, molasses, four or five different kinds of preserves and several other dishes. We also had plenty of good coffee and cold, rich milk to drink. None but a soldier who has experienced a hard campaign can conceive of how a gang of hungry men could appreciate such a meal. I must say that this late dinner was a perfect Godsend.

After we had finished eating I felt ashamed to offer them Confederate money, but could do no better, and offered it with an apology. They very readily accepted it, and when I insisted that they should take a dollar they refused and would have only fifty cents. This house was guarded to prevent our men committing depredations such as they had been doing, and which was having a demoralizing effect upon the army. Soldiers must be made to behave or they will not fight.

Upon returning to camp I found that an order had been received during my absence to cook one day s rations and have it in haversacks and be ready to march at five o clock next morning. This at once aroused our suspicions, for we concluded that we were about to meet the enemy. Next morning about five o clock we began moving. We had not gone more than a mile and a half before our suspicions of the evening previous were fully verified and our expectations realized by the booming of cannon ahead of us in the direction of Gettysburg. Upon looking around I at once noticed in the countenance of all an expression of intense seriousness and solemnity, which I have always perceived in the faces of men who are about to face death and the awful shock of battle. As we advanced the cannonading increased in fury. It was Heth's Division, ahead of ours, fighting. At last we arrived upon a hill where, upon another hill in front of us and about a half mile distant, we could see Heth's cannon arranged and booming away at the Yankees, who were replying with considerable briskness, and we could also see the infantry of Heth's Division advancing in line of battle. It was really a magnificent sight. The country was almost destitute of forest and was so open that it was easy to see all that was going on. Our division (Pender's) continued to keep within about half a mile of Heth's. McGowan's Brigade was at the right of the division and the Thirteenth Regiment at the right of the brigade. This being the case, I could see from one end of the division to the other as it moved forward in line of battle. It was nearly a mile in length. The scene was certainly grand, taking all the surroundings into consideration. After Heth had driven the enemy some distance, it became necessary for our division to go to his support. McGowan's South Carolina and Scales's North Carolina brigades were the first to relieve Heth. The hardest fighting did not begin until McGowan's and Scales s divisions went into it. Then such a rattle of musketry I never heard surpassed. It lasted for about two hours and a half without cessation and how many brave fellows went down in death in this short period of time! Officers who have been in all the fights tell me that they never saw our brigade act so gallantly before. When the order was given to charge upon the enemy, who were lying behind stone fences and other places of concealment, our men rushed forward with a perfect fury, yelling and driving them, though with great slaughter to themselves as well as to the Yankees. Most of the casualties of our brigade occurred this day (July 1). As the enemy were concealed, they killed a great many of our men before we could get at them. There were a good many dwellings in our path, to which the Yankees would also resort for protection, and they would shoot from the doors and windows. As soon as our troops would drive them out, they would rush in, turn out the families and set the houses on fire. I think this was wrong, because the families could not prevent the Yankees seeking shelter in their houses. I saw some of the poor women who had been thus treated. They were greatly distressed, and it excited my sympathy very much. These people would have left their houses, but the battle came on so unexpectedly to them, as is often the case, that they had not time. I passed through a house from which everyone had fled except an extremely old man. A churn of excellent buttermilk had been left, and I with some other doctors helped ourselves. Someone near by shot at us as we came out and barely missed us.

The fighting on the first day ceased about night, and when our brigade was relieved by Lane's North Carolina Brigade it was nearly dark. I returned to the hospital, and on my way back came to Anderson's Division of our corps (Hill's) lying in line of battle at least two miles in rear of where the advance column was. Pender's Division and Heth's had been fighting all day, and they were exhausted, besides being terribly "cut up" and when they drove the Yankees to the long high range of hills, which the Yankees held throughout the fight, they should have been immediately reinforced by Anderson with his fresh troops. Then the strong position last occupied by the enemy could have been taken, and the next day when Ewell and Longstreet came up the victory completely won. If "Old Stonewall" had been alive and there, it no doubt would have been done. Hill was a good division commander, but he is not a superior corps commander. He lacks the mind and sagacity of Jackson.

When I arrived at the hospital my ears were greeted as usual at such time with the moans and cries of the wounded. I went to work and did not pretend to rest until next morning after daylight. I found that Longstreet had come and that McLaw's Division of his (Longstreet's) corps was encamped near the hospital. Kershaw's Brigade was almost in the hospital grounds. On looking around I discovered many of my old friends from Laurens whom I had not seen since the war began. They all seemed surprised and glad to see me; but I had work to do and they had fighting, so we could not remain long together. They were all lively and jocose. Milton Bossardt [3rd Lt. Milton P. Buzhardt, Co. B, 3rd S.C. Infantry] was in a gay humor and left me as one going on some pleasant excursion, but before two o'clock of the same day he was a corpse. He was shocked to death by the bursting of a shell. Captain [D. M. H.] Langston [Co. I, Acting Lt. Col.] and a number of others in the Third Regiment who were my acquaintances were killed.

On the second day of the battle the fighting did not begin until about twelve or one o'clock, from which time until night it raged with great fury. The reason it began so late in the day was because it required some time for Ewell and Longstreet to get their forces in position. Longstreet was on the right, Ewell on the left, and Hill in the center.

On the third day the fighting began early in the morning and continued with the greatest imaginable fury all day; at one time, about three o clock in the afternoon, with such a cannonading I never heard before. About 150 pieces of cannon on our side and as many or more on the side of the enemy kept up one incessant fire for several hours. It was truly terrifying and was like heavy skirmishing in the rapidity with which the volleys succeeded one another. The roar of the artillery, the rattle of the musketry and the wild terrific scream of the shells as they whizzed through the air was really the most appalling situation that could possibly be produced. Our troops (Pickett's Division) charged the enemy's strong position, which they had now entrenched, but with no avail, although we slaughtered thousands of them.

On the night of the 3d General Lee withdrew the army nearly to its original position, hoping, I suppose, that the enemy would attack him, but they didn't dare come out of their strongholds, for well they knew what their fate would be if they met the Confederate Army of Virginia upon equal grounds. On the 4th our army remained in line of battle, earnestly desiring the advance of the Yankees, but they did not come. During this day the rain fell in torrents, completely drenching the troops. Awhile after dark we began to leave, but took a different and nearer route to the Potomac than the one we had just passed over. Though nearer, it was very rough and not macadamized, and the passing of wagons and artillery over it cut it up horribly and made it almost impassable. Yet over this road our large army had to pass. I was lucky enough to get into a medical wagon and rode until next morning. It rained nearly all night, and such a sight as our troops were next day! They were all wet and many of them muddy all over from having fallen down during the night. Billie looked as if he had been wallowing in a mud hole, but was in a perfectly good humor. On this day (July 5) we recrossed the Blue Ridge Mountains. Climbing the mountains was very tedious after so much toil, excitement and loss of sleep, but we met with no obstacle until we came to Hagerstown, Md., where we stopped on account of the Potomac's being too high to ford. While here the Yankees came up and our army was placed in line to meet them, but they did not dare to attack. In this situation we remained for several days with them in sight of us.

After a pontoon bridge was finished at Falling Waters and the river was sufficiently down to ford at Williamsport, we left the vicinity of Hagerstown. It was just after dark when we began leaving. It was a desperately dark night and such a rain I thought I never before knew to fall. I did not meet with such luck as the night we left Gettysburg, Pa., but had to walk all night, and such a road I think troops never before traveled over. It appeared to me that at least half of the road was a quagmire, coming in places nearly to the knees.

Hill's Corps went by Falling Waters and Longstreet s and Ewell s by Williamsport, where they had to wade the river, which was still very deep, coming up nearly to the shoulders. The pontoon bridge was at Falling Waters, where we crossed. Our division was in the rear at this place, and when we got within about a mile and a half of the river we halted to enable the wagons ahead to get out of the way. Being very tired, we all lay down and nearly everyone fell asleep, when suddenly the Yankee cavalry rushed upon us, firing and yelling at a furious rate. None of our guns were loaded and they were also in a bad fix from the wet of the previous night. They attacked General Pettigrew's North Carolina Brigade first. Our brigade was lying down about fifty yards behind his. I was lying down between the two brigades near a spring. General Pettigrew was killed here. I was close to him when he was killed. It was a serious loss to the service. We fought them for some time, when General Hill sent an order to fall back across the river, and it was done in good order. The attack was a complete surprise and is disgraceful either to General Hill or General Heth. One is certainly to blame. The Yankees threw shells at the bridge and came very near hitting it just as I was about to cross; but, after we were close enough to the river not to be hurt by our own shells, our cannon on this side opened upon them, which soon made them "skedaddle" away.

We feel the loss of General Pender in our division. He died in Staunton, Va., from wounds received at Gettysburg. He was a very superior little man, though a very strict disciplinarian.

IN CAMP AFTER GETTYSBURG CAMPAIGN

Camp near Orange Court House, Va.

August 10, 1863.

All is quiet here now. When two armies have a great battle both sides are so crippled up that neither is anxious to fight soon again. The enemy must be somewhere about, or we would not be here. I do think there will not be another fight soon, for the Yankees dread us too much. It seems that Meade will not attack us, and that whenever we fight we must make the attack. I believe it will be a long time before we have another battle, if we have to wait for the enemy to advance on us.

Our long trip lately was very fatiguing, and we all became very thin and lean, although our health remained fine. Your brother tells me the Pioneer Corps had a very hard time of it on the way back from Pennsylvania. He took a more direct route to Culpeper Court House than we did, in order to assist some of Ewell's men in crossing the Shenandoah River.

Wilcox of Alabama is the major-general appointed over us, but he cannot surpass General Pender, who commanded us at Gettysburg. Pender was an officer evidently superior even to Hill. He was as brave as a lion and seemed to love danger. I observed his gallantry on the opening of the battle. He was mortally wounded on the first day as the fight was closing.

I have seen letters from some of our wounded who were left at Gettysburg. They are now in New York, and all say they are treated well. I had a chance to remain with our wounded, and, had I preferred to do so, I might have had a very interesting experience. Our chaplain, Beauschelle [J. N. Bouchelle, 13th S.C.], was captured and is somewhere in Yankeedom, and I suppose is in prison, as chaplains are now held as prisoners, but he is apt to be released soon.

Our army is in splendid health and spirits, and is being increased rapidly every day by conscription and by men returning from the hospitals. Last year when a soldier was sent to a hospital he was expected to die, but all who come from the hospitals in Richmond now are highly pleased with the treatment they received. The hospital sections set aside for officers are admirably kept.

We get plenty to eat now and I am beginning to get as fat as ever again. Beef, bacon and flour, and sometimes sugar and potatoes, are issued to us. Dr. Tyler and I have obtained twenty pounds of sugar, a fine ham and one-half bushel of potatoes, and we hope to get some apples and make pies, as we have so much sugar. Vegetables are abundant in the country around here, and I succeeded in getting so much blackberry pie to eat recently that it made me sick.

Our regiment is on picket duty to-day. It went on last night. The weather is intensely hot, as hot as I ever experienced in South Carolina, but we are encamped in a fine grove and do not suffer from the heat as we would if marching.

The first chance I have I will send you two hundred dollars. You must buy everything you need, even if calico does cost three dollars a yard and thread one dollar a spool.

I am extremely gratified to hear that you and George are both in such excellent health, and I am glad you had him baptized.

Chapter 5

14th South Carolina Infantry

EDGEFIELD ADVERTISER
JULY 15, 1863

Edgefield's Roll of Honor Gleaming!

The mail of Monday last brought dispatches from Charlottesville and Martinsburg, continuing the following sad intelligence:

Casualties in Co. D, 14th S. C. V., at the Battle of Gettysburg, Pa.

Killed:--Lieut. Harvey Crooker, Sergt. Beaufort Wallace and Private N[athan] L. Bartley.

Wounded:--Sergt. Charles L. Durisoe, leg amputated; Corpl. James Youngblood, hand off; Preston Pruier and Pinckney Posey, mortally; Preston Deloach, Joe Brunson, J[ames] A. Colgan, J[ohn] E. Colgan, J. F. [John H.] Cheatham, E[dward M.] Dinkins, [George] W. Murrell, slightly.

A dispatch to Mr. W. P. Butler says Thomas Butler, younger brother of Col. M[atthew] C[albraith] Butler, and in his command, was killed on the 2nd of July—shot through the heart, and died immediately.

No tidings of the 7th Regiment have been received since the Battle of Gettysburg.

* * *

EDGEFIELD ADVERTISER
JULY 29, 1863

Casualties in Co. D, 14th S. C. V.

Through the kindness of Lieut. E[rasmus] S. Mims, commanding Co. D, 14th S. C. V., we are placed in possession of the following correct list of casualties in Co. D, at the battles of Gettysburg and since:

July 1st. --Killed: N L Bartley and F[elix] Ridgell; Wounded: Lieut W[illiam] H Brunson, severe; Lieut H D Crooker, mortally, died 3rd July; Sergt C L Durisoe, leg amputated; Corp Jas Youngblood, right arm amputated; Corp J[ames] A Colgan, slight; M[illedge] L Bartley, severe; J Brunson, slight; J[ohn] H Cheatham, severe; B[eauford] W. Christian, slight; J[ohn] E Colgan, slight; F H Corley, severe; B[aley] Corley, slight; T[homas] P Deloach, slight; E[dward] M Dinkins, severe; W[illiam] B Griffis, severe; G[eorge] W Murrell, slight; G D McCarty, slight; Sam Overstreet, severe; P[ickens] P Posey, slight; P[resley] M Prater, slight; T[utor] T Ridgell, severe; [Alexander Spann] Walker, slight; J[ohn] Bridwell, severe.

July 3rd. --Oscar Cheatham, J[abez] Deloach, J[ohn] Whittle, slight; D[avid] Etheredge, severe.

Taken prisoners on 13th July—W P Goodman, Wm Ryan, L[emuel] D Hagood.

* * *

EDGEFIELD ADVERTISER
JULY 29, 1863

Soldiers Just Returned

Lieut. W[illiam] H. BRUNSON of Co. D, 14th Reg't., who was so painfully wounded before Richmond a year ago, celebrates the anniversary of that event by returning home with a bullet hole through each thigh—which pleasant punctures he received from the hands of the Yankees at Gettysburg. The friends of this intrepid soldier will be glad to hear that his wounds are doing well, and that he is already getting about a little on his crutches.

Mr. W[illiam] S. COVAR, son of our old townsman, Mr. SHERRY COVAR, has also just got home from Virginia; he has been brought low by typhoid pneumonia, but "Home, sweet Home" has already set him upon his feet.

* * *

EDGEFIELD ADVERTISER

AUGUST 5, 1863

For the Advertiser
Casualties in Co. B, 14th S. C. V.

MR. EDITOR:--I send you the casualties of Co. B, 14th Regiment, S. C. V, in the fight of Gettysburg, Pa., as received in a letter from Mr. Jesse Black, of that Company:

Killed:--Privates Wesly Padgett and Gilford Etheredge.

Wounded:--R[obert] B. Watson, thigh, severely; Lieut. J[ohn] M. Bell, leg, severely; Lieut. H. J. Rauch, both thighs; Sergt. E[rwin] A. Roach, severely; S[amuel] N. Rauch, thigh, severely; Henry Jennings, leg amputated; Marion Snelvegrove, groin; Gilford Gilder, [William] P. Havird, John Gileon, Z[edekiah] Crouch, Jas. Ouzts, Thos. Perry, R[obert] T. Jones, G[eorge W.] Harris, Thos. Miller, Thos. Whittle, Ivy Whittle, B[ailey] Matthews, A[mbrose] Gibson and Wm. Crouch.

–A. P. W.—

For the Advertiser
Casualties in Co. K, 14th S. C. V.

Killed:--Sergt. E. R. Mobley, G[eorge] W. Free, James Ouzts, Jesse Parkman, Wilkerson Rice, M. W[esley] Stevens.

Wounded:--Lieut. S[imeon] Cogburn, foot, severe; Sergt J[ohn] C. Buzzard, arm, severe; Corp. J[ames] N. Werts, shoulder, slight; Corp. W[hitfield] D. Gradick, thigh, severe; A[ndrew] J. Timmerman, ankle, severe; W[illiam] H. Ouzts, head, slight; Private A. B. Adams, back, severe; W[illiam] H. W. Adams, leg, severe; R[ansom] D. Amacker, hand, slight; John L. Doby, thigh, severe; Joshua Edwards, thigh, slight; John Falkner, head and shoulder, severe; T[homas] B. Harvey, legs, slight; Whit[field] Harvely, neck, severe; James Harling, thigh, severe; Rufus Harling, face, severe; Allen King, left arm amputated; B[enjamin] W. Mayson, thigh, severe; Martin Ouzts, thigh, severe; Franklin Ouzts, leg, slight; George

Ouzts, head, mortally; Larkin Rice, side, slight; B[enjamin] M. Timmerman, hand, slight; Edw. Timmerman, face, severe; G[oodley] M. Timmerman, head, slight; George Taylor, shocked with shell; James Taylor, back, slight; R[alph] S. Towles, leg, severe; A[ndrew] C. Werts, arm, slight.

Missing:--Marion Ouzts and J. T. Timmerman.

Killed, 6; wounded, 29; missing, 2; total, 37

J[ames] H. ALLEN,

Lieut. Commanding, Co. K.

* * *

EDGEFIELD ADVERTISER
AUGUST 12, 1863

Death of Sergt. C. L. Durisoe

The mail of Monday last, brought to Mr. W. F. DURISOE, of this place, the sad intelligence that his son, Sergt. CHARLES L. DURISOE [14th S.C. Infantry, Co. D], whose leg was amputated after the battle of Gettysburg, breathed his last at David's Island, New York Bay, on the 23rd July. This amiable and upright young man was, for some years previous to the breaking out of the war, closely identified with the corps of the Advertiser, and each week, wielded his manly right arm in bringing out the old sheet. For over two years past, the same manly right arm has been nobly wielded in defense of his native South; but now, alas! Its labors are done. His name has become a "household word" in the household of the Advertiser. Let the memory of this brave and devoted young soldier—and of the many like him—be hung like a cherished picture upon the walls of Edgefield's heart.

From the letter which brought these sorrowful tidings, we are permitted the make the following extract:

My Dear Sir: This brings you the melancholy tidings of the death of your very gallant son CHARLIE. He reached this place the 19th instant, and received every attention that he could desire. I was glad when I saw that he and I were in the same ward, for I felt as if I could give him some attention myself; and besides he expressed a wish to be with me. We all did everything in our power for him, but God, in his wise Providence, has seen fit to take him from us.

Last night, about 10 ½ o'clock, he breathed his last; he was not conscious at the time of his death. Some days ago he thought he would recover. I conversed with him on the subject of religion; he seemed anxious to talk about it, and said he had determined to be a Christian. Even before the battle two months previous, he had promised God to serve him better. He said he prayed often and he believed God had answered his prayer; and also told me that if it were God's will that he should die, he would endeavor to submit. I trust he is now in heaven. Accept my profound sympathies.

Yours, truly,

T[homas] P. QUARLES [3rd Sgt., Company C, 7th S.C. Infantry][52]

* * *

EDGEFIELD ADVERTISER
AUGUST 19, 1863

For the Advertiser

SACRED TO THE MEMORIES OF
Crooker, Wallace and Durisoe:

The wreath of "Immorielles" is scarcely withered, which mourned the loss of our gallant countrymen at Chancellorsville, ere its faded leaves are to be renewed by fresh offerings to the patriotic soldiers, who have fallen on the field of Gettysburg. With feelings of deep sadness, we present to the view of their fellow citizens, the names of the bold and intrepid soldiers who have sealed with their blood, their devotion to their country, as men who will not remain neglected, and unrecorded, whilst a grateful but afflicted country cherishes the recollection of their heroism.

At the commencement of the war, CROOKER, WALLACE AND DURISOE volunteered in the Edgefield Rifles, a Company raised in this vicinity by Capt. CICERO ADAMS [later of the 22nd S.C. Infantry, Co. A], went thro' the campaign together, and upon the disbanding of that company, subsequently volunteered in Co. D, 14th Regt., S. C. V., Capt. [Abner Monroe] PERRIN. With that gallant and veteran Regt. they stood shoulder to shoulder amid the trying ordeal through which it passed, and

52. Sgt Quarles was also confined on David's Island. He was shortly thereafter sent home to await exchange.

fell together on the bloody field of Gettysburg, inseparable in death as in life.

Lieut. HARVEY DRAKE CROOKER died on the 2nd July from wounds received on the 1st, at the battle of Gettysburg, in the 32nd year of his age. In his bold and gallant conduct on that bloody battlefield, he illustrated the heroism of the family from which he sprang, and renewed in his daring intrepidity, the gallantry of a patriotic ancestry. To the bereaved and widowed mother, whom he has left to bewail his untimely loss, the proud reflection that he nobly fell in defense of his country, whilst it may not dry the tears of a mother, may yet temper with consolation the grief that saddens the anguished bosom.

Sergt. BEAUFORT WALLACE, died on the 2nd July from wounds received on the 1st, at the battle of Gettysburg, in the 25th year of his age. In the spring-time of life, with everything to make life desirable, the spirit of this gallant soldier has passed from the battle-field to the judgment of his God. Filial in his domestic relations, exemplary in his mortality, correct in his deportment, a widowed mother alone in the sanctuary of her affections can only estimate his loss. May almighty God pour the oil of consolation upon her afflicted and bruised heart, and close up the wound which the enemies of our country have opened.

Sergt. CHARLES L. DURISOE, died at David's Island, New York from wounds received on the 1st July at the battle of Gettysburg, in the 24th year of his age. The last, though not the least of this gallant triad, warm and impetuous in his feelings, and devoted in his patriotism, has given his life to the cause of his country. Identified with the war from its commencement, engaged in the campaigns, in the camp and in the field, he illustrated the character of the Southern soldier, and has left to his countrymen, for imitation, the unspotted character of a youthful martyr. Though the family hearth may have a vacant seat, and sadness hang around the homestead, yet in the reflection that their "son has done his duty," let his parents find refuge from regret.

The hand of friendship pays this humble tribute to three brave soldiers, who sleep far away from their native land. May some gentle spirit kindly watch over their graves, and preserve over verdant the mound that marks the spot of their last repose.

---M---

* * *

EDGEFIELD ADVERTISER
SEPTEMBER 9, 1863

Lieut. S[imeon] Cogburn, Lieut. W[illiam] S. Jordan and Lieut. [James P.] Sloan, of the 14th S. C. V., left in the enemy's hands after the battle of Gettysburg, are in the U. S. Hospital, Chester, Penn., and, we hope, doing well.

* * *

EDGEFIELD ADVERTISER
MARCH 16, 1863

Out of Limbo at Last

Two of our young soldiers, Mr. WM. RYAN [14th S.C. Infantry, Co. D; captured at Falling Water, July 14, 1863] and Mr. WM. GOODMAN, Jr. [14th S.C. Infantry, Co. D], who have been prisoners in Yankeeland ever since the battle of Gettysburg, have finally reached their homes in our midst. They have been most of the time in the old Capitol Washington; more latterly however, they have been experien-cing the tender mercies of Beast Butler at Point Lookout. Poor boys! They have had a rough and dreary pilgrimage of it. They deserve now the "fatted calf" and the "gold ring" and the "best garment"—and all manner of petting, caressing, feeding, loving.

* * *

EDGEFIELD ADVERTISER
MAY 4, 1864

Gen. Abner Perrin at Gettysburg

From an article in the Richmond Dispatch, entitled a "Review of the Pennsylvania Campaign," we take pleasure in transferring to our columns the annexed well-merited and highly complimentary allusions in reference to the part taken in the Gettysburg fight by the gallant PERRIN and his brave men, he being Colonel of the 14th S.C. Regiment at the time, and in command of McGowan's Brigade. Edgefield's sons wherever engaged, reflect credit on this old District; and, with a proper appreciation of all that is true and noble, she had just cause to be proud of her intrepid and lion-hearted boys. Here is the extract we allude to, and to which we respectfully invite the reader's attention:

About three o'clock, the enemy having made a strong demonstration on the right, Gen. [James H.] Lane was sent to the extreme right, and Gen. [Edward L.] Thomas closed upon the left of Gen. [Alfred Moore] Scales. Soon thereafter the division (with the exception of Gen. Thomas, who was retained to meet a threatened advance on the left) moved forward slowly to the right to the support of Major Gen. [Henry] Heth, who was now vigorously engaged with the enemy. About 4 o'clock the three brigades of Lane, Scales, and Perrin, were ordered by Major Gen. [William Dorsey] Pender to advance and to pass Major Gen. Heth's division, if it should be found at a halt, and charge the enemy, who were posted on a prominent ridge between a quarter and half mile out from Gettysburg. The division at once moved rapidly forward and soon passed the division of Major Gen. Heth, now under command of Brigadier Gen. [James Johnston] Pettigrew, whose men seemed much exhausted and their ranks greatly thinned by the severe fighting through which, during some four or five preceding hours,that division had passed. Gen. Lane, on the extreme right, was much annoyed by a heavy force of dismounted cavalry on his extreme right flank, which kept up a severe and continuous enfilade fire.

This so much delayed him in his advance that he was unable to attack the enemy, except a small force of them, which he dislodged from a skirt of woods, the same that was occupied the next day by [Major William J.] Pegram's battalion of artillery. Perrin, after passing Heth's division, reformed his brigade in a ravine and moved rapidly forward. Upon ascending a hill in front of this ravine, the brigade received a deadly fire of musketry and artillery, posted behind temporary breastworks, and from their artillery which was posted to the left of the road near Gettysburg. The brigade, however, advanced steadily, reserving its fire, and easily dislodging the enemy from his several positions—encountering but little real opposition except from an enfilade fire from the artillery on the left, until it came within two hundred yards of the enemy's last position: the ridge upon which is situated the Theological Seminary. The brigade, in crossing a line of fencing, was subjected to a most withering and deadly fire; but it pressed gallantly forward, without delaying to return the fire of the enemy. Upon reaching the edge of the grove which covers the crest of the ridge, Col. Perrin finding himself without support either on his right or his left, Gen. Lane having been delayed by the attack on his flank, and Gen. Scales having halted to return the fire of the enemy after Gen. S. had been disabled from command by a wound which he received, attacked the enemy, who were in his immediate front, with great vigor and decided success. He was now, however, subjected to a most damaging enfilade fire on both flanks, but quickly dividing his command, he ordered the two right regiments to change front to the right, and his two left regiments to change front to his left, and attacked most furiously on their flanks the enemy who were posted on the right behind a stone wall, and on the left behind a breastwork of rails. The enemy were soon put to flight, and rapidly retired through the town to Cemetery hill. The retirement of the enemy caused the artillery on the left to limber up and move rapidly to the rear. Much of this artillery would have been captured but the two regiments met a second force of the enemy posted behind a stone fence to the left of the College, and, though they were easily dislodged, they continued to offer sufficient resistance to enable the artillerists to make off with their guns. It is needless to say that Col. Perrin and his gallant brigade deserve all credit for the manner and spirit with which this attack was conducted. The efficiency and value of the services of Col. P. have been fully recognized by the Government in the promotion of that officer to the rank of a Brigadier General; he being now in command of [Cadmus M.] Wilcox's old brigade. The only reward which the officers and men of the brigade can ever receive must be found in the gratitude of their countrymen, and the consciousness on their part that they did their duty well and truly.

* * *

Anderson Intelligencer

November 6, 1895

CAROLINIANS AT GETTYSBURG
Honorable Record of Gen. Perrin's Brigade

To the Editor of the News and Courier: In view of the interest taken

Joseph Newton Brown, a lawyer from Anderson, S.C. commanded the 14th S.C. Infantry at Gettysburg where he was wounded. Lt. Col. Richard P. Todd of the 3rd S.C. Infantry had been his pre-war law partner. He was promoted to Colonel on Sept. 10, 1863. Brown was captured the next year at the Battle of North Anna River on May 23, 1864 and was exchanged after a stint at Fort Delaware.

(Men of Mark in South Carolina Volume 1)

by the State in having marked the positions of South Carolina troops in the battle of Gettysburg, July 1-3, 1863, I enclose a copy of Gen. Abner Perrin's report of the battle, then Col. Of the 14th South Carolina Volunteers, and promoted brigadier general on recommendation of Gen. Lee for his success in capturing the town.

It will be seen that Gen. McGowan was prevented from being in this campaign by reason of severe wounds received at Chancellorsville, May 3.

This copy was received at Cooper Union on a recent visit to New York, and will be of a special interest to the surviving soldiers engaged, and to the friends of those who have fought their last battle, and are now "resting in the shades of the trees."

Thanking you for your offer to publish the same in your Sunday's editions, I am,

Joseph N. Brown

Anderson, October 21, 1895

GENERAL PERRIN'S REPORT
General Abner Perrin's report of the battle of Gettysburg, July, 1863:

Headquarters McGowan's Brigade

August 13, 1863

Sir: This brigade, consisting of the following named regiments, to wit: the 1st, (Provisional Army), 12th, 13th, 14th and 1st (Rifles), the 1st under command of Major C. W. McCreary, the 12th under Col. John L. Miller, the 13th, Lieut. Col. B. T. Brockman, the 14th, Lieut. Col. Joseph N. Brown, and the Rifles, Capt. William M. Hadden, being a part of Major General Pender's light division of the Army of Northern Virginia, in the later campaign across the Potomac and was from June 5 until the present time under my immediate command.

About 8 o'clock on the morning of Jul 1 I received orders to get under arms, and the brigade, except Capt. Hadden, who was left with the Rifles to guard the wagon train, commenced the march on the turnpike leading to Gettysburg at the head of the division, and just in rear of the division of Major Gen. Heth.

The march was continued to within three miles of Gettysburg, when I was ordered to file down a road, from line of battle, leaving sufficient room between my left and the Gettysburg road for Gen. Scales's brigade, and to throw out skirmishers to cover my right flank.

Skirmishing between the advanced infantry of Gen. Heth's division and that of the enemy as well as heavy artillery firing had already commenced in our front. I was soon notified that Gen. Heth would advance, and that I would make a corresponding movement forward, preserving my alignment with Gen. Scales on my left. We moved through an open field about a mile, where we halted in rear, and in supporting distance of Gen. Heth's division, which had now become closely engaged with the enemy in our front. Here Brig. Gen. Lane's brigade took position on my right to protect our flank from the enemy's cavalry and some infantry reported by Capt. W. T. Haskell in that direction.

We remained in this position until about 8 o'clock, and were again ordered forward, and again advanced probably half a mile, when we came close upon Gen. Heth's division pressing the enemy within a short distance in front of us.

I remained in this position until after 4 o'clock when I was ordered by Gen. Pender to advance and to pass Gen. Heth's division, should I come up with it at a halt, and to engage the enemy as circumstances might warrant. I soon came up with and passed Gen. Pettigrew's brigade, the men of which seemed much exhausted by several hours of hard fighting.

Here I availed myself of a ravine, which sheltered us from the enemy's artillery, to reform my line, and instructed regimental commanders when the advance was resumed not to allow a gun to be fired at the enemy until they received orders to do so.

We now moved forward, preserving an alignment with Gen. Scales, and as soon as the brigade commenced ascending the hill in front we were met by a furious storm of musketry and shells from the enemy's batteries to left of the road near Gettysburg; but the instructions I had given them were scrupulously observed; not a gun was fired. The brigade received the enemy's fire without faltering; rushed up the hill at a charge, driving the enemy without difficulty to their last position at Gettysburg.

We continued the charge without opposition, excepting from artillery, which maintained a constant and most galling fire upon us until we got within two hundred yards of their last position, about the theological college. Some lines of infantry had shown themselves across the field, but disappeared as we got within range of them. While crossing the last fence, about two hundred yards from a grove near the college, the brigade received the most destructive fire of musketry I have ever been exposed to. We continued to press forward, however, without firing until we reached the edge of the grove. Here the 14th regiment was staggered for a moment by the severity and destructiveness of the enemy's musketry. It looked to us as though this regiment was entirely destroyed.

I here found myself without support either on the right or left. Gen. Scales's brigade had halted to return the enemy's fire, near the fence about two hundred yards distance from the enemy. Gen. Lane did not move on my right at all, and was not at this time in sight of me. This gave the enemy an enfilading fire on the 14th. This regiment under the lead of Lieut. Col. Brown and Major E[dward] Croft most gallantly stood its ground.

I now directed the 1st regiment, under Major McCreary, to oblique to the right to avoid a breastwork of rails behind where I discovered the enemy was posted, and then to change front to the left and attack in flank. This was done most effectively under the lead of this gallant officer. The enemy here were completely routed. This caused the whole of their artillery on our left, at least thirty pieces, to be limbered up and removed to the rear. Much of their artillery would have been captured, but the 1st and 14th in their pursuit again met a force of the enemy's infantry, strongly posted behind a stone wall near to the left of the college. It was the work of a few moments, however, to dislodge them.

These two regiments, now reduced in numbers to less than one-half the men they carried into battle, pursued the enemy to within the town of Gettysburg, capturing hundreds of prisoners, two field pieces and a number of caissons.

While the 1st and 14th regiments were assailing the enemy and driving him from his breastwork near the college, I ordered the 12th regiment, under Col. Miller, and the 13th, under Lieut. Col. Brockman, to oblique the right and charge the enemy, strongly posted be-hind a stone fence to the right of the college, from which position he had kept up a constant and withering fire of musketry upon the front and right flank of the brigade. These two regiments had necessarily to change direction to the right somewhat, so as to meet the enemy full in front. This movement was most brilliantly performed by these two regiments, and was most skillfully managed by the officers I have mentioned. They rushed up the crest of the hill and the stone fence, driving everything before them, the 12th gaining the stone fence and pouring an enfilading fire upon the enemy's right flank. The 13th, now coming up, made it an easy task to drive the enemy down the opposite slope and across the open field west of Gettysburg.

This was the last of the fight of this day. The enemy completely routed and driven from every point, Gettysburg was now completely in our possession.

After penetrating the enemy's lines near the college, the change of direction of the 1st and 14th to attack the enemy in flank to the left, and the oblique movement and change of direction of the 12th and 13th to attack the enemy in the flank to the right, necessarily separated the brigade into two parts. As soon as I knew the enemy had been routed on the right, I ordered the 12th and 13th to unite again with the 1st and 14th, who were now pursuing the fleeing force through the town. Finding the two last named regiments now reduced to less than half the number with which they entered the battle, and the men much exhausted, I ordered them back from the town to await the 12th and 13th, and sent a small detachment through the town to take such prisoners as the enemy had left in the retreat. It was after the recall of these two regiments that the brigade of Brig. Gen.

Ramseur filed through Gettysburg from the direction of my left.

The loss of the killed and of the brigade did not fall short of 500—100 killed, 477 wounded; total 577.

Better conduct was never exhibited on any field than was shown by both officers and men in this engagement. Each one of the color sergeants taken into the fight was killed in front of his regiment. Some regiments had a number of color-bearers shot down one after another. The officers generally were conspicuous in leading their men everywhere in the hottest of the fight.

After the 1st and 14th were withdrawn from Gettysburg Gen. Pender ordered me to get the brigade together and let the men rest. Now it was that the first piece of artillery which we had driven was opened upon my command and it was the same artillery which we had driven from our left near Gettysburg. I saw it move off from my left, and file into position over the hill.

The next day, having taken position in rear of some artillery as support, we were exposed to and suffered a small loss from the enemy's shells. About 6 o'clock in the afternoon I was ordered to push forward my skirmish line, and to drive the enemy's pickets from a road in front of Cemetery Hill. I communicated this order to Capt. William T. Haskell in command of a select battalion of sharpshooters acting as skirmishers, and sent Major McCreary forward with his regiment, about 100 strong, to deploy in rear of Capt. Haskell, and to act as a support. This battalion of sharpshooters, led by the gallant Haskell, made a most intrepid charge upon the Yankee skirmishers, driving them out of the road and close up under their batteries; but soon after gaining the road Capt. Haskell received a wound from the enemy's sharpshooters from which he died in a few moments on the field. This brave and worthy young officer fell while boldly walking along the front line of his command, encouraging his men, and selecting favorable positions for them to defend. He was educated and accomplished, possessing in a high degree every virtuous quality of the true gentleman and Christian. He was an officer of most excellent judgment and a soldier of the coolest and most chivalrous daring.

This position was held by my skirmishers until about 10 o'clock at night. I was ordered to place my brigade in line of battle, then on the right of Gen. Ramseur's brigade and on the left of Gen. Thomas. I remained quietly in this position during the remainder of the night, having thrown forward skirmishers again.

Early next morning (the 3rd) the heaviest skirmishing I have ever witnessed was here kept up during the greater part of the day. The enemy made desperate efforts to recapture the position, on account of our skirmishers being within easy range of their artilleries on the Cemetery Hill, but we repulsed them every assault, and held the position until ordered back to the main line at Gettysburg. At one time the enemy poured down a perfect torrent of light troops from the hill which swept my skirmishers back to the main line. I now ordered the 14th to deploy and charge the enemy, which was done in the most gallant style, not without losing some valuable officers and men. Lieut. Col. Brown and Major Croft, of the 14th, were severely wounded.

We remained at Gettysburg the remainder of the night and during the 4th, and at night moved back with the division toward Hagerstown; went into line of battle at Hagerstown on the 11th, when my skirmishers were again engaged, and where we lost a few men killed and wounded. Among the former was Capt. John W. Chambers of the 1st, a most gallant and worldly officer, who fell at the head of his company.

On the night of the 13th we commenced the march in the direction of Falling Waters. While resting about two miles from Falling Waters we were attacked by the enemy's cavalry. I was ordered to move my command to the right, and had to extend my right flank to the canal near the river to keep the enemy from getting around my flank. The enemy kept pressing upon me with his skirmishers. As soon as I got in position and was prepared to receive the enemy's attack I was ordered toward the bridge at Falling Waters. The brigade fell back in perfect order and gained the road, and formed in line across it, and then moved in retreat toward the bridge in rear of the whole corps.

I lost in this affair about thirty men captured, being the greater part of two companies that I had sent forward to strengthen the skirmish line. It resulted in their not going where they were ordered to go. I lost from men breaking down, sick, barefoot, straggling, etc., about sixty more from the time of leaving Gettysburg to reaching and re-crossing the Potomac at Falling Waters. My total missing in the whole campaign was about ninety men. My killed and wounded: six hundred and fifty-four.

I take occasion to mention the names of Major Croft, of the 14th, Major Isaac F. Hunt, of the 13th, and Major E. F. Bookter, of the 12th, as officers who proved themselves fully worthy of their positions throughout the engagements around Gettysburg. I remarked particularly the cool and gallant bearing of Major Bookter, and the force and judgment with which he managed the men under his control.

Capts. W. P. Shooter, T. P. Alston and A. P. Butler of the 1st regiment, South Carolina Volunteers, Capts. James Boatwright and E. Cowan, of the 14th South Carolina Volunteers, and Capt. T. Frank Clyburn, of the 12th, were distinguished for uncommonly good conduct in the action, as I can testify from personal observation.

A. PERRIN

Colonel Commanding Brigade

Extract from Major Joseph A. Engelhard's report, adjutant general of Gen.

W. D. Pender, who was mortally wounded:

"Too much credit cannot be awarded to Col. Perrin and the splendid brigade under his command for the manner and spirit with which this attack was conducted. To the former the Government has recognized his valuable services in a manner the most grateful to the true soldier by a prompt promotion. Of the latter, all who are acquainted with their gallantry on this occasion unite in their commendation to both.

Their commander, (Major Gen. W. D. Pender) who fell mortally wounded the succeeding day, was most enthusiastic in their praise.

"JOSEPH A. ENGLEHARD, A. A. G."

From Gen. A. P. Hill's report:

"The rout of the enemy was complete, Perrin's brigade taking position after position of the enemy, and driving him through the town of Gettysburg.

"A. P. HILL, Lieutenant General"

* * *

CONFEDERATE VETERAN MAGAZINE
FEBRUARY, 1900

[Excerpt of longer obituary]

CAPT. JAMES BOATWRIGHT.

We record the death of Capt. James Boatwright, Company B, Fourteenth South Carolina Regiment, McGowan's Brigade, of Ridge Spring, Edgefield County, S. C. He was born in Columbia, S. C, January 18, 1833, and died September 13, 1896. His grandfather Boatwright, for whom he was named, was one of the earliest settlers' of Columbia, and one, of its wealthiest and most prominent citizens. To his mother's people were granted in colonial times most of the Ridge lands of Edgefield County, S. C. His great grandfather Watson was an officer in the revolutionary war, and was buried with military honors.

An uncle of Capt. Boatwright's uniformed a company of Hampton's Legion, C. S. A. It was originally known as the Watson Guards.

Capt. Boatwright was well educated. He was a cadet at the South Carolina Military Academy at Charleston. At the age of twenty-seven years he left his wife and child on a lonely, isolated plantation and went as lieutenant.

. . .

At the battle of Gettysburg Capt. Boatwright's company went in with fifty-four men, and after the three days' battle reported eight men for duty. The company had sixteen men killed on the field of battle, and every officer wounded except Capt. Boatwright, who was in command of the regiment at the close of the battle. The gallant Gen. Abner Perrin, in his account of the battle of Gettysburg, says: "Capt. CAPT. JAMES BOATWRIGHT. James Boatwright was distinguished for uncommonly brave conduct in this battle, as I can testify from personal observation."

. . .

* * *

LAURENS ADVERTISER

APRIL 1, 1903

DR. JOHN R. SMITH HAS PASSED AWAY

[Co. C, 14th South Carolina Infantry]

Was One of the County's Best Men

DEATH WAS SUDDEN

Something of His Life and Career

He was an Able Physician and a Fine Type of Patriot and Citizen

------

A few weeks after the battle of Gettysburg an aged pair in this county received a letter from a Confederate captain that their boy, a member of his company, had probably given his life for his country, fighting in the forefront of battle, where he was always to be found doing his duty and that his body had not been recovered. Two years later, after the surrender at Appomattox, the father was at a neighboring railway station when a train arrived. Out of it, hobbling on crutches and on a "peg leg" was the son, who had been mourned as dead. The parents were Mr. and Mrs. Joel A. Smith of Mt. Gallagher and the son was John Robert Smith, who had entered the Confederate Army just as young manhood was reached four years before and had served as a private in Capt. [George] Wash[ington] Culbertson's company [Co. C 14th S.C.], McGowan's brigade. It was this John Robert Smith, lovingly known all over Laurens County as Dr. "Pegleg" Smith, who passed away at his home last Wednesday night, at the age of about 64. His health had been failing a long time but death was not expected—although Dr. Smith had himself said that the summons would come suddenly.

After the War young Smith went to the S.C. Medical College, Charleston, and graduated, having read medicine under Dr. Wait. Since then and until his death he practiced medicine at and around Mt. Gallagher. He was at one time president of the county medical association, he served in the House of Representatives, was master of Brewerton Masonic Lodge and grand pursuivant and grand junior and senior deacon in the Masonic grand lodge of South Carolina.

He is survived by his wife and four daughters and three sons. The daughters are Mrs. Joel Daniel of Summerville, Mrs. Robert Ellis of Due West and Mrs. G. A. Fuller of Alma and one unmarried. Wilmot Smith of Alma is the oldest son and there are two young lads. Two of his brothers, G. P. Smith and Fleming Smith live in this city.

Laurens and South Carolina lose in Dr. Smith a noble gentleman and citizen. He was a brave soldier. The leg lost long ago in the first day's fighting at bloody Gettysburg tells that story. His comrade, B[urket] L. Henderson [Co. C, 14th S.C.], carried him from the field but the next day he was captured. The leg had already been amputated but in the federal prison a second amputation was necessary. He was lying in the federal prison the years that his family and comrades believed him dead.

He was an excellent physician. Not only was he a devoted, earnest, sacrificing doctor, who ministered to poor and rich, but he was a man of brains and information—one of the best physicians that this county has had. The people of his neighborhood will sorely feel the loss of his professional services.

In 1876 Dr. Smith and his red-shirts from the Saluda Hills were heard from time and time again. They were always on hand when needed. He was one of the men to whom the county and state owed a big debt.

He was always active in politics. He was impulsive, outspoken and plain spoken. His position was always known. He was an intense Democrat, a party man first, last and all the time. He was frequently in the minority and he was always in the minority when he believed the minority right. In county conventions he was an influential leader, talking hard sense, boldly like the man that he was. His good humor was unfailing. He was a man one loved to meet and shake hands with and we shall all miss him.

From the birth of THE ADVERTISER he was its friend. In the last campaign the editor had a kind letter from him in which he took issue with an editorial position but it was such a letter from such a friend as not every newspaper has.

His brother masons and kindred and neighbors buried him at King's Chapel, where his father rests, Friday. He was a member of the Methodist church, unpretentious in that as in other things and counted it as nothing to advertise blatantly that he was a servant of God.

Truly, Laurens will miss brave, loyal and true "Peg-leg John Smith." In other conditions and a larger field, his fine intellect might have made him more conspicuous in affairs but he has lived the life of a patriot and left to his people a name and memory that they have a right to value high.

* * *

LAURENS ADVERTISER

APRIL 8, 1903

REMINISCENCES OF THE WAR

John B. Bagwell [14th South Carolina, Co. C] Recalls the Days of Gettysburg—Life in Federal Prison
------

MR. EDITOR, SIR: I don't feel as spry as I did forty years ago, when I followed the lead of Mars Bob Lee over the hills of Virginia and Maryland.

Still I am very thankful that I can eat my three meals a day; remembering the time when I did not have one meal in a day—and that was a mighty slim one. We went through much hardships, still some "sweets" were mixed with them.

On the first of July 1864 [Editor's note: should be 1863], I lay in a wheat field, five miles from Gettysburg, Pa., when the Minnie balls cut the grain around my head. When my Company, Co. C, 14th S. C. Infantry, double quicked into action, I could not follow with my lame ankle. I was disabled in a foraging trip before the fight. Lieutenant John Poole, [Wade] Hamp[ton] Phillips and Jack [John L.] Bramlett and Capt. [George W.] Culbertson were wounded the first evening, July 1st. For two nights, I sat up all night with Dr. John R. Smith to keep him from bleeding to death. Hamp Phillips was shot through the chest. I saw a silk handkerchief pulled through his body. On the 16th of July it was rumored that the Confederate Cavalry were on the way to capture our wounded. All our officers were then sent to Chester, Pa., where Lieutenant Poole died on the 22nd of July.

Lieutenant [Nathaniel] Austin also died there. Our wounded were carried into the town of Gettysburg on the 18th where we stayed two weeks, burying our dead. Then to Baltimore Jail, for 21 days. Then to Point Lookout prison where we stayed eighteen months. Myself, Dr. Billy Ball [William H. Ball, 3rd South Carolina, Co. G], Sam[uel D.] Puckett [3rd Battalion South Carolina Infantry, Co. A] and Broadford[53] bunked together for this long time in prison. To show what we went through we were put into companies of 100 men—and some of these died in our company. We landed home on the 8th of March 1865 on a 30 days' furlough which did not give us time to return to the field again before the surrender.

JOHN B. BAGWELL

* * *

NEWBERRY HERALD
JULY 17, 1903

Forty-Two Years Ago

Editor Herald and News; On the first day of July, 1903, I was hoeing my potato patch on the road which I took nearly forty-two years ago when I left home, which was at Col. J. C. S. Brown's, to go to war. It was in August that I went. I joined that grand company—the first that left Newberry—Company B., "Rhett Guards," First South Carolina Regiment, Maxey Gregg commanding the regiment. The first of July forty years ago the company and I were on the battlefield of Gettysburg. We opened the ball at Gettysburg under A. P. Hill commanding the corps, W. D. Pender the division and Col. Albert Perrin of the 14th South Carolina Regiment the brigade—McGowan's Brigade. McGowan had been wounded at Chancellorsville just two months before. The old brigade showed herself that day. She was the first brigade to enter the field at Gettysburg. The brigade commander was complimented that evening by General Pender for the gallant work the brigade had done that day. Pettigrew's brigade went into the battle just ahead of our brigade. We passed by that brigade just before we got to Gettysburg. Pettigrew's men gave three cheers for South Carolina as we passed them.

---

53. Walter A. Bradford, 3rd South Carolina Infantry, Co. A.

There were three Leitzsey brothers in the brigade. Two of them were commissioned officers in the Thirteenth South Carolina Regiment. I was a private in the first Regiment. We suffered a great deal that day. One was killed and the other two were wounded. I was taken prisoner after General Lee fell back into Virginia.

* * *

EDGEFIELD ADVERTISER
AUGUST 23, 1911

CAPT. W. H. BRUNSON
Gallant Confederate Veteran Answers Last Roll Call; Postmaster for Twenty-five Years

Captain William Henry Brunson is dead, having entered peacefully into eternal rest Sunday morning. His life as citizen and soldier earned for him

William H. Brunson was a 2nd Lieutenant in Co. D of the 14th S.C. Infantry at Gettysburg. He was wounded in the thigh, but returned to Virginia with the retreating army. Many of the other wounded were left behind to become prisoners of the enemy. Brunson was part of a hand picked battalion of sharp shooters from the brigade. This battalion was credited with the capture of 830 prisoners during the war.

(Confederate Veteran Magazine)

that rest which is prepared for all who are faithful during their earthly probation.

...

"When the Confederates retreated from Fredericksburg, Brunson in command of his company, covered the rear of Anderson's division. At the battle of Gains Mills he was slightly wounded early in the day but while in a charge about sun down he was shot in the mouth, the ball passing out the back of his neck. Before this wound had healed he had one hand shattered while his regiment, 14th S. C., was charging a redoubt in the battle of

Chancellorsville. In the first day's fight at Gettysburg he was shot through both legs. He fell on a Federal captain, who was shot through one leg. After getting himself off the Federal officer he said, "Captain, you are bleeding profusely, I have some whiskey in my canteen that I thought I might need if badly wounded. Drink it," handing him the canteen; the officer taking the canteen and seeing it was light said, "there is no more than a drink here. Have you had any?" When Brunson said he had not he for a time refused to take it, until he was convinced that he would soon faint if he did not. Two heroes had met. They both recovered. After Brunson was again well enough for duty, he was assigned to the command of the 2nd Company of the S. C. Battalion of Sharpshooters commanded by Maj. W. S. Dunlop, McGowan's Brigade. Beginning with the battle of the Wilderness, on the 14th day of May, 1861, he was constantly under fire until 22nd of June. While in command of his battalion of three companies, and opposing the advance of the whole of Hancock's corps on Petersburg, he was shot through the foot.

Thomas W. Carwile was Sergeant Major of Co. D, 14th S.C. Infantry at Gettysburg. He was wounded, but was able to retreat with the army. Carwile was promoted to captain the next year and became the commanding general of the United Confederate Veterans for South Carolina post-war.

(Confederate Veteran Magazine)

General Wade Hampton
(Library of Congress)

~ *Section 3* ~

Cavalry

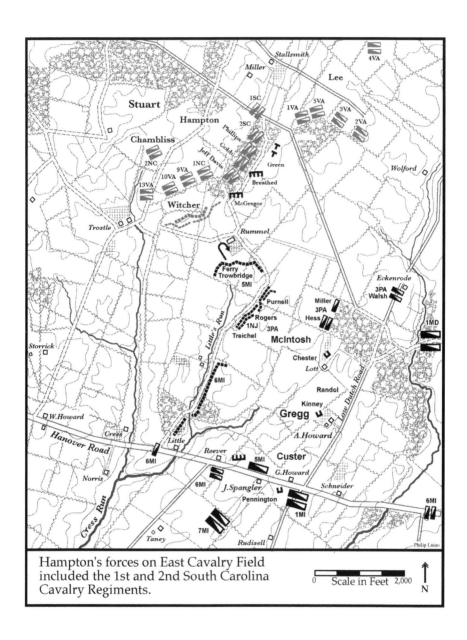

Hampton's forces on East Cavalry Field
included the 1st and 2nd South Carolina
Cavalry Regiments.

Introduction:
South Carolina Cavalry

The cavalry of South Carolina contained two regiments fighting at Gettysburg, the First South Carolina Cavalry and the Second South Carolina Cavalry. The First South Carolina Cavalry was under the command Colonel John Logan Black, but was separated from him at its beginning due to an earlier wound he received at the Battle of Upperville. Black rose from his sick bed as soon as he was able and traveled to meet his command along the way. He, however, was only able to connect with a small element that had been separated from Hampton's Brigade in the dark while crossing the mountains near Williamsport and Hagerstown, Maryland. These were one company of the First South Carolina Cavalry, one company of the Second South Carolina Cavalry and Company C of the First North Carolina Cavalry under Lt. Robert H. Maxwell. Hart's Artillery Battery of South Carolina gunners was also with the separated cavalry of which Black took charge.[54]

Hart's Battery had been greatly crippled during the same battle at Upperville in which Black was wounded. "Every piece but one was disabled, two were dismounted, and borne off on caissons." A prized Blakely had been struck in the limber chest by a direct hit from a Union artillery shell and was dismounted. According to U. R. Brooks of

---

54. Black, John Logan. Crumbling Defenses Or, Memoirs and Reminiscences of John Logan Black, Colonel C.S.A. Macon, GA: n.p., 1960. 32. Print.

Hampton's Brigade, "Hart's Battery did not accompany the movement of the cavalry, owing to its disabled condition."[55]

As they entered Pennsylvania along the route to Gettysburg, Col. Black, with the eighty to one hundred men he had assembled, provided a cavalry escort for an ordinance wagon train he came upon that had fallen behind the army. Being isolated as it was, the commander feared attack due to rumors of Yankee cavalry in the area. They parted company once Black's improvised cavalry unit got them safely to Chambersburg where they linked up with Barksdale's Mississippi Brigade. There he reported to Gen. Barksdale who sent him to protect the rear from the rumored enemy cavalry. This report turned out to be unfounded. Black then proceeded on to Gen. Robert E. Lee's headquarters for further orders. There Col. B. G. Baldwin, Lee's Chief Ordnance Officer conveyed orders from Gen. Lee to proceed and attempt to locate Maj. Gen. J. E. B. Stuart, whose cavalry was out of contact with the main army. Black was well known to Lee due to his having been a cadet at West Point in 1850 during Lee's tenure as the Academy's superintendent.[56]

Black was further ordered to gather up any loose bodies of cavalry like he had done the night before and bring them into his ad hoc regiment. These scattered troopers brought his unit to between two hundred and three hundred horsemen. Black recorded that "a day or so afterwards I was ordered to report in person" to Gen. Lee. Lee gave him further orders, then took a few moments to reminisce about their days at West Point before dismissing Black to return to his men.[57]

The next day Black was instructed to position his men at the rear of the infantry of the Army of Northern Virginia where they provided the rear guard for the march to the Gettysburg battlefield. They diverged and rode to the town of Fairfield where the Virginia cavalrymen under Brig.

55. Wittenberg, Eric J. Gettysburg's Forgotten Cavalry Actions: Farnsworth's Charge, South Cavalry Field, and the Battle of Fairfield, July 3, 1863. New York: Savas Beatie, 2011. 30. Print; Brooks, U. R. Butler and His Cavalry in the War of Secession, 1861-1865. Columbia, SC: State, 1909. 177. Print; Brooks, U. R., and D. B. Rea. Stories of the Confederacy. Columbia, SC: State, 1912. 260. Print; Nunnelee, Lewis Tune, Louis Sherfesee, James Franklin Hart, and Robert J. Trout. "James P. Hart to John B Bachelder, March 13, 1886, GNMP." Memoirs of the Stuart Horse Artillery Battalion: Moorman's and Hart's Batteries. Knoxville: U of Tennessee, 2008. 213. Print.
56. Black, 32-33.
57. Black, 33-34.

Gen. William E. "Grumble" Jones fought a major engagement two days later on July 3, 1863.[58]

At 4:00 P.M., Black was ordered to move his men to the rear of Lt. Gen. James Longstreet's First Corps. Black noted that he was within sight of the camp of Kershaw's Brigade of fellow South Carolinians. He wrote that he had his men ready to go, including Hart's Battery, but then orders to proceed did not materialize until between 8:00 and 9:00 P.M. They marched at Kershaw's rear throughout the night "at a snail's pace."[59]

At daylight Black was ordered to report to Gen. Lee's Headquarters near Gettysburg, where he witnessed from a distance a conversation Lee had with Lt. Gen. A. P. Hill and Longstreet. Once the war council broke up, Lee introduced Black to his First Corps commander and officially turned his command over to Longstreet. Black rode with Longstreet amongst the various brigades back to his troopers. They were positioned near Longstreet's Headquarters to protect a bridge and guard a road at the foot of a hill near Black Horse Tavern. Black remained there on July 2, witnessing, but not participating in, the day's actions.[60]

At 4:00 P.M. on that day, July 2, 1863, Black's usual commander, Brig. Gen. Wade Hampton of Columbia, South Carolina, engaged the enemy with his cavalry brigade in Hunterstown, Pennsylvania. The Second South Carolina Cavalry along with the First North Carolina, Cobb's Legion and Phillips Legion (both of Georgia) cavalry regiments clashed with Michigan cavalry under Brig. Gen. George Armstrong Custer.[61]

The Second S.C. Cavalry had entered the month of June with 320 men, but by the time they arrived at Hunterstown, their force of effective troopers was down to 137. At the Battle of Brandy Station on June 9, Col. Matthew C. Butler lost a leg and Gen. Hampton's younger brother Lt. Col. Frank Hampton was mortally wounded and died that night. This left Maj. Thomas Jefferson Lipscomb in command of the regiment.[62]

58. Black, 34; Shevchuk, Paul M. "The Cavalry Fight at Fairfield, Pennsylvania, July 3, 1863." Gettysburg Magazine 1 (1989): 105. Print.
59. Black, 36.
60. Black, 37-39.
61. Harman, Troy. "Hunterstown 1863, Battle History." Hunterstown 1863. Hunterstown1863, 2008. Web. 14 Nov. 2015.
62. Brooks, Butler and His Cavalry, 171.

Custer led Company A of the Sixth Michigan Cavalry in a headlong charge down the Hunterstown Road to strike a frontal assault against Hampton's men, then quickly withdraw to lure them into a trap. Hampton's Brigade, with the Georgians of Cobb's Legion in front, dogged the Michigan troopers down the Hunterstown Road for a quarter-mile, bouncing between the rail fences separating it from the surrounding farms. At the end of this chase awaited the rest of the Sixth Michigan Cavalry along with the Seventh Michigan Cavalry. The crossfire that Custer had set up between the two Michigan regiments caught the Confederates there before spreading out in fierce hand-to-hand combat across the farms of J. G. Gilbert and J. Felty. Custer's artillery overlooked the field on Felty-Tate Ridge.[63]

Total losses between the two sides amounted to between eighty and one hundred men. Hampton's surviving horsemen withdrew back up the Hunterstown Road to their previous position. The two enemy lines remained a mile apart, trading artillery shots until 11:00 P.M. that evening when Gen. Judson Kilpatrick ordered Custer to withdraw his men. Like much of the Battle of Gettysburg, this was an accidental clash in which neither side intended to engage. By doing so, this deprived both sides of planned and much needed cavalry support. Ewell's Corps lacked the support from Hampton it so desperately needed for its actions against Culp's Hill and East Cemetery Hill, and likewise Daniel Sickles' Union Third Corps was vulnerable on the left flank due to the absence of Kilpatrick's cavalry. Both sides were forced to expend much needed infantry resources for intelligence operations watching the enemy, with less accurate results.[64]

On the morning of July 3, Hampton was ordered to move through Hunterstown and find the right flank of the Union army. He arrived on the left of the Virginia Cavalry Brigade under the command of Col. John R. Chambliss at 1:00 P.M. Brig. Gen. Fitzhugh Lee soon joined on Hampton's left. Hampton and Fitz Lee were ordered to report to their commander, Maj. Gen. J.E.B. Stuart. Hampton thought it unwise for the two senior brigade commanders to be absent from the field at the same

63. Harman.
64. Harman.

time and told Lee that he would report first and upon his return that Lee should go to Stuart.[65]

Hampton was unable to find Stuart and upon returning, found that a charge had been ordered. Not knowing the source or reason, Hampton countermanded this order. Chambliss soon sent word to Hampton requesting support, as he was making a charge and needed aid from the nearest brigade. Hampton sent two regiments (First North Carolina and the Jeff Davis Legion of Mississippi) to reinforce Chambliss. This action by the North Carolina and Mississippi troopers was highly successful, but in their fervor, they drove beyond a prudent point of safety and ran into the enemy's reserves. Hampton himself rode forward to take charge and engaged in the desperate hand-to-hand combat. Misinterpreting this move, Hampton's assistant adjutant general, Capt. T. G. Barker, ordered the full brigade to charge. Hampton was severely wounded in hand-to-hand combat with a Yankee trooper during this operation and was forced to leave the field, turning over command to Col. Laurence S. Baker of the First N.C. Cavalry.[66]

During this charge, Maj. Lipscomb, commanding the Second S.C. Cavalry, experienced a near miss. A federal squadron charged directly towards Lipscomb, one Yankee private closing in yelled, "Oh damn you, I've got you now!" Lipscomb carefully leveled his revolver and "sent a bullet crashing through his brain."[67]

While the fighting took place on East Cavalry Field, Colonel Black and his makeshift regiment had been positioned beside Hood's Texans. They were assisting the Georgia brigade of Brig. Gen. George "Tige" Anderson in a heavy engagement with Brig. Gen. Elon J. Farnsworth's Yankee cavalrymen of Kilpatrick's division. Black, along with artillery support – including the South Carolina battery of Capt. James Hart – provided much needed support to Anderson's Brigade. Black said that they took up a

65. Reports of Brig. Gen. Wade Hampton, C. S. Army, commanding brigade, with congratulatory orders JUNE 3-AUGUST 1, 1863.--The Gettysburg Campaign O.R.-- SERIES I--VOLUME XXVII/2 [S# 44].
66. O.R., Hampton.
67. Brooks Butler' and His Cavalry, 546.

position in "a small field of the finest Timothy I ever saw. It was very thick
& 3 feet high."[68]

Black had spotted the approaching federal cavalry of Gen. Wesley
Merritt, then coming up from Maryland, and reported this around 11:00
AM that morning. Black then deployed his approximately 100 troopers and
other assorted "ragtag and bobtail" of the hospital and wagon trains that
he could assemble into a line of battle, totaling about 300 men. Black did
not have much faith in this group, referring to them as more of a
"nuisance" than a "benefit," so he took his most reliable men and
established a skirmish line. Anderson's infantry, Black's skirmishers and the
other odd assortment of soldiers were covered by Hart's, Reilly's (Rowan
Artillery of North Carolina) and Bachman's (Palmetto Light Artillery of
South Carolina) Batteries.[69]

Capt. William K. Bachmann led a veteran command of German
immigrants from Charleston. This well-known battery, known as the
German Artillery, had fought in every major engagement in which the
Army of Northern Virginia had participated. Bachmann and his men
"enjoyed a fine reputation" which was "due to the men who composed it to
say that, like their comrades in the Confederate army, they bore their
hardships and did their duty without flinching."[70]

Rather than participating in the artillery barrage supporting Pickett's
Charge, Bachmann's and Reilly's guns were instead deployed overlooking
the Michael Bushman farm near the right end of the Confederate line on
Warfield Ridge. This was among the infantry around the Alexander
Currens farm at the intersection of the Ridge Road and the Emmitsburg
Road.[71]

Heavy skirmishing took place between the Sixth Pennsylvania Lancers
and Black's ragged command. The Pennsylvanians advanced on the stone
Alexander Currens farmhouse, which was filled with Confederate
sharpshooters. The well-aimed shots had been taking a toll on the
advancing Yankees, but the Pennsylvania cavalrymen drove them from the

68. Wittenberg, Eric J. Gettysburg's Forgotten Cavalry Actions: Farnsworth's Charge, South
Cavalry Field, and the Battle of Fairfield, July 3, 1863. New York: Savas Beatie, 2011. 30.
Print; Pfanz, Harry W. Gettysburg, the Second Day. Chapel Hill: U of North Carolina, 1987.
254. Print; Black, 36-37.
69. Wittenberg, 94; Pfanz, 254; Black, 36-37.
70. Wittenberg, 30-31.
71. Wittenberg, 31; Brooks, Stories of the Confederacy, 282.

farmhouse. The Federal troopers occupied the house for a time, but steady fire from Law's Infantry and Bachmann's and Reilly's batteries soon drove them from the house and forced them to take shelter behind a low stone wall which ran perpendicular to the Emmitsburg Road. The Yankees now momentarily halted, so Col. Black rode to Longstreet's headquarters to request reinforcements to shore up the Confederate right flank against the growing threat. The Sixth Pennsylvania's position was well in advance of the main body of Merritt's brigade, and two squadrons of the First U.S. Cavalry slipped into line beside the Pennsylvanians. When a squadron of the Second U.S. Cavalry and a squadron of the Fifth U.S. Cavalry joined them there, the Union threat to Law's position grew.[72]

In the meantime, Hart unlimbered his battery in the front of this lengthening line. The Yankees charged and briefly captured Hart's guns before the Confederates counter-charged and retook them. The First U.S. Cavalry formed a heavy skirmish line and charged through the dismounted Pennsylvanians, struck the Confederate line, and drove it back toward its artillery support. Black feared they would soon break and went in search of reinforcements. He found two regiments marching toward their position in what he considered a leisurely fashion. He spotted an officer wearing the stars of a colonel leading the men. Black besieged the man, "Damn it all, Colonel, if you don't move faster the enemy will lap before you are in position." The officer responded in a jolly fashion, "Oh, no, I think not." When another officer referred to this man as "General" Black discovered that he was cursing at Brig. General Evander Law himself, and quickly apologized. Law was unfazed and laughed it off, prompting Black to speculate that Law had simply not changed his uniform adornments after his promotion. Law ordered the two regiments into line of battle. They opened fire while Law detached the Eleventh and Fifty-Ninth Georgia regiments and sent them around the right to take advantage of the situation.[73]

Law had high praise for Capt. James Hart and his men, saying, "Hart's guns were well handled and did good service as long as the enemy

72. Wittenberg, 95.
73. Wittenberg, 96-97; Black, 42.

remained in reach of them."[74]   Eventually, the First U.S. Cavalry pulled back with Black and his cavalrymen in pursuit. Black said, "We drove them clean away & Law took his Regiments and went back saying he hoped I could hold the ground."[75]

On July 2, Black petitioned to be returned to his command of the First S.C. Cavalry now that his regiment was on the field. At 2:00 PM on July 3, his request was granted, and he was ordered to report to Hampton's Brigade headquarters with his improvised command. The passage of between 700 and 800 Union prisoners on the road hindered his progress. He asked Gen. William Pendleton, Lee's chief of artillery, about this and discovered that a controlled retreat had begun due to a shortage of ammunition. Black arrived at Stuart's headquarters and learned of Hampton's wounding. He and Scriven had missed the fighting on the East Cavalry Field of Gettysburg.[76]

South Carolina Cavalry was active in scouting and guarding the retreat of Lee's army. Black recalled sitting on his horse by a fence in the rain until 2:00 am or 3:00 am on the night of July 3. Once moving, Black often rode ahead to help scout the retreat route. He was suffering a fever from his wound at Upperville and took advantage of the opportunity to lie down until the head of the retreating column arrived. During one of these scouts, while lying along the outskirts of Greencastle, Pennsylvania, a belligerent local approached him and said that he hoped they never made it home. Black assured him that it would be Greencastle's loss, as their army would likely burn the town if forced to in order to create a diversion to cover their retreat. The angry man inquired as to his possible relation to a local judge named Jeremiah Black. Judge Black was indeed a cousin of Col. Black's, prompting the colonel to say, "he used to be, but now claimed no Yankee kin."[77]

Gen. Wade Hampton traveled back to Virginia in the same ambulance carrying Maj. Gen. John Bell Hood. The ride covered more than 200 miles

74. Johnson, Robert Underwood, and Clarence Clough Buel. "The Struggle for Round Top." Battles and Leaders of the Civil War. Being for the Most Part Contributions by Union and Confederate Officers. New Introd. by Roy F. Nichols. Vol. 3. New York: T. Yoseloff, 1956. 327. Print.
75. Black, 42.
76. Black, 44-45.
77. Black, 46.

on rutted roads before arriving at the Confederate General Hospital in Charlottesville, Virginia. Hampton was surprised to be alive.[78]

Col. Black with the First S.C. Cavalry and Maj. Lipscomb with the Second S.C. Cavalry continued fighting skirmishes throughout Maryland during the Army of Northern Virginia's retreat. Along the way, Black was diagnosed as having contracted typhoid fever and was taken to the hospital at Winchester, Virginia. He was sent from there to a private home to recover. Black was fortunate. He soon had company in the form of one of his privates from Company A. Although he chose to serve throughout the war as a horse trooper, Andrew Paul was also a physician from Abbeville, S.C. At the time, Dr. Paul was himself a patient at the hospital. Seeing the plight of his colonel, Dr. Paul went to the medical director and insisted that he be sent to the house as Black's personal physician. Thanks to Paul's attendance, Black soon recovered.[79]

78. Tagg, Larry. *The Generals of Gettysburg: The Leaders of America's Greatest Battle.* Campbell, CA: Savas Pub., 1998. 361. Print; Cisco, Walter Brian. *Wade Hampton: Confederate Warrior, Conservative Statesman.* Washington, D.C.: Brassey's, 2004. 121-22. Print.

79. Black, 48-49.

Chapter 1

1st South Carolina Cavalry

SUMTER WATCHMAN AND SOUTHRON
FEBRUARY 2, 1910

SOLDIER-POETS ACCOUNT OF CHARGE AT GETTYSBURG

Graphic Description by Peter J. Malone [1st South Carolina Cavalry, Co. E] of the Terrific conflict, in Which He Received the Wound That Finally Ended His Life

------

Among those who offered their lives for the south during the War between the States, there was no figure more heroic than Peter J. Malone, the soldier-poet. A mere lad of 19 years, he bore himself with dauntless spirit in the famous last charge at the battle of Gettysburg and received on that bloody field the wound which after ten years of suffering resulted in his untimely death. A native of Charleston and at one time a worker on the staff of the Charleston Courier, Peter Malone crowded into the brief period of his mortal life, work of so notable a quality as to insure him a place among South Carolina's men of genius and achievement. He was a poet of ability from whose pen flowed some really beautiful things; and,

Peter J. Malone
(Poems of Peter J. Malone)

although he was not allowed time to fulfill the promise of his early years, the volume containing his poems published only recently and reviewed in the Sunday News of January 9, is an important contribution to the literature of the South.

Peter J. Malone died young, before his mental development was nearly completed. Cut off at the age of 29, his artistry was not allowed time to ripen. It has been said of his work "one of the chief points in which it impresses me is its indication—so rare anywhere— of far greater strength behind." Had he lived longer, he might have risen to heights far beyond those to which he actually attained. His early death was directly due to the wound that he received at Gettysburg; and the following description from his pen of that great charge is a piece of writing "strong and simple in its truth, and yet exhibiting, even thus in prose, the fervor and grace of expression of the born poet."

The account of the charge as will be seen, is in the form of a letter to Col. John Logan Black [1st South Carolina Cavalry]. The letter follows:

Col. John Logan Black, Ridgeway, S.C. Dear Colonel: I have taken the earliest opportunity to attend to your request, and trust that the sketch herewith given, though hastily drawn from material preserved only in memory, may fully comprehend the object you contemplate. You may find that I am occasionally led into the recital of facts irrelevant to the matter of inquiry, but they are concomitant facts and serve to illustrate the statement I desire to make more fully than could be accomplished did I avoid all digression. It is the story of a single charge that I propose to write, but no leaf in the history of any revolution bears record of a prouder heroism, a more invincible courage, than was that day exhibited along our depleted ranks. I find it impossible to speak with certainty of our arrival on the field of Gettysburg, or of our position at the fatal hour of encounter. The more prominent incidents of the terrible scene are still pictured on my memory; but it is rather as evidences of a strange, wild dream, in which much has faded from the waking memory, than as any past event of real life, that I now contemplate them.

About 3 o'clock on the afternoon of July 3, 1863, our brigade moved to its position on the left of the army. There was one incessant roar of artillery, and the ground was shaken, while to the northwest clouds of smoke arose above the unbroken thunder of six hundred guns. For a time the tremendous reverberations rendered it difficult for one at a distance to determine the direction of the battle; but knowing the position, it was easy to divine that, as the din became less distinct, we were steadily forcing the enemy from every point. At the time our brigade was thrown from the serried form of the phalanx across the fields which was so soon to become our battle ground, it seemed the resistance of the enemy grew more stubborn; the smoke became denser and darker, and curling upward filled the immense sky. We were in ignorance of the juxtaposition of the enemy's cavalry, but any one without risking his dexterity, might have ventured to predict that the quietude of this part of the field was soon to be broken by the crash of sabres, the shout of triumph, and the agonizing cry of death. The quick eye of our leader, his rapid movements from regiment to regiment, his hurried, yet confident tone of command, and above all, his frequent anxious glance towards a certain dense oak forest one mile away, were indications sufficient of this, even before the skirmishers had engaged one another on the intermediate ground.

Soon a battery opened on us from the enemy's line. They managed their guns with admirable precision, but although branches of trees were rifled from their trunks, and shells exploded in our ranks, little damage was done. At this time our regiment was calmly awaiting orders for the engagement. The battle had opened. I was of the color-guard, on the right of J. H. Koger,[80] the bearer of the standard, whose heroism in keeping it proudly in the face of the enemy, and afterwards in bearing it in triumph from the field, where he had narrowly escaped death and capture, became so well known. On my right was Sergt. T. P. Brandenburg [1st South Carolina Cavalry, Co. E], whom you will remember as a peerless soldier and a truly imperial spirit.

80. H. J. Koger, 1st South Carolina Cavalry, Co. E

We were not long left quiet—Gen. Fitz Lee encountered the enemy on our right, and being overwhelmed by numbers, it became necessary for us to attack them at our front to divert their attention from his brigade. Gen. Hampton proposed to lead our regiment. We started out in fine style, and one continued shout arose from the charging column. The enemy now appeared in a black, compact line, and at a casual view seemed rather a continuation of the forest. The intervening ground over which we were passing was so crossed and seamed with fences and ditches as to greatly impede our progress; and the sharpshooters, concealed whenever concealment was possible, found in the moving mass of beings an excellent mark for their rifles. It was, no doubt, by one of those chance balls that I was wounded.

We had not advanced beyond two hundred yards from the cluster of trees where we had taken shelter, when I was struck, the ball entering my right side. Believing it to be no more than the fragment of a shell which had struck without breaking the surface, I kept on with the regiment. We were soon at the sabre point, and fighting desperately. The color-guard, from some mysterious circumstance, became precipitated from its position to the head of the column, and met the enemy at a small opening in a fence, which soon became so blockaded by the regiment as to prevent those in the rear coming to the assistance of the few who had first entered the enclosure or any of us who might be wounded from securing our escape to the hospital. Gen. Hampton, I was informed, here engaged a number of the enemy, and cut his way through them with Achillean valor, bearing upon his noble form the marks of cruel wounds. At this critical moment my right side and arm became paralyzed, the sabre fell from my hand, and large drops of cold sweat collected upon my face.

The surgeon, seeing my unfortunate condition, rode up and assisted me over the fence. Having my blankets rolled up and fastened to the front of my saddle, I fell upon them, being no longer able to sit erect; while my horse, infuriated by the crash of cannon, the explosion of shells, and the sight of the blood, rushed desperately to the rear. Before I reached the temporary hospital established on the field, I overtook Pvt. W[illiam] D. Shirer, of company E, whose right arm had been broken. He was in the very acme of pain. This unfortunate young man died from the effects of the wound about three weeks afterward, at Gettysburg. I have no recollection of my arrival at the hospital. Sinking into a state of insensibility, I was carried thither by those appointed for that purpose. When aroused to consciousness, Corporal H[enry] L. Culler, of Company E, Private Charles Franklin of Company B, and hundreds of other friends and foe, were around, receiving medical attention.****Upon inquiry of a surgeon as to the probability of my recovery, I was candidly, but kindly informed that the chances were against me. The medical opinion was opposed to the performance of an operation, as it would render the "chances" of recovery still more precarious. I was utterly prostrate, and sank from sheer exhaustion if any effort were made to raise me up.

The next day we were informed that our army was retreating, and that, as we could not be moved, our capture was certain. Surgeon _____ remained with us. When taken we were sent to Gettysburg hospital, where our treatment, though kind, was rendered repugnant by the flippancy of some of the United States surgeons. One, for instance, passed where Corporal Culler and myself were lying and remarked that we "must die in any event." Culler was shot through the body, and though expecting this announcement, he groaned heavily when he heard it. In three days he was a corpse. We were then removed to New York, where we received the most considerate attention. My health improved slowly, and as I was young at the time, I have so far outgrown the misfortune as to feel no (great?) inconvenience from it. My regret is that thousands were less fortunate.

In conclusion, Colonel, I have the honor to be,

Yours respectfully,

P. J. MALONE

Orangeburg, S. C., Jan. 6, 1867

* * *

Excerpt from "Crumbling Defenses or Memoirs and Reminiscenses of John Logan Black, Colonel C. S. A."

[Note: This excerpt begins while Col. Black convalesced following the Battle of Upperville where he received a concussion. As a result of this wound, Black was left behind by Lee's Pennsylvania bound army. He would soon endeavor to catch up with his command.]

Col. John Logan Black was the commander of the First South Carolina Cavalry. He had been a cadet at West Point when Robert E. Lee was the Superintendant.

(Confederate Veteran Magazine)

After leaving here the sun got too hot for me and I stopped on the wayside at an artillery camp. The Captain commanding the battery very kindly laid me down under his tent fly (all the tent his co. had) & I was asleep in a moment. How long I slept I know not. I was awakened by the moving of his guns. The battery had been ordered to the front & he was about to march off, leaving me his tent fly with [John L.] Carey [Black's orderly, Co. C, 1st S.C. Cav.] & [Harvey] Hood[81] to watch me. This I would not permit & made him take it, which he did reluctantly. I do not know his name if he gave it to me but he was both a soldier and a gentleman, one with a soul.

From here I passed on & soon got to Gen'l. John B. Hood's Hdquar. Who had heard I was killed & was arranging to have me buried. Hood seemed surprised as I rode up.

I found my quartermaster's camp was near Hood's & so went there. Dr. Jno. T. Darby,[82] Hood's Division Surgeon, very kindly attended me and I was very much improved by a good night's sleep, so much so I rode several miles next day. The next night I was invited to the house of Mr. Breilys, a magnificent mansion, & here found Capt. [Thomas Jefferson] Adams of the [Co. A] Jeff Davis Legion from Mississippi, dreadfully wounded. I managed, thro Hood, to get a telegram sent to Mrs. Adams who came and nursed him till he got well, tho I think he was so disabled he never served again—a gallant man.

I was at Mr. Brielys several days. I here telegraphed to Dr. Robertson to let your Mother know I was not badly wounded, I think in these words, "I am wounded in head tho not severely" and wrote, I suffered a great deal from dizziness or rather a sleepy feeling and this lasted for a month & over.

However, in a few days moved on to Winchester & finding Gen'l. Lee was bound to cross the Potomac—resolved to go or die myself. I, therefore, as soon as I could ride, pushed on to reach my Hdquar. & so get with my Regt. As you will see, tho, I got to it after the Battle of Gettysburg was over and half an hour before we began our retreat. I was in that fight on the extreme right. My Regt. was on the left.

I pushed on and crossed the Potomac at Williamsport & started for Hagerstown, supposing Hdquar. there. Stuart had made his historic detour with the cavalry and was lost to the infantry out of Williamsport. I found, marching on, nearly an entire co. of my own Regt. and one of 2nd. S. C. Calvary that had been cut off from Stuart in crossing the mountains, as well

81. This was probably Pvt. W. H. Hood of Co. D, 1st S.C. Cavalry who was frequently detailed to the regimental or brigade commissary by Col. Black.
82. John T. Darby, originally in Hampton's Legion, later Medical Director with Stewart's Corps, Army of Tennessee.

as Lt. [Robert H.] Maxwell's [Co. C] 1st. N.C. Cavalry. I took command of these detachments & moved on.

At the end of the first night's march in the edge of Pennsylvania I came on an ordnance train, a large one and a reserve train of much importance. It was too far in rear and somewhat exposed to flank attacks of predatory marauding parties of the enemy. The officer who was in charge if it was apprehensive of an attack and many rumors were floating round as to Yankee Cavalry. He came to my camp for assistance and advice & I offered to escort him as he was only one march from the (illegible) of Gen'l. Lee's Army. He & I decided to rest until 10 or 11 & then march. We did so and I took the rear guard, giving him a few flanking videttes. I had, I think, about 80 to 100 men & some good officers, Major [Thomas E.] Scriven [Co. F] & Capt. Leonard Williams [Co. K] 2nd. S.C.C. We marched the entire night and just before dawn my ordnance train passed thro Gen'l. Barksdale's Brigade & moved on in safety to Chambersburg. I halted in a little village & lay down at the door of a house and slept an hour.

I then rode to Gen'l. Barksdale's Hdquar. & reported my presence and asked where I could find Gen'l. Lee's Hdquar. & was told, Chambersburg. I neglected to state that Hart's Battery was with these cut off troops. I also took command of these troops. I was very courteously received by Gen'l. Barksdale & invited to breakfast with him. By that time a rumor came that Yankee Cavalry were in our rear & by Gen'l. Barksdale's sanction, I moved several miles to the rear, sent out scouts, but soon learned it was a kind of straggler's dispatch & without foundation.

Now my ordnance officer, whose name I have forgotten, reported to headquarters and, I believe, swore he never would have gotten thro except for my aid & protection. I was at 11 o'clock about to leave command and to ride on to Chambersburg to report in person to Gen'l. Lee for orders & to be sent to my Regt. & Brigade when Col. [Briscoe G.] Baldwyn, chief ordnance officer of the Army of Northern Virginia, came to me and introduced himself. He took me one side and asked me if I had ever seen or served under Gen. R. E. Lee. I told him I belonged to Class of '50 at West Point when Gen'l. Lee was Supt. He replied:

"Very well, then. Gen'l Lee suspected who you were and directed me in that case to give you the private means of communication thro the country

& also direct you to send out some scouts to see if you can communicate with Gen'l. Stuart."

He gave me the names of several men but would not let me write them down. By his orders I sent a man back to Hagerstown, an intelligent and reliable man, to see Dr. Magill or someone at Dr. Magill's house. Magill was a surgeon in Confederate Army, man of high character, & much trusted and, I think, from what Col. B. said, means of intelligence were made thru him & trusted friends at his home.

I was also ordered to take command of all loose bodies of cavalry and picked up a number until my command was 200 to 300 strong. I organized them into a kind of Regiment & by Gen'l. Lee's orders moved thro Chambersburg next day (Sunday) and camped a few miles above, near a place called Pleasant Hill.

While I had a good many good men, I had a good many game-legged cusses & wagon rats. Yet I managed to keep them in some kind of order and discipline. Tho I heartedly wished both them and myself back at our own Regiments.

A day or so afterwards I was ordered to report in person at Gen'l. Lee's Hdquar. and did so. Gen'l. Lee gave me some orders and directions, spoke of being separated from Stuart and the main body of Cavalry, but did not seem to censure Stuart. As soon as I got my orders, I rose to leave but Gen'l Lee ordered me to take a seat, said he was not engaged, & commenced to talk to me of bygone days and cadet life, asking me if I knew where Robert Williams, a Virginian contemporary with me, was. I replied I did not. He said:

"I am sorry to say he is in the Federal Army. He came to Washington to resign but they bought him up with a mess of porridge and put him in the Adgt. Gen'l.'s Office."

He spoke of the war & said we must succeed and establish our independence, that if we failed the consequences would be terrible and generations unborn would feel it.

We were sitting on camp stools near his tent & no one else was near. He looked grave and had his usual dignified manner. Some officer came to him on business & I arose, bowed, and left.

The next day he sent Gen'l. [Robert Hall] Chilton[83] to inspect my drove of picked up troops and the day following I got orders to march in rear of the infantry army, then turn to the right to fight the Battle of Gettysburg. I marched to a little town, called Fairfield, and halted. It was at the foot of the mountains & a small place, apparently inhabited by a poor class of people. I bivouacked in the rear of a house, picketing my head quarter horses to the garden. The yard was presided over by a redheaded Yankee woman who had a temper of her own and a tongue of her own. John Carey, my orderly, went into her yard for some purpose and she castigated him with her tongue for some time. I had to prevent the men from annoying her to hear her scold. Poor woman, she was true to her side. We were invaders & these are not always saints in an enemies' country. I often felt sad as I saw the ravages of war, even in an enemies' country. We saw women & children—They looked sad. It was not with them that we made war but with men, but these men, their brothers, husbands & sweethearts.

That night the ordnance officer & I joined commands or rather I volunteered to defend him from predatory attacks. We halted after dark to feed & rest—and campfires were soon lighted and all in a blaze. I sent someone to get me water. A large house was near but no water could be found at it. Famished, I went with a party of mounted men to the house. It was very dark & we could find no gate. The doors and windows of the house were closed & the house was apparently deserted. I ordered a man to break down the fence. A blow or two opened a window in the second story and a lady like voice asked what we wanted.

"Water, nothing but water. Where is your well?"

Without answering, she seeing our faces said, "Oh, my, Jane," to another lady in the room, "The whole Rebel Army is on us."

And she appealed to me to go to the comdg. officer and get her a guard.

"But Madam," said I, "We want water. Tell us where it is and we will trouble for nothing else."

She then said, I must excuse her, told where the gate & well was & how to get it, etc., and back she came to begging me to go for a guard for her.

83. Chilton was Robert E. Lee's Chief of Staff.

This I declined to do. She begged and pleaded, asked me if I was a husband and father, a member of the church, etc. I answered her questions politely & by this time one or two more ladies were at the window, all entering in the entreaty for a guard. They were evidently first class people. So I said to them:

"Ladies, you do not need a guard. I am the comdg. Officer myself. I pledge the word of a gentleman for your safety while my command is here. My headquarters are yonder. If your premises are molested, open these two windows & show a lamp in them, protection will come to you."

There came a very polite volley of thanks, Would I come in? I thanked them. I would not as it was contrary to orders from headquarters. How many men had I under my command & when was I going away?

I replied, "Ladies, excuse me. Military strategy forbids me answering your questions. I will go away when ordered or whipped away. I have men enough. My name & rank is a secret to you. I am a gentleman and with defenseless women & children we make no warfare."

"You said you were not a member of the church," said one, "But you are truly a Christian gentleman in feeling. From which state do you come?"

"I am from South Carolina. Well, I must go to my camp. When I leave here I will be the last man to leave. Close your blinds and sleep in peace. Ladies, Goodnight."

I kept my promise & sat on my horse until our rear guard was ready to leave and left with it.

I got my last written order from Gen'l. Lee's Hdquar. At Fairfield. By it I was ordered to move at 4 p.m., 2 miles in Gen'l. Longstreet's rear. At 4 p.m. my command was mounted, Hart's Battery hitched & ready to move. Kershaw's Brigade was bivouacked in sight of me. It had not moved. I dismounted my command & waited. It did not move and I rode to it to see why and at sunset took a lunch supper with Col. Wm. F. Dessasure, 14th. Regt. S. C. & Lt. Col. Wm. Wallace [2nd S.C.], both of Columbia. They knew nothing, only had not been ordered to move. Now I am positive as to the terms of my orders. If Longstreet had an order to move also, was his countermanded and mine not? I have heard that he was censured for being slow in this march & I am disposed to think of my own, knowing he was behind time if his orders from Army Hdquar. correspond with mine.

I have never seen any published account of undoubted authority that proved that Longstreet was behind time in moving as to his orders—or do I know he had an order to move before 4 p.m., tho I am positive my order was so worded and signed by R. H. Chelton, the Adj. Gen'l. I got all of my written orders from Army Hdquar. during the week or 10 days. I was subordinate to none save Gen'l. Lee & reporting direct to his Hquars. I returned to my command and left a courier at Kershaw's Hdquar. to inform me when that Brigade moved. It did so between 8 and 9 o'clock. I then put on a patrol guard to preserve my interval between front of my own command & rear of infantry. Also a proper rear guard and so we marched the balance of the night. How far I can't say, as the march was at a snail's pace, often being compelled to halt to keep from running on the rear of Kershaw. About an hour before day or earlier Longstreet's front halted & turned aside to rest. Here I lost them & ran on them as they debouched into the road to march towards Gettysburg. I also at this time met a courier from Army Hdquar. It was ordering me to turn over my command to my next in rank & to report at daylight at Genl. Lee's Hdquar. near Gettysburg.

I had just turned Hart's Battery and my cavalry into a small field of the finest Timothy I ever saw. It was very thick & 3 feet high. Leaving orders & the command feeding, I pushed forward at a gallop with my orderly & got to Gen'l. Lee's Hdquar. in half an hour. In reporting I was told Gen'l Lee had walked off a short distance and he was pointed out. I rode toward him and found he was conversing with Lt. Gen. A. P. Hill whom I had never seen before. Capt. Rogers, a Virginian I knew & had known well at Adams Run had accompanied Gen'l. Lee & was sitting some paces off. I rode up and dismounted, sat down by Capt. Rogers, waiting for Gen'l Lee to be unengaged.

Lt. Gen. Longstreet soon came up and joined Gen'l. Lee & A. P. Hill. I had never before seen Longstreet. As well as I remember the conference lasted 20 minutes or over. They were standing in an old graveyard, not enclosed, a few trees near by and in plain view of the city of Gettysburg below, and we could see the outlines of the enemies' line of battle beyond the town. Our line then ran through the outer edge of the town which we had gained the day before & held & continued to hold.

Of course Capt. Rogers and I were out of ear shot & ourselves talking in a low tone. I here saw a council of war and that too on a memorable field of Battle—Gettysburg. I here saw three men grouped together, immortal names on the pages of future history. Gen'l. Lee was standing with his back to me. He was the best looking, of course. For me he was the best looking man in the universe—that I always knew. Longstreet was fat & full, A. P. Hill rather slender. I never saw him again or was nearer to him than at that time. Directly the conference ended & all three turned to leave, each in separate directions and each on foot. As Gen'l. Lee turned toward me I advanced & saluted him. He returned the salute & shook hands and, turning, called Gen. Longstreet and introduced me to Gen L. & said, "General, Col Black has an improvised command of cavalry and a Battery of artillery. I turn him over to you to explore your ground, watch your flanks and rear," and he added, "I commend Col. B. to you as once a cadet under me at West Point."

He bowed. We returned the bow & he left & Gen'l. Longstreet commenced asking me about my command. I told him I had a good battery, Hart's, as good as there was in the army, which was true. Some detachments of good cavalry & some hash of picked up men of whom I knew little. He ordered me to send my orderly back to bring up my cavalry on the road side. Leaving my battery to follow in rear of his corps still marching up and massing in Brigades two hundred yards in rear of the spot Gen'l. Lee & he had met on & covered from view of the enemy by a hill on which the conference was held. I rode back there with Gen'l. Longstreet & through half a dozen brigades. The brigades were one before the other in line as represented by the lines at the right & not over 10 paces apart. They were cleaning & firing off their guns, preparing for action. Some on the ground with open haversacks, eating. Many a poor fellow among them had marched his last march & was about to fight his last battle to sleep the "sleep that knows not breaking." I saw in passing thro several brigades, no one I knew. The men seemed cheerful & bouyant and a more gallant corps never was arrayed for the fatal fray.

As I came up I had passed the brave Gen'l. Barksdale sitting on a fence on the road side waiting for his Brigade to come up or move. As I rode by he recognized me and offered his hand. In reply to my inquiry he said he was unwell & felt badly. It was his last day on earth and yet he should live forever in the memory of Mississippians. Something in this man reminded me very much of Governor J. H. Means tho he did not resemble Means.

By this time my command of Cavalry had come up and I accompanied Gen'l. Longstreet to the right & top of a hill on a pike heading out of Gettysburg. Here he made his headquarters & ordered me to take possession of a bridge in sight & supply him with two trusty cavalry subalterns. I did, so selecting Capt. Fred Horsey, then 1st. Lt., & Lt. J. Wilson Marshall of same company. Longstreet ordered Horsey to go out 3 or 4 miles in one direction & Marshall in another at full speed with a few men and to come back and report as to whether they could see any enemy or not. I was also ordered to put Hart's Battery in position as it had to command a road bearing to the right. I did so. In an hour Horsey came back and reported no enemy to be seen. He had explored the ground Longstreet deployed on as his entire line of battle was to the right of where his corps was massed in Brigades.

At 8 a.m., after Horsey made his report & left, Gen'l. L. turned to me and asked if he could rely on his statements. I answered if there was an officer in the army he could rely on he could on Horsey. He seemed then to begin to deploy. I was not with him for an hour tho I heard no (missing).

I went to the foot of the hill and bridge to see about something & ordered Lt. Marshall to examine a large house that was near the bridge, a kind of tavern & I think called the "Black Horse Tavern". Marshall did so and found a number of whiskey barrels. These I promptly ordered stored and soon after informed Gen'l. L. what I had done.

"I suppose," said he, "You saved some for yourself & me."

"Excuse me, General, as I do not drink, I forgot to do so."

I applied for orders and was ordered to stay at his headquarters & await orders. I did so and so was a spectator at a safe distance of the fight that took place that day (2nd day's fight). I saw Anderson's Division (our own Fighting Dick) as it advanced in line of battle first thro the low grounds of a creek, then ascending some slope it struck the enemy. I also met Maj. General Cadamus Wilcox at the head of his Division as he marched to the flank to deploy & move into line. I spoke to him and introduced myself. He remembered me tho I had not seen him for 3 years. He was an officer, comdg. a cadet co. I was in at West Point.

Hood, I did not see, tho I was perhaps near him several times in the day.

Late in the evening I was ordered to the right 3 miles to watch the flanks & bivouacked. I had orders to report in person at Gen'l. L's Headquarters at dawn and did so. He had left & moved forward to the line of battle of day before. I followed & caught him all alone. He was passing along the line & over the crest of the small hill where the day before our lines had captured the famous 16 gun battery, dead horses and dead men were thick in every direction. The wounded had been removed.

I had seen this battery go the day before and before it was captured, several cassions or limber boxes had blown up, each sending up a huge column of smoke. They were no doubt exploded by rifle balls as our line was near them when they exploded. I have another indelible recollection of this day—the cannonade—It was impossible to distinguish the isolated report of a gun. The 2 to 400 firing was terrific but the roar was exactly like the continuous noise made by beating on a large waiter. I remarked this to Capt. Rogers or Roper (?) who was with Gen'l. L.

Altho I had been idle all day yet from excitement or from weakness, for I was still weak and had my head bandaged, I was completely exhausted. I slept like a log the night before. I felt fresh the morning of the third day's fight & well I was for I caught my share.

While Gen'l. L. & I were riding, Lt. Col. Sowelle of his staff came to him & he ordered Col. Sowelle to take me & my command & locate me and it on the extreme right & to transfer me to the command of Maj. Gen'l. Hood. Col. Sowelle was also ordered to inform me as to what was expected of me. We moved to Hood's (right) and about 1000 yards beyond along a road leading into Gettysburg by which road made an agle of 15° with our line of battle. Hood's extreme right was 4 batteries, 16 guns under a Major Henry, masked in an orchard. Beyond this 1000 yards were two companies of Alabama Infantry and only 40 or 50 strong. These companies were turned over to my command & Sowelle gave me orders if I was attacked and overpowered to fall back on our right flank. Firing line was really oblique to the right & rear of our line. I was also ordered to report by Courier to Gen'l. Hood's Hdquar. If I was attacked, urged to hold my ground so long as possible and to lap or swing back in good order.

A considerable body of Yankee Cavalry came out of a piece of woods and commenced to form in a field in my front. I ordered Hart's Battery to open on them, which was done effectually & the formation broken up, so accurate was Hart's fire. My orders were to keep Hart's Battery or to let it fall back on Henry's 16 gun Battery as I thought best. As I had only two guns of this most excellent battery & thought my supports not sufficient to keep them so exposed when I ordered them to open, I only used one gun, the one on the left next to Henry. The one on the right moved in rear of it & unlimbered & commenced to fire. As soon as it opened, the other limbered up & moved a corresponding distance to the left and opened. Thus I had the battery firing from one gun at a time but it was served rapidly & before the enemy were aware I had moved the battery 5 or 6 hundred yards. As they did not advance, we quit firing & I ordered Hart to take position in supporting distance of Henry.

In the meantime, Yankee Cavalry in small bodies were seen on our right and rear. I reported this & was ordered to swing back and form a line nearly perpendicular to the one I had before held. I did so and was soon attacked by dismounted cavalry. I reported by courier to Gen'l. Hood's Hdquar. & received message from Brig. Gen'l. Law comdg. Hood's Division that two Regiments of Alabama troops were marching to reinforce me & to hold my ground. This I was doing as best I could. The part of my command I could rely on dismounted & deployed as skirmishers. Hart's 2 guns I ordered up & unlimbered, ordered them to fire over my line. The first shell used exploded over my line, the second in the muzzle of the gun. Fortunately no damage was done by either save to demoralize my line. I ordered the guns to cease firing but one of the Lts., Halsey, I think, of the battery, informed me they had shells with better fuses &, as the enemy was pressing hard, I ordered the guns opened again. The shells worked well and guns were never better served or with greater rapidity & kept on at it.

My line was in woods, my right resting on a wheat field of tall bearded wheat about ripe and as high as a man's head. Old Parson Johnson, by sending a man up on slim tree, found out what I suspected, that the enemy were lapping my flank and deploying a line far to my right & in 5 or 600 yards of my line. Things were a blue aspect—it looked as if I would be whipped back on Henry when, chancing to look to the rear, I saw two of our infantry Regiments in 75 yards marching leisurely in rear of my line. Riding up to the officer at the head of the Regt. in front, I pointed out the trouble & suggested he would form on my right. To this he assented & I pointed out my right flank and was leading him towards my right flank. I thought he marched too leisurely & said:

"Damn it all, Colonel, if you don't move faster the enemy will lap before you are in position."

"Oh, no," he replied. "I think not."

By that time he halted as I did at the right of my line and his columns moved on. About this time someone called him "Gen'l Law" & I apologized. He laughted. He had only recently been promoted and was still wearing a Colonel's uniform. He ordered me to go along (missing) and said as soon as his regiment unmasked my line we would charge the Yankees and drive them off.

Law gave the command, "By the left flank forward, Commence firing." I ordered the cavalry to yell. One man spoke to me and said he was out of ammunition. I told him to come on and yell like hell. He did so. Tho I am free to think the Alabama Infantry who were in open ground did the hardest fighting, yet the cavalry held pace in the advance and did a long ways the most yelling. Their behavior was very gratifying to me in this charge as they were improvised. If I had had 100 of my own men and officers I would have felt sure of their behaving well but this mixed command did more than well. We drove the enemy in a hurry. Part of my line soon entered the open field and we saw the Yankee Blue Coats mount the big rail fence and over.

This attack was made, I think, by the 1st. and 2nd. Regular Dragoons U.S.A. We dove them clean away & Law took his Regiments and went back saying he hoped I could hold the ground.

A word as to Law—by Hood's fall & loss of a leg that morning, the command of his division devolved on Law & he commanded his division with much credit. He was an excellent officer. I served under him a few days in last of the war when he was a Major General comdg. cavalry & have seen him several times since the war and talked over the mixed charge of cavalry on foot and infantry.

This run away tho of the Yankees kept my immediate front unmolested till night. But about an hour afterwards I was surprised to hear the almost immediate (missing) of Major Henry's 16 guns & to hear it repeated and a pretty rapid discharge of small arms. It was over half a mile to my left. I sent a courier at full speed to see what was up but the firing was over before the soldier galloped halfway. He soon came back with a message from Law that he had killed Gen'l. Pleasonton of the Yankee Army but in this he was mistaken. It was Brig. Gen'l. Farnsworth. When Law left me with the two Alabama Regiments he had laid them down to rest & left them near. Gen'l. Farnsworth had perhaps spotted a small body of mounted men, 150 about I had moved several times in course of the day on Henry's right, & concluded to make a dash at them and to dash in for a kind of feeling reconnaisance. He came down the road at a gallop and ran square upon Henry's Battery before he saw it, who saluted him with a sweeping discharge of grape & cannister which literally annihilated the head of his column. A second discharge did its work & the Alabama Regiments springing to their feet, pound in a murderous volley.

The Yankees had Henry in their front, 16 guns raining an iron storm of grape. A stone wall on their right and the Alabama Regiments on their left and it was said that only 14 or 17 were seen to escape. It was wholesale slaughter. This was the last fighting of the night.

Farnsworth, as papers on his person showed him to be named, had his bowels shot out. After the firing ceased, a Confederate ordered him to surrender. He had a pistol, "No, Dam you" & turning the pistol up, blew out his own brains.

In the charge in the wheat field two of my men were shot thro the thigh and, as soon as we had time to look after the wounded, were gathered up and reported to me as bleeding to death. We had no surgeon. An inquiry was made if there was a doctor in ranks. A new recruit of my own Regiment said he was a doctor. I ordered him to improvise some means and stop the hemorrhage. He did and saved the men and attended to others. I said to him, "I will make you an assistant Surgeon" & did so, recommending him as having won his spurs on the battlefield. It was Dr. Horace Drennan of Abbeville.

Night came & I was exhausted & suffering with my head. I went to Gen. Law to get orders for the night. He saw my situation and told me to instruct the officer next in rank to me, Major Scriven 2nd S.C.C. and for me to ride a certain point & sleep till morning. I did so and slept like a log.

The next morning at dawn when I got back to my comd—I found the right flank of Hood's Texas Brigade resting on my left flank & closing the gap between Henry's Battery & my line. I also saw at a glance that (illegible) in faulty line had dug some dirt in the night and entrenched and were strongly posted. These arrangements had all been carried out in the night.

I rode up & formed the acquaintance of the Col.—comdg. Hood's Texans & ocassionally we met at our flanks. I do not remember his name but he was a genuine specimen of a Texan, tall and lank—some of his men had obtained poisoned food from a house near our line and in front. He sent a corporal's guard to oust the occupants of the house. The corporal came back and reported no one to be found on the premises—the house was smoking as he made his report & I opine they had paid the penalty for murder if anyone was found there when the guard went.

About 10 a.m. this day (the day after the third day's fight) rain commenced falling or rather commenced pouring down in torrents. It fell for some time and by 12 p.m. the clover sward was boggy and my horse sank deep at every step.

I had made application the night before to have my regiment sent to me and about 2 p.m. an order came for me to march my command across, or rather, in rear of our line of Battle and to report to Hampton's Brigade Hdquar. Then, with the main body of the cavalry on the left of the line of battle, I marched at once and in three miles came to the Black Horse Tavern about one mile from town of Gettysburg. Here the road was blockaded by an immense column of Yankee prisoners moving diagonally to our right and rear. I halted my command before I got to the road and rode forward myself. I saw Genl. Pendleton, Chief of the Artillery of the Army, sitting on his horse and riding up spoke to him and asked how the battle had gone—to Genl. Lee's satisfaction?

He replied it had.

"But," said I, "General, what is the meaning of that column of prisoners heading in that direction-They can't march that way an hour without our right flanks falling back to protect them. Are we retreating?" I inquired.

He leaned towards me & said in a low tone of voice:

"I have not 3 rounds of shell to the gun. The battle has involved an extraordinary expenditure of fixed ammunition. We must fall back until we can get supplies of ammunition from our reserve stores coming up. We have no shells but an abundance of grape & cannister."

I think I gave his entire words. By this time the 7 or 800 Yankees had passed and I marched on, sad but not disheartened, and reached my Brigade Headquarters about night fall. I found that Hampton had been wounded and that Baker was in command. Soon after dark, in gloomy silence, we commenced our retreat. I think my Regt. led off. At all events, Col. Baker, Lt. Col. Waring, Jeff Davis Legion, and I were at the head of the column.

We compared notes & I heard of our losses. Lt. Col. Walker had been wounded, captured, and soon after released by our men's running over the Yankees again. He had been sent off and was safe. Old Hill (Lt. Hill, Co. E.) had been badly hacked over the skull by a Yankee sabre but Hill's head was hard, very hard—tho a good head and a brave one. I believe he was on duty with a bandana bound round it,

We moved on in silence until 2 or 3 A.M. when we halted and bivouacked in the mountains. I sat by a fence all night as it rained incessantly and I got no rest but at the head of my Regt. marched on the next day. Excessive hard service and the wound in my head had done the work for me and I had a slow fever. I was very weak and anywhere else would not have been on duty. I would now & then gallop on a mile, lay down and rest until the column came up with me, & so move on. This afforded great deal of relief and but for my grey horse Roderick, a mountain Virginia horse, I would not have made the march. Moving in this way, we came near Fincastle. Col. Baker ordered me to ride ahead for some purpose & to look out for something. I did so and halted and laid down in the surburbs of Fincastle.[84] I had only my orderly with me.

While laying here, a citizen came to me, a man of 60 years. He was bitter and said he hoped we would never get back. I told him not to be uneasy, we were even able to turn and fight our way forward. He said our trains would never pass even Fincastle. I replied if we were attacked there

84. This should be Greencastle, Pa. Fincastle is in Virginia.

we could burn the town to create a diversion and that, as I knew he was a man of wealth, he would be a sufferer & that he had better pray for our safe return. I think he did pray for us to get away from Fincastle. He wanted to go away but I told him he could not, to detain him for a time.

By this time a detachment of men had come up to report to me to do look out for our right flank. Ordered them thro the town and told the officer if he was whipped back to burn the town to create a diversion. My old citizen heard my name and said to me I was very much like Judge Jeremiah Black* and asked me if I was kindred. I told him I used to be but now claimed no Yankee kin. Several Citizens came to look at me. Judge Jeremiah Black, who was from the same American ancestor as my father, had lived & practiced law in Fincastle.

The brigade came up and we passed on. Of the next 24 hours I have little recollection save marching on slowly with fever on me, my head reeling and scarcely able to sit in my saddle. The next day I was sent by Col. Baker to ride on to Williamsport to try and recruit & rest. But as I rode into Williamsport where our entire wagon train was parked, unable to cross the swollen Potomac, crowded with thousands of our wounded. All we could bring from the field and we had brought off, all capable of being moved and many whose wounds were of such character they ought not to have been removed. Several of whom I shall yet speak. It was reported the Yankee Calvary was approaching. In the town was Gen'l. Imboden's Calvary Brigade, only two regiments strong. I rode at once to Gen'l. Imboden's Hd-quar. and explaining my presence, offered my services, which were accepted.

The General asked me to go on the pike north of the town and to stop and organize all the slightly wounded & stragglers that came in. I did so, & soon got a number of lame horse cavalry men, some of them good soldiers. I also got about 113 or 114 Infantry under a Captain Jackson of Hood's Texas Brigade. Jackson was shot thro one arm but naively remarked he could (illegible) willing to whip off Yankee Cavalry. Our train was pouring into the town and we soon picked up a number of men. We also had a number of guns & small arms in abundance which had been brought off from Gettysburg. Our supply for the guns of shells was less than 3 to the gun but a plenty of grape and cannister. We got our force marshalled and had many a wagoner under quarter-masters who volunteered for the occasion. At Gen'l. Imboden's request, I took command of the left of his line and here directly in (missing) was my commissary Sergeant, John (illegible) in command of 10 to 15 of my own dismounted men.

Late in the day the enemy began to advance, brought up a battery and shelled us for a while but the shells flew mostly harmlessly over us & over our wagon train which was parked on the alluvial land on the margin of the River. We also had all streets leading out of town barricaded with wagons and Gen'l. Imboden had been very active and made admirable arrangements for defense. The most of the fight took place on my right, yet my part of the line sustained a light attack or was begging to be attacked as all at once the Yankees drew off to their left. The reason why we could not at once understand. They suddenly learned that Gen'l. Stuart was camped up on the Hagerstown Pike directly in their rear, so the Yankee officer adroitly slided off to his left & cleared our front — Stuart marched up as well as I recollect about dark & it was soon too dark to follow them. Our trains were saved & the "Wagoners Fight", as this had been termed, was over. Captain Jackson of Hood's Texas Brigade with his improvised company of Hood's Texas Brigade, behaved very gallantly & captured more prisoners than he had men. After the fight had began as our right was pressed, feeling able to spare him, I had ordered him to the right to the main Hagerstown Pike where I apprehended the main attack would be. A body of the enemy took possession of a house in his front. Jackson charged the house and captured all of them. After the fight I commended Jackson and asked him if I could serve him. He said he and his men were hungry. I wrote a note to Gen'l. Imboden who ordered a full supply of rations to Jackson's command. I was much pleased with this brave & modest man. I told him if I could do anything for him I would. He simply said:

"If you ever see Gen'l. Hood, tell him I did the thing right."

I told him I would, tho it was not till the war was over that I had a chance to speak to Hood about him & did so.

My Brigade came up that night and, as the enemy was about, I took command of my Regiment tho entirely unfit to do so. We marched out toward Hagerstown and had some skirmishes at a place called Funkstown.

In one of these skirmishes Capt. M. T. Owens, Co. A., was wounded in the heel. He lived to get to his home in Abbeville C.H. S.C. & died of tetanus (lockjaw) a few days after. Owens was a gallant man. In one of the same skirmishes a beautiful beardless boy named Foreman of Barnwell was killed—shot in the skull. Poor boy, he was handsome as a girl. I merely mention these two but many another gallant soldier of my command had hit the dust & sleeps the sleep that knows not breaking under the cold Yankee sod. Brave men whose lives were laid down in our sacred cause and struggle for liberty.

[End of excerpt]

* * *

Excerpt from "Hampton and His Red Shirts" by Alfred B. Williams 1935

A delightful and thrilling incident, recently recalled to mind, marked happily the close of the day meeting. As Hampton was leaving the stand many men crowded about, as always was the case, to shake hands with him. Among them was a small, modest man, making his way forward rather diffidently. The General caught sight of him and promptly pulled him out of the press, exclaiming: "Well! Here's the boy who saved my life at Gettysburg!"

The two had not met since the surrender, but Hampton said he never could forget the face of his old soldier, put a hand affectionately over his shoulder and introduced him to those near by as David Flenniken [Co. D, 1st S.C. Cav.], a business man of Winnsboro, who, he said, "saved my life while he was a boy in his teens."

Remarking that meeting Mr. Flenniken gave him more pleasure than all the demonstrations of the day, he narrated briefly the incident of Gettysburg. He was receiving a report from Flenniken, who was one of his best scouts and couriers, when the latter exclaimed suddenly, "Look to your right !" The General looked just in time to see a Federal soldier deliberately aiming at him with a rifle at short range and instantly rode the man down and sabered him.

Mr. Flenniken died not long ago, but his family and surviving fellow citizens recall proudly the day of the Winnsboro meeting and Hampton's final words regarding his former comrade : "He never in the four years failed to deliver an order."

Chapter 2

2nd South Carolina Cavalry

EDGEFIELD ADVERTISER
JULY 29, 1863

Casualties in Co. I, 2nd Regt. S.C. C.

Maj. T. J. Lipscomb, of the 2nd S.C. Cavalry sends the following casualties in Co. I, Capt. CLARK commanding:

THOROUGHFARE GAP, June 25—Wounded: Privates Kelly and Hogan, slightly.

GETTYSBURG, July 3—Killed: Sergeant Thomas Butler

BOONSBORO, July 8—Wounded: Private John Lyons.

* * *

NEWBERRY HERALD AND NEWS

APRIL 29, 1910

HE IS HALE AND HEARTY
It is Captain J. Wistar Gary and He Lives In Newberry and Is Commander Jas. D. Nance Camp.

In the Columbia correspondence of the News and Courier of Friday appeared the following:

Columbia, April 21.-In a letter to the adjutant general, W. H. Bricker of Carlisle, Pa., asks of the whereabouts of one "Capt. Gary, or Garey,' who was in the battle of Gettysburg. The letter was referred to Mr. A. S. Sally, Jr., who states that the Gary referred to was Gen. "Mart" Gary, who, at the time mentioned was captain of the 2nd South Carolina cavalry.

The letter from Mr. Bricker states that "I met him at Gettysburg on July 3, 1863, but we did not have much chance to talk matters over then."

Mr. Bricker also says that he met the Capt. Gary later at the reunion of the cavalry of both armies.

The information will be furnished many years ago.

Gen. J. W. Moore, of Hampton, in as requested, Gen. Mart Gary died the next issue of the News and Courier (Saturday) published the following:

To the Editor of the News and Courier: I notice in your paper of the 22nd a special from Columbia, which states "in a letter to the adjutant general, W. H. Bricker, of Carlisle, Pa., asks of the whereabouts of one Capt. Gary or Garey, who was in the battle of Gettysburg," and goes on further to state that the letter from Mr. Bricker states that "I met him at Gettysburg on July 3, 1863, but we did not have much chance to talk matters over then." Mr. Bricker also says that he met this Capt. Gary later "at the reunion of the cavalry of both armies."

The information you give that this was Gen. Mart Gary is erroneous. Gen. Mart Gary went into the war as captain in the infantry of the Hampton Legion. The legion at that time was composed of six companies of infantry, a battery of artillery, (afterwards widely known as Hart's

Lt. James Washington Moore was the adjutant of the 2nd S.C. Cavalry. He was wounded in the hand at Brandy Station on August 1, 1863, the month after Gettysburg. He was surrendered as part of Gen. Joseph Johnston's army. He was not at the site of the surrender in North Carolina, but instead signed his parole at Augusta, Georgia. Moore was later an attorney for the railroad and for Hampton County, S.C.

(Men of Mark in South Carolina Volume 1)

battery) and two squadrons (four troops) of cavalry, the whole under the command of Col. (afterward lieutenant general) Wade Hampton.

In the spring of 1862 the Infantry was raised to a full regiment and M. W. Gary (commonly spoken of as Mart Gary) became colonel, Wade Hampton being promoted to brigadier general and assigned to a command of a brigade of cavalry. The cavalry of the legion and Hart's battery composing a part of his brigade.

During that year by additions of other cavalry commands the cavalry of the legion was raised to a full regiment under the name of the 2nd South Carolina cavalry.

One of the new troops which composed this regiment was under the command of Capt. T. J. Lipscomb, afterwards colonel of the regiment, and a lieutenant of that troop was J. Wistar Gary, who became captain of the troop. known as "Troop G." This was one of the largest troops of the regiment and was almost always on the skirmish line when we fought dismounted. Capt. J. W. Gary was in command of the dismounted men of, the 2nd cavalry at the battle of Gettysburg, and this was the time to which Mr. Bricker evidently referred when he says "we did not have much chance to talk over matters then." The reunion of the cavalry of both armies, Mr. Bricker mentions, and at which he says he met Capt. Gary later, was, I presume, in July, 1885, when a number of cavalry officers, both Confederate and Federal, met for the purpose of locating the positions of the respective cavalry commands by request of Col. Batchelder, the historian of the battlefield of Gettysburg.

Capt. J. W. Gary and the writer were the only two present who had been members of the 2nd South Carolina cavalry. It was evidently Capt. J. Wistar Gary to whom Mr. Bricker refers.

Capt. J. W. Gary lived at Newberry, in this state. I have not met him for many years, and my information is that he is dead.

He was a gallant and accomplished officer and well worthy of the name of the distinguished family to which he belonged. I have written this hurriedly, simply with the view of keeping the record straight.

Yours truly,

James W. Moore,

Former Adjutant of the 2nd S. C. Cavalry.

Hampton, S. C., April 23, 1910.

Mr. Salley is evidently mistaken as to the identity of Capt. Gary mentioned in the inquiry. Gen. Moore is evidently correct as to the Identity of Capt. Gary, but mistaken in his information that he is dead. Capt. J. Wisar Gary is now living with his relative, Mr. Craig Gary at _____ in Newberry county, and is among the youngest of the survivors of that great conflict.

Capt. Gary is commander of the Jas. D. Nance camp, U. C. V. [United Confederate Veterans] has been the commander from organization of the camp. He was in Newberry a few days ago and is in the enjoyment of the best of health.

He enlisted at the beginning of the war as a private in Company B, Third regiment with S. N. Davidson Captain. At the end of the first years' service he was transferred to Company G, Third regiment, with T. J. Lipscomb as captain and Gary was first lieutenant and after Mr. Lipscomb was promoted to Colonel, Mr. Gary was made captain of the company and served in that capacity through the remainder of the war.

* * *

NEWBERRY HERALD AND NEWS
MAY 10, 1910

CAPTS. GARY AND BRICKER.
Friendship Between Men Who Faced Each Other in Battle Closed by Capt. Bricker's Death.

Some days ago The Herald and News printed an extract from a letter written by Captain Bricker to the adjutant general inquiring about Captain J. W. Gary and also corrected an impression that General Moore had that Captain Gary was dead. The letter of Captain Bricker was referred by Mr. A. S. Salley, Jr., to Captain Gary, and is as follows:

Carlisle, Pa., April 16, 1910.

Adjutant General of South Carolina.

My Dear Sir: I desire very much to secure the address of an officer of a South Carolina Confederate regiment, I think the Second of Hampton's Legion. I believe it was a Capt. Gary, I met him at Gettysburg on July 3, 1863, but we did not have much of, or any chance, to talk matters over them, but afterwards at the reunion of the cavalry of both armies we did meet and had a very pleasant conversation. Now, if you can give me his address, if living, I will certainly feel under everlasting obligations to you.

Truly and sincerely yours,

W. H. Bricker,

624 N. W. Street, Carlisle, Pa.

His name was Capt. Garey or Gary, Second S. C. cavalry, C. S. A. At least I think I am correct about it. Captain Gary replied to the letter and The Herald and News gives his reply:

April 26, 1910.

General W. H. Bricker,

Carlisle, Pa.

My dear Sir: The enclosed clipping taken from the News and Courier, a daily paper published at Charleston, S. C., is my apology, as well as excuse, for writing this letter, for it brings to mind a very enjoyable visit to the battlefield of Gettysburg in July, 1885, when I, as well as other Southerners, had the pleasure of first meeting you when neither party "was under arms." I should have written you a letter of thanks years ago for the kind and gracious manner in which you received us on that occasion, and for the generous hospitality and entertainment given. But, like many other things, the letter was so long postponed, that finally I lost your address, and only discovered it from this chance clipping containing the letter from my friend and former comrade, General James W. Moore, disclosing the fact that I am the Gary to whom your former letter referred.

General Moore, however, as you are now aware, is mistaken in his information that I have "passed over the river." This mistake I am truly glad to correct in person, and to say that I am commander of "Camp James D. Nance, No. 336, U. C. V.," located at this place and have held that office since its organization in July, 1883, and further to announce that it is the banner camp in South Carolina, containing a membership of two hundred eighty-eight ex-Confeds in good and regular standing.

Even at this late day, permit me to thank you most sincerely for the hospitality, and especially for the cordial manner of the hand-grip and the soldierly spirit in which you met and entertained us at Gettysburg in 1885. We felt it then, and still appreciate it as we live it over again in memory.

Now, I want to give you an invitation to visit us, so as to be here on the 10th of May proximo, as this is the largest annual gathering we have (anniversary of Stonewall Jackson's death), the day on which are bestowed by the U. D. C. Southern Crosses of Honor on worthy ex-Confederates; and the day that the "boys" are given a big dinner and barbecue. I vouch for you a most hearty welcome, and, at the same time, will thoroughly convince you that the war is over, and that amity and good feeling for our re-united country reigns supreme, at least In the South.

Wishing you and yours continued happiness and prosperity, I beg to subscribe myself,

Sincerely your friend,

J. W. Gary.

On Saturday Col. O. L. Schumpert received a copy of the Evening Sentinel of Carlisle, Pa., dated April 27, in which is recorded the sudden death of Captain Bricker and from which The Herald and News makes the following extract. It will be seen that Captain Bricker died before he got the information which he was seeking in regard to Captain Gary.

The Sentinel of April 27 says:

The hand of death has again stricken down one of Carlisles best citizens, the Hon. William H. Bricker. Capt. Bricker, as he is best known, was working about the chicken yard at his home on North West Street late Monday afternoon. Mrs. Bricker was visiting a friend in town, and Mr. Bricker was alone. Mrs. John D. Shearer, who resides next door, was in the yard at her home, and heard Mr. Bricker moan. Then she saw him fall. Hastily she summoned Mr. Dysert, another neighbor, and he and Mr. Yost, and others who gathered quickly carried the stricken man into the house. Dr. A. R. Allen was summoned, and when he arrived Mr. Bricker was still breathing, but in a few moments passed away. His death is attributed to heart failure. While Capt. Bricker had been in declining health for some time, his death at this time was unexpected, and the news received over town was a shock.

Sketch of His Life--Active In Politics--A Great War Record.

Honorable William H. Bricker was born August 6, 1837, and was therefore in his 74th year. He followed farming, and it was while he was still on the farm, that he enlisted in Company H, Third Pennsylvania cavalry. He was soon chosen first sergeant, and on May 1, 1863, was promoted to lieutenant of Company B, of the same regiment. On August 22, 1863, he was captured by the rebels and confined alternately in Libby prison, and in prisons in Danville, Va., Macon, Ga., Charleston and Columbia, S. C. While at Columbia, he escaped and was out 12 days. He was recaptured, after suffering great privations. After 16 long and weary months he was exchanged, and his term of enlistment having expired, was honorably discharged. On January 25, 1865, he returned to the farm. Subsequently he moved to Newville. In1870 he was appointed United States store keeper, which office he resigned in 1875.

In Politics.

In 1876 Captain Bricker moved to Beaver Falls, in Beaver county, Pa., where he was engaged in the book, stationery and news business, and where he was successful, and a prominent -citizen. He was a delegate to the Republican State convention in 1881 and again in 1894. In 1884 he was elected register and recorder of Beaver county, and again elected in 1887.

He was also engaged in the real estate and insurance business at one time. In 1898 he was elected to the State Legislature, and in 1900 was reelected by nearly 2,000 plurality.

At Gettysburg.

As may be seen from a brief reference to his war record above given, Captain Bricker was a brave soldier, and of this there are many unmistakable proofs. For instance, at Gettysburg he led a detachment sent out unmounted, for support in front of Rummel's barn. Taking a position in the line, they suffered great loss. Subsequently the squad remounted and made a charge on the enemy. Every man was wounded excepting Capt. Bricker and the bugler.

Whilst a prisoner at Charleston, S.C., he was promoted to a captaincy, but never was mustered as such for the reason that the regiment was mustered out, before his return. A comrade of Captain Bricker, a Carlisle gentleman who was in the same company, says that Captain Bricker was a gallant soldier, always ready for any hazardous duty, and was respected and loved by all the officers, well as the men.

Augustus H. Lark of Greenville, S.C. was a private in Co. F throughout the war and was present at the time of Gettysburg. The month before he was one of four men who carried Brig. Gen. Matthew Calbraith Butler from the field when he was wounded at the Battle of Brandy Station. At the time of the surrender, Lark had been detailed to herd cattle for the army from South Carolina. After working for the election of Wade Hampton as governor, he left S.C. for Arkansas where he became a Methodist minister and "reared an interesting family of fourteen children."

(Confederate Veteran Magazine)

Benjamin Hamett Teague of Aiken, S.C. was a member of Co. B, 2nd S.C. Cavalry throughout the war. He was a dentist for forty-eight years post war and was pivotal in veteran's affairs as the S.C. Commander of the United Confederate Veterans. Teague also created the Star of the West medal for the best drilled cadet at the Citadel. The medal was named for the ship fired on by Citadel cadets while trying to resupply Fort Sumter.

(Confederate Veteran Magazine)

William Stone was a private in Co. D of the 2nd S.C. Cavalry. He was a resident of Florence County, S.C.

(Library of Congress)

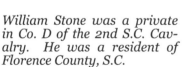

~ *Section 4* ~

Artillery

Chapter 1

South Carolina Artillery

THE ATLANTA JOURNAL
AUGUST 24, 1901

Carnage at Gettysburg and Siege of Petersburg

By James G. Ramsey

Color Bearer, Palmetto Battery, South Carolina Volunteers

Will you give space to one more army experience of one who occupied a very humble position in the make-up of the Confederate Army?

This much prized recital of what each individual saw, has made your very prized paper very much appreciated, and while we were putting our thoughts in print, I consider that living participants are the true ones to make history that will be very interesting in time to come.

At least six of these have touched upon the battle of Gettysburg, and of all the battles I believe the carnage was equal, if not greater, in the three days. A distinguished foreigner who witnessed this fight remarked that the results were so impressive that if he were professor of military science he would choose the battle of Gettysburg for the special study of his students. So I will touch upon some incidents in corroboration of what has been said about this subject.

There has been a standing controversy, imputing an erroneous charge to one of the commanders being tardy, and I want to show in my feeble way that such was not the case. We all know the tension and strain on men and horses after thirty days of marching, hardly stopping to eat, and would like to show that we arrived on the battlefield very early in the morning, and were six miles from the scene at 3 o'clock on the night of the 1st of July. The road was blocked with Hill's and Ewell's wagon trains. The second day General Longstreet was ordered to attack up the Emmittsburg Road. The troops that were in this charge were mostly Georgian, four brigades from Georgia, one Mississippi, one Alabama and one Texas brigade, with the artillery of this corps, one South Carolina brigade composing the two divisions of General E[vander] M[cIver] Law and General Hood. This fearful undertaking to dislodge the enemy from his stronghold on Round Top was no child's play. The steady strokes of fresh troops that was hurled against our attacking column of 13,000 men, and as line upon line was forced back, yet onward they pressed until the summit was reached, and Round Top was captured, and three rifled cannon was brought to the rear - and the sequel of this charge, about 4,500 men were knocked out of line. General Meade testifies that Round Top was the key to his position, and then the imputation of tardiness. Why we did not hold Round Top is very well explained. Some one was ordered to move at the same time upon our extreme left, with definite orders to co-operate so as to neutralize our attacking column. This same commander admits under his official act that he did go in at dusk after we had been fighting for three hours, and the smoke of our battle had overshadowed the countless slain. From the Northern accounts, General Hancock was wounded in the thigh, General Gibbon in shoulder and General Sickles, fighting desperately was struck in the leg. General Sedgwick came up with the Sixth corps. The Rebels camel back was broken by this feather. His line staggered, reeled and drifted slowly back, amid the roar of musketry over their dead bodies.

I reproduce this to corroborate the statement of the terrible odds we were fighting, and I shall always believe that Longstreet's corps did some of the hardest fighting at this terrible battle, and went in with as much military precision as any of the troops that got in at all. It is shameful libel for our muster roll to ever revert to this charge in any other way. Now I will make just one remark what happened to our gun No.4 of the Palmetto Battery during the bombardment, which never was surprised in any battle. Every horse at this piece was killed. Every man wounded, and a plunging shot cut Robert Small and Robert McIntosh nearly in "twain" two noble boys. It was a tidal wave of blazing hell to stand before those horrible discharges of shot and shell, and if you will excuse me, I want never to witness such dismal scenes anymore.

When Major [Benjamin] Eishleman, in command of Washington Artillery, was ordered to fire the signal gun for the artillery duel, the world never witnessed such a bombardment, where over 300 guns were firing at once. I asked a federal artillery officer, since the war, "Why they did not press us after the battle was over?" His reason was good. He said out of eighty-seven horses he lost fifty-six and was in no condition to follow. After the fight I was sent with others to procure some fresh horses to remove our guns and here I met ambulances and empty ammunition wagons loaded with wounded. The rumbling sounds intermingled with the groans made a dismal scene, and it seemed that one-third of our army had been placed hors do combat.

* * *

THE ATLANTA JOURNAL
SEPTEMBER 21, 1901

A Correction

By James Graves Ramsey

[Color Bearer, Palmetto Battery South Carolina Volunteers]

Mr. Loyless:

The article published by Mr. Hemphill concerning the battle of Gettysburg is so nearly complete.

He places the losses of Hood's and McLaws' divisions at 4,467. In the feeble testimony I gave in last being 4,500. While he makes no report of artillery, we only differ about 38 men in the report. The battle of Gettysburg was fought without cavalry, only White's battalion being present. General Stuart was on a hunt with the entire cavalry arm of the service. The one reason I wrote my piece to help substantiate the correctness of the second day's fight the bloodiest of all. A five column article being published that the First corps was a disjointed affair, and that we scarcely got in at all. Now please give space to my simple narrative as one more witness that we did go in and lost as heavily as any troops under fire. Very Respectfully,

James Graves Ramsey

* * *

ANDERSON INTELLIGENCER
JULY 16, 1902

WAR STORIES
Garden's Battery Heroes—Recollections of Gettysburg, July 2 and 3, 1863

There's many a thrilling, aye, curdling incident in the many battles of the States' war that history does not chronicle; inscriptions on field tablets do not record; cycloramas fail to exhibit, and even the traditions will soon be lost if not rescued from oblivion by surviving participants or spectators; and yet any attempted delineation by a mere pen sketch of most of these must needs be but adumbration of the reality.

Captain Louis Gourdin Young in his admirable address to the camp of Georgia Veterans in Savannah, April, 1900, "pleaded for the preservation of our memoirs of the Southern Confederacy and suggested that each veteran put on record what he saw and what happened in his own experience" and Mr. J. E. Norment in his interesting letter October 3, of the same year, calls attention from the field of Gettysburg to the "one-sided story" told there and pleads that the Southern States build their own monuments.

The writer had been repeatedly requested to record the services rendered by Garden's Battery, S. C. V., and particularly those of one solitary gun on the 3rd of July, '63, and connecting incidents therewith, and which, though, like all other exploits of that fateful day, achieved little save to illustrated the spirit de corps and peculiar afflatus which possessed Lee's veterans at that time.

The following extracts from the correspondence mentioned is self-explanatory. Quoting from a letter of Capt. Hugh R. Garden to Mr. Lloyd Collis, 195 Broadway, New York, son of Gen. C. H. T. Collis, date July 18, '01: "The photographs this morning are a genuine surprise. I did not know that an effort had been made to locate batteries on the field of Gettysburg. ***On second day, after engaging Big and Little Round Top, I crossed the valley in front, (shown in photograph) prior to the charge of cavalry under Brig. Gen. Farnsworth. Finding the 'Devil's Den' impassable I returned to this position.***That night I carried away, under Gen. Law's orders, from the slope of Little Round Top, in the wheat field, four rifled cannon captured that afternoon in the 'whirlpool' of the battle by Hood's division.

"I have always understood that these were the only cannon captured and taken by the Confederates from that battlefield. The last day of the battle was my best and worst day, and there seems to be no reference to it. On that last 'dies irae,' the day of Pickett's charge, I was sent about a mile to the left of my first position near the turnpike, immediately on the right of the Washington Artillery, and engaged Big Round Top during the first part of the great artillery duel. While thus engaged the chief of Gen. Longstreet's staff, who was on the pike observing the effect of the artillery fire, ordered me to cease firing on Round Top and to move by section to the left of the peach orchard and advance in echelon across the plain. I obeyed the order, but only one section of my battery, under Lieutenant [William A.] McQueen, made the advance, for when it moved obliquely to the left and went into position at a point down a gentle descent, (as I can never forget,) about 200 yards to the left of the peach orchard, and about 300 yards at least in front of our line of artillery, the attention of the opposing artillery was drawn to its fire, and within ten minutes every horse and man was killed or wounded. I took volunteers and fresh horses in to remove my men and gun. After two attempts we succeeded, under the same concentrated terrific fire, made more terrible by the explosion of caissons and the fire overhead of our friends in the rear. There for the first and only time during the entire war I felt compelled to encourage my men by personal example. It was in that carnival of hell also that while two of us were trying to carry a wounded man across the open field I heard a wounded Federal officer say: "I have laid her since yesterday. I am a D. K. E." I could only unsling and give my canteen and say: "I would help you, but I cannot get my own men out of this fire." I never saw him again, but he must have been saved, for at sunset our army was not in possession of the field. Some of my best men fell there and I have always thought that as Pickett's charge marked the high-tide of the confederacy, the advance of that solitary section in obedience to what I understood to be Gen. Longstreet's order to advance the artillery marked the high-tide in the greatest artillery duel in history."

Extract from letter of Major W[illiam] M. Robbins, 4th Alabama, dated Gettysburg, September 10, 1901, to Captain Hugh R. Garden, Mutual Life Building, N. Y. City: "You know that no report has ever been made of the services rendered by the artillery of Hood's division on this field, so that the only information on this interesting subject is the testimony of survivors. ***As to the tablets and monuments, he continues: "The work is being done under the supervision of the Secretary of War, whose agency here is the National Park Commission, composed of two Union soldiers and one Confederate—all three having fought in the battle here." *** "I have long since had a tablet erected to your battery, but have reason to fear the inscription falls short of doing justice to you and your command for want of information."

There are also letters from Gen. E[dward] P[orter] Alexander to Captain Garden and from the latter to the Hon. J. Harvey Wilson, then the chivalrous Sergt. Wilson, of the battery, but the gist of these will be covered in the sequel.

This writer was only a private, attached to this third section of Garden's battery, and can presume to describe nothing more than was seen and experienced from that humble standpoint. This battery formed a part of Major John C. Haskell's Battalion, a veritable beardless Coeur de Lion, with one arm in the grave and ready to bury forty more if necessary to be nearest the flashing of the guns.

The battalion composed Bachman's German Battery from Charleston, Riley's and Latham's, of North Carolina, and Garden's composed mostly of Sumter and Chesterfield volunteers and followed more particularly the fortunes of Hood's old brigade, the invincible Texans, of Longstreet's corps; but all under command of our gallant chieftain, that skilled artillerist, urbane gentleman, Gen. E. P. Alexander, who had gained the profound respect and soldierly love of his command, the corps artillery. June thirty-nine years ago, on this second day of July, 1863, under a fierce Pennsylvania sun, we reached the then obscure village of Gettysburg.

"Gettysburg! Name instinct with so many tears, with so much mourning, with those sobs which tear their way from the human heart as lava makes its way from the womb of the volcano. There are words in the world's history whose very sound is like a sigh or a groan; places which are branded "accursed" by the moaning lips of mothers, wives, sisters and orphans. Among them none is more gloomier or instinct with a more nameless horror than the once insignificant village of Gettysburg. It has been called "pivotal Gettysburg," though it savors of a paradox, because there was neither victor nor vanquished, only the culmination.

As we approached the mighty drama was in full progress and the field already stained and scarred from the intermittent combats of the morning and preceding day. Between us and the gigantic arena there yet intervened a skirt of woods along which a serried column of infantry were maneuvering for position, while shot and shell from Cemetery Heights ploughed through the ranks and we remember the flying hats and scattered limbs of the dead and wounded as hideous gaps were made through the files, also the steady "Close up" and continued firm and confident tread of those oaken-hearted troops, nearer to danger and surer death. The shrill bugle blast of our own command sounded in quick succession: "Cannoneers Mount!" "Double quick!" "Action front!" "Commence firing!" and with a whirl and rush, and scarce breathing time, our own guns were joining in the grim war music.

Field and staff must write history of locations and surroundings. The man at the muzzle sees little beyond his hammer staff and swab bucket and the grinning mouth of his piece. We only know we were on the left of the long battle line, with the Round Top in our front and the peach orchard and wheat field bristling with bayonets, while the heights above glowered with guns.

A word as to the morale of Lee's army at this juncture may help to explain why Gettysburg seems so often to be spoken and written of as "the battle of the war," and to account in a measure for those desperate assaults and fearful fatalities. The splendid and decisive victories over Burnside, with heavy odds, at Fredericksburg; the almost rout of Hooker, with the odds, too, at Chancellorsville; the triumphant march through the foe's territory, caused Lee's veterans to look forward to victory as a foregone conclusion, until there obtained a contagious intoxication from past successes and an exultant and overweening anticipation of future easy triumphs. Alas! That we should have forgotten that we occupied the heights at Fredericksburg and that it was Hooker, not Meade, at Chancellorsville. We forgot, too, that these combats occurred on our own soil, and that though game we felt ourselves, we were now on the dunghill's own barnyard, and though still forcing him to take to the fences he would die game holding them. I will make no attempt to recount the gallant charge of the corps as it hurled itself against Sickles' salient and forced him back to the ridge and eventually to its rugged summit, leaving the ground strewn with the slain and the valley slopes fertilized with the rich Southern blood, mingling with that of the foe. (Verily the seeds which germinate on that soil should produce hybrid plants and mongrel fruit.) Nor the desperate charge and assault of our invincible Texans who gained the crest, hand to hand, point to point, and—oh, Lord, but for the reinforcements to the enemy and the lack of them to our own troops that day, this might have been dated from the "Confederate States."

So wildly enthused were our men, so thoroughly imbued with the war spirit, so exultant and dauntless in their splendid pride, that even the cumbersome cannon were rushed down and attempted to follow up the infantry charge by scaling the steep and jagged sides of little Round Top. Victory seemed just within our grasp. One more blow, only one more, but—"The century reeled when Longstreet paused on the slope of the hill," sang one of their own poets. Human brain, nor brawn, nor courage could do more.

The morning of the 3rd discovered the enemy retired to the summits of Cemetery Ridge, and strongly entrenched behind natural and artificial fortifications. What next? Who knew? Doubtless councils of war were held on both ridges and reconnoitering parties and field glasses busy, while the royally irresponsible rank and file loitered away the welcome calm in restful repose or grim badinage, though impressed with the weighty pregnancy and potent influence of the hour and circumstances so heavily freighted with the shadows of coming events. Many, very many, who whiled away those moments enjoyed their last smile on earth.

The rays of the midsummer sun beat down fiercely upon the long and silent battle lines on ridge and heights and upon the intervening slopes of orchard and wheat fields. The very air seemed to hold its breath.

Then! A signal gun! Again the bugle blast sounded the command: "Commence firing!" Each cannoneer was in place with automatic promptness and busy precision, and the next instant the earth trembled as a mighty roar from 150 cannons' mouths belched flame and smoke and murderous metal toward the frowning heights with deadly accuracy. But this defiant challenge was quickly answered and the long range of hills became an undulating line of flame, under heavy hanging palls of smoke issuing from the muzzles of Meade's bronze war dogs, as they fiercely roared "Come on!" While Lee's guns from the ridge thundered grimly, "We are coming!" At that moment the spectacle was grand, as a graphic writer describes it: "The heights, the slope, the fields and the rugged crest opposite, were enveloped in smoke and fire from the bursting shell. The somber roar, sounding like the bellowing of a thousand bulls, leaped back from the rocks and rolled away in wild echoes through the hills. All the furies seemed let loose, and yet this was only the preface." The above writer had reference to Pickett's renowned charge, but alas, it was also only the preface and full as ominous for one small gun squad. The same writer continues: "In the evening the thunder dropped to silence. The time had come." It was then some order was issued from some source. The devoted third section of the battery promptly "limbered up." Each man assumed place and we moved quickly and obliquely across the descent, through orchard and waving wheat. On, on, under the black, yawning mouths of 24 guns on the heights above, silent, but gaping and yawning at the amazing audacity, and only awaiting developments. They came quickly.

The right wing of Pickett's column brushed past. One solitary gun wheeled into "Action front!" "Load!" "Fire!" Then hell broke loose! No sooner had flame and smoke gushed after the hurtling shell than Round Top Hill became a veritable scathing volcano of destruction, emitting dense volumes of smoke, lurid tongues of flame and hurling metal missiles that hissed or shrieked, or wailed through space, or burst with deafening peals as they scattered their jagged, death ladened fragments around. The ground was ploughed and torn and great clouds of dirt and debris thrown up everywhere; both earth and air were rended by the detonations and mighty rush of iron hail intermingled with the pelting of leaden bullets; man after man went down with his death-hurt or disabling wound from deadly aim or fatal chance. Not a horse was left to move a wheel.

And yet the remnant of that seemingly doomed section stuck to their gun, loaded and fired with a growing and defiant desperation of courage and determination, as their duties doubled in handling the piece, and hurled back shell or shot or shrapnel, as the meager supply of the limber chest, permitted, and until it was exhausted.

There was no single skulker there; no man flinched his duty or shrunk from the terrible unequal combat; faces might blanch at the horrifying carnage, but nerves blanched not in that relentlessly ireful hour. Exhausted, bleeding, ammunition spent, comrades prone, six horses dead or dying, farther effort futile, our gallant officer, the calmly brave Alex McQueen, himself faint and bleeding, ordered the pitiful fragment to seek protection from the infernal death sluice; as, indeed, any other move was a human impossibility –remaining a fatal folly.

The men who composed this section of Garden's battery and went with the gun into the valley were:

Lieut. W[illiam] Alexander McQueen, Sumter

Sergt. And Gunner Matthew E. Haynesworth, Sumter

Corp'l. James Henry Haynesworth, Sumter

Corp'l. Robt. F. Small, Charleston, mortally wounded at the gun

Charles Haynesworth, Sumter

Thomas R. McIntosh,

       Lynchburg, Sumter County, mortally wounded

In action

William Moultrie Reid, Sumter County

J. Merrick Reid, (then) from Charleston

Driver, W. W. Grady, Chesterfield County

The names of the other two gun drivers cannot now be ascertained.

The names of those who volunteered to accompany Capt. Garden and ventured into the bloody death hold to rescue the wounded are, so far as authentically ascertained: Capt. Hugh R. Garden, Sergt. J. Henry Wilson, Corp'l. John J. Green, James Diggs Wilder, all of Sumter County, and Lawrence W. Scarborough, Darlington County. Capt. Garden was unquestionably a brave boy, (for he was but a boy of bare majority then, with but a downy "bang" upon upper lip and the roseate hues of babyhood yet in his cheeks), and he had followers every whit as brave as he, as some proved that day, for when he called for volunteers to the rescue of men and gun any hesitation was only from ignorance of the fact that he intended to lead them into the jaws of perdition and enough futile and worthless havoc had already been caused. The brave John J. Green when appealed to replied: "We'll go anywhere that you will." They went and on reaching the gun found the lone figure of Bill Grady calmly and fearlessly sitting on the trail, never having left the ground, and awaiting assistance to remove his wounded comrades.

Small and McIntosh were shot down by the same solid missile and the writer doubtless had his closest call and most amazing miraculous escape. These men were for the instant in line, one behind the other, and I directly in line with them when they were struck down, yet was untouched, save by a gob of warm, quivering flesh from one of the victims, which was hurled against my shoulder and stuck tenaciously for some time and the stain for days. Where did the line shot go? Eternity may answer.

In a private letter to the writer from our general, E. P. Alexander, occurs the following:

"This is how it was; it was not prior to Pickett's charge, it was during it. I gave Pickett the signal or order when to charge. He was some distance behind our firing line, in which I had 75 guns. As Pickett's front line passed the guns I galloped down the whole line, from the left flank to the right, ordering every battalion commander to advance every gun, with 15 or 20 rounds of ammunition left. After reaching our right flank with those orders I galloped back to or beyond the centre, where by that time some dozen or more gaps were going forward, and I went with them and brought them into action, firing upon a Federal force, (Staunard's brigade), which moved out to attack Pickett's flank. As soon as I saw that the attack was a failure I ceased fire and reserved ammunition, but held position to cover Pickett's retreat. I remained there for some hours and Gen. Lee came out, without a single member of his staff, or any courier, and remained with me for over half an hour of the time. Evidently he expected Meade to advance and intended himself to help rally the infantry and make the best stand possible."

"You ask why? For what purpose were those guns sent into the very mouth of hell? The answer is very simple. The infantry had gone into the mouth of hell and it was the duty of the artillery to go with them, and I am proud of the fact that the artillery of our corps, in about three hours fighting on the 2nd, and about 2 hours during the charge, on the 3rd, suffered more than the artillery of the other two corps did put together in the whole campaign. Look at the list of casualties and you will see. So at least we were fought up to the handle."

There were two other guns from some command, which had followed in our wake down the dread slope, but had unlimbered some distance in rear and to the right and left of us; thus making our gun the apex and a dread salient for the concentrated fire from the heights. General Alexander says: "I thought there were four guns and all from your battalion (Haskell's) and that two of the four were dismounted by the concentrated fire poured on you by at least twenty guns." Alas, Gettysburg was a disjointed battle and as Col. Taylor has said: "There was an utter absence of accord in the movements of the several commands." In that great scene of smoke, dust, uproar, blood, of columns maneuvering, cannon thundering, men shouting, yelling, cheering, dying; with ears deafened and eyes bedimmed and senses benumbed, one heard nor saw little distinctly. It is the trifles that cling to memory, obscuring the greater events. Capt. Garden mentions a wounded Federal. This writer, too, remembers in rushing down into that vortex, he was appealed to by a man in blue and halted a moment to give him water. Memory preserves the appearance of the luxuriant wheat, the orchard and fruit, but all else than the more accentuated occurrences of that day of wrath are lost.

The following is the inscription set up at Gettysburg Park to mark the location and give the record of Garden's battery on the hill opposite Big Round Top and the Devil's Den:

Army of Northern Virginia, Longstreet's corps, Hood's division, Henry's battalion, Garden's battery. The Palmetto Light Artillery, two Napoleons, two 10 pound Parrots.

July 2, in reserve near here, but not engaged.

July 3, in position here and actively engaged in firing upon the Union lines within range. About 5 p.m. aided in repelling cavalry under Brig. Gen. Farnsworth, which had charged into the valley between this point and Round Top.

July 4, occupied position near and west of this place until 6 p.m., then withdrew from the field.

"Reductio ad absurdum" could properly and literally be added to this inscription, Sic transit Gloria mundi. Mr. Norment was right.—J. Merrick Reid, in News and Courier.

Wee Nee, July 2, 1902

* * *

James Ezra Tindal was the first sergeant of Garden's Battery at Gettysburg. Tindal had graduated Furman University in 1858 and was attending the University of Bonn in Germany when the war broke out. Immediately following the war, he advocated for plans to bring about suffrage for former slaves, contending that they could not be suspended "between slavery and citizenship." Tindal aided in reestablishing the Citadel and South Carolina College (University of South Carolina). He was also a founding trustee of Clemson University.

(Men of Mark in South Carolina Volume 3)

THE ATLANTA JOURNAL

NOVEMBER 8, 1902

Capt. Garden's "Palmetto Battery" at Gettysburg

By James G. Ramsey,

Palmetto Battery, A. N. Va.

While we are enjoined by the Confederate veterans association to urge and aid in the erection of enduring monuments to our leaders as well as heroic soldiers with suitable inscription of their valorous deeds, where found, such has been carried out in hundreds of cities, paying tribute to the Confederate dead.

Battle tablets and bronze cannon on battlefield mark the spot where regiments and batteries went down in bloody conflict. What can be more impressive? The silent story of the dead on the field of battle.

Before I close I shall endeavor to show that many instances where such has been done are not accurate, in some instances, and very misleading. Humanity moves slowly and the world is ready to receive the luminous truth. The world never before so hungered for truth and receive so little. History is being traduced, statements garbled and intoxicated with misleading facts. It is best to be candid and look courageously every problem squarely in the fact. Let the grain discard the chaff. The ostrich who hides his head in the sand does not escape the hand of his pursuer; the march of progress will overcome the wrongdoer. While so much has been written about the gigantic struggle of three days at Gettysburg, how strangely, but how truly has any reference been made of the artillery branch of the service, and I will here mention our battalion in this fight, not forgetting to mention the infantry which we charged with on the second day of the battle.

Patriotism and endurance were characteristic of the Confederate soldier, but there was a limit to the endurance, even of those lion-hearted fellows. We had been marching continuously for 30 days after we left the Rapidan, and to be rushed into this fight footsore and tired, and the

James Hart was a captain commanding Hart's Battery at Gettysburg.

(Stories of the Confederacy)

brilliant achievement, surely such men are worthy of note. Now, I will give an outline of our action. When the order was given for Hood and McLaws' division to storm the impregnable heights of Round Top mountain, the fearful undertaking of dislodging the enemy from his stronghold position, these oaken-hearted soldiers went forward under a baptism of fire from the frowning batteries of 250 cannon over the meadow and up the cannon crowned hills, these legions moved with martial tread, shell and shot ploughing through their sturdy advance, making hideous gaps, and the steady command, "Close up." Such were the scenes in this whirlpool of this high tide battle, a brilliant chapter wrote in letters of blood. This wonderful battle full of action and full of interest to the many thousands who participated in this grand panorama of desolation; men cheering, fighting, falling, the senses almost benumbed from the smoke-thundering cannon.

No word can tell the story of their splendid heroism in the second charge, requiring a degree of patriotism rarely witnessed in the annals of war.

While this charge was not entirely made with infantry, two batteries from this, Haskell's battalion, were ordered to charge with the infantry, [Hugh R.] Garden's [South Carolina] and [James] Reilly's [North Carolina] six gun batteries, something not often done, and very seldom brought into execution. On this occasion we moved forward to this charge under a heavy fire from the enemy's batteries. We charged as far as we could, being impeded at Devil's Den, by a morass, and the steep ascent beyond made this move impracticable. The infantry in the meantime had swept forward, driving line upon line and overran three rifle cannon. Just under the ledge of Roundtop, these cannon were pulled down the steep ascent by hand and General Hood ordered our major, John C. Haskell, to bring up some horses and carry them to the rear. Did any other troops save any captured artillery at Gettysburg? General Hood was severely wounded in the arm by an exploding shell.

General Alexander, being questioned as to the artillery advance, remarked that the infantry had been sent into the mouth of hell, and it was the duty of the artillery to go in with them. We did go in, and fought to the finish. This battalion of 18 guns had expended 1,500 rounds of ammunition in the fight, and the third day preceding Pickett's charge, the four batteries commanded respectively by Captain Reilly, Captain [W. K.] Bachman [South Carolina], Captain Garden and Captain [A. C.] Latham [North Carolina]. These batteries had discharged their duties when nightfall came, and the day to approach the finale seemed ominous with some evil foreboding. The stillness foretold the storm on the morrow by a signal gun in the distance, a bugle call and another day of carnage. The earth trembled with the horrible discharge of 400 guns, thundering from every hilltop. Now, preceding Pickett's charge, every gun was brought into action, so as to have neutralizing effect in this forlorn disastrous attack, many officers agreeing that it was an unguided affair, and as some others have said, there was utter absence of accord in movements of several commands, which brought about some confusion and resulted disastrously to our grand army at Gettysburg.

Now, during this bombardment an order had been issued for the artillery to advance, and before carried into general execution was abandoned, but amid the roar, din and confusion of battle, Lieutenant [William] Alex McQueen, of the Palmetto battery, had ordered, "Limber up, cannoneers, mount, action, front!" No more than a few minutes these brave fellows obeyed, and went down in bloody strife. The line was obliqued to the left, down through the orchard and ascent, two other guns followed in the wake, placing down right and left, in the rear, leaving this gun in the apex of the triangle. There were no skulkers there. These men were at their post and for duty, and the business end of that rifled piece, and went down fighting under a baptism of shot and shell. The engines of war were thundering from every hilltop, sending death-dealing messages upon its wings. In a few minutes six horses lay dead, piled up in harness, a solid shot cleaning up one side of a gun killing Robert [F.] Small and Tom [Thomas Robert] McIntosh, two noble boys, and every man was more or less wounded or stunned around this piece. This gun was many yards in advance of the firing line of 148 pieces in action, and shows the nearest approach of all the artillery in the greatest artillery duel the world ever witnessed. Now the monument that marks the heroic struggle of Garden's Palmetto battery is erected on the eastern slope of the avenue, with two Napoleon guns fastened to an iron carriage, will last for ages. A tablet set to iron post nearly a yard square tells the rest, and fails to name the gallant and knightly John C. Haskell, who had lost an arm at Seven Pines, had commanded this battalion in twenty pitched battles in historic Virginia. Let us render unto Caesar the things belonging to Caesar.

These unwritten records will soon be hushed so far as actual participants are concerned. While the park commission has done wonderful work with its available resources and information, let us hope that the effort being made to induce the government to own this vast battlefield of 16,000 acres in place of a narrow strip and a few hundred acres as now exist will be successful. The absence of monument to the Confederates will imperfectly supply the information to future students of military science and will poorly determine where brigades and regiments went down in bloody conflict at Peach Orchard, Wheat Field, Devil's Den, Round Top, and Little Round Top. The 450 monuments that mark the spot of the Federal's noble defense in repelling the fearful attacks of the Confederates shows that the best blood of the AngloSaxon met here, and the master stroke in this high tide battle, unless remedied, is but one-half represented. The bloody carnage of three days, where over 40,000 fell on both sides, killed, wounded, and missing, and nine generals were killed and 21 severely wounded, tell its own story in the grand cyclorama of desolation. The marking of these spots can be done while survivors are living; in a few more years it will be impossible.

If we remain true to our own convictions we should not be too deeply engrossed by the story and anecdotes to neglect this opportunity. Sentiment is good enough in its place. The fruition is patriotism perfected by deeds of action. The story of this battle is so vividly impressed by the piteous appeals for water in a scorching July sun that it will never be forgotten. A

Federal officer, appealing to be taken from under the dreadful fire, was only supplied a canteen of water from my gallant captain, remarking: "I cannot get my own wounded men under cover."

Such were the closing scenes in this greatest of battles. The battery that was captured was Smith's [4th] New York battery. Now I have written too lengthy. I will relate a particular incident. One of our drivers in urging the horses to greater speed in the charge on Round Top cut himself in the eye and completely destroyed his sight.

* * *

John Cheves Haskell was a member of Garden's Battery. At Gettysburg he was beside Gen. John Bell Hood when Hood received the disabling schrapnel wound to his arm. Afterward Haskell was part of the great artillery duel on July 3rd and witnessed the discussion between Col. E. Porter Alexander and Lt. Gen. James Longstreet launching the famous assault known as Pickett's Charge. Haskell was wounded shortly after by a spent piece of an artillery shell. His brother William was killed during the battle. After the war, Haskell married the daughter of Wade Hampton.

*(The Haskell Memoirs:
The Personal Narrative
of a Confederate Officer)*

CONFEDERATE VETERAN MAGAZINE
AUGUST, 1909

Col. J. C. Haskell.

Col. John Cheves Haskell, who died recently in Columbia, S. C. was widely known as the one-arm quartermaster who never knew when he was whipped. He was one of the artillery officers of Longstreet's Corps, and fought his four batteries of eighteen guns in all the hard battles from the Rapidan to Antietam and the gory field of Gettysburg. It was here that this battery with Hood's Texas. Law's Alabama, and Benning's Georgia Brigades swept forward and captured three rifle guns from Smith's New York Battery. These guns were carried down the hill by hand.

Colonel Haskell lost his arm through an act of bravery. Once in battle he saw a regiment of infantry almost demoralized by the swift action of cannon. Colonel Haskell, mounted on his magnificent sorrel, stopped the tide of retreat, and bidding the regiment follow him, dashed forward to victory—a victory which cost him his right arm. Hood being short of staff officers, Haskell offered his services, even with his arm hanging shattered, but was ordered to report to the hospital instead.

* * *

SUMTER WATCHMAN AND SOUTHRON
JUNE 7, 1913

SURVIVOR TELLS OF GETTYSBURG

W. M. Reid [Garden's Battery] Describes Game Incidents of the Fearful Clash

------

As Gettysburg is interesting everyone just now, I thought that perhaps the experience of a minor actor in that bloody drama would be of interest to your many readers. The writer was a member of Capt. Hugh R. Garden's battery light artillery, Col. John C. Haskell's battalion, Longstreet's corps, A.N.V. This battalion consisted of Reilly's and Flanner's North Carolina and Bachman's and Garden's batteries of South Carolina. We arrived on the battlefield on the morning of July 2 and were placed immediately in action on the extreme right of our line. Our guns opening on Round Top, the guns on which we silenced in a short time with our 14 guns with the loss of one man, two horses and one gun dismounted in Reilly's battery we remained there the rest of the day. While lying there a regiment of Yankee cavalry charged in amongst us, but our cavalry, I think Hampton, soon surrounded and captured them. When their Col. Farquhar saw that he was surrounded he got off his horse, drew his pistol from the holster and blew his brains out. We believed for some time that the act was caused by humiliation at being captured but were told later that there was a price on his head for executing one of our men contrary to the rules of war.

On the morning of the 3rd we were moved to our left and into the historic peach orchard from which we engaged the batteries on Little Round Top. About 1 o'clock orders came for every gun in Longstreet's corps to open on a certain point in front of Pickett's division. This was always done previous to a charge so as to demoralize the enemy. The roar of the guns was awful—far exceeding anything the writer ever heard and he was in all the great battles of Virginia. The very earth seemed to tremble under the concussion. This lasted for about one hour when orders came down the line to cease firing and prepare to follow Pickett's charge. On examination it was found that there was only ammunition enough for one gun in the whole battery. This was placed in the limber chest of our gun. When these arrangements were completed Lieut. W[illiam] A. McQueen, who was in command of the piece, turned to Maj. Haskell and asked when he should move, the reply was "Move at once." We moved out of the orchard and down the slope for 100 yards or more. Not a shot was fired at us until the first shell left the muzzle of our gun and then there was a hail of shot and shell in reply. Gen. [Edward Porter] Alexander, in his history of Longstreet's artillery, says that the Northern account says that there were 210 guns bearing on this gun and also says that the first shell we fired killed and disabled 27 of their men by enfilading their line—anyhow in less than five minutes (this may not be exactly accurate as I don't think any of our crowd was timing things just then), five horses out of the six lay dead, two cannoners dead and three wounded. Lieut. McQueen then called to us to leave which we did without a second summons, and as we were leaving, Pickett's division passed on that grand and awful charge—that is the way that the third gun of Garden's battery "followed up" Pickett's charge. Counting the drivers, there were 11 men in this detachment. The writer, who rammed that fatal shot home, and M. E. Haynesworth, who aimed the gun, are the only living survivors. Gen. Alexander says that the spot is now marked by the United States government by a stone tablet, and the writer hopes to stand on that spot about 3 o'clock on the 3rd day of July, 1913, just 50 years after that awful day. The two splendid boys who gave their lives—cut almost in twain by the same shell—were Bob Small of Charleston and Tom McIntosh of Lynchburg. Lieut. McQueen was killed near his home at Dingle's Mill in Sumter county the day Lee surrendered.

W. M. REID, St. Charles, May 29

* * *

CONFEDERATE VETERAN MAGAZINE
JUNE 1915

CANNONEERS AS CAVALRYMEN.

BY JAMES W. BRUNSON,

FLORENCE, S.C.

A few days before the battle of Gettysburg the artillery of the 3d Corps, A. N. V., was in camp near South Mountain, Md. The long, hot march from Fredericksburg had proved very hard on all the animals of the army, and many of the horses of the artillery were practically exhausted. It seemed, therefore, almost an absolute necessity that fresh animals be secured from the farmers of the surrounding country. These, however, were not to be taken without remuneration. Specific values were to be fixed and quartermaster receipts given in exchange, redeemable in gold at the close of the war.

Pursuant to the idea, a detail of twenty men was made from Pegram's Battalion for the enterprise, commanded by Lieutenant Chamberlayne, Adjutant B. Boswell, I. C. Pettigrew, and myself constituting the contingent from the Pee Dee Light Artillery. Starting early, about ten o'clock we came to a very prosperous-looking farm and asked if we could get lunch. The owner was absent (?), but the lady of the house surprised us with a layout of good things to which we had been strangers for years. She was evidently a lady of education and refinement, neatly dressed in black and wearing a long, old-fashioned gold chain and watch. She presided with an ease and dignity which reminded us of home, and when she calmly remarked, "I hear you gentlemen are looking for horses for your artillery; I am happy to inform you that mine are out of your reach." and some one replied, "Be assured, madam, we are equally so in view of your kind hospitality," it seemed the sentiment of us all. Upon asking the name of an unfinished railroad near by, she answered somewhat sarcastically, I thought, "Stephens's Folly," evidently an unpopular project of Thad Stephens.

David Gregg McIntosh commanded McIntosh's Artillery Battalion at Gettysburg.

(The Long Arm of Lee, Vol. 2 by Jennings Cropper Wise)

Much impressed and with many thanks, she refusing our Confederate money, we bowed ourselves out, mounted our horses, and proceeded some distance on our way when the lieutenant ordered me to take four men and surround a house distant about seven hundred yards on the left. The house was of brick, and we found all doors and blinds closed and no sign of life save a blind bay horse in the adjoining orchard. When we met at the front door, some of the men reported having seen a horse led through the gate into the yard as they rode up. Being unable to find this horse in the yard, the conclusion was unmistakable that he was in the house. After repeated knocking at the door, a pale and greatly frightened woman presented herself. Seeing her distressed condition, I hastened to say: "Do not be frightened, ma'am; we would not hurt a hair of your head. We are looking for horses for our artillery, for which we are willing to pay."

"I have no horse but that one in the orchard," she replied. "You can take him if you want to."

"Where is the horse, ma'am, that was led into the yard a few minutes ago?"

"No horse was brought into the yard."

"O yes. ma'am ; these men saw it led through the gate."

"Then where can it be?" looking around quite innocently.

"Why, in the house, of course."

At this she seemed very much distressed and said: "If you men come into the house, you will scare my poor crazy sister to death." Telling the boys to remain outside. I followed her into a hall with two doors opening on each side and one at the end. The crazy sister was a reality, judging from the facial contortions of a pale woman seated within.

The side doors were readily opened with the remark: "You see no horse is here."

"You have not opened that one," pointing to the end door. Rather spiritedly she said: "Surely you would not go into a lady's bedroom."

"By no means, ma'am: but it is no harm to look in." After some parley, she cracked the door a few inches; but, being unable to see anything but a blank wall, I pushed open the door, and there stood before me a fine bay horse, his feet upon a mantilla to deaden the sound. He seemed to be a pet animal, as he stood with his head and neck over a bed upon which were three little children playing with his mane. The woman rushed forward and, throwing her arms around the horse's neck, screamed out: "You shan't take my dead husband's horse!" The children set up a yell in which the crazy sister joined with a vigor which clearly showed that, though her mind might be out of order, her lungs and vocal organs were sound.

I was certainly in a fix and regretted that I had prosecuted the search, and then atrocities and barbarities perpetrated on our own women and children by the Yankee soldiers flashed through my mind. But before me were the tearful faces of that woman and children, and their appealing cries were ringing in my ears. Going to the front door, I told the outsiders that I had found the horse and directed one of them, whom I knew, to come with me and help me decide whether the horse was really fit for our work. On the way I told him that we must find something the matter with that horse. After a close examination, he, being taller than I, found a little saddle gall on the back, and we pronounced him sore-backed and unfit for artillery. I seized the opportunity to impress upon this woman the barbarities of her own people. She replied that she had had no hand in it.

Our party, having secured about twenty-five horses, had reached the crest of a long hill when we were greeted by a solitary Minie ball flying harmlessly above our heads, and, looking down the hill before us, we descried what appeared to be a small party of Yankee cavalry. We immediately charged, but found, to our sorrow, that we had run into a considerable body of troops which had been hidden by a bend of the road. Within three minutes Chamberlayne and twelve of our men were captured, Boswell among the number. Eight of us were saved by the led horses rushing in and cutting us off from the Yankees and blocking the road. We wheeled and took to our heels, the loose horses so blocking the road as to give us some fifty yards the start and then so hindering the pursuit that we kept pretty well ahead. Pettigrew, however, had unfortunately, in order to rest his horse, changed his saddle to a large Pennsylvania draft animal, which had neither speed nor bottom. My horse was thoroughbred, of Planet stock, and I was holding him in to keep pace with my friend and kinsman. After a race of about two miles, Pettigrew's horse fell, blood gushing from his mouth and nostrils. At that time the Yankees were about sixty yards behind. Throwing one foot out of stirrup, I called to Pettigrew: "Get your overcoat and jump behind me." "Never mind the overcoat," said he and sprang up behind me. I gave my horse the spur, and we soon faded from the sight of our pursuers. The enemy must have had poor horses, or they would have picked us up before Pettigrew's horse fell, and they were certainly poor shots; for, although they kept up a fusillade with their repeating carbines, they failed to hit anything, unless possibly Pettigrew's horse, the immediate cause of whose death we deemed it unwise at that particular time to investigate.

We reached camp about ten o'clock at night, a pair of tired and disgusted men; for we had not only failed to get any fresh horses, but had lost our gallant Chamberlayne, with twelve of our brave fellows, to say nothing of twelve of our best artillery horses. But tired as we were, we fed and faithfully rubbed down the splendid animal that by his speed and bottom had saved us from the horrors of a Yankee prison.

James Lane Napier was a member of the Pee Dee Artillery at Gettysburg. He graduated from the Medical College of South Carolina in 1868. He later became the president of the South Carolina Medical Association and the state board of medical examiners.

(Men of Mark in South Carolina Volume 2)

~*Section 5*~

Miscellaneous

James Connor of Charleston, S.C. graduated from South Carolina College in the same class as Col. D. Wyatt Aiken of the 7th S.C. Infantry. At Gettysburg he was in command of the 22nd North Carolina Infantry. He was later promoted to Brig. Gen. to command Kershaw's former brigade. Before the war, Connor was the state's attorney who prosecuted the captain of the Wanderer, the last ship caught attempting to illegally import African slaves into South Carolina.

(Library of Congress)

Chapter 1

Miscellaneous

Charleston Daily News
July 13, 1870

THE CAROLINA DEAD
Names of our Soldiers whose Graves at Gettysburg can be Identified

The following list, for which we are indebted to Mrs. Brown, the secretary of the Hollywood Memorial Association, of Richmond, Va., shows the names of the South Carolina soldiers buried at Gettysburg, whose graves can be identified:

[Captain] T[homas] J. Warren, Company [D], 15th Regiment

Nicholas Hill, Battery A

Lieutenant M[ilton] P. Buzzard [Buzhardt], Company B, 3rd Regiment

Lieutenant [Captain] G[eorge] F. McDowell, Company F, 2nd Regiment

Lieutenant [1st Sergeant] W. F. Wessin [Wessinger], Company [I], 15th Regiment

Second Lieutenant George C. Brazington, Company H, 2nd Regiment

Joel Miller, Company [M], 7th Regiment

H[ampton] Vanderford, Company H, 15th Regiment

J. C. Wansill, Company __, 8th Regiment

E. M. or W. Burgess,[85] Company H, 15th Regiment

E. Aames, Company __, 8th Regiment

Captain T[homas] E[rasmas] Powe, Company C, 8th Regiment

R. W. Person, Company C, 2d Regiment

Lieutenant W[illiam] R. Thomas, Company K, 3rd Regiment

Sergeant __Roberson,[86] Company E, 15th Regiment

J[ames] H. Cassan, Company A, 2d Regiment

J[ohn] T. Eady, Company G, 15th Regiment

Captain R[obert] C. Pulliam, Company B, 2d Regiment

Lieutenant __ Mondymady, Company F, 3d Regiment

Sergeant S. K. Wearrell, company F, 8th Regiment

E.P. Pulley, Company B, 3d Regiment

Sergeant W[alter] Isbell, Company C, 2d Regiment

W[illiam] W. Koon, Company I, 15th Regiment

Lieutenant A. A. Fuller, (James's Battery B)

George W. Smith, (Jordan's Battery), Company E, 21st Regiment

J. Bligh, Company D, 2d Regiment

W. E. Felder, Company D, 2d Regiment

W. R. Ballard, Company D, 2d Regiment

W. E. C. Fulmer,[87] Company F, 34th Regiment

Sergeant T[homas] L. Butler, (Cavalry), Company [I], 2d Regiment

G[eorge] W. Parker, Company F, 1st Regiment

R. M. Love, Company G, 2d Regiment

H[enry] W. Wilkerson, Company H, [2d] Regiment

---

85. Franklin Burges
86. Hugh Robinson
87. William E. C. Fulmer, Co. F, 3rd S.C. Battalion

Sergeant D. R. Ryan, Company E, [2d] Regiment

J. W. Polk, Company E, [2d] Regiment

W. R[iley] Allen, Company E, [2d] Regiment

Sergeant John C. Mayo, Company G, 1st Regiment

T. A[ugustus] Rhodes, Company [H], 1st Regiment

P. M. Nell (Parker's Battery)

J. B. Longbridge (Parker's Battery)

Felix Reulan (3d Company, W. A., of New Orleans)

Corporal J. M. Dance, Company E, 1st Regiment

C. Hamman, Company A, 1st Regiment

T. Hayes (Rhett's Battery)

W. P. Casey (Rhett's Battery)

William Layman, Company __, __ Regiment

W. A. of New Orleans 2d Company

S. Martin (Rhett's Battery)

P. Hill, (Battery 3d), Company F

J. W. Stewart, (Battery 3d), Company B

Sergeant M. W. Wolf, (Battery 3d), Company D

Y. L. (Culbertson's Battery 3d), Company D

E. R. Stokes, (Battery 3d), Company F

J. W. Toarth, (Battery 3d)

Lieutenant B. B. McGowan, (Battery) Company K

[Lieutenant] J[ohn] H[enry] Walker, Company D, 3d Regiment

A. H. Starnes, Company D, 3rd Regiment

Captain T. J. Vance, __ Company, 1st Regiment

B. R. Smith, Company M, 7th Regiment

Sergeant W[illiam] L. McCurrie, Company [D], 7th Regiment

M[astin] C. McCall, Company K, 8th Regiment

M[alc] McP[herson], [K] Company, 8th Regiment

* * *

EDGEFIELD ADVERTISER
APRIL 20, 1871

The South Carolina Dead at Gettysburg

The Baltimore Sun of Monday says: "Mrs. M. A. Snowden and several other ladies reached this city on Saturday morning, from Charleston, as delegates from the Memorial Association of that city, on their way to Gettysburg, Pa., for the purpose of making final arrangements for the removal to their own State of the remains of all South Carolinians who fell in the memorable battle at that place. The party, accompanied by several ladies of Baltimore, design leaving for Gettysburg tomorrow.

* * *

CHARLESTON DAILY NEWS
MAY 11, 1871

MEMORIAL CELEBRATION

The remains of eighty South Carolinians, who fell upon the bloody field of Gettysburg, were yesterday reinterred at Magnolia Cemetery. The preparations which have been in progress for the past week, culminated in the solemn ceremonies around the graves, and seldom have we seen a more impressive spectacle than was exhibited yesterday on that hallowed square. The memories of the past, which seem of late to have been smothered up by our present troubles, were once more awakened, and few who stood upon that solemn ground who did not feel the influence produced by them. The long rows of freshly made graves spoke louder than trumpets, and the cause for which they died was invested with a brighter glory by the immensity of their sacrifice. They died upon the soil of an enemy, and yesterday saw the latest prayer of many of them granted, that they should sleep their long lost sleep in the bosom of their native Carolina. The wives, mothers and sisters who sent them forth to battle remembered these dying words, and after a long interval of untiring energy and labor in the great and hallowed cause, they have fulfilled their wishes. All honor to the ladies who have assisted in this sacred work.

The bright morning was propitious to a celebration of the kind, and at an early hour, masses of evergreens, beautiful crosses and chaplets, and lovely bouquets of flowers were to be seen borne about the streets. The extensive decorations in the Hibernian Hall, from the late fair of the Sisters of Mercy, were taken down to form material for the decorations, and various wagons, with their vernal freight, variegated with baskets of flowers, could be seen traveling the city. At 2 o'clock, by general consent, the leading establishments on our principal streets were closed, and the population turned out en masse, to do honor to the remains of the fallen heroes. The street cars on the up trips were jammed; everybody was hurrying to the railroad depots.

The trains on the South Carolina and Northeastern Railroads were much longer than usual. On one train alone there were thirteen passenger cars, and every one full. Up to the minute that the last train left the depot, ladies and gentlemen, and the inevitable small boys, could be seen hurrying up, but at last the whistle blew, and the long train of cars moved rapidly up to the Forks of the Road.

Alighting here, the visitors walked up the avenue, and were soon at the burial ground of the Confederate dead. In addition to the railroad trains, vast numbers of impromptu vehicles were plying along the roads, and over 6000 persons must have been upon the grounds. The road from the gate of the cemetery, within the grounds, was thronged with vehicles, and the vast concourse of people were densely crowded around the speaking stand, at the northeast corner of the Confederate burial ground.

The ceremonies were introduced by Lieutenant-General R[ichard] H[eron] Anderson, who excused the absence of the venerable Dr. Bachman, and announced that the Rev. Ellison Capers had been requested to take his place.

Mr. Capers then offered the following prayer:

"O! Thou great, good and merciful God—Thou Father of compassion and god of all consolation and grace in Christ Jesus our Lord, to thee we bring our humble tribute of praise and thanksgiving. We are unworthy and sinful—Thou art holy and worthy to be exalted for evermore. O! God! be with us, in this hour, when with sad hearts we exclaim, lover and friend hast Thou put far from us and our acquaintance into darkness. We have gathered today around the remains of the beloved and honored dead, who were not alone bound to us by the strong ties of kindred and affection, but to whom we owe a deep debt of gratitude, for these sleeping patriots shed their blood in our defense.   And whilst we place upon their graves memorial garlands of love, affection and gratitude, wilt Thou Heavenly Father, engrave upon our hearts the remembrance of their virtues, and teach us to emulate their patriotic love of country? Impress upon our hearts, everlasting God, the solemn lesson of mortality here taught us, and, whilst we linger around the hallowed mounds under which our dead heroes lie, let us look beyond—above, and prepare, by lives of innocence, virtue, benevolence and faith, to join our departed ones in that land where sorrows are ended and partings are unknown. Have mercy, dear Father in heaven, upon the beloved relatives and friends of the dead. Comfort the widow and the orphan, and provide for their necessities. And we beseech Thee look in mercy upon our distracted land; remove the evil; let wisdom guide our counsels, and prosperity smile again upon our land. Finally, may Thy holy religion be widely diffused until the whole earth be filled with Thy glory. In the name and for the sake of the Lord Jesus Christ, Amen.

The following beautiful ode, written expressly for the occasion by Dr. J. Dickson Bruns, and set to music by Prof. Thomas P. O'Neale, was sung by the children of the Confederate Home, led by Mr. O'Neale and assisted by a powerful chorus of bass voices on the stage:

Ode

BY DR. J. DICKSON BRUNS

Hushed be the clamor of the mart,
Stifled as when stricken peoples pray;
For through a fallen nations heart
We bring our heroes' dust today.

Let all her sons a Sabbath keep
In their proud city by the Sea,
And come, whoever loves to weep
The broken lance of Chivalry.

Come Honor with thy dinted shield,
And Valor with thy shivered glaive;

And from the sod where Faith hath kneeled,
Rise justice from her trampled grave!

And come, O dove-eyed Peace; who long
From this, our desolate land, hath strayed,
And let us dream that Hate and Wrong
With these our brothers' bones are laid!

Twine Amaranth for the noble dead,
Nor be the victor-leaf forgot,
And, while the parting prayer is said,
Strew Heart's Ease and Forget-me-not.

For these no sculptured shaft shell rise,
Nor stolen urn emblazon them,
But sobbing waves and waning skies
Will sound their fitting requiem.

And, year by year, a form unseen
Shall deck the turf we heap today,
To keep their fadeless memories green,
Who fell, in vain, for liberty.

So guard, O God! this sacred dust,
Which we with prayers and tears would bless,
And be Thou still the Widow's trust,
And Father of the Fatherless.

The Rev. J. L. Girardeau, D. D., next delivered the address. To give a synopsis of this speaker's words would be an injustice to his splendid effort, and convey but a faint impression of its power and beauty. His soul-stirring words met with a warm sympathy from his audience, and his master delineation of the present situation, its tendencies, and our proper course, excited the deepest interest. His closing appeal and invocation to those whose obsequies were being celebrated was touching and beautiful, and many an eye filled with tears.

Mr. Edward R. Miles then read a poem prepared for the occasion. It referred to the solemn ceremonies of the day and was filled with beautiful thoughts. The allusion to the bells of St. Michael's seemed particularly happy and touching. The affecting ode written by the Rev. C. S. Vedder upon the return of the Gettysburg dead was then sung by the children of the Home. It is as follows:

Ode,

UPON THE RETURN OF THE GETTYSBURG DEAD

BY REV. C. S. VEDDER

Room! for the banished room!
Room, on their Mother's breast;
She calls them from their stranger tomb,
To hold them to her rest!
Room! where their native sky
May arch their peaceful sleep;
Room! where the martyr comrades lie—
Their living comrades weep!

Room! for their Sisters' tears
Have mourned them long in vain,
And tributes down through all the years,
Shall fall in loving rain!

Room! where their native Pine
May sentinel their dust,
And Cypress and Magnolia twine
Their garlands for the just!

Room! where the spreading Oak
May mourn a nation's loss,

And droop o'er budding promise broke,
Its sad funereal moss!

Room! by the sobbing sea,
Room! near the saddened street,
Room! where their sepulchres may be
Meccas for pilgrim feet!

Room! 'tis their Mother calls,
She sent them from her sides,
For her they stood, as living walls,
For her they grandly died!

Room! for the exiled, room!
Room, in our inmost hearts,
While tearful Love can guard their tomb
Till Life itself departs!

While the ode was being sung the open graves were being filled up, after which the ladies of the Memorial Association began the work of decorating the graves. On each lowly stone was placed a chaplet, frequently varied by beautiful crosses of evergreen and flowers. Not one was forgotten, and the tender and loving manner with which the work was done showed the deep feelings of the fair decorators. In the centre of the burial ground was a large evergreen cross, covered with white lilies, and standing upon a raised mound. It formed a beautiful central figure and emblem to the lowly graves around.

The remains which were reinterred are not yet furnished with head-stones, but this will be attended to shortly.

The following is the list of those South Carolinians who were buried at Gettysburg, Pennsylvania, in consequence of wounds inflicted during the battle of July 1st, 2nd and 3rd, 1863, and whose graves were marked and could yet be identified:

Camp Letterman Burying Ground

W.C.C. Fullmer,[88] section 1, grave 34, company F, 34th regiment

Sergeant T[homas] E. Gaillard, section 2, grave 5, company F, 2nd regiment

F. L. Nettles, section 3, grave 31, company E, 2nd regiment

T. J. Turner, section 4, grave 4, company G, 22nd regiment

Jacob H. Clancy, section 4, grave 5, company G, 13th regiment

H. S. Jones, section 5, grave 16, company G, 7th regiment

Lieutenant [Nathaniel] Austin, section 3, grave 27, company E, 14th regiment

F. T. Derrick, section 5, grave 31, company I, 15th regiment

H. M. Paysenger, section 7, grave 12, company E, 3rd regiment

Austin Nabos, section 7, grave 13, company G, 2nd regiment

E. R. Enrick,[89] section 7, grave 15, company C, 15th regiment

Sergeant P. T. Dickson, section 9, grave 1, company C, 2nd regiment

**Buried at Rose's, under large cherry tree, back of the barn:

R. M. Love, company G, 2nd regiment

H[enry] W. Wilkerson, company H, 2nd regiment

Sergeant D. R. Ryan, company E, 2nd regiment

J. K. Polk, company E, 2nd regiment

W. R. Allen, company E, 2nd regiment

**Buried in McMillan's Orchard, under apple tree, near General Pickett's Division line of fortifications:

Sergeant John C. Mayo, company G, 1st regiment

[Sergeant] T. A[ugustus] Rhodes, company G, 1st regiment

**Buried in Rose's Meadow Peach Orchard:

W[illiam] N. Riley, company F, 2nd regiment

88. William E. C. Fulmer, Co. F, 3rd S.C. Battalion
89. E. R. Amick

J[ohn] M. Reynolds, company F, 2nd regiment

W[illiam] W. Waller, company F, 2nd regiment

W[illiam] G. Lomax, company F, 2nd regiment

J[eremiah] F. Roberts, company A, 2nd regiment

W. M. Roach, company A, 2nd regiment

**Buried in Apple Orchard, at Black horse Tavern:

Sergeant D[aniel] Q. McDuffie, company I, 8th regiment

T[homas S.] Hampton, company H, 8th regiment

**Buried northwest of Rose's Barn, under Peach Tree:

Captain Wilson, 2nd regiment

**Buried north of Rose's, inside the fence, on south side of Emmetsburg Road under apple tree, near the Meadow Stream:

J. Bligh, company D, 2nd regiment

W. E. Felder, company D, 2nd regiment

W. R. Ballard (or Bannard), company D, 2nd regiment

**Buried in the woods, east of Crawford's tenement house:

G. W. Smith, company E, Jordan's Battery

**Buried North of Black Horse Tavern, near the Creek and Graveyard:

E. P. Pulley, company B, 3rd regiment

Sergeant W[alter D.] Isbell, company C, 2nd regiment

W[illiam] W. Koon, company I, 15th regiment

Lieutenant A. A. Fuller, James' Battery

J[ames] H. Casson, company A, 2nd regiment

J[ohn] T. Eaddy, company G, 15th regiment

Captain R[obert] C. Pulliam, company B, 2nd regiment

Lieutenant W[illiam] R. Thomas, company K, 3rd regiment

[Color Sergeant] E[lijah] Adams, company K, 8th regiment

F[ranklin] M. Burgess, company H, 15th regiment

J. C. Wansill, 8th regiment

H[ampton] Vanderford, company H, 15th regiment

Joel Miller, 7th regiment

Second Lieutenant George C. Brasington, company H, 2nd regiment

Lieutenant W. F. Wissen, 15th regiment

Lieutenant George M. McDowell, company F, 2nd regiment

Lieutenant M. P. Buzzard, company B, 3rd regiment

Nicholas Hill Batty, company A, 3rd regiment

W. R. Person, company C, 2nd regiment

**Buried opposite Rose's house, under peach tree:

Captain T[homas] J. Warren, company A, 15th regiment

**Buried near the barn on Crawford's tenant farm:

T. Hayes, Rhett's Battery

The following are the names of those South Carolinians whose graves were marked, but which could not now be identified separately, and hence will be grouped as they were buried:

P. Hill, battery 3rd, company B

W. P. Miller, battery 3rd, company B

J. W. Stewart, battery 3rd, company E

Sergeant W. Y. Wolf, battery 3rd, company D

Sergeant Y. L. Culbertson, battery 3rd, company C

Sergeant J. W. Foarthe, battery 3rd, company C

Lieutenant M. P. McGowan, battery 3rd, company K

Lieutenant P. B. Longford, company E, 8th regiment

Lieutenant J. M. Potter,[90] company H, 15th regiment

Sergeant E. W. Eure, company H, 15th regiment

Sergeant J. T. Spears, company E, 15th regiment

90. Joseph M. Porter

F. W. Lewis, company E, 15th regiment

T[homas] W. Sligh, [3rd S.C. Infantry, Company E]

**Buried west of Rose's barn, under a large cherry tree:

Edward J. Mills, company I, 2nd regiment

T[homas] S. Gadsden, company I, 2nd regiment

**Buried in Rose's garden:

S. C. Miles, company I, 2nd regiment

This list is prepared by a Northern gentleman who is not familiar with the names and regiments of South Carolina. On this account a few slight inaccuracies could scarcely be avoided.

As soon as the decoration was over, the dense crowds hurried out of the cemetery, under the threatening approach of a heavy black cloud. The train was in waiting and the thousands were quickly whirled to the city.

* * *

CHARLESTON DAILY NEWS
JUNE 25, 1872

THE GETTYSBURG DEAD
South Carolina Soldiers Interred at Hollywood

The following is a list of the names of the South Carolina soldiers, whose remains have been removed from Gettysburg, and interred in Hollywood Cemetery, Richmond, Va.:

Lieutenant G[eorge] M[atthew] Meyers, Company H, 8th Regiment; Lieutenant H. W. Werther, Company H, 8th Regiment; Lieutenant W[illiam] C. Hodges, Company B, 7th Regiment; Lieutenant W[illiam] C. Barmore,[91] Company [B], 7th Regiment; Sergeant W[illiam] L. McCurry, Company D, 7th Regiment; Corporal W[illiam] H. Mathers,[92] Company I, 7th Regiment;

91. Compiled Service Records indicate his rank was Private.
92. William H. Mathis

M[astin] C. McColl, Company K, 8th Regiment; H. McL, Company G, 8th Regiment; J. R. Blouch, Company A, 8th Regiment; C. Bening, Company A, 8th Regiment; R. Mainson, Company B, 8th Regiment; J. M. McIntosh, Company G, 8th Regiment; A. McPherson, Company H, 8th Regiment; J. D. Rhodes, Company F, 8th Regiment; T. N. Pressley, ____, ____ ; W. Dickson, Company D, 8th Regiment; ____ Thurling, Company I, 7th Regiment; S. C. Ridgeway, [Company I], [7th Regiment]; M. McP____, Company ____, 8th Regiment; B. R. Smith, Company M, 7th Regiment; J. K. Easterling, Company G, 8th Regiment; J. B. Robbins, Company I, 8th Regiment; A. McLand, Company G, 8th Regiment; H. R. Adams, Company G, 8th Regiment; A. J. Jennings, Company B, 2nd Regiment; C. A. M____, Company B, 2nd Regiment; C. A. Markley, Company B, 2nd Regiment; ____ Trapain, Company ____, 7th Regiment.

For the unselfish devotion which has sustained them in their arduous task, and for the loving care with which they have held sacred the bones of our dead, the people of the whole South owe the ladies of the Hollywood Memorial Association a debt of everlasting gratitude. South Carolina, at least, will never forget what they have done for her fallen sons.

＊

Anderson Intelligencer
May 27, 1880

Wade Hampton and His Leg

It is rather mournful to look at Wade Hampton in the Senate, nursing his stump of a leg and subjecting his splendid physique to the disgrace of crutches. He is the only cripple in the body- I mean visibly so. To be sure his colleague, the dashing [Maj. Gen. Matthew Calbraith] Butler [South Carolina], has but one leg, but you might watch him move about for ten years and not know it, so perfectly does he manage his cork. To be sure, too, there are men who suffer, sometimes intensely, for trying to stop bullets in the late unpleasantness, like [Lt. Gen. John Brown] Gordon [Georgia] and [Brig. Gen. Matthew Whitaker] Ransom [North Carolina] and [Maj. Gen. Samuel Bell] Maxey [Texas]; but their infirmities are not visible. Not so with Hampton. He is in the very prime of his life, scarcely over fifty, and a hopeless cripple. Nobody feels pain in looking at Aleck Stephens, for his case is just the result of a slow and natural process of decay, which he rather seems to relish. But you insensibly feel a deep sympathy with Hampton's loss as with the late Senator Morton's infirmities, because both came along prematurely, like the hurricane on the oak, and marred powerful frames. And the General croons over his abbreviated limb all the time- not in any growing or testy spirit, for he is the soul of patience, but it must be remembered that his whole life has been one of nerve, vim, dash, and his present forced inactivity must only intensify the memory of his daring exploits and "moving accidents by flood and field." Can it be supposed that when Morton sat in the Senate, a big, chained dog, the defenseless prey of the smallest cur that had legs and could use hem, he never fretted at the picture of his past activity, when he used to bound into the saddle at the Governor's office in war times, and dash to camp or arsenal, the very embodiment of physical vigor as he lashed his horse to a white foam through the excited streets? No wonder, then, that while the General nurses his leg, he also nurses mainly regrets. Several interesting incidents happened lately in a single day, as told by one of Hampton's intimate friends. The General, in the hope of picking up some views about cut legs, has a way of stopping people similarly afflicted. As he was standing on his crutches in the main hall, near the Senate entrance, a large man came along, his right leg lost above the knee, and he had some patient arrangement that seemed like a framework, light and portable, to help him out of his scrape. Accosting him, Hampton spoke of their mutual infirmities, and asked how that arrangement worked. "Very well," replied the stranger. "It is an invention of my own"- and he went on the explain it. "May I ask where you lost your leg?" inquired the General. "Yes, certainly, it went off when Hampton charged our battery at Gettysburg." "Indeed; I'm grieved to hear it," said the General, very sincerely. "My name is Hampton." They shook hands very warmly over the bloody chasm, and the stranger turned out to be Representative Caulk, of Wisconsin.

Later in the day the General was on his way home in the street car when a man entered with only one arm, the other gone at the socket. The General invited him to a seat and managed the payment of his fare.

"Where did you lose your arm?" asked Hampton.

"Well, sir, it was at Gettysburg," answered the man, "when Hampton made that terrific charge with his cavalry."

Whereupon those two shook hands and made up and the man now

says that if Hampton is put on the Democratic ticket, he will swallow it hook and line. It was on the same bloody field that [Maj. Gen. Alfred] Pleasanton and Hampton met as rival cavalry leaders, and they met only on Wednesday last over the pipe of peace. Pleasanton was enchanted with his old enemy, and said that he was the only soldier he ever heard of who told the whole truth in case of defeat. Let me tell another instance of Hampton's kindheartedness, and then the reader can possibly judge why it is that he is the idol of the colored race of the South. Recently, it will be remembered, he went to Mississippi on the death of his son. While there he met with three old slaves of his. They called to pay their respects, and in and apologetic way told "Massa Wade" that they had to fight for their freedom and hoped he did not feel bad about it. On inquiry he learned of them that all three had been wounded on board the "Monarch" during the war. They knew nothing of how their account stood, or might stand under the law, with the United States Treasury, and the General's first act when he came back was to obtain them pensions. That's the way the "rebel briga-diers" are depriving the Southern negroes of their rights.

-Brooklyn Eagle Letter-

* * *

News and Courier
Anderson, South Carolina
July 27, 1882

M'GOWAN'S BRIGADE AND THE PART IT PLAYED AT GETTYSBURG

The Confederate Victory July 1, 1863—Advancing Mid a Storm of Shot and Shell—The Losses Immense—Incidents of Personal Daring—importance of the Engagement

ANDERSON, S. C., July 12

To the Editor of the News and Courier: Under the Act of Congress approved June 9, 1880, entitled "An Act to complete the survey of the Gettysburg battlefield, and to provide for the compilation and preservation of data, showing the various positions and movements of troops at that battle illustrated by diagrams," I was requested by Col. D. Wyatt Aiken, M. C., to meet Col. John B. Batchelder, the historian and a landscape painter, to whom the work was committed under said Act, and to point out the positions and movements of McGowan's Brigade in order to preserve our Confederate success on that hard-fought battlefield. Col. Batchelder also wrote me to meet him and the Union officers commanding the opposing forces on the first day of the battle, and fixed June 14th for the day of the meeting.

We met, as requested, and spent two days in the work, one of which was taken chiefly with the battle of the first day. There was not the least difficulty in establishing every position and movement of the brigade, in all of which the Union officers concurred with me. We had stakes driven into the ground at all proper points and Col. Batchelder assured me that he would take pleasure in giving us a correct showing in his illustration of the battle.

The Union officers frankly admit their defeat, and the retreat through the town, qualifying it with their weary condition from long forced marches. As heavy were our losses, theirs were much greater.

In May last you requested me to write up one of the battles of McGowan's Brigade for the Weekly News, which was also urged on me by officers of the brigade, and I have taken Gettysburg.

Very truly yours,

JOSEPH N. BROWN

McGowan's South Carolina Brigade at Gettysburg

[By Lieut.-Col. Joseph N. Brown, 17th S.C.V.]

Gen. McGowan and Capt. A. C. Haskell, were both severely wounded at Chancellorsville, May 3, 1863, and Col. Abner Perrin, of the Fourteenth South Carolina, commanded the Brigade on the Pennsylvania campaign, with Lieut. J. G. Barnwell, of the First, as his A. A. G. The field officers of the several regiments were: Major C. W. McCreary, First; Major W. M. Haddon, Orr's Rifles; Col. J. L. Miller, Lieut.-Col. H. C. Davis, and Major E. F. Booker, Twelfth; Col. B. T. Brockman and Lieut.-Col. I. F. Hunt,

Thirteenth; Lieut.-Col. Joseph N. Brown and Major Edward Croft, Fourteenth, and Capt. W. T. Haskell, of the First, commanded the Battalion of Sharpshooters.

On the thirtieth day of June, 1863, the armies of Gens. Lee and Meade were in Pennsylvania. The long march from the Rappahannock had relieved both armies of all their weak and faint-hearted, and none but brave and strong men had marched there to battle. They went there prepared in their minds for hard fighting, and the make-up of the mind has much to do in making the fight of the soldier. The Union soldier had now been recalled from Virginia to defend his own soil.

On the morning of the 30th day of June A. P. Hill's corps moved from the Cumberland Valley and, crossing the mountains to the eastern side, encamped near their base. Pender's light division of this corps comprised the four brigades of Gen. E. L. Thomas, of Georgia, Gen. James H. Lane, of North Carolina, Gen. A. M. Scales, of North Carolina, and Gen. Samuel McGowan, of South Carolina.

THE LINE OF BATTLE

On the morning of the first day of July an early conflict appeared imminent. McGowan's brigade was called to arms. Artillery and infantry were passing towards Gettysburg, six miles distant. Artillery firing opened in front. Maj. Haddon, with Orr's regiment, was detached from the brigade for guard duty. The remainder of the brigade, with the field and staff officers already mentioned, moved towards the town. A line of battle was formed, with Gen. Lane's brigade on the right, McGowan's in the centre, and Gen. Scales on the left. The left rested on the Chambersburg turnpike. Gen. Thomas' brigade was not in line. Gen. Perrin gave orders to the field and staff, and then communicated to the rank and file, that they were to move forward without firing. That they were not to stop under any circumstances, but to close in, press the enemy close, and rout it from its position. The firing of artillery increased and that of small arms began. This continued for several hours, during which time the brigade approached nearer the scene of action, resting at intervals in the shaded woods. Rumors of disaster and success alternately passed along the lines, derived from the wounded and prisoners. Gen. Reynolds, commanding the Union army, had been killed. Gen. Archer, of our army, had been wounded, and he, with most if his brigade of Gen. Heth's Division, had been captured. But upon the whole the advantage was on our side, and by 4 o'clock p.m. the Union army had fallen back to a line of hastily constructed breastworks of earth, rails and the like on the slope fronting and west of the Lutheran Seminary, one-fourth of a mile west of the town. This line was continued by a strong stone fence beginning some two hundred yards south of the Seminary near a brick house, and running southwardly along the crest of Seminary Ridge, and a little further back, or east, than the breastworks. On the turnpike, and near the Seminary, the Union artillery was strongly posted, being on our left. As thus presented Gen. Scales on our left had on his left flank all this artillery and in his front the rail and earthworks above described full on Union soldiers pressed back, but not defeated, and replenished with fresh troops from the rear.

In front of McGowan's brigade were the breastworks, defended by the same line continuing southward. In front of Gen. Lane was the strong stone fence, behind which was posted a strong line of dismounted cavalry with repeating rifles, which outflanked him. The ground from which these works and the stone fence presented a gradually declining slope to the valley westward; then on a level of about two hundred yards, then a like gradual ascent up to the crest of the ridge, making perhaps half a mile from crest to crest, and presenting the fairest field and finest front for destruction on an advancing foe that could well be conceived.

THE ASSAULT

If, in this position of affairs the brigades of Gens. Scales and Lane should fail to keep pace with McGowan's in the assault to be made, it would be no disparagement of their gallant officers and men. It was an impossibility. The centre must be broken.

The order to advance was now given. The order to hold fire until ordered forward and close in on the enemy was repeated. The Thirteenth Regiment was on the right, next to it the Fourteenth, next Twelfth, and next the First. Passing a burning house on our right and crossing a small run, the brigade mounted the hill beyond and passed over the crippled lines of Gen. Pettigrew's brigade, which, after hours of gallant fighting, had been withdrawn and were resting from their toils.

In front and in view amid the grove of trees was the Seminary, now changed from the halls of learning to a scene of bloodshed and carnage. Beyond was a beautiful town partly concealed from view by the shade trees surrounding the Seminary. Its 3,000 inhabitants were a thrifty, industrious and moral people. Crests of ridges in successive ranges stretched southwardly with the richest valleys between. Beyond and to the south of the town rising still higher was Cemetery Heights, so soon to become historical ground. It was but the glance of the eye for a moment, and then its grandeur was lost in the tumult of battle.

STORM OF SHOT AND SHELL

The advancing columns now moved on and encountered the storm of shot and shell from the batteries on the turnpike fronting Gen. Scales, and pressed on as ordered, without firing until the line of breastworks in front became a sheet of fire and smoke, sending its leaden missiles of death in the faces of the men who had often, but never so terribly, met it before. The impenetrable masses of artillery and infantry in front and on the flank of Gen. Scales impeded his progress, enfilading and sweeping his whole front. He was wounded, and every field officer of his brigade, save one, had fallen. In like manner, on our right, Gen. Lane was held in check by the stone wall in his front, and the cavalry on his flank, threatening certain destruction if his advance continued. The valley had nearly been reached. The want of support on the right and left exposed the brigade to a raking enfilade fire from both right and left without abatement in front.

STILL FORWARD

To stop was destruction. To retreat was disaster. To go forward was "orders." Then Gen. Perrin on horseback dashing through the lines of the brigade, and with his flashing sword in the evening sunshine and his voice above the din of battle, directed and led the charge. Three hundred yards yet intervened between the advancing column and the breastwork in front, and the assailing forces with quickened pace pushed forward amid the Minnie balls sweeping the earth in front and flank. The dead, the wounded and the dying were falling at every step. Our firing had begun in earnest, and was pouring in on the enemy thick and fast.

THE CREST OF THE RIDGE

The enemy in front of the Seminary were closely massed, and strongly supported at the building as well as from the rear and on its flanks. The lines from this point curved slightly back on either side near to the crest of the Ridge, and this made the Seminary the salient or point of attack, and to break the line and take the breastworks here the brigade threw itself against it with all its fury. Here the opposing forces grappled with each other, one determined to hold its position, and the other determined to take it. The close quarters at which they were now engaged made the losses on both sides heavy. By this time the brigade had attained a point which exposed it to a raking fire from the cavalry with repeating rifles behind the stone fence on our right. Its greatest force was spent on the Thirteenth and Fourteenth with deadly effect. But they maintained their unbroken front, closing in, and replying in all directions whence the missiles of destruction came. The ever solid Twelfth with unbroken front pressed on and was dealing deadly blows in its front, carrying terror before it. The First on our left, outflanked and enfiladed, pressed on in the usual contest, drawing closer to the breastworks, approached firmly and steadily along at equal pace with its comrades, though confronting such fearful odds against it, both in front and on the flank.

THE FIELD WON

The desired point was at last reached. The brigade carried the works, and the centre was thus broken and the field was ours. The whole line then gave way, and the Union soldiers, Pennsylvanians they were, after making such heroic resistance were pressed back, closely followed, with fearful loss. While the contending forces were thus grappling at close quarters at the breastworks, the artillery limbered up and was making for the rear. This timely prudence alone saved it. The stone wall on our right was carried, and the whole field was ours. The Thirteenth and Fourteenth had suffered most from those repeating rifles. The Union columns were broken, pressed back, at first rapidly and disorderly, with our men close to them, still pouring into their ranks a deadly fire. As they neared the town they became more massed, and moved more slowly and stubbornly, with lines still broken. As they were entering the town they looked backwards, as if half minded to turn on the pursuing foe and renew the conflict. But doubtless their movements were obstructed by the crowded streets in their front. Gen. Abner Doubleday, who commanded the Union forces, in his official report of the battle says: "I remained at the Seminary superintending the final movement until thousands of hostile bayonets made their appearance around the sides of the building. I then rode back and rejoined my command, nearly all of whom were filing through the town. As we passed through the streets our frightened people gave us food and drink."

ON TO THE TOWN

The Union forces had been pressed out of their breastworks, and our weary soldiers had entered them, and passed on to the town. The Fourteenth passed on both sides of the Seminary, Col. Croft, with a portion, passing to the right, and pushing forward for the possession of a desirable piece of artillery. Others were pushing for the same point. Major Croft probably reached it first, as he with an eye for the immediately useful secured the only injured horse, which he mounted with the harness still on, presented a captured sword to his lieutenant colonel, and soon afterwards loaned the horse to the gallant Capt. T. P. Alston, of the First, to ride into town in command of the skirmishers.

The brigade had now reached the town, which Gen. Perrin ordered the First and Fourteenth to enter. This they did simultaneously with flags unfurled, the First by the Chambersburg turnpike, and the Fourteenth passing to the left, or rather directly along and between North Boundary street and the old railroad embankment or bed, until it reached the Main street running south through the town, and marching up that street was passed by Gen. Pender, at the shade trees on the right, who extended a compliment in passing. A few paces further on Major McCreary with the First had reached the same street by the Chambersburg turnpike where Gen. Pender complimented the regiment for its gallant conduct. In like manner he complimented each regiment through its commander for its glorious day's work. The fourteenth having the shortest cut reached the Main street first, but Major McCreary reached it further on and first held the more central or advanced position, where the Fourteenth again joined it. The streets and fencing look now as they did then. Only a hedge has been allowed to grow up and spread on the north side of Boundary street by which the Fourteenth passed into town.

Gen. Rode's Division of Gen. Ewell's Corps now coming up, the First and Fourteenth were ordered back and joined the Twelfth and Thirteenth between the town and Seminary, where we rested.

GEN. LEE AND THE CAROLINIANS

Gen. Pender was at the Ridge were we first entered the battle and saw the close fighting throughout. He saw the Brigade as it appeared from his point to almost mingle with the Union soldiers, and passing the Seminary and the Ridge almost together, and out of sight and the firing ceasing he supposed that the Brigade was captured. Riding forward however, he met Lieut. Simmons, of the Twelfth, who was wounded, and of whom he made the inquiry if the Brigade was captured, to which the Lieutenant answered, "No, it's over the hill yonder." (The large body of the enemy known to be there well justified his fears.) The General then rode forward with speed, and ordered the Twelfth and Thirteenth back to a point between the town and the Seminary to protect the right flank, and then into town where he overtook the Fourteenth and First, as above stated. Gen. Lee then came up, and all honor was given to "the South Carolina Brigade that captured Gettysburg."

THE LOSSES

The points of greatest danger were held by the regiments on the right and left, the Thirteenth on the right and the First on the left. The Thirteenth was nearest the cavalry with repeating rifles at the stone fence, and lost more in killed than any other. Col. Bruckman, although too sick for duty, was at his post, but the movements for that reason were largely conducted by Lt.-Col. I. F. Hunt. It added to the regiment's already high reputation acquired under its former gallant commander, Col. O. E. Edwards, who fell commanding the brigade, after the wounding of Gen. McGowan at Chancellorsville.

The First, being on the left, had to encounter a long line of infantry overlapping its left, and was nearest the artillery.

The centre, comprising the Twelfth and Fourteenth, was swept by the same enfilading fire that enfiladed our flanking regiments, and the losses in men were nearly equal in all the regiments in proportion to the numbers engaged. The Twelfth sustained heavy loss from the artillery fire directed towards the centre.

It would seem impossible for any of the regiments to have sustained more than it had to meet or to have borne more than it had to encounter. There would have been enough glory in any one of them to have carried its own front. All of them had more than this to do.

NO ESCAPE FOR THE WOUNDED

The losses were immense. The Fourteenth, which was the largest regiment, lost over 200 killed and wounded out of 475 carried into action. The Thirteenth had sixty-four killed or to die of their wounds. All the regiments lost one-third. There was no loss of prisoners. They were all killed or wounded. Over six hundred had fallen in front of the breastworks. The thousands of hostile bayonets that appeared and passed around the sides of the Seminary building comprised what remained of fifteen hundred carried into action. The nature of the ground was such and the contest so brief that the wounded could not be moved, and were wounded twice, thrice and as many as four times, after being stricken down. Large numbers died of their wounds. A few who, with shattered arms or wounded bodies, ran back in safety to the surgeons, have not ceased to admire their legs for the good service rendered. It was the only battlefield in which all avenues of escape for our wounded were closed. There was nothing that the ambulance corps could do. The ground was swept at every point by the deadly Minnie balls. The artillery fire is terrible, but the almost silent whirl of the Minnie ball is the death-dealing missile in battle. Not a foot of ground presented a place of safety. The Union troops fired low, and their balls swept close to the ground in the dish-like field in their front. The terrible strife was over in a few minutes—fifteen, say maybe twenty at most. Men never fell faster in this brigade, and perhaps never equaled, except in Orr's regiment at Gaines's Mill. On our side the firing was not slack nor wild. The trees in the Seminary grounds where the Union lines ran are still thickly covered with scars, from the ground to the height of a man, made with the bullets of our unerring rifles. They are well marked on their western sides. And the ground strewn with their dead and wounded well attested the accuracy of the deadly aim.

THE GALLANT ENEMY

It was no ordinary soldier that we had met. The prisoners captured were more intelligent than on other fields. They were mostly Pennsylvanians fighting for everything they held dear. The celebrated Iron Brigade was in our front. The 121st Pennsylvania, 143rd Pennsylvania, 149th Pennsylvania, 151st Pennsylvania, and others not remembered. Maine troops were there, who stated that they came in not more than fifteen minutes before the action began, then the artillery on our right, cavalry behind the stone wall, all holding to the death. But there was no crossing of swords and bayonets, for this is seldom done except on paper. It was no time for a thousand hair-breadth escapes with nobody hurt. It was not the clipping off of clothing, but the bodies of men that were struck. While the losses in line officers and men were great it was remarkable that not a single field officer was disabled for duty, though they did not escape unstruck.

INCIDENTS OF PERSONAL DARING

The Rev. W. B. Carson, chaplain of the Fourteenth Regiment, remained with the wounded, of whom ninety of his own regiment were too badly wounded to be removed in ambulances south of the Potomac. He went into the heavily shelled woods for blankets for his wounded men and remained to administer to their wants until death freed many from their sufferings.

Dr. Louis V. Hunt, the eminent surgeon of the Fourteenth, performed many skillful operations, drawing praise from Union surgeons. He returned with us on the final retreat.

A soldier boy of the Fourteenth captured the large flag of the 149th Pennsylvania in the works, where all its guard were slain. Another captured a smaller one, and folding it in his bosom, fell two days afterwards advancing in the picket line if front of Cemetery Heights.

R. Owens, color bearer, son of Capt. R. S. Owens, of the Fourteenth, who had fallen at Frazier's farm, was shot dead while carrying the flag of his regiment, and all his color guard but one was slain.

In the Twelfth Regiment one color bearer after another was shot dead until four were killed and two others wounded. And a scarcely less fatality attended the colors of the other regiments. The land of the Shamrock, as in other fields, contributed its quota on the strongly contested ground.

IMPORTANCE OF THE ENGAGEMENT

The importance and magnitude of this sanguinary engagement and glorious victory was lost sight of by the public eye in the grand movement which culminated in the great events immediately succeeding. But it was not lost sight of nor forgotten by the great Lee. He promoted Col. Perrin to Brigadier-General, who on the 12th of May, 1864, while leading his Alabama Brigade to the charge at Spottsylvania, as he did McGowan's Brigade at Gettysburg, fell in the front of battle and his great spirit ceased from war.

We rested on the field of battle and the next day held Seminary Ridge along the stone fence which covered Gen. Lane's front the first day. We supported the artillery, and the only fighting by the brigade, except by the Sharpshooters, was done by Capt. T. F. Clyburn (afterwards Colonel) who with two companies of the Twelfth drove back a line of battle and restored our pickets who had been driven from their posts. Our line passed by a farm-house surrounded by a fine orchard, and owned by a gentleman named McMillan, who canned his fruit, and who abandoned all on the morning of the 1st. Abandoned property is lawful prize in war, and our weary soldiers enjoyed those fruits, on the volunteer system, in the intervals of quiet. The old gentleman and his wife still live, and although nineteen years have passed he still laments the loss of his earthly store. Every building and tree now looks as it did then, and the same well of water again quenched the wayfarer's thirst. During the night of the 2nd the brigade was moved forward to the dirt road on the slope fronting Cemetery Ridge and was joined by Orr's Regiment, but was not engaged in the great battle of the 3rd.

The pickets were driven in at one time, and the Fourteenth ordered forward to restart the line, which was quickly done. But it drew a heavy fire from the heights in front, inflicting some loss, in which both the field officers were wounded. The wounds of Major Croft were severe, and his valuable services lost to his regiment for more than a year. Then returning with an unhealed wound in the side and his arm in a sling, he continued at his post until the close of war.

KILLED IN ACTION

As before stated, our losses were immense. But the greatest individual loss to the brigade was that of Capt. William T. Haskell, of the First Regiment, commanding the Battalion of Sharpshooters. He was killed in front of Cemetery Ridge on the second day, and the gravity of his loss can scarcely be estimated. It was only known to those who knew him best. Gen. Pender also fell mortally wounded on the second day while reconnoitering, and our army lost in him another of our great generals.

And then the long list of line officers who fell, leaving whole companies without a commissioned officer. Among them the First Regiment, besides Capt. Haskell, Killed, Lieut. A. W. Pogue. Wounded, Capt. J.S. McMahon, Lieuts. J. Cox, James Armstrong, M. M. Murray, J.F. J. Caldwell.

Twelfth Regiment—Killed, Capt. J. Hunnicutt. Wounded, Capt. J. M. Moody, Lieuts. J. A. Watson, M. T. Sharpe, A. W. Black, W. J. Stover, J. M. Jenkins, ____Simmons.

Thirteenth Regiment—Killed, Capt. Cromer, Lieuts. McNinch and Leitsey. Wounded, Capt. Dewberry, Lieuts. Leitsey, Hill, A. M. Bowers, John Dabney, J. F. Banks.

Fourteenth Regiment—Killed, Sidney Carter and N. Austin. Wounded, Adjutant W. J. Ready; Capts. H. P. Griffith, W. M. Jordan and G. W. Culbertson; Lieuts. Robert B. Watson, John M. Bell, H. J. Roach, William H. Bronson, J. F. Jordan, A. F. Jordan, W. R. White, J. H. Williams, S. Cogburn, James P. Sloan and Jesse Gwin.

And the hundreds of brave men, most of them young, and on the threshold of life, whose names were not recorded in the official reports of the battle. But they still live in the memories of the loved ones at home, and years afterwards their bodies were removed to Southern cemeteries by patriotic and loving hands. Here let them rest until the morning of the general resurrection.

In the afternoon of the 3rd the great world-renowned assaults were made on the iron-crested and rock-bound heights in front, resulting in disaster, and then the star of the Southern Confederacy began first to wane.

Of the regimental commanders in this campaign, Col. J. L. Miller, of the Twelfth, was killed at the Wilderness, May 5, 1864; Col. B. T. Brockman, at Spottsylvania, May 12, 1864; Major W. Haddon, of Orr's Rifles, at Deep Bottom, July 28, 1864, and Col. C. W. McCreary, of the First, at Gravelly Run, March 31, 1865. It was distressingly sad that Col. McCreary, after so long and brilliant service, should fall in almost the last battle, even as the fabric of the Confederate power was tottering and being broken to pieces and the last blow being struck. The smile that always lit up his pleasant face paled in death near the enemy. Of these and the long list who stood shoulder to shoulder with us at Gettysburg and who fell on these and other battlefields, and those who have survived the sad and closing scene at Appomattox—a brigade which the writer as senior colonel at times had the honor to command—he would say, with feelings akin to Scotland's bard—

> "The bridegroom may forget the bride
> Was made his wedded wife yestreen;
> The monarch may forget the crown
> That on his head an hour has been;
> The mother may forget the child
> That smiles so sweetly on her knee,
> But I'll remember thee, Glencairn."

REGIMENTAL COMMANDERS

The promotion of Gen. Perrin and his death has already been stated. He was a martinet in discipline and every inch a soldier. His accomplished wife, a daughter of Col. P. M. Butler of the Palmetto Regiment, preceded him a short time to the grave, and two children survived them. He was the last colonel but one of the Fourteenth Regiment. He was captain of company "D," from Edgefield, at the organization in 1861. The former colonels were field officers at the organization—Col. James Jones in the camp of instruction, and Cols. Samuel McGowan and W. D. Simpson, who so often led it to battle. The First boasted of its Maxey Gregg, a name so inseparably connected with it and the Brigade. Orr's Rifles had its Col. James L. Orr in the camp of instruction and J. Foster Marshall, D. A. Ledbetter, who had fallen at Second Manassas. The Twelfth with Col. R. G. M. Dunovant, of honorable service before, who was succeeded by the gallant Col. Dixon Barnes, who distinguished himself and regiment on many fields and so much at second Manassas, and who fell at Sharpsburg, regretted by all. Col. O. E. Edwards of the Thirteenth, so brave, and so efficient in all departments of the service and especially in battle has already been mentioned. These officers left with their regiments the impress of their own gallant spirits, which was preserved unimpaired on many battlefields, and on one of which they submit was never excelled.

GETTYSBURG IN 1882

An inspection of the field at Gettysburg on the 14th and 15th of June, 1882, presented precisely the view it did nineteen years ago. It looked as if seen but yesterday. Time seemed to have made scarcely a change. The impressions on the mind had been so strong that the hills, valleys, parcels of woods, Seminary, slopes, houses, streets, fencing, then thrown down, and roads, were all of them fresh in the memory. When it looked a little too far from McMillan's house to the woods on the south, and inspection disclosed a small clearing from that side of it. The existence of the dirt road was denied by some, but a search at once located it. The field only lacked the surging masses of men and arms to complete it. The portion if the stone fence nearest our right, on the first day, had been removed.

On the other side the view from Cemetery Ridge, Culp's Hill, Little Round Top and other points held by the Union forces, disclosed positions which the "Rebel soldier" would have regarded as havens of safety. No wonder Gen. Pickett failed in his charge.

In peace, the men who had met there before the war now met again. On the Southern side were Gen. Trimble, accompanied by his niece, Miss Trimble. The General, though hale and hearty, still carries with him the evidence of the hard-fought battle. Gen. A. M. Scales, M. C., of North Carolina, Col. Oates, M. C., of Alabama, with only one arm, Capt. _____, of Pegram's Artillery, and the representative of McGowan's Brigade and his school-girl daughter, who took a lively interest in the incidents of battle as related by both Union and Confederate officers, and with them inspected all the fields.

On the Northern side were many officers assembled for their reunion. Several of them inquired specially for that gallant officer of ours who rode through the lines of his brigade and led the charge. They stated that it was the grandest sight they ever saw in battle. Among them were Gen. Richard Coulter, of Pennsylvania, with his wife and daughter; Gen. Edward L. Dana, Col. Of 143rd Pennsylvania Volunteers, commanding second brigade at Gettysburg; Lt. Col. Geo. F. McFarland, 151st Pennsylvania Volunteers, accompanied by his amiable wife. We thought that Col. McFarland had been killed by us nineteen years before. We had shot him and his horse near the Seminary, wounding him severely, from which he lost a leg, but his cheerful disposition well supplies the loss. Major E. P. Halstead, A. A. G. of the First Corps; Capt. M. L. Blair, of 143rd Pennsylvania; Capt. J. M. Clapp, of 121st Pennsylvania; Capt. Beaver, son of Gen. Beaver, of Pennsylvania, and others whose name and rank are not remembered. These officers were all in our front on the first of July, 1863, and gave a most hearty welcome to the Southerners. And the citizens were alike courteous. All points of the battlefield are accessible and in two days all the important and strategic points can easily be taken in by the tourist.

With many thanks to Col. John B. Batchelder, the historian, for the aid rendered, to his amiable wife for courtesies in the brief time allowed, to the officers we had the pleasure to meet, and to the citizens of the town of Gettysburg, we bid an affectionate adieu. And now, as to the senior officer in rank of McGowan's Brigade now living who participated in the battle, the duty requested of him has been performed. The points of the battlefield, the positions of the several regiments, their movements and the movements of the Brigade have been carefully and correctly pointed out to Col. Batchelder, the historian, and the Brigade will now have its place in the picture.

The record thus given of one battle will show that defeat did not everywhere confront the Confederate forces at Gettysburg, and at least one gem will be preserved from that ill-fated field.

* * *

Sumter Watchman and Southron
March 10, 1887

How Gettysburg Was Lost

General E[vander] M. Law, of South Carolina, writing in the December Century of his experiences at Gettysburg, tells of a proposition which he made to General [John Bell] Hood for an attack on the Union left, and says: "I found General Hood on the ridge where his line had been formed, communicated to him the information I had obtained, and pointed out the ease with which a movement by the right flank might be made. He coincided fully in my views, but said that his orders were positive to attack in front, as soon as the left of the corps should get into position. I therefore entered a formal protest against a direct attack, on the grounds:

- That the great natural strength of the enemy's position in our front rendered the result of a direct assault extremely uncertain.

- That, even if successful, the victory would be purchased at too great a sacrifice of life, and our troops would be in no condition to improve it.

- That a front attack was unnecessary,--the occupation of Round Top during the night by moving upon it from the south, and the extension of our right wing from that point across the enemy's left and rear, being not only practicable, but easy.

- That such a movement could compel a change of front on the part of the enemy, the abandonment of his strong position on the heights, and force him to attack us in position.

"General Hood called up Captain [James] Hamilton, of his staff, and requested me to repeat the protest to him, and the grounds on which it was made. He then directed Captain Hamilton to find General Longstreet as quickly as possible and deliver the protest, and to say to him that he (Hood) indorsed it fully. Hamilton rode off at once, but in about ten minutes returned, accompanied by a staff-officer of General Longstreet, who said to General Hood, in my hearing: 'General Longstreet orders that you begin the attack at once.' Hood turned to me and merely said, 'You hear the order?' I at once moved my brigade to the assault. I do not know whether the protest ever reached General Lee. From the brief interval that elapsed between the time it was sent to General Longstreet and the receipt of the order to begin the attack, I am inclined to think it did not. General Longstreet has since said that he repeatedly advised against a front attack and suggested a movement by our right flank. He may have thought, after the rejection of this advice by General Lee, that it was useless to press the matter further.

"Just here the battle of Gettysburg was lost to the Confederate arms.

It is useless to speculate upon the turn affairs might have taken if the Confederate cavalry had been in communication with the rest of the army, and if General Stuart had kept General Lee informed, as he should have done, of the movements of the Federal army. In considering the causes of the Confederate failure on that particular field, we must take the situation just as we find it. And the situation was as follows: The advance of the two armies encountered each other on the 1st of July. An engagement ensued in which the Confederates were victorious. The Federal troops retired through Gettysburg and took position along the heights east of the town—a position which, if properly defended, was practically impregnable to a direct attack.

"The whole matter then resolves itself into this: General Lee failed at Gettysburg on the 2nd and 3rd of July because he made his attack precisely where his enemy wanted him to make it and was most fully prepared to receive it. Even had he succeeded in driving the Federal army from its strong position by a general and simultaneous assault along the whole front (which was the only possible chance of success in that direction), he would have found his army in very much the same condition that Pyrrhus found his when, after driving the Romans from the field of Asculum, he exclaimed, 'another such victory, and I am undone!'"

* * *

Aiken Standard
February 1, 1893

<h1 style="text-align:center">THE JOURNAL AND REVIEW
BIGELOW'S BATTERY</h1>

<h2 style="text-align:center">THE NINTH MASSACHUSETTS AT THE
GETTYSBURG PEACH ORCHARD</h2>

The Cannoneers Were Novices at the Guns, but Longstreet's Confederates Didn't Have a Walkover on Their Line—Sacrificed at Last for the Good of All

[Copyright, 1872, by the American Press Association. Book rights reserved.]

On to the front to battle for the defense of Washington, of Philadelphia, of New York, to drive the butternut intruders from the Keystone soil, hastened the minute men of 1863, the one year's men, the nine months' and three months' and thirty day militia. On to the front; yes, and, although they didn't dream of it, to save the day at Gettysburg. In the throng of bustling New England boys marched a company of Massachusetts light artillery, the Ninth Independent battery, led by Capt. Bigelow. The men had enlisted for nine months, thinking, perhaps, that it would take that long to give the Confederates a drubbing that would teach them to stay at home south of the Potomac forever after; perhaps, that glory worth carrying home could not be won in a shorter time.

On July 2 the battery lay with the artillery reserve of Meade's army behind Cemetery Ridge when Longstreet's 30,000 veterans were crawling through hollows, among wheatlands and fences and farm buildings to pounce upon Sickles' unfortunate line between the Peach Orchard and Round Top. A scattering fire, beginning as the afternoon advanced, warned the Union generals of what was coming—a sundown assault in force—and then ho, for the reserves; Bigelow's guns galloped down the old, half hidden road along the rear of Sickles' line of battle toward the angle, the men with fresh curiosity spying here a gap, there an exposed site; here a fleet staff officer carrying orders, there a handful of men getting somewhere at double quick; here a row of iron throats in position, there a regiment of infantrymen lying flat on the ground, only with necks craned to know what the hurry was about.

On to the front, the men heedlessly beating the very ground where their battery was soon to be annihilated and wondering at the moment whether it was not a false alarm—a battlefield scare. The pieces were unlimbered where the converging fire of a score of Longstreet's guns under a network of falling shot and shell, zipping bullets speeding as the wind and as thick as snowflakes drove Sickles' infantry back to be caught in that firey net behind them as fish are snared in a seine. A Sergeant killed, a gunner wounded before a shot could be fired, and the Massachusetts boys were baptized soldiers of the veteran Army of the Potomac. It was no scare. That grass grown, not fenced, cross country road from Round Top to the Peach Orchard, along the edges of Devil's Den and the wheat field across from Plum Run, was a road to the mouth of hell.

The battery opened fire upon those Confederate guns that enfiladed the Peach Orchard. The pieces were handled with the coolness of veterans. The Confederate cannoneers showed judgment. Some of their canisters exploded under Bigelow's shots, and they quit firing. Bigelow and his boys thought that this meant victory but it was not so. Those Confederate shots were a prelude to something more. They ceased, and three interval shots in succession gave a signal for Longstreet's infantry assault. Directly in front of Bigelow the brigades of Kershaw and Semmes leaped a stone wall that had stopped them, halted coolly for a moment then dashed forward to sweep up the debris of Sickles' line spared by the shot and shell, like the second ball in play at tenpins.

Kershaw's line started at a point 400 yards distant in an oblique direction and marched under Bigelow's fire until it was directly in his front, 200 yards away. The range was easy, and with double charges of canister the guns played upon the solid ranks until they melted into a mob of fleeing men. The Confederates saw that their supports could never pass that battery, and a band of sharpshooters was detached from the charging column to move by the flank and disable it. Like bloodhounds on a trail, they hung to the work and were not to be shaken off, for artillery is no match against skulking riflemen. Semmes' brigade followed Kershaw's and shared the same fate from the double charges of canister. Semmes was killed.

While this was going on Barksdale's Mississippi brigade, taking an inner track, had captured the Peach Orchard and was forging its way down the line on the flank and rear of Bigelow's position. The chief of artillery warned Bigelow of his danger from Barksdale's men and ordered him to withdraw the guns. But Bigelow saw the nearer danger, the sharpshooters on his front, who, the moment the guns ceased their canister hail, would find the coast clear to run up and shoot down his drivers and horses, leaving the cannoneers helpless with the guns. The only hope was to retire firing, so as to hold Kershaw's men in front at a distance and discourage the march of Barksdale's on the flank. The limbers of the battery, with their teams harnessed in, were aligned in rear of the guns and attached to the trails of the pieces by long ropes. At each discharge of a gun the recoil would send it back several yards, and the limber teams would start ahead far enough to take up the slack of the rope. In this way the battery retired 410 yards and was at the time 1,000 yards in advance of any Union battery or regiment.

At the rear of an open field on the Trostle farm the battery brought up before a stone wall having only a narrow gateway sufficient to pass one limber and gun at a time. The loss in men and horses had been heavy, yet the battery might have withdrawn with honor and a lighting complement of men. But the chief of artillery rode to the spot with a charged tone and ordered Bigelow not to retire farther, but to hold the position around the Trostle house until a new line of batteries could be planted behind it to cover the gap between Round Top and Hancock's line on Cemetery Ridge. It was then 6 o'clock when the battle at the Wheat Field and Devil's Den, on Bigelow's left, was raging with frightful intensity. Barksdale's victorious column, unopposed and sheltered by a rise of ground fifty yards away, was advancing on the right and Kershaw's men still blazing away with their rifles in front. Delay at the Trostle house for six isolated guns but half manned meant sacrifice and nothing less. What a difference between the prospect then and two hours before! "Halt there!" said Bigelow as each gun rolled up to the stone wall. "Double shot with canister and lay the contents of your limber chests by you guns for quick work." Not an instant too soon was the order obeyed, for Barksdale's men were crossing the ridge fifty paces away.

The fuses were cut to explode the cases near the muzzles of the cannon. Barksdale's men charged again and again and were as often sent back under murderous slaughter until finally one section of the battery—two guns—became entangled among some boulders in changing position, and Kershaw's sharpshooters, taking advantage, closed in on the front. At the same moment one of Barksdale's regiments—the Twenty-first Mississippi—pushed through on the right flank, the men taking shelter among the limber chests and from there shooting down Bigelow's cannoneers at the guns confronting Kershaw's men. That reduced the fight to a hand to hand affair between individuals. A Mississippian rushed up to a cannon to spike it, and one of the cannoneers—Private Ligal—beat him to death with the head of an iron rammer. Another was killed by the blow of a handspike while dragging a prisoner to the rear by main force. There must be an end to such work when the odds are a hundred to one, and a half hour all told finished the defense of the Trostle house and wiped out what was left of Bigelow's battery.

Two of the guns had been dragged by hand through the Trostle house yard to the rear. In the yards and field lay 60 of the battery horses dead and wounded, and seeing no hope of defending the remaining guns Bigelow told his men to save themselves and get back to the lines as best they could. Bigelow was severely wounded. One of his lieutenants was killed and another mortally wounded. Six sergeants were present in the action and 2 of them were killed and four wounded. Seven corporals and privates were killed and 12 wounded. The killed and wounded numbered 28, or about half the fighting men belonging to the guns. The horses taken into action numbered 85, and 65 were disabled. The loss was the second highest incurred by any volunteer Union battery in the service during a single engagement.

The execution more than compensated for the loss. The battery expended over three tons of missiles, including ninety rounds of canister, and fired in all 528 rounds. The brigades of Barksdale and Semmes were checked by the fire of the battery, and Kershaw, who had started out hopefully, pledged to carry Round Top on the front, had been repulsed and his regiments sent back to cover, smarting. Kershaw explained his failure by saying that when his brigade got abreast of Bigelow's guns an order to march by the left flank and capture the battery was construed by the line as one to march by the right flank, and obedience to it carried his column out of action. Had it obeyed the first order and gone to the left, Bigelow would have blown the desperate fellows, to atoms from the mouths of his pieces.

When the battery at last gave up the struggle a new line had been formed in the gap behind it, and a couple of fresh Union brigades, under Cols. Willard and Lockwood, charged to the Trostle house and retook the four abandoned guns. The Massachusetts boys who were on their legs next day received the guns back, and they fought them afterward and on more than twenty battlefields without losing a single piece.

The men were not sated with glory at Gettysburg and re-enlisted for the war. They fought through the campaign of 1864, and on the field of Cold Harbor repeated their plucky deed of Gettysburg, but at less cost of blood to their own. At Bethesda Church, June 2, the battery was with Gen. Warren, and at one stage in the fight found itself alone engaged with a heavy Confederate skirmish line and a masked work of field guns. It held the ground until darkness kindly covered the linkedness of the line and then drew out of the trap. At Petersburg, June 17, the guns advanced with the assaulting columns against the Confederate works, and when the attack failed covered the withdrawal of the infantry by vigorously shelling the enemy's batteries and breastworks to prevent a countercharge. The total loss of the company in killed during its three campaigns was 10, a crack record for artillery.

It rarely happens to one organization to strike a crisis like that at Gettysburg a second time, and it is good for the service that such is the case. The reputation of always getting "cut to pieces" is an unlucky one. It is enough to have stood the test once just to show what may be expected in times of need, and the companion troops of the North Massachusetts battery chuckled to themselves on many of the hard fought fields of Virginia when Bigelow's guns wheeled into action. A banner bearing the legend, "Gettysburg Peach Orchard," waved above them, and that told the whole story.

GEORGE L. KILMER

* * *

SUMTER WATCHMAN AND SOUTHRON
MARCH 27, 1895

Carolina at Gettysburg.
A State Commission to be appointed to Locate Positions, etc.

The government is now preparing to mark the famous battlefield of Gettysburg just as the battlefields of Chickamauga and Chattanooga were marked last summer. The following letter received by Governor Evans yesterday, on which he has not acted yet, however, shows what is being done to this end:

To His Excellency the Governor of the State of South Carolina:

Sir: The undersigned, consisting of the U. S. Gettysburg Battlefield Commission, and representing the Union and Confederates soldiers of the civil war, are charged by the War Department with the duty of ascertaining and suitably marking, with permanent historic tablets, the several positions and evolutions of each and every command of infantry, cavalry and artillery of the armies in the battle of Gettysburg during the three days' conflict. The result, when finished, will be a monument to American manhood, and this commission is anxious to perform its duty with accuracy and impartiality.

To this end we invite your co-operation, and suggest the propriety of the appointment of a State commission of intelligent and worthy veterans who were present, and, if possible, representing each of the organizations from your State present in the battle, who will visit Gettysburg and locate the positions and movements of commands with which they served.

We hope such a commission will be sent by each of the Southern States. These commissions will be welcomed and the information and data they furnish correctly noted, carefully recorded and permanently marked by historic tablets which are to be erected.

We have the honor to be your obedient servants,

John P. Nicholson, Wm. M. Robbins,

Commissioners

* * *

CONFEDERATE VETERAN MAGAZINE
OCT. 1897

HE WAS A HERO IF A PAUPER.

Hon. J. L. McLaurin, of South Carolina, in a speech to Confederate Veterans, said:

In the battle of Gettysburg a stalwart lad from Darlington, S. C, was bravely advancing in the face of a hot fire when a shot tore off his first finger. An officer ordered him to the rear. "No, sir." was his reply; "they will call me a coward if I go back for that." A moment later a piece of shell took his arm off clear and clean above the elbow. A comrade caught him. And the poor fellow said: "I will go back now, but I would rather lose my arm than to be called a coward."

Two weeks ago there was a death in the poorhouse. The bed was hard, the walls bare, the wan face cold and still, while across the breast was pinned the armless sleeve of a pauper's coat. The heroic soul of Henry Miller had winged its flight to God, far beyond the reach of want and ingratitude.

* * *

ANDERSON INTELLIGENCER
JULY 24, 1901

WAR STORIES
Some Personal Recollections of Gettysburg by One of General Longstreet's Couriers

Atlanta Journal

In the issue of the Journal of March 30, 1901, Mr. Robert R. Hemphill, of Abbeville, S.C., says: "Pickett's loss at Gettysburg has been greatly exaggerated and for nearly 38 years the fancy story of his 'sacrifice' has been written up in glowing words until many persons believe that Pickett did all the fighting at Gettysburg."

Mr. Hemphill also gives the official losses of the various divisions of General Lee's army, as shown in the official records, and of course they must be taken as correct. These official figures show that Pickett's loss at Gettysburg was less than that of any other division of the army except Early's and R[ichard] H[eron] Anderson's.

Now I do not recall any "fancy stories" of Pickett's famous charge which intimate even by inference "that Pickett did all the fighting at Gettysburg." Neither do I believe Mr. Hemphill intended to detract one iota from Pickett's brilliant and glorious charge at Gettysburg, in which he won undying fame, and the admiration and plaudits of the civilized world in the short space of an hour. But, if left to stand as it is, without some explanation as to how much fighting he did and the conditions and circumstances surrounding it, or leading up to his magnificent charge, I believe it would certainly have that effect. I am not criticizing Mr. Hemphill's letter adversely or writing from any standpoint or motive, whatever, other than the "truth of history" and simple justice to all concerned.

Now let us see what the conditions and circumstances were. Up to Gettysburg General Pickett had done no fighting during that year except, perhaps, some little skirmishing. When the battle of Chancellorsville (including Salem Church and Fredericksburg) was fought Pickett's and Hood's divisions were with General Longstreet at Suffolk, Va. After that most decisive battle of the war was fought and won General Longstreet was ordered back to Fredericksburg and reunited with the main army. The army rested and recruited there for some weeks and then started for Pennsylvania. Pickett's division was composed entirely of Virginians. They were all near their own homes and the division was easily recruited and equipped. Consequently, when General Lee entered Pennsylvania Pickett had one of the largest and best equipped divisions in the army.

When General Lee had reached Chambersburg a halt was made for several days. General Longstreet remained there; General Ewell moved further on toward Carlisle and General Hill moved up toward Gettysburg. This disposition of the army placed it in a short triangular shape, with each of the three corps resting about twenty miles apart, on the base and side lines of the triangle.

General J. E. B. Stuart, with his cavalry, was scouting somewhere in the direction of Washington, and for several days was "lost," so far as his whereabouts was known to General Lee or the army, was concerned. General Longstreet's corps was encamped around Chambersburg, I think, for a week or more, and General Lee's headquarters were located but a few hundred yards from General Longstreet's, as they were nearly always close together. One evening late a scout for General Longstreet, named Harrison, I think, galloped up to his headquarters and reported that General Meade's army was coming rapidly from Washington. General Longstreet reported the matter to General Lee at once when he sent notice of the same to Ewell and Hill. General Longstreet moved up to Greencastle, about half way between Chambersburg and Gettysburg the next day and camped for the night with Hood's and McLaw's divisions. The next day he moved on to Gettysburg. That was the first day of July. About 2:30 or 3 o'clock in the afternoon General Longstreet was riding along some distance in advance of reaching the head of the column, and on reaching the summit of a slight elevation, Gettysburg came in plain view, as we were not far from the Emmetsburg road, which came in at right angles to the pike we were on from Chambersburg. A slight halt was made, and after a brief conference with the staff Col. G[ilbert] M[oxley] Sorrell, the adjutant general, turned to me and directed me to go back to Chambersburg and tell General Pickett to move up his division to Gettysburg at once. Fighting was then in progress between portions of Ewell's and A. P. Hill's corps, and the federal advance. The rattle of musketry was pretty lively and was distinctly heard where we were. That must have been about 3 o'clock in the afternoon of July 1. General Pickett was still in camp two miles beyond Chambersburg, that is, on the Virginia side. In going back I had to pass through the columns of Hood's and McLaw's divisions greeting my loved comrades of the glorious Tenth Georgia regiment. Soon afterward I met a part of Ewell's corps coming in from the direction of Carlisle. Passing through these troops greatly retarded my progress, but I was well mounted, and after getting clear of them, I made fine speed, and reached General Pickett just at sundown. When I delivered my verbal message, he called for his own couriers immediately and sent them flying to his different brigades. In less than an hour, his division was on the road to Gettysburg. It was dark when I passed through Chambersburg on my return, and as I had been in the saddle since early in the morning, and my horse having had neither rest nor food, I stopped at a farm house and procured some corn for him and when I came to a strip of woods, I turned into it, unsaddled my horse, and fed him on the ground. I lay down on the ground by him and rested until Pickett's men had passed.

It has been sometimes said that General Longstreet was tardy in getting on the field into position at Gettysburg, but I have never been able to understand what could have given rise to such an unjust and false charge as that. When I reached headquarters on my return from Chambersburg it was between 7 and 8 o'clock on the morning of July 2. General Longstreet was at the front. As soon as I could feed my horse and get some breakfast I hurried to him at the front. When I found him it was probably 9 o'clock. From that time on through the day I was with him continuously and can testify of my own personal knowledge that he worked harder to get a good line and get his men on it promptly than I ever have known him to have done on any other battlefield. Any delay can never be justly charged to General Longstreet. He was especially alert and active at Gettysburg and grew impatient and angry at any slowness on the part of his subordinates.

When the line was established Pickett's division had arrived in supporting distance, but was held in reserve, and did not take part in the fighting on that (the second) day.

When the line of battle was ready to move forward the men were lying down resting, and General Longstreet rode along in rear of the entire line to see if everything was in good shape and ready for the advance. Being satisfied with the situation, he rode down into a little ravine, dismounted, walked up to the line, ordered the men up, and placing himself at the head of the Twenty-fourth Georgia regiment, gave the order to advance. The line being near the crest of the elevation, a moment's forward movement brought the men into plain view of the enemy, in their strong position on the opposite ring, and the two "Round Tops." As soon as our line became exposed to the view of the enemy, it was met by a most furious and terrific storm of shot and shell and our men were swept down like grass before the scythe. But the line rushed forward across the open field, and the advance line of the enemy was swept back, and melted away like snow in the warm sunshine. General Longstreet went in on foot, and followed the line of battle to the red brick house, where a slight halt was made. When he started in he had left the staff for the moment behind the crest of the hill, but as soon as the battle opened, they knowing that he might be killed in the charge, or would need their services, with one accord, mounted their horses, and galloped across the field to him in the face of that terrible fire. When we reached him, he was at the corner of the peach orchard. Someone had brought his horse to him, and as he mounted he directed me to go back and tell General [William Nelson] Pendleton, who was in command of the reserve artillery, to bring up at once every piece of artillery he had. As I hurried back, under that awful fire, I passed by one of our batteries which had been posted on the crest of the hill we had started from, saw that every man and horse had been killed or wounded except a lieutenant and one private, and they were working heroically, trying to fire one gun. Hurrying on, I found General Pendleton, about one mile in the rear, sitting quietly on his horse at the head of an artillery battalion, awaiting orders. I delivered my message quickly, and he at once moved forward to the front. When I returned to the front I found General Longstreet considerably in advance of the brick house, where I had left him. The firing had now ceased, and our part of the line was in a dead quiet. The battlefield was strewn with the killed and wounded, and everything had the appearance of a cyclone having passed over it. We had passed considerably beyond the line first occupied by Federals, and many prisoners were taken. Just beyond the red brick house a regiment of Zouaves had been posted, and the ground was thickly strewn with their dead. I think their organization was entirely destroyed, as I never saw them after that.

There was no more fighting that day, as both armies were badly crippled, and had lost heavily in killed, wounded and prisoners.

Next morning General Longstreet rode to the front early and was met by General Lee and the other general officers of the army. A consultation was held and the situation fully discussed. The question was as to what was best to be done, whether to renew the fighting or not. I think they were nearly or quite all opposed to the renewal of the fight, except General Lee. He felt that he could not honorably and consistently retire from the field under the circumstances without a further effort to crush the federal army. I am sure he was very strongly opposed in that position by his generals. But his wish and judgment was the law of the army and he insisted that the battle must be renewed and preparation for its renewal was ordered commenced at once. General Lee graciously and generously assumed all the responsibility of the possible result. All the artillery of the army was then ordered massed in as secure positions as possible along the front and the ammunition inspected and made ready. It was evident the enemy was preparing to meet whatever movement was made by General Lee. When everything was in readiness a signal gun was to be fired, which was to open the greatest artillery duel ever fought on this continent, or perhaps in the world. When the artillery duel was over, then an infantry assault was to be rushed upon the center of the enemy's line. General Pickett's division, which had not fired a gun up to that time, was selected to lead that assault in conjunction with Heth's division, supported by [James Henry] Lane's and [Alfred Moore] Scale's brigades, of [William Dorsey] Pender's division, and Wilson's brigade, of Anderson's division. Pickett's men were in fine condition for the terrible work before them. The ranks were full, and the men well equipped. In fact, it was perhaps the finest division in the army. When they were drawn up in line of battle, under cover before the signal gun was fired to open the great artillery conflict, they certainly presented a grand appearance. General Pickett, as he proudly rode up and down in front of his men, mounted on his fine black horse with his own long black hair flowing back upon his shoulders, appeared a veritable cavalier at the head of his invincible clans. But all this was soon to be changed, and shorn of its martial grandeur. At last the boom of the signal gun sounded along the line, and then the 150 pieces belched forth their dreadful thunder and the air was quickly filled with exploding shells and shrieking solid shot. The enemy was ready and replied promptly and vigorously. The earth fairly trembled under the recall, and the greatest artillery battle of modern times was on. It is impossible, at this late day, to describe it, though the memory of it still lingers vividly in the mind, and will remain fresh as long as life shall last. The terrific fire of the 250 pieces of artillery was grandly awful, and the roar is said to have been heard at Staunton, Va., 130 miles away. When it was over, which was probably two hours from the start, General Pickett was ordered to move forward with a rush. His line moved out from cover and was soon in plain view of the enemy. Their whole fire was now concentrated upon him, but his men moved steadily and rapidly forward. They had to cross an open space of three-quarters of a mile, under the most galling fire of the entire federal army in range of them. But onward they swept invincible with impetuosity and the steadiness of a dress parade. As the men fell dead or wounded the ranks were closed up and still pressed onward with wonderful precision and gallantry. I was on an elevation where I could see the entire line as it swept across the open, and I am sure I never saw it surpassed for bravery upon any battlefield of the war. There was neither lagging nor hesitation, but the brigade moved forward steadily and rapidly. At last the federal position was reached, when there was a sudden mixing of the two lines. The federals were pressed back, many of the Confederates were killed some distance inside the federal lines. Reinforcements were rushed in by the enemy from every direction. All of General Pickett's supports did not reach the line in time to enable him to withstand the onslaught that was made upon him, and having lost heavily in that charge upon the enemy's position the Confederates were compelled to retire, being badly cut to pieces.

It will thus be seen that General Pickett fought scarcely and hour at Gettysburg, while some of the other divisions of the army were engaged in the three days' fighting, and all of them on the second and third days. The fighting every day was heavy, and I think this will fully explain why General Pickett's loss in killed and wounded was not as large as that of some of the other divisions. While it is true General Pickett was only engaged in the fight for a few minutes he won not only immortal fame and glory, but the admiration of the world for his gallantry.

Now I have written no "fancy words" in describing General Pickett's part in the battle of Gettysburg, but have simply endeavored to do him and General Longstreet and their brave men even justice.

The battle of Gettysburg was the greatest battle of the war, and I am sure will be so recognized by the impartial historian of the future, and Pickett's gallant and brave charge was perhaps the acme of the crowning glory to the Confederate arms on that great battlefield.

J. W. ANDERSON

* * *

ANDERSON INTELLIGENCER
JULY 15, 1903

War Stories

When Lee Needed the Boy General, Micah Jenkins.

Yesterday was the anniversary of one of the greatest battles in the history of the world--Gettysburg. Around this little village in Pennsylvania 40 years ago the forces of Robert E. Lee hurled themselves against the great armies of Meade, the federal commander, and there resulted a battle sanguinary in the extreme, the result of which was a victory to neither side. Yet it was a loss to Southern arms, for it forced Lee to give up his offensive warfare into the country of the enemy end caused him to fall back upon his own country already impoverished by the ravages of mighty armies.

South Carolinians did their part at Gettysburg, although the glory was in great measure given to others—and gloriously did all the Southern troops deport themselves in this great battle. It is on record in Gen. Lee's own handwriting that had a certain brigade of South Carolinians been there, the fortunes of the battle would have been quite different. It is singular that the great commander-in-chief should think that the tide of the

*Brig. Gen. Micah Jenkins recruited the 5th S.C. Infantry and be-
gan the war as their colonel. He was promoted to brigadier
general on July 22, 1862 at the age of 26. Jenkins' Brigade was a
part of Pickett's Division, but was kept behind to defend Richmond and was spared from Pickett's Charge. Jenkins was later
killed at the Battle of the Wilderness.*

(Library of Congress)

battle could have been turned by just one brigade-when so many thousands of troops were engaged-but the following is a Copy of the letter written by Gen. Lee to "the boy general:"

Headquarters
Army of Northern Virginia,
August, 1863.

Dear General: I regret exceedingly absence of yourself and your command from the battle of Gettysburg. There is no telling what a gallant brigade, led by an efficient commander, might have accomplished when victory trembled in the balance, I verily believe the result would have been different if you had been present.

Sincerely yours,
R. E. Lee,
General.

To Gen. M. Jenkins.

This letter is on file somewhere in the archives of the State capitol and Col. M. P. Tribble who is working on the Confederate rolls is looking for it so that it may be returned to the family of the gallant little general who was killed in the battle of the Wilderness, the fatal fire being from a body of Confederates. Gen. Longstreet wounded at the same instant, and the Wilderness fight was lost.

Much against their will Jenkins and Corse of Virginia were detailed by President Davis to act as a guard for Richmond during Gen. Lee's invasion of Pennsylvania. Gen. Longstreet in his history has said that it was a great mistake for the two finest brigades in the entire army to have been left at. Richmond, and the letter of Gen. Lee also indicates what great dependence the commander-in-chief had in the little brigadier, who was one of the "gamest" men and one of the best soldiers in the entire army--State, July 9.

* * *

THE ANDERSON INTELLIGENCER
JULY 19, 1905

AT CHANCELLORSVILLE
Three Instances of conspicuous Bravery That Mocked at Death

From the Augusta Chronicle

[Excerpt from longer article]

...

In narrating incidents that occur under such exciting conditions as a battle one can tell only what transpires immediately under his own eye or within his hearing, and even he must be careful lest his imagination give such coloring to his statement as to suggest some doubt of its correctness. I have seen official reports that did not tell the story of a battle as it should have been told. Where is the official report, or historical account, that has done justice to McGowan's brigade at Gettysburg, in its brilliant charge against [John Fulton] Reynolds the first day?

Who was there and heard them that can ever forget the words of Gen. Abner Perrin to the brigade? "Men," said he: "the order is to move forward. You will go to the brow of the hill just in front of us. If you see that [Henry] Heth (whose division led the attack) does not need you, protect yourselves the best you can under the hill. But if Heth should need you go to his assistance at once without waiting for orders. Don't fire your guns, give them the bayonet. If they run then see if they will outrun the bullet." And the gallant Heth did need us, and with what a rush we passed directly through his line, to the cry of his men of "Go in South Carolina!" right up and into the teeth of Reynold's men, sweeping them from the face of Seminary Ridge. This charge was so sudden and so successful that many of the enemy could not get away and sought shelter in the College buildings. The late P[atrick] H[enry] Reilly, of my old company [Co. L, 1st South Carolina (McCreary's)], who died a few years ago in Greenville, S. C., and whose memory I shall revere while life lasts as one of the bravest men and best soldiers I have ever known, made a capture by himself in one of the rooms of twelve or fifteen of the "blue coats." I can now hear the clarion voice of the fearless McCreary calling out for volunteers to enter the streets of Gettysburg, and the 1st regiment went with him to a man.

Col. [Issac F.] Hunt [Co. D, 13th South Carolina] proved himself a worthy successor of the heroic [Augustus F.] Edwards. It has never been my privilege to know him personally, but I have the pleasantest recollections of him as a gentleman, the sincerest admiration of his bravery and the greatest respect for his ability. His handsome face and the fine form made him a noticeable personage in the brigade. He is still living—as honored citizen of Greenville, S. C. His letter to me, from which I have made up a part of these reminiscences, was not intended for publication, and I owe him an apology for the use I have made of it. But such vivid and well written accounts should not be withheld. They are intensely interesting to the old soldier element, and keep the younger generation reminded of the quality of manhood it took to discharge the duties of citizenship in our Southern country forty odd years ago.

On the retreat from Gettysburg the brigade was detained for several days in the vicinity of Hagerstown, Md., waiting for the Potomac River to fall so that pontoons could be thrown across it at Falling Waters. The day before the night of the crossing to the Virginia side Company L was ordered out on skirmish line as a relief detail. The enemy's skirmish line, of which we had an unobstructed view, lay about three hundred yards from our rifle pits and extended through a farm yard. The roofs of the buildings in the yard and other places affording cover were all manned by their sharpshooters. To reach our rifle-pits we had to go over a stretch of wheat field of about two hundred yards. Notwithstanding the enemy had the "drop on us," we succeeded in getting safely into the pits, though a very short while after we reached them the lamented Capt. John W. Chambers was mortally wounded. This left the company without a commissioned officer to command it, Lieut. (afterwards captain) Wm. Aiken Kelly being temporarily in charge of Company F, the highest non-commissioned officer present was the writer, who, at the time enjoyed the distinction of being 3rd corporal.

In rushing to get into the rifle-pits P. H. Reilly, J[ames] E. Osborne, Frank M. Martin and myself landed in the same one together. The pit was too small for the four, and fearful that one of us might get killed, I told Frank Martin to go to the one next on our left and about twenty feet distant. He got himself ready, and picking his chance made a bolt for the rifle-pit. The marksmanship of the enemy was accurate, and they did not permit him to make the distance, short as it was, without giving him their attention. He had gone, perhaps two-thirds of the way when there was a sound as if a bullet had struck him, and heels over head he went into the pit. I hollered out to him, "Frank, are you hurt?" In a moment he had his knapsack off his back and taking from it a red flannel shirt held it up and answered: "No, but they have killed my shirt as dead as h__l." A bullet had passed through his knapsack and perforated the shirt at each of the folds. This superb soldier was wounded and captured at Spottsylvania Court house, Virginia, and died in Washington, D. C.

The enemy gave us another exhibition of their good marksmanship when Jim Osborne was looking through a hole between the Chestnut rails, of which the rifle-pit was made, and exposing the upper portion of his head, a shot broke one of the rails into two pieces right against his forehead.

B[enjamin] F. Brown

Carolina Volunteers, McGowan's brigade, 1861-65

* * *

Confederate Veteran Magazine
October, 1913

HAD JACKSON BEEN AT GETTYSBURG

By D[avid] H. Russell, Anderson, S. C. [6th South Carolina Infantry, 2nd Co. I]

I read with a great deal of interest the late Maj. E. C. Gordon's article, "Controversy about Gettysburg," in the October VETERAN, written in reply to some statements by H. Reiman Duval, of New York. I was in the battle of Gettysburg, and have always held some strong opinions as to the reasons for our failure there.

Major Gordon's belief may be readily accepted, since he was at the council of war; while Mr. Duval's statements are made from hearsay. The inaccuracy of the latter's statements becomes apparent when he says that General Lee was at this special council of war, when it is well known that he was not on the battle field of Gettysburg during the first day.

I write to add my small testimony to Major Gordon's statement, and should like to repeat a conversation I had with Gen. John Gordon at a banquet some years ago and at which I was, fortunately, near enough to ask questions I had been thinking of so long. General Gordon told us that he had never seen his command in finer fighting trim than on that day, notwithstanding the forced marches they had made. He said they went into battle like the sturdy veterans that they were, and that in a short time they had the Yankees on the run. He said he soon saw that Little Round Top was the key to the situation, and was pressing forward to the tune of the Rebel yell to seize it when the order came to him three different times to halt. He disregarded the orders until the fourth one came, more peremptory than the others, commanding him to halt where he was. He said it was one of the most painful moments of his life, as in twenty minutes more he knew he could have had Little Round Top hard and fast. His first thought was, "O for one hour of Stonewall Jackson!" for he knew, he said, that if Jackson had been at his old place watching the firing line, Little Round Top would not have so easily escaped our capture. General Gordon told also of how, after nightfall, he could hear the sound of new entrenchments being thrown up in the enemy's line and of the arrival of new troops, and that he rode back to headquarters and urged a night attack, but was overruled.

My recollection of this conversation is very vivid, and its statements fully carry out Major Gordon's assertions in the article under discussion.

* * *

CONFEDERATE VETERAN MAGAZINE
NOV., 1913

LOVE AT LAST—GETTYSBURG 50 YEARS AFTER.

BY J. LEMACKS STOKES, WILLIAMSTON, S. C.

Once more the "tide is high" at Gettysburg—
They front again, the valiant blue and gray—
But O the pathos of this "charging" line
Of grim, gray veterans of that far-off day!
They hold the heights once more, the steadfast
blue.
And see the gray tide come; the undimmed eye,
The heart alone in its perpetual youth
Survive the day they stood ready to die.
Life has been hard upon these grand old men;
They've fought and lost on many a stricken field
Life has been kindly too, for what is best remains
Of valor high that knew not how to yield.
The "tide is high" indeed : the gray have reached
the crest.
But what a sight! And who could this forecast?
No sword is drawn, no shot is fired, but hand
Of blue clasps gray in love at last, at last.
In love at last
In love that makes the wayward world go round,
In love that stills the cannon's awful sound,
In love that holds alone the mystic clue,
And reconciles what blue, what gray, each sought
to do—
In love at last, in love at last!

* * *

CONFEDERATE VETERAN MAGAZINE
SEPTEMBER 1914

MEMORIES OF BATTLES.

BY COL. U[lysses] R[obert] BROOKS[93] [6th South Carolina Cavalry,
Co. B], COLUMBIA, S. C.

[Excerpt from longer article]

93. "Col." Brooks was actually a private in the war.

On the 3d of July, 1863, at Hunterstown, near Gettysburg, General Hampton, cool, with noble eye flashing fire, sang out: "Charge them, my brave boys; charge them!"

The whole Yankee cavalry came down upon us with all its energy and fury. Still the line bore the renewed shock. Each of the whole line seemed to be striving with his man, and more of the enemy pressed on. Two dashed at the gallant Hampton, but paid the penalty before his dexterous arm. Another fresh squad rushed from the line and bore upon him. The flashes from the muzzle of his pistol kept them at a moment's bay, while two Mississippians, Privates Moore and Dunlap, of the Jeff Davis Legion, fearlessly rushed to his rescue with sabers lifted high in the air, bringing their sharp edges down upon the heads of the pressing assailants; but sadly they went down beneath the angry tread. Gleaming sabers from several arms were playing over his head, already spurting with gore; but his unerring pistol sent another reeling from his saddle. Frantic with rage, they pressed him against the fence, and! just as the column was being borne back two brave men, Sergt. Nat Price, of Company A, 1st North Carolina, and Private Jackson, of Company B, Cobb's Legion, descrying the awful dilemma of their beloved commander, recklessly dashed into the unequal contest. A sure shot from the pistol of the former went through the nearest one just as he was repeating a blow upon the General's bleeding head. Throwing themselves between him and the pressing antagonists still chafing for their victim, the former earnestly shouted: "General, they are too many for us. For God's sake leap your horse over the fence. I'll die before they shall have you." The spur was suited to his suggestion. His noble steed cleared the fence amid a shower of balls that shred the air, one severely wounding him in the side. The party furiously dashed after the deliverers just as they too were wheeling to follow the uplifted saber. One came down on Price; another barrel sent him reeling from his saddle. The next in van raises his vengeful arm to cleave him down; his uplifted arm received the blow, and before another was raised to finish the work his faithful steed followed in the leap and safely bore him alongside his companion on the other side of the fence.

* * *

CONFEDERATE VETERAN MAGAZINE
Oct. 1915

LONGSTREET AT GETTYSBURG.

BY O[liver] G. THOMPSON [3rd South Carolina Battalion, Co. G], LAURENS, S. C.

A review of the article by W. H. Thompson in the June number of the Veteran prompts me to make this defense of my old commander. I give Mr. Thompson due credit for his laudatory description of Longstreet as a loyal, stubborn fighter. This commendation is in happy contrast to the mass of embittered literature in which Longstreet's critics have dealt with the subject, "Who Lost Gettysburg?" There is, however, a vein running through the article that is suggestive of "damning with faint praise."

Now, as to Gettysburg, I shall mention several facts which ought to convince not only those who had experience at the front, but the younger generation also, that their existence would have been utterly inconsistent with the theory of Longstreet's being responsible, or in any manner at fault, for the failure at Gettysburg.

First, Longstreet was second in command of the grand Army of Northern Virginia, leading the first great corps. If for any cause Lee had been disabled, Longstreet would have been in command of the army; certainly temporarily. What becomes of our exalted estimate of the peerless Lee and of the Confederate authorities who would retain in command an officer of high rank after such a blunder or insubordination (some say treason) as Longstreet is charged with at Gettysburg?

Secondly, if Longstreet had been guilty, as his critics charge, why was there not some criticism at the time, some court of inquiry, suspension from command, or court-martial?

Thirdly, does not every survivor who had experience at the front know that had Longstreet been guilty of the half that has been charged the rank and file would have heard and known of it? Was there ever during the war an officer of rank guilty of a great blunder or defection in any of our battles but every private knew of it? Who of the 1st Corps or any other corps ever heard of these baseless charges until after General Lee's death?

Fourthly, let's see now what followed this alleged blunder or defection. Just sixty days from Gettysburg Longstreet, the "old war horse" of Lee, was leading as fine a body of troops as was ever organized for battle—the division of Hood and McLaws—to Chickamauga's bloody field, there to command the left wing of the army in the only great victory won in the West. Following Chickamauga, he was tendered the command of the Army of Tennessee, which, for well-known reasons, he declined. Mr. Thompson says he was slow at Chickamauga and Knoxville. I was with my command at both. Who of the old corps ever heard of his being slow at either place? He also says Longstreet was ordered to reach the field at daylight on the second day at the Wilderness; that he "came down the turnpike at nine o'clock. Field's Texans leading." If his orders were to reach the field at daylight, he was very nearly on time. Leaving our bivouac at 2 a.m. on that eventful 6th of May. Longstreet swept down the plank road, with Kershaw's South Carolinians leading, and into the tempest of fire at sunrise, fixing bayonets as we filed to the right of the road just in time to stem the tide of Hancock's onset.

To revert to Gettysburg, much has been written about a famous sunrise order that Longstreet failed to carry out. General Longstreet has disproved this by Lee's staff officers. There is nothing to show that Lee expected him to move in the morning. Moreover, his troops were within a mile of Lee's headquarters. The evil effect of any delay on his part was also fully offset by Sickle's projection of the Federal left in a salient angle toward Longstreet's line, so that an attack in the afternoon threatened the Federal left much more seriously than a morning attack would have done. Longstreet did not order Pickett's charge on July 3, Lee ordered it against Longstreet's protest.

In a hitherto unpublished collection of Lee's letters and dispatches, which belongs to Mr. Wymberly Jones DeRenne, of Wormsloe, Ga., much can be found throwing light on or "bringing into clearer light" Lee's intentions, plans, and opinions during the three years in which he led the Army of Northern Virginia. It has been said that the letter in the collection which possesses the greatest historical value is the one which Lee wrote to President Davis discussing the failure of the Gettysburg campaign. It was a private communication and preceded by nine days the formal letter made public at the time, in which Lee asked to be relieved as commander of the

Army of Northern Virginia. In the earlier confidential statement he might have been tempted to put on other shoulders the blame for defeat if he had felt that that blame could be justly shifted. Yet he stood nobly by his impulsive and honest declaration to Pickett on July 3, on the latter's return from his famous charge: "It was all my fault." Lee was not looking for scapegoats; he never looked for them. He wrote to Davis on July 31. 1863: "No blame should be attached to the army for its failure to accomplish what was projected by me, nor should it be censured for the unreasonable expectation of the public. I alone am to blame, perhaps, in expecting too much of its prowess and valor. It, however, in my opinion, achieved under the guidance of the Most High a genuine success, though it did not win a victory. I thought at the time that the latter was practicable. I still think that if all things had worked together it would have been accomplished. But with the knowledge I then had and in the circumstances I was then placed I do not know what better course I could have pursued. With my present knowledge, and could I have foreseen that the attack on the third day would have failed to drive the enemy from his position, I should certainly have tried some other course. What the ultimate result would have been is not so clear to me."

Stuart has been blamed because his cavalry was out of touch with Lee's army for six days, from June 27 to July 2 Ewell has been assailed because he did not attack Cemetery Hill and Culp's Hill late in the afternoon of July 1; but Lee was right in holding that the Army of Northern Virginia was not to blame and that his subordinate commanders were not to blame for the defeat. He expected too much of the "prowess and valor" of his troops. He was defeated, not because his plans were wrong in conception or went wrong in execution, but because he was fighting against an army well handled and possessed of a new spirit since it realized that it had at last found a dependable leader.

* * *

EDGEFIELD ADVERTISER
JANUARY 2, 1918

Longstreet at Gettysburg

In looking over the reminiscences of the Civil War, by Gen. John B. Gordon, he says that Gen. Longstreet was slow in making the attack on the morning of July 2, and that Gen. Lee had ordered Longstreet to open the battle at sunrise, and it was two o'clock before Gen. Longstreet could be found, and Gen. Lee was wondering all morning what had become of his war-horse. Gordon lays the blame all on Longstreet's tardiness in not having his corps on the field in time.

On the evening of July 1 Gen. Longstreet's command left Gettysburg about three or four o'clock, and marched without halting nearly all night, reaching Gettysburg some time before day. My brigade, Kershaw's, halted in a swamp, and remained there until gray dawn. We were then moved back and forth, up and down the battle line some three or four times. At last we halted, and were told to be "ready to move forward at a moment's notice." _____ _____ General Lee by _____ in our rear boot-to-boot. Gen. Lee knew just where Gen. Longstreet was before daylight. And he knew that Gen. Longstreet was "ready for the fray."

Why did Gen. Gordon wait until after Gen. Lee's death to bring these charges against the greatest fighter in the army? Simply, he did not like Longstreet, because he commanded the first corps, and stood in rank next to Lee.

No, Gen. Longstreet was not tardy on any battlefield. There was a kind of intuition among the soldiers in Longstreet's corps; that after all the other troops had made their long marches, tugged at the flanks of the enemy, threatened his rear, and all the display of strategy and generalship failed, then when the hard, stubborn, decisive blow was to be struck, the troops of the first corps were called upon to strike it.

Longstreet had informed Lee at the outset: "My corps is as solid as a rock—a great rock. I will strike the blow, and win, if the other troops gather the fruits of victory." How confident the "Old War Horse," as Gen. Lee called him, was in the solidity and courage of his troops, and soon his seventeen thousand men were to be pitted against the whole army of the Potomac. Still, no battle was ever considered decisive until Longstreet, with his cool, steady head, his heart of steel, and troops, who acknowledged no superior, or scarcely equal, in ancient or modern times, in endurance and courage, had measured strength with the enemy.

Gen. Hancock was counted the best fighting general in the Federal army, and Gen. Longstreet was nearly always pitted against Hancock.

Gen. Lee said after the battle of Gettysburg: "If I had listened to Gen. Longstreet's advice things would have been different there." It was not in Gen. Longstreet's heart to make the assault on "Little Round Top." He did not favor Pickett's charge on the 3rd day. He bitterly opposed this useless sacrifice to life and limb. In his memoirs he tells how he pleaded with Lee to relive him from the responsibility of the command.

In 1866 Gen. Hancock and Gen. Longstreet were discussing the battle of the Wilderness. Hancock said: "Gen. Longstreet, at the time you were wounded in that battle you had me wrapped up in a wet blanket; you were about to capture my whole command."

Generals Lee, Longstreet and Gordon are all dead, but in defense of Gen. Longstreet I must say that Gen. Gordon did him a great injustice. When Gen. Longstreet was sent to Chickamauga to re-inforce Bragg, he commanded the left wing, and opened the battle and led in the Van Hood's division of Longstreet's corps; broke the Federal lines. Later in the day Longstreet drove his column like a wedge into the Union center, ripping asunder the whole Federal division. No officer or body of men could have contributed more to the triumph of the Confederates than did Gen. Longstreet and the brave men who followed him from the Rappahannock.

The praises of Longstreet and his men were freely proclaimed by the Army of Tennessee. While this battle (Chickamauga) was in full blast Gen. [Benjamin Franklin] Cheatham and Gen. [Leonidas] Polk came riding in rear of our line. Polk was an Episcopal Bishop, and commanded a division in the Western army, and was a great admirer of Gen. Cheatham. As Gen. Cheatham was passing he said, "Give 'em hell, boys." About that time the Bishop was lost in the soldier and shouted, "Give it to 'em, boys! Give 'em what Gen. Cheatham says."

In time the south will learn to appreciate the worth of one of her greatest military leaders. Thus far she has done herself an injustice in not allowing full credit for the services rendered to her Lost Cause by Gen. James Longstreet. In time to come the name of Gen. Longstreet will be honored by America, as Washington, Lincoln, Lee and Grant. Why should we of the South, the land of his birth, for whose defense he gave his services and imperiled his life.

He was born in Edgefield county, South Carolina, but in a little town of Georgia upon the high ground stands an old building that once sheltered whom Lee honored with ____ship, and whom he called his "War Horse." Here Gen. Longstreet lived after his battles were fought and the cause finally lost. Here he entertained many distinguished veterans of the late war. Here, too, at one time visited the man who holds the reins of this government, Woodrow Wilson. And under the roof of the then home of Gen. Longstreet, so I have been told, was born the first daughter of Mr. and Mrs. Woodrow Wilson.

Gen. Longstreet was one of the greatest fighters, and could do as much real bull-dog fighting with his corps as any other commanding officer in either army. All honor to Gen. James Longstreet. His men almost worshiped him. Whenever he gave an order or a command his men responded "ready."

Gen. Longstreet's command was in Tennessee from September 19 to April 27, 1864, without winter quarters, fighting the most of the time.

When the campaign opened up in Virginia Gen. Lee called for his "War Horse" to come back as hurriedly as possible. We were then camped at Greenville, Tenn. We at once began the march to Bristol, a distance of one hundred miles. Then we boarded box cars, and were hurried to Virginia with all possible speed. We landed at Charlottesville, and marched from there to Gordonsville. We were then sixteen miles from the Wilderness. The first day's battle had been fought—this was May 5. We halted for rest and sleep. At one o'clock the long roll beat, and we all were up and in line. Longstreet's whole command struck a turkey-trot and kept it for sixteen miles, getting to the battle line at sunrise, May 6. We were moved down the plank road through the thicket. Gen. Lee and staff were sitting on their horses. We were halted at that time. Longstreet rode up and clasped the hand of Lee. Gen. Lee said: "General, I never was so glad to see you. Hancock has broke my line, and I believe I will have to fall back to 'Mine Run' to breastworks." Longstreet said: "General, we will whip him right here in the Wilderness." Lee then said, "Put your men in," and we went in like a cyclone and drove Hancock's corps back nearly two miles.

It was a fact all through the war, whenever there was a hard, knotty, stubborn place to strike, Longstreet was called upon to make the strike, and he was never found wanting. At this very battle (The Wilderness) Gen.

Gordon did his best to reap the fruit of victory from Gen. Longstreet after he was so badly wounded in the neck.

J. Russell Wright [7th South Carolina Infantry, Co. G]

Seneca, S.C.

* * *

Edgefield Advertiser

June 11, 1919

Longstreet at Gettysburg.

In looking over the "Reminiscence of the Civil War" by Gen John B. Gordon, he says that Gen. Longstreet was slow in making the attack on the morning of July 2nd, and that Gen. Lee had ordered Longstreet to open the battle at sunrise and it was two o'clock before Gen. Longstreet could be found, and that Gen. Lee was wondering what had become of his "war-horse." Gordon lays all the blame on Longstreet's "tardiness," as he calls it, in not having his First Army Corps on the field in time.

Now, I do not like to take issue against a dead man, but in this case I will, and with gloves off. Gen. Gordon waited until Gen. Lee died before bringing this false statement against Gen. Longstreet. The truth of the matter is, Gen. Gordon never did like Lee's "war-horse," he was very jealous of him, which all the army officers knew. This was not the first time that Gen. Gordon tried to snatch the "roses" from Longstreet.

Listen what Gen. Lee says after this great battle: "If I had listened to Gen. Longstreet, things would have been different at Gettysburg." That is a matter of history.

Now, I'm going to come down to brass tacks. I was on that march with Gen. Longstreet. Gordon was not along that night before the battle. On the evening of July 1st, Longstreet's command left Chambersburg about 4 o'clock, perhaps it was 5 o'clock, and marched all night, reaching Gettysburg a little while before day light. My brigade (Kershaw's), halted in a swamp and remained there until about gray-dawn. We were then moved back and forth, up and down the line some three or four times. At last we halted and were told to be ready to move at a moment's notice.

By this time the sun was about at the tops of the trees. Now, mark you, Gen. Gordon says that Longstreet could not be found until mid-day, July 2nd.

At sunrise, maybe a little after, Gen. Lee and Gen. Longstreet, with three or four of their staff, rode by some thirty yards in rear of the then, line of battle, "boot-to-boot." Gen. Lee knew just where Gen. Longstreet was before daylight of that morning, and he knew that Longstreet was ready for the fray. As I have stated, Gen. Gordon waited until Gen. Lee's death to bring these charges against the greatest fighter in the army, simply because he did not like Gen. Longstreet, because he commanded the First Army Corps and stood in rank next to Lee. It was universally acknowledged in the First Army Corps that if Gen. Lee had a hard nut to crack, he always called for his 'war-horse' to crack it and he never failed. No, Gen. Longstreet was not tardy on any battle field.

There was a kind of intuition among the soldiers of Longstreet's corps that after all the other troops had made their long marches, tugged at the flanks of the enemy, threatened his rear, and all display of strategy and generalship failed, then when the hard, stubborn, decisive blow was to be struck, the troops of the First Army Corps were called upon to strike it. Gen. Longstreet had informed Gen. Lee at the outset: "My corps is as solid as a rock--a great rock. I will strike the blow and win if the other troops gather the fruits of the victory."

How confident the "Old Warhorse" was in the solidity and courage of his troops, and soon his seventeen thousand men were to be pitted against the whole army of the Potomac. Still, no battle was ever considered decisive till Longstreet, with his cool, steady head, his heart of steel and troops, who acknowledged no superior nor scarcely equal, in ancient or modern times, in endurance and courage, had measured strength with the enemy. I repeat again what Gen. Lee had to say after this battle, his words, and they are historic: "If I had listened to Gen. Longstreet's advice, things would have been different."

It was not in Gen. Longstreet's heart to make the assault on "Little Round Top." He did not favor Pickett's charge on the 3rd day. He bitterly opposed this useless sacrifice of lfe and limb. In his "Memoirs" he tells how he pleaded with Lee to release him from the responsibility of command. I have Gen. Longstreet's history, "From Manassas to

Appomattox," also Gen. Gordon's "History of the Civil War." I've never known anyone to use the pronoun "I" as often as he, "I" and "my." "I" planned the battle; "my" division whipped the fight, etc. Now, the truth of history is, if Gen. Lee had ordered Gen. Longstreet to make the attack at sunrise, the order was countermanded. He was ready and his troops were as solid as a great rock.

I can't tell where Gen. Gordon was on the morning of July 2nd, but I do know that Gen. Longstreet was "Johnny-on-the-spot."

At any time in the day or night, if Gen. Lee had ordered Longstreet to open the battle, he would have struck Gen. Meade like a cyclone, just like he did at 2 o'clock that same day.

My next will be Gen. Longstreet at Gettysburg.

J. RUSSELL WRIGHT [7th South Carolina Infantry, Co. G].

* * *

EDGEFIELD ADVERTISER
JULY 9, 1919

Longstreet at Gettysburg.

It is a matter of history that Gen. Lee and Gen. Longstreet rode together on the morning of July 2nd to reconnoiter Gen. Meade's right wing. It is stated that Gen. Longstreet asked Gen. Lee to let him make a flank attack on Meade's left, that he thought it could be done with less sacrifice to life and limb. Gen. Longstreet says this was the first time that he had ever noticed Gen. Lee to manifest a spirit of anger, and turned to him and said, "No. I'll make the attack in Meade's front and whip him on his own ground." After the battle Gen. Lee admitted that if he had listened to Longstreet's advice things would have been different at Gettysburg.

Now, I will give, as near as I can, about the time that Gen. Longstreet made the charge through the wheat field and to the peach orchard up to the foot of Big Round Top. It was after the cannon duel. I suppose this was the greatest cannonading that was ever known in ancient or modern times. About 200 cannon from each side belched forth fire and lead which made the everlasting hills quiver and rock for two hours. I suppose it was about two o'clock when Gen. Longstreet ordered the charge. History gives the number of men in this charge from seventeen to twenty thousand. From then until night it was war to the knife. That night after the battle we slept on the battlefield. This was just as gallant a charge as Pickett's on the 3rd day on Little Round Top.

In time the South will learn to appreciate the worth of one of her greatest military leaders. Thus far she has done herself an injustice in not allowing full credit for the services rendered to her cause by Gen. James Longstreet. In time to come, the name of Gen. Longstreet will be honored by America as Washington, Lincoln, Lee and Grant. Why should we, of the South, the land of his birth, forget him, for whose defense he gave his services so freely and imperiled his life?

He was born in Edgefield, South Carolina, but in a little town of Georgia upon the high grounds, stands an old building that once sheltered the head of the soldier whom Lee honored with his friendship and called his "war-horse." Here Gen. Longstreet lived after his battles were fought and the cause went down to its grave at Appomattox, wrapped in its bloody mantle. Here he entertained many distinguished veterans of the war of the "60's." Here too, at one time visited the man who holds the reins of this government--Woodrow Wilson. And under the roof of the then home of Gen. Longstreet, so I have been told, was born the first daughter of Mr. and Mrs. Woodrow Wilson.

Gen. Longstreet was one of the greatest fighters and could do as much real bull-dog fighting with his corps as any other commanding general in the army. All honor to Gen. Longstreet. His men almost worshipped him. Whenever he gave an order or a command to go forward, his men responded "Ready."

Gen. Longstreet's command was in Tennessee from September 19th to April 27, 1864, without winter quarters, fighting most of the time. When the campaign opened up in Virginia, Gen. Lee called for his "war-horse" to come back as hurriedly as possible. We were then camped at Greenville, Tennessee. We at once began to march to Bristol, Tennessee, a distance of one hundred miles. There we boarded box cars and were hurried on. We landed at Charlottesville, Virginia, and marched from there to Gordonsville. On the night of the 5th of May, our command was in sixteen miles of the battle field of the wilderness, the battle of the wilderness had been fought. We halted for the night and everybody was soon fast asleep, but at one o'clock the long roll began to beat and the command was in the road to the wilderness in a short while, and we struck a turkey trot and kept it until sun rise. This was May 6th. Arriving on the battle field, we were moved down the old plank road through the thicket. Gen. Lee and staff were sitting on their horses. We were then halted. Longstreet rode up and grasped the hand of Lee. Gen. Lee said, "General, I never was so glad to see you. Hancock has broken my line and I believe I will have to fall back to 'Mine Run' to the breast work (which was about three miles back)." Longstreet said, "General, we will whip him right here in this Wilderness." Gen. Lee said, "Put your men in." This was the first time I had ever heard the two generals talking, and the order was given by Gen. Longstreet, forward, file right and we went into the bushes and struck Gen. Hancock's line like a thunder bolt and turned the tide of battle.

In 1866 in the city of Washington Gen. Hancock told Gen. Longstreet "When you were wounded at the Wilderness on May 6th, you had my command rolled up in a wet blanket."

This was another time that Gen. Gordon claimed the "roses" from Gen. Longstreet, about which I will tell later on.

My next, "Longstreet in Tennessee."

J. Russell Wright [7th South Carolina Infantry, Co. G].

* * *

CONFEDERATE VETERAN MAGAZINE
Nov., 1919

J. M. Riddle,[94] of Lancaster. S. C, wants to know if any of those who were with him on the retreat from Little Round Top, at Gettysburg, are now living. He will be glad to hear from any old comrade.

* * *

94. There were two South Carolinians named James M. Riddle at Gettysburg. 3rd Lt. James M. Riddle of the 2nd South Carolina, Co. E, who enlisted out of Camden County and Pvt. James M. Riddle of the 3rd South Carolina, Co. K, who enlisted out of Spartanburg County.

CONFEDERATE VETERAN MAGAZINE
FEB., 1922

PENSIONS FOR FAITHFUL NEGROES.

BY COMMANDER J. F. J. CALDWELL,[95]

CAMP JAMES D. NANCE,

U. C. V., NEWBERRY, S. C.

In providing for pensions to negroes who served faithfully during the war of secession, the States of Tennessee and Mississippi have discharged a duty incumbent on every State embraced in the Confederate States of America. The other States are blameworthy for their neglect to do likewise. I reproach myself for my inactivity; for I had personal knowledge of negroes serving with the Army of Northern Virginia who not only performed their menial tasks with fidelity, but also risked their lives for their masters or employers. One of these, a hired free negro, insisted on accompanying me in the battle of Gettysburg; and I had, literally, to drive him back. And after I was shot down, he was the first man to come to me, and that while rifle balls were still humming around. He, however, needs no pension, for he died several years ago.

Col. M[unson] M[onroe] Buford,[96] of South Carolina, who served under Hampton, Stuart, and Lee, was one of the first persons I know of to urge this provision for negroes by articles in the newspapers. I am sorry to say that we still have it not in South Carolina. A bill providing for it was passed by our State Senate, last winter, but did not reach a vote in the House of Representatives. We are confident of the passage of the measure at the next term, which begins in January. Such pensions will cost little; for very few of those faithful servants survive. And it is a duty which we should discharge without further delay.

95. 2nd Lt., 1st South Carolina (McCreary's or Gregg's), Co. B
96. "Col." Buford was actually a private in the 5th South Carolina Cavalry, Co. K

* * *

CONFEDERATE VETERAN MAGAZINE
FEB. 1922

GEN. E. M. LAW AT GETTYSBURG.

[The following tribute appeared in the Charleston (S. C.) News and Courier soon after the death of General Law.]

Maj. Gen. Evander McIver Law will always be remembered as a South Carolinian, one of the most gallant of the many gallant officers contributed by South Carolina to the Confederate army. He was born in Darlington, educated at the Citadel, from which he graduated in 1856, and was one of the first teachers at the King's Mountain Military School at Yorkville when Colonel Coward and Gen. Micah Jenkins established that famous institution. In 1860 he left Yorkville to start a military school of his own at Tuskegee, Ala., but a few months later, in January, 1861, he headed a company of Alabama volunteers and took part in the capture of Pensacola and the fort at that place shortly thereafter being made lieutenant colonel of the 4th Alabama regiment. His service thenceforward in the armies of the Confederacy was continuous, and he fought in most of the great battles of Virginia and distinguished himself again and again at the First and Second battles of Manassas, at Gaines's Mill, and Malvern Hill, at Boonesboro and Antietam, at Fredericksburg and Gettysburg, at Chickamauga, and in all the hard campaigns from the Wilderness to Cold Harbor.

In the dispatches which told of General Law's death mention was made of the fact that at the battle of Gettysburg, where he commanded Hood's division after General Hood was wounded, "he was signally successful, having been brevetted on the field at Gettysburg by General Longstreet for maneuvering his division on the Round Top in such a manner as to effect the disastrous repulse of Kilpatrick's division of mounted Federal troops." In the Century Magazine for December, 1886, General Law himself told the story of how Hood's division, which occupied the Confederate right at Gettysburg, held the front line throughout July 3, 1863, that long day which followed the disastrous but immortal charge of Pickett. The most spectacular event of that day was the repulse of Kilpatrick's division when General Farnsworth, emerging suddenly from the woods at the base of the Round Tops, led the charge upon the Confederates in which he and all but a handful of his men met their deaths.

When the charge began General Law was talking with the officers of Bachman's Battery, a Charleston organization, commanded by Capt. James Simons and Gen. Rudolph Siegling. He hurried off one of the members of his staff with orders to detach the first regiment he should come to on the main line, and send it on a run to head off the advancing cavalry. This happened to be the 4th Alabama regiment, and as Farnsworth and his men came galloping up the valley the Confederates ran out in the open ground on the farther side, opening fire as they ran, the course of the cavalry being abruptly checked and saddles rapidly emptied.

"Recoiling from this fire," General Law wrote, "they turned to their left and rear and directed their course up the hill toward the position occupied by our batteries. Bachman's Battery promptly changed front to its left, so as to face the approaching cavalry, and, together with the infantry supports, opened a withering fire at close range. Turning again to their left, Farnsworth and the few of his men who remained in their saddles directed their course toward the point where they had originally broken in, having described by this time almost a complete circle. But the gap where they had entered was now closed, and, receiving another fire from that point, they again turned to the left and took refuge in the woods near the base of Round Top. There they came in conflict with the skirmish line of the 15th Alabama regiment, and General Farnsworth, refusing to surrender, killed himself with his pistol, In the charge on Bachman's battery some of Farnsworth's men were shot within thirty-five or forty yards of the battery's guns."

General Law in his prime was one of the handsomest of men, as straight as an arrow, with jet black beard, and of dashing appearance. The grace of his manner was flawless. He had not lived in South Carolina since the early 90's, when, for a time, he edited the Yorkville Yeoman. He was held in the highest esteem by his surviving comrades throughout South

Carolina and only a few weeks ago, at a meeting of Camp Sumter in this city, warm tributes were paid him by Colonel Armstrong and others, and he was elected to honorary membership in the Camp.

* * *

CONFEDERATE VETERAN MAGAZINE

FEB. 1923

McGOWAN'S SOUTH CAROLINA BRIGADE IN THE BATTLE OF GETTYSBURG.

BY B[enjamin] F. BROWN [1st South Carolina (McCreary's and Gregg's, Co. L], AUGUSTA, GA.

The interesting article on "The Battle of Gettysburg, July 1, 1863," by John Purifoy, Montgomery, Ala., in the January Veteran, has caused me to look up some history of what McGowan's South Carolina Brigade, Pender's Light Division, A. P. Hills' Corps, did on that memorable July 1, 1863. The brigade was commanded throughout the three days' battle by Col. Abner Perrin.

Col. Perrin's report, written a little over a month after the battle, and being official, is, therefore, authentic war history.

That report was as follows:

"Headquarters McGowan's Brigade, August 13, 1863.

"Sir: This brigade, consisting of the following named regiments, to wit: The 1st (Provisional Army), 12th, 13th, 14th, and 1st (Rifles), the 1st under command of Major C. W. McCreary, the 12th under Col. John L. Miller, the 13th under Lieut. Col. B. T. Brockman, the 14th, Lieut. Col. Joseph N. Brown, and the Rifles, Capt. William M. Hadden, being a part of Maj. Gen. Pender's Light Division of the Army of Northern Virginia, in the late campaign across the Potomac, was from June 5 until the present time under my immediate command.

"About 8 o'clock on the morning of July 1, I received orders to get under arms, and the brigade, except Capt. Hadden, who was left with the Rifles to guard the wagon train, commenced the march on the turnpike leading to Gettysburg at the head of I he division and just in rear of the division of Major General Heth.

"The march was continued to within three miles of Gettysburg, when I was ordered to file down a road, form line of battle, leaving sufficient room between my left and the Gettysburg road for General Scales's brigade, and to throw out skirmishers to cover my right flank.

"Skirmishing between the advanced infantry of General Heth's division and that of the enemy, as well as heavy artillery firing, had already commenced in our front. I was soon notified that General Heth would advance and that I would make a corresponding movement forward, preserving my alignment with General Scales on my left. We moved through an open field about a mile, where we halted in rear and in supporting distance of General Heth's division, which had now become closely engaged with the enemy in our front. Here Brigadier General Lane's brigade took position on my right to protect our flank from the enemy's cavalry and some infantry, reported by Capt. W. T. Haskell in that direction.

"We remained in this position until about 3 o'clock, and were again ordered forward, and again advanced, probably half a mile, when we came close upon General Heth's division pressing the enemy within a short distance in front of us.

"I remained in this position probably until after 4 o'clock, when I was ordered by General Pender to advance, and to pass General Heth's division, should I come up with it at a halt, and to engage the enemy as circumstances might warrant. I soon came up with and passed General Pettigrew's brigade, the men of which seemed much exhausted by several hours' hard fighting. Here I availed myself of a ravine, which sheltered us from the enemy's artillery, to reform my line, and instructed regimental commanders when the advance was resumed not to allow a gun to be fired at the enemy until they received orders to do so.

"We now moved forward, preserving an alignment with General Scales, and, as soon as the brigade commenced ascending the hill in front, we were met by a furious storm of musketry and shells from the enemy's batteries to the left of the road near Gettysburg; but the instructions I had given were scrupulously observed; not a gun was fired. The brigade received the enemy's fire without faltering, rushing up the hill at a charge, driving the enemy without difficulty to their last position at Gettysburg.

"We continued the charge without opposition, except from artillery, which maintained a constant and most galling fire upon us until we got within two hundred yards of their last position, about the Theological Seminary. Some lines of infantry had shown themselves across the field, but disappeared as we got within range of them. While crossing the last fence about two hundred yards from a grove near the college, the brigade received the most destructive fire of musketry I have ever been exposed to. We continued to press forward, however, without firing until we reached the edge of the grove. Here the 14th Regiment was staggered for a moment by the severity and destructiveness of the enemy's musketry. It looked to us as though this regiment was entirely destroyed.

"There I found myself without support either on the right or left. General Scales's brigade had halted to return the enemy's fire near the fence, about two hundred yards distant from the enemy. General Lane did not move on my right at ab, and was not at this time in sight of me. This gave the enemy an enfilading fire on the 14th Regiment. This regiment, under lead of Colonel Brown and Major E. Croft, most gallantly stood its ground. I now directed the 1st Regiment, Major McCreary, to oblique to the right to avoid a breastwork of rails, behind which I discovered the enemy was posted, and then to change front to the left and attack in Hank. This was done most effectionly under the lead of this gallant officer. The enemy here were completely routed. This caused the whole of the artillary on our left, at least thirty pieces, to be limbered up and removed to the rear. Much of their artillary would have been captured, but the First and Fourteenth, in their pursuit, again met a force of the enemy's infantry strongly posted behind a stone wall near to the left of the college. It was the work of a few moments, however, to dislodge them.

"These two regiments, now reduced in numbers to less than one-half the men they carried into battle, pursued the enemy to within the town of Gettysburg, capturing hundreds of prisoners, two field pieces, and a number of caissons.

"While the 1st and 14th Regiments were assailing the enemy and driving him from his breastworks near the Seminary, I ordered the 12th Regiment, under Colonel Miller, and the 13th, under Lieutenant Colonel Brockman, to oblique to the right and charge the enemy, strongly posted behind a stone fence to the right of the college, from which position he had kept up a constant and withering fire of musketry upon the front and right flank of the brigade. These two regiments had necessarily to change direction to the right somewhat, so as to meet the enemy full in front. This movement was most brilliantly performed by these two regiments, and was most skillfully managed by the officers I have mentioned. They rushed up the crest of the hill and to the stone fence, driving everything before them, the Twelfth gaining the stone fence and pouring an enfilading fire upon the enemy's right flank. The Thirteenth, now coming up, made it an easy task to drive the enemy down the opposite slope and across the open field west of Gettysburg.

"This was the last of the fight of this day. The enemy completely routed and driven from every point, Gettysburg was now completely in our possession.

"After penetrating the enemy's lines near the College, the change of direction of the First and Fourteenth to attack the enemy in flank to the left, and the oblique movement and change of direction of the Twelfth and Thirteenth to attack the enemy in the flank to the right, necessarily separated the brigade into two parts. As soon as I knew the enemy had been routed on the right, I ordered the Twelfth and Thirteenth to unite again with the First and Fourteenth, who were now pursuing the fleeing force through the town. Finding the two last-named regiments now reduced to less than half the number with which they entered the battle and the men much exhausted, I ordered them back from the town to await the Twelfth and Thirteenth, and sent a small detachment through the town to take such prisoners as the enemy had left in the retreat. It was after the recall of these two regiments that the brigade of Brigadier General Ramseur filed through Gettysburg from the direction of my left.

"The loss of the killed and wounded of the brigade did not fall short of 500—100 killed, 477 wounded; total, 577.

"Better conduct was never exhibited on any field than was shown by both officers and men in this engagement. Each one of the color sergeants taken into the fight was killed in front of his regiment. Some regiments had a number of color bearers shot down one after another. The officers generally were conspicuous in leading their men everywhere in the hottest of the fight.

"After the First and Fourteenth were withdrawn from Gettysburg, General Pender ordered me to get the brigade together and let the men rest. Now it was that the first piece of artillery which we had driven was opened upon my command, and it was the same artillery which we had driven from our left near Gettysburg. I saw it move off from my left and file into position over the hill.

"The next day (2nd), having taken position in rear of the artillery as a support, we were exposed to and suffered a small loss from the enemy's shells. About 6 o'clock in the afternoon I was ordered to push forward my skirmish line and to drive the enemy's pickets from the road in front of Cemetery Hill. I communicated this order to Capt. William T. Haskell, in command of a select battalion of sharpshooters acting as skirmishers, and sent Major McCreary forward with his regiment, about one hundred strong, to deploy in rear of Captain Haskell and to act as a support. The battalion of sharpshooters, led by the gallant Haskell, made a most intrepid charge upon the Yankee skirmishers, driving them out of the road and close up under their batteries, but soon after gaining the road (called the dirt road), Captain Haskell received a wound from the enemy's sharpshooters, from which he died in a few moments on the field. This brave and worthy young officer fell while boldly walking along the front of his command, encouraging his men and selecting favorable positions for them to defend. He was educated and accomplished, possessing in a high degree every virtuous quality of a true gentleman and Christian. He was an officer of most excellent judgment and a soldier of the coolest judgment and most chivalrous daring.

"This position was held by my skirmishers until about 10 o'clock at night. I was ordered to place my brigade in line of battle, then on the right of General Thomas. I remained quietly in this position during the remainder of the night, having thrown forward skirmishers again.

"Next morning (the 3rd) the heaviest skirmishing I ever witnessed was kept up during the greater part of the day. The enemy made desperate efforts to recapture the position, on account of our skirmishers being within easy range of their artillerists on the Cemetery Hill, but we repulsed every assault, and held the position until ordered back to the main line at Gettysburg. At one time the enemy poured down a perfect torrent of light troops from the hill, which swept my skirmishers back to the main line. I now ordered the Fourteenth to deploy and charge the enemy, which was done in the most gallant style, not without losing some valuable officers and men. Lieutenant Colonel Brown and Major Croft, of the Fourteenth, were here severely wounded.

"We remained at Gettysburg the remainder of the night and during the 4th, and at night moved back with the division toward Hagerstown. We went into line of battle at Hagerstown, on the 11th, when my skirmishers were engaged and where we lost a few men in killed and wounded. Among the former Capt. John W. Chambers, of the First, a most gallant and worthy officer, who fell at the head of his company.

"I take occasion to mention the names of Major Croft, of the Fourteenth, Major Isaac F. Hunt, of the Thirteenth, Major E. F. Bookter, of the Twelfth, as officers who proved themselves fully worthy of their positions throughout the engagements around Gettysburg. I remarked particularly the cool and gallant bearing of Major Bookter, and the force and judgment with which he managed the men under his control. Capts. W. P. Shooter, T. P. Alston, and A. P. Butler, of the First South Carolina Volunteers; Capts. James Boatwright and E. Cowan, of the Fourteenth, and Capt. T. Frank Clyburn, of the Twelfth, were distinguished for uncommonly good conduct in the action, as I can testify from personal observation."

"A. Perrin, Colonel Commanding Brigade."

"Major Joseph A. Englehard, Assistant Adjutant General

Light Division."

Extract from report of Maj. Joseph A. Englehard, Assistant Adjutant General of General Pender, who was mortally wounded:

"Too much credit cannot be awarded Colonel Perrin and the splendid brigade under his command for the manner and spirit with which this attack was conducted. Of the former the government has recognized his valuable services in a manner most grateful to the true soldier by a prompt promotion. Of the latter, all who are acquainted with their gallantry on this occasion unite in their commendation to both.

"Their commander Maj. Gen. W. D. Pender, who fell mortally wounded on the succeeding day, was most enthusiastic in their praise."

"Joseph A. Englehard, Assistant Adjutant General."

From General A. P. Hill's report:

"The rout of the enemy was complete, Perrin's brigade taking position after position of the enemy and driving him through the town of Gettysburg.

"A. P. Hill, Lieutenant General."

Extract from the report of the Federal commander, Gen.

Abner Doubleday, commanding the First Corps of the Federals at this point, who says:

"I remained at the Seminary superintending the final movement until thousands of hostile bayonets made their appearance around the sides of the building. I then rode back and rejoined my command, nearly all of whom were filing through the town. As we passed through the streets our frightened people gave us food and drink.

"Abner Doubleday,

"Major General Commanding First Army Corps."

Some Recollections of Gettysburg.

BY SERGT. B. F. BROWN, COMPANY L, FIRST REGIMENT, SOUTH CAROLINA VOLUNTEERS.

Colonel Perrin says: "Here I availed myself of a ravine which sheltered us from the enemy's artillery to reform my line and instructed regimental commanders when the advance was resumed not to allow a gun to be fired at the enemy until ordered to do so." This is what followed as well as I can now recall the circumstances. Colonel Perrin, who was only a few paces from where my company (L.), of the First, was lined up, said: "Men, the order is to advance; you will go to the crest of the hill. If Heth does not need you, lie down and protect yourselves as well as you can; if he needs you, go to his assistance at once. Do not fire your guns; give them the bayonet; if they run, then see if they can outrun the bullet."

When we reached the crest it was plain that Heth did need us, for his men were at a standstill and were exposed to a terrific fire from the Union batteries on Seminary Ridge. As we swept through his lines, onward in our charge, the men cheered us with the stirring words: "Go in, South Carolina! Go in, South Carolina!" And so well did we go in that we not only reached Seminary Ridge, but actually entered the Theological Seminary, and my schoolmate and messmate, P. H[enry] Reilly, captured some ten or more of the panic-stricken enemy who had sought shelter in one of the rooms in the Seminary building.

Colonel Perrin says: "I ordered the Twelfth and Thirteenth to unite again with the First and Fourteenth, who were now pursuing the fleeing enemy through the town."

The First, commanded by the brilliant, fearless, and magnetic Maj. C. W. McCreary, entered Gettysburg in response to a call for volunteers from Maj. McCreary. The heavy fighting was over; the enemy were disappearing from our front in the direction of Gettysburg, and we had come to a halt.

Why we were halted I have never learned. Why Major McCreary did not take the regiment into Gettysburg without calling for volunteers, I do not know, but I do know that, so far as I could see, the 1st Regiment went with him to a man and remained in Gettysburg until withdrawn by order of Colonel Perrin.

The superb manner in which Colonel Perrin handled McGowan's Brigade won for him the stars of a brigadier general, he laid down his noble life in the front of the battle while leading his Alabama brigade in the charge at Spotsylvania, May 12, 1864.

* * *

AIKEN STANDARD
AUGUST 3, 1934

The battlefield of Gettysburg is an intensely interesting place to Charles P. Johnson,[97] local cotton weigher, who recently visited it on the

97. Possibly Pvt. Charles P. Johnson of the 15th South Carolina, Co. A. Co. A was from Columbia, SC.

first vacation he's ever taken. He reports at length on the sights he saw while spending several hours going over the scene of America's greatest conflict, and states that he was ashamed to find that, after seeing all the great monuments erected by the states to their native sons who took part in the fighting, South Carolina has only a small and cheap marker to tell the sight-seer that troops of the Palmetto state were on the field for the Confederacy. Many brave and illustrious Carolinians fought, bled and died at Gettysburg and it is only fitting that their deeds of valor should be commemorated in as grand a style as that of the men from other states, be they Northern or Southern.

~*Section 6*~

Reunions

Lt. Thomas J. Duckett was a Sgt. in Company I, 3rd S.C. Infantry at Gettysburg. He is pictured at the 1913 Gettysburg Reunion wearing the hat he wore throughout the war. He had decorated it with markings from the battles he fought and reunions he attended.

(National Park Service)

Chapter 1
Reunions

NEWBERRY HERALD AND NEWS
APRIL 25, 1913

ITEMS OF INTEREST FROM STATE CAPITAL

GEORGIA LABOR FEDERATION THANKS GOVERNOR BLEASE.

Veterans in Aiken This Week Looking Forward to Gettysburg. - Governor Blease on Education.

Governor Blease is in Aiken in attendance upon the Confederate Veteran's reunion. He is accompanied by a good many members of his military staff. The governor will return to the city tonight.

[Excerpt of longer article]

A good many of the old soldiers have been in Columbia on their way to the reunion. Comrade was meeting comrade here, and all were looking forward to the meeting of other comrades in Aiken. None of these men is young anymore, but when they don the gray of the Confederacy and begin to live over again in reminiscence the days when they battled for the South, they are young again in spirit, at least, and their eyes kindle with the old-time fire.

Already some of the veterans are planning to attend the celebration of the fiftieth anniversary of the battle of Gettysburg, at Gettysburg, Pa., July 1, 2, 3 and 4. This promises to be the greatest reunion of the Blue and the Gray since the war, and an occasion memorable in the history of the nation. Any veteran may secure all information he desires either from the State's representative, appointed by the governor, the Hon. W. Jasper Talbert. Parksville, S. C., or the State member of the U. C. V. committee. Col. C. K. Henderson, Aiken. S.C. An elaborate program has been arranged for the occasion.

Virginia's Gettysburg monument to Robert E. Lee and his men is now being erected on the Gettysburg battlefield, on the spot where General Lee stood during Pickett's and Pettigrew's charge. It is stated in the pamphlet giving information of the coming celebration that "this is the originally accepted design of the eminent sculptor. T. Wm. Seivers, Richmond, Va., but it has been somewhat altered and improved." The cut of the monument shows a handsome and elaborate work of art.

* * *

KEOWEE COURIER
MAY 28, 1913

LETTER SENT TO VETERANS.

Arrangements for Entertainment at Gettysburg Reunion Set Forth.

Major Gen. B. H. Teague, commanding the South Carolina Division, U. C. V., has addressed to the veterans a letter setting forth officially the arrangements that have been made to care for them during the Gettysburg reunion. July 1-4, next. The letter follows:

To the Confederate Veterans of South Carolina: The State of Pennsylvania has extended an Invitation to all Confederate veterans to unite with the Grand Army of the Republic in the celebration of the 50th anniversary of the battle of Gettysburg, July 1, 2, 3 and 4 of this year, on the battlefield.

The Legislature of our State at its last session appropriated $1,000 to pay for the transportation of such Confederate veterans residing in South Carolina as participated in that battle. The Gettysburg survivors only are to share in this fund for their transportation, and those who purpose attending the celebration must furnish a certificate, attested by a Confederate veteran, sworn to before the Clerk of Court of the county In which they reside, and forward the same to the commanding officer, Gen. B. H. Teague, Aiken, S. C. on or before the 15th day of June. With this certificate must be sent the name of the railroad station from which each one will start. This certificate will be recorded and returned to the sender with a check for his proportionate share of the State's appropriation for railroad fares.

All veterans who purpose attending the celebration who were not participants in the battle of Gettysburg, will have to pay their own railroad fare. Free entertainment will be furnished to all veterans in a large camp to be established for this purpose.

Remember, all Confederate veterans who were not in the battle of Gettysburg, who attend this celebration, must obtain, before leaving home, a certificate signed by the commander or adjutant of a camp of United Confederate veterans. This certificate will be presented at Gettysburg to secure entertainment.

While any veteran wearing civilian's clothes will be entertained, it is desired that all who can will wear the gray uniform.

B. H. Teague, Major General,

S. C. Division. C. C. V.

Official: S. E. Welch.

Attorney General, Chief of Staff.

Camp Norton.

In connection with the above notice with reference to the July reunion at Gettysburg. It will prove of interest to many to read a short sketch prepared by J. W. Holleman a year ago regarding the organization of "Camp

Norton." The article follows:

Walhalla. April 7. 1912.

On the 7th day of April, 1902, some Confederate Veterans met in the Court House at this place and organized a "Camp of Confederate Veterans," and as this is the tenth anniversary of said organization, I have concluded to give an account of the same, and it may be interesting to some of those old veterans who still live, and to the descendants of some who have crossed over and answered "Roll Call" on the other side of the river.

The organization was made as follows:

Col. Robt. A. Thompson, Commander, Colonel 2d Rifles.

Major Stiles P. Dendy, 1st Lieutenant Commander, Major 2d Rifles,

Sergt. R. Y. H. Lowery, 2d Lieutenant Commander, Co. C. Orr's Rifes.

Sergt. J. W. Holleman, Adjutant, Co. C. 12th Regiment.

Adjt. J. G. Law. D. D. Chaplain. 38th Georgia Regiment.

Alexander, W.H., Co. F, 22d. Regt.

Aldrich, R. H., Ordnance Dept.

Adams, Jasper, Co. C. 2d Rifles.

Brandt, H. L., Co. C. Orr's Rifles.

Burton. W. J. N., Co. I. Palmetto Sharpshooters.

Brucke, A. C., Co. C., 2d Rifles.

Burley, W. W., Co. B. 17th Regt.

Burrell, Jas., Co. H, 1st Artillery.

Crenshaw, N., Co. M, Palmetto Sharpshooters.

Campbell, J. L., Co. E, 2d Rifles.

Chastain, H. A., Co. K, 12th Reg.

Cain, Richard, Co. K, 22d Regt.

Cantrell, Staten, Co. G, 12th Regt.

Dendy, S. K., Co. F, Orr's Rifles.

Durham, Marion, Co. B. 2d Rifles.

Davis, John G., Co E, 1st Artillery.

Driver, B. E., Co. E, 20th Regt.

Elrod, A. W., Co. C. Palmetto Sharpshooters.

Ellison, A. H., Co. F. 2d Cavalry.

Fendley, J. W., Co. A, Orr's Rifles.

Fendley, D. W., Co. A. Orr's Rifles.

Fincannon, I. D., Co. G, 20th N.C. Regt.

Gibson, H. A. H., Co. B, 2d Rifles.

Grubbs, W. T., Co. D, 2d Rides.

Hamilton. W. W., Co. L, Palmetto Sharpshooters.

Hudson, J. M., Co. C, Orr's Rifles.

Hawkins, John, Co. B, 2d Rifles.

Hunnicutt, J. M., Co. H, 2d Cav.

Harris, David, Co. F, 2d Rifles.

Keaton, John, Co. K, 12th Regt.

Kelley, J. H., Co. F, 2d Cavalry.

Logan, J. B., Co. C, Orr's Regt.

Manning, I. C., Co. G. 2nd State Reserves.

Mongold, W. H., Co. C, Orr's Regt.

Mason, James. Co. K. 22d Regt.

Martin. V. F., Ordnance Dept.

Moss, W. W., Co. E. Orr's Rifles.

Morton, John B., State Reserves.

McKee, H. M., Co. B, State Reserves.

Nix, E. J., Co. B. 2d Rifles.

Nichols, Jas., Co. K. 12th Regt.

Pool, S. M., Co. E. Orr's Rifles.

Perry, John D., Co. C. 7th Cav.

Phillips, N., Ferguson's Battery.

Phillips, Evan, Co. E. Orr's Rifles.

Powell, W. P., Co. D, 11th N. C. Regt.

Pieper, F. W., Co. C. Orr's Rifles.

Rogers, Leonard C., C

Rogers, Leonard, Co.C. Orr's Regt.

Rutledge, R. S., Co. C. Orr's Rifles.

Ridley, C. M., Co. K. 12th Regt.

Ramey, Albert, Ferguson's Battery

Strother, W. A.

Sanders, J. M., Co. D, 22d Regt.

Sanders, Wm., Co. B. 37th Va. Cavalry.

Singleton, W. O., Co. B, Palmetto Sharpshooters.

Terrell, M. A., Co. F. Orr's Rifles.

Todd, Thos. C., Co. E, Orr's Rifles.

Taylor, Franklin, Co. B, 2d Rifles.

White, N. L., Co. K, 12th Regt.

Wilson, M. H., Co. C, Orr's Rifles.

Miss Sallie Norton was elected sponsor of the Camp.

I hope that some of the children or grandchildren of those old soldiers who are yet alive, and especially of those who are dead, will keep the copy of The Courier which has this list in it, and when you are old, like we are, you may like to read over the list. Wishing all good luck and good health. I am,

Yours sincerely,

J. W. Holleman, Secretary,

600 from Pickens District.

It is an Interesting fact to note that there were 600 soldiers from Pickens District at the Battle of Gettysburg. Four companies from Orr's Regiment of Rifles were there—Companies A, C, E and F--and two companies from the Twelfth South Carolina Regiment--Companies G and K. Each of these six companies mustered in with 100 men or more, and by a system of recruiting each was kept up to its full strength up to the time of the engagement in the Battle of Gettysburg, thus showing that there were not less than 600 from Pickens District participating In that great battle.

* * *

NEWBERRY HERALD AND NEWS
JUNE 3, 1913

To Go To Gettysburg.

Mr. W[illiam] G. Peterson [3rd South Carolina, Co. B] has been granted leave of absence by the post office department at Washington to attend the Gettysburg reunion of survivors of the battlefield, all such old soldiers in the employment of the government being granted leaves of absence. Mr. Peterson, coming under those heads, expects to avail himself of the advantages of opportunity.

There will be quite a "bunch" of the old soldiers from Newberry present on that momentous occasion. May all who go be able to return to mingle again at other meetings of "old vets," in some instances the old vet is living yet, one or two occasionally quite so, "you bet." (Perhaps this will be allowed to pass one time.)

* * *

NEWBERRY HERALD AND NEWS
JUNE 20, 1913

CRITICIZE HANDLING OF GETTYSBURG FUND
One Confederate Says Custodian Favored "Select Few."

Columbia State, 18th

To the Editor of the State: Are we getting a square deal? Judging from Gen. Teague's letter in Saturday's State, many of us who were at Gettysburg are not. The intention of the appropriation was to help all the veterans who participated in the battle—all were to be treated alike, is my understanding. And besides, Gen. Teague issued a circular letter for all those who contemplated going to the meeting to get their applications to his office by June 15, which he won't deny. Instead of waiting until June 15 to see how many would apply, and then apportioning the fund to all alike, however small the amount, he gives out all the funds to a portion of the applicants and leaves some without any help, several days before the time designated.

I don't know how other old soldiers look at it, but it looks like caucus work to me: giving the State's money to a part of the intended beneficiaries and saying to the others, "Get there if you can, pay your own way or stay at home; it is not for you, but those whom I have selected."

Now, Mr. Editor, among all the men of our State I think the old soldiers should be the last ones to be humiliated by such treatment as those who were left out in the apportionment of this fund received.

O[tway] Henderson [15th South Carolina, Co. K].

McCormick, June 16

"Awkward Situation."

To the Editor of the State: The State of Pennsylvania has generously provided for a reunion of the survivors of the two great armies that fought each other in the memorable battle of Gettysburg. A reunion in the spirit of civic friendship and good will towards each other after an elapse of 50 eventful years would doubtless be a pleasant episode, although combined with a feeling of sadness in the experience of all in attendance. In view of the invitation to ex-Confederates to attend, the last session of the South Carolina legislature assumed the work of providing to defray the railroad expenses of her soldiery to and from the reunion, but the legislative big hearted solons instead of arranging to draw upon the State treasury for the necessary amount fixed it at $1,000, enough to provide for 64 veterans, while in fact we have 111 who have been led to apply for transportation. The provision thus made is a legislative disgrace to the State and an insult to those who have accepted the invitation. Such little legislation reminds me of the legislative ex-Confederate pauper pension act, which was passed a few years ago under the guise of helping the needy veterans who put their lives upon their country's altar in the interest of State rights and Southern sentiment. Being a great, proud and financially prosperous State and not being willing to expend all of our energy in regard to the old soldier in high sounding and skyscraping adjectives in praising his self-sacrificing heroism, our lawmakers passed an act to give needy soldiers a pension. But the soldier must certify that he was a member of a certain company and regiment and get two other soldiers to verify to the same, and then swear that his entire income from all sources during the preceding year was not in excess of $75, and amount really less that the expenses of feeding a common mule, and upon complying with these requirements he is given a little more than $2 a year. Yes, we have a State pension law to help the needy ex-Confederate soldier. We are going to see to it that he has for himself and family at least as much from all sources as $75 to meet the necessary expenses of life.

Such a little niggardly pension law under the circumstances which exist would be a reflection upon the government of old Huerta of Mexico. Niggardly ingratitude is one of the meanest sins in the whole catalogue. Possibly some thoughtful, resourceful man may find a way to patch over the legislative act with reference to the shortage in the reunion appropriation and call it a mistake, otherwise it must go down as a fact in South Carolina history. It is time to treat the old soldier with due respect or forever leave him alone.

W. H. Kirton [7th South Carolina, 2nd Co. L].

Newberry, June 17.

"Cavalryman" Writes.

To the Editor of the State: I see in the State that Maj. B. H. Teague has made a distribution of the funds appropriated by the South Carolina legislature for paying the expenses of the veterans who engaged in the battle of Gettysburg. I would like to see a list of the select few, and the proof that they furnish that they were in the battle. I know that I am entitled to a share in that fund, as I furnished ample proof, in time, to the clerk of court.

"Cavalryman."

P. S.—I would like to hear from the infantry and artillery on this subject.

"C."

Ninety-Six, June 16.

Was in the Battle

To the Editor of the State: Please give me some information in regard to the appropriation made by congress for paying the expenses of the Confederate soldiers who were at the battle of Gettysburg that would like to attend the reunion July 1. I have my certificate made stating that I was in the battle and I would like to get funds from this appropriation. Any information given will be appreciated.

M[el] Fleming [3rd South Carolina, Co. G]

Lanford, June 16.

(Maj. Gen. B. H. Teague writes to the State that the funds placed in his hands by the general assembly, to be used in paying the expenses of veterans attending the Gettysburg celebration, has been apportioned by him among 64 persons, and that proper vouchers for payments made out of the appropriation will in due time be filed in the office of the South Carolina historical commission.—Editor, the State.)

* * *

NEWBERRY HERALD AND NEWS
JUNE 24, 1913

WOULD PROVIDE FUND FOR ALL SURVIVORS
GOVERNOR BLEASE WRITES GENERAL B. H. TEAGUE.
Offers to Give Joint Note Making up Deficiency in Gettysburg Reunion Fund.

Special to the Herald and News.

Columbia, June 23—Gov. Blease on Saturday night addressed a letter to General B. H. Teague, at Aiken, suggesting the giving of a note by himself and General Teague to make up the deficiency in the appropriation by the legislature for paying the traveling expenses of the survivors of this State to the anniversary of the battle of Gettysburg, soon to be held on the battlefield. The appropriation by the legislature was only $1,000, which has provided for only sixty-four applicants, according to General Teague, while the total number of applicants is 200 or more. The governor suggests the giving of a joint official note, feeling sure the legislature at its next session will be glad to make an appropriation for this purpose.

The letter of the governor followed the statement by Gen. Teague, published in the daily newspapers of Saturday morning, setting for the facts given above.

Following is the letter of the governor to General Teague:

June 21, 1913

General B. H. Teague, Commander South Carolina Division, United Confederate Veterans, Aiken, S. C.—Dear Sir: I have noted with regret, though it was to be expected, that the appropriation by the legislature for the survivors of the battle of Gettysburg to defray their traveling expenses to the anniversary soon to be held, is greatly deficient, providing for considerably less than one-half the number applying. South Carolina ought to give all her survivors of this great battle an opportunity to attend this reunion, and it has seemed to me nothing more than just that it should be done. I am satisfied the money can be secured through one of the banks, and that the legislature at its next session will be only too glad to make good the deficiency. It has seemed to me proper, however, that the matter should be taken up with you first, you being the direct representative of this State in charge of the distribution of the fund appropriated by the legislature and the State's representative upon the battle of Gettysburg commission, and I suggest to you that we give a joint official note for an amount necessary to make up the deficiency in the appropriation. I have no doubt the money could be secured upon such a note, and all the survivors from this State given an equal opportunity to take advantage of this reunion.

As time is pressing, I shall be glad to hear from you immediately.

Very respectfully,

Cole L. Blease

Governor

* * *

NEWBERRY HERALD AND NEWS
JUNE 24, 1913

As to Gettysburg.

The meeting at Gettysburg begins on July 4. General Teague has published a list of those to whom he has given checks and the amounts. In Newberry are the following as published in his communication:

W. C. Sligh, Company E, Third infantry regiment, South Carolina Volunteers $15.65, Newberry.

J. G. Rikard, Company D, Third infantry regiment, South Carolina Volunteers, $15.65, Newberry.

M. M. Harris, Company E, Third infantry regiment, South Carolina Volunteers, $15.65, Pomaria.

D. A[ugustus] Dickert, Company H, Third infantry regiment, South Carolina Volunteers, $15.65, Newberry.

E[phrain] P. Bradley, Company D, Third infantry regiment, South Carolina Volunteers, $15.65, Newberry.

* * *

NEWBERRY HERALD AND NEWS
JUNE 24, 1913

MANY VETERANS DENIED

Gen. Teague Says He Distributed Legislative Fund as Directed by U. C. V Convention

To the Editor of the State:

I thank you in the name of the Confederate veterans of South Carolina for the effort you are making to raise an additional fund towards paying the way to Gettysburg of those who were not reached by the legislative fund. I have had over 200 attested certificates of those who fought in that battle, 66 have received checks from me and there are still 144 unprovided for and every mail brings another application or inquiry.

A circular letter will be issued by me in a day or two explaining that a resolution passed by the Aiken reunion convention sustains me in disbursing the legislative fund as I did: Taking Columbia as a central point the average railroad fare would be for each veteran about $16, so to send the balance would require a fund of $1,400. The legislature should have appropriated an ample amount, since it gave no fund for our reunion this year (we were allowed the unused fund appropriated the year before.) The citizen tax payers of the State should now rally and do the proper thing—since the legislature did not. Pennsylvania will spend nearly a half million dollars on this celebration. New York State has appropriated $125,000 to carry her veterans to it. Massachusetts gives $30,000, Connecticut $2,500 and all other Northern States large funds. Of course they are more able to give than our State but these appropriations show a spirit of liberality and these funds are not restricted by the Union veterans alone but are given also to the Confederates who are citizens of those commonwealths. How the hearts of our old veterans will beat with gladness and pride if South Carolina proves that she has not forgotten them!

B. H. Teague

Maj. Gen. Comdg. S. C. Division, U. C. V.

Aiken, June 20.

* * *

NEWBERRY HERALD & NEWS
JUNE 24, 1913

GEN. TEAGUE WRITES OF GETTYSBURG FUND
Commander of Confederate Veterans Sends Circular Letters Explaining Disbursement.

Aiken, June 20—Gen. B. H. Teague, Commander S. C. division, U. C. V., and disburser of the $1,000 fund appropriated by the legislature to send veterans to Gettysburg, has issued a circular letter in explanation of his disbursement of the fund. Gen. Teague's letter is as follows:

"Comrade: The act of the legislature appropriating the $1,000 reads: 'Expenses to Gettysburg, reunion of Confederate soldiers who participated in battle fought at that place. Money to be expended under the direction of B. H. Teague, major general commanding S. C. division, United Confederate veterans.' I voluntarily brought the subject up before the convention of veterans at the Aiken reunion, that I might be guided by the opinions of comrades as to the disbursement of this fund. It was suggested by a comrade that $15 be given to each applicant, then by another $10 was suggested, then another man thought it should be prorated by the amount required for each applicant's railroad fare. Finally, as no definite amount was agreed upon, by resolution, the whole matter was left in the hands of the commander. This resolution is recorded in the minutes of the convention 'to do as he thought best with it' now in possession of the adjutant general.

"For two weeks after the reunion the applicants came in slowly. In this time I issued a circular letter to my comrades, saying they must send in their names by June 15. This was done simply to hurry them up; nothing was said, or intended, that any one would be debarred after that time.

"After much thought, I concluded that it would be best to adopt the last suggestion offered at the reunion, especially since it looked as if there would not be many applicants. I did not know any more than the legislature, how many there would be and there was no means for finding it out, so I began to send out checks, in rotation, the amount of each applicant's railroad fare, as each application came in and continued this, until the $1,000 was paid out.

"The number checked was 46. Since then, the number of applicants has run up to 200 or more in all. Now, had I waited until the last day possible, and divided the money equally among the over 200 who applied, there would not have been $5 apiece—not enough to take one hardly 100 miles and back. Then suppose on the other hand, that having been done, an applicant had said 'that it was not the intent of the act—that it was intended each one's way should have been paid in full.' You see I could not satisfy all. The trouble has not been with your commander—it has been with the legislature—it did not instruct me definitely and did not appropriate enough money to go around. I have done my best for you, comrades, giving my time, labor and expenses in this unsolicited and bothersome task.

"My heart goes out to the disappointed ones. I wish I had it within my gift to pay the way to Gettysburg of every comrade in the State—you would all be there. I have called on the people of the State to help you and have listed your names and if any money comes into my hands, I will send check to you as I have done to the others—first on the list, first served.

Yours truly,

B. H. Teague,

Commander.

* * *

Newberry Herald and News
June 24, 1913

ARRANGEMENTS TO BE MADE FOR VETERANS
GEN. TEAGUE AND GOVERNOR BLEASE WILL SIGN NOTE.

To Raise Money For Confederate Veterans to Attend Gettysburg Reunion.

Special to The Herald and News.

Columbia, June 23.--General Teague has wired Governor Blease that he is willing to sign official note in Gettysburg reunion matter as suggested by the governor. The governor wired General Teague to sign note and forward at once to Columbia, or to come over to Columbia tonight so the matter may be arranged immediately.

* * *

LAURENS ADVERTISER
JUNE 25, 1913

GEN. B. H. TEAGUE ANSWERS CRITICISMS
Explains Method of Distributing Fund of $1,000 Appropriated by the State Legislature.

Gen. B. H. Teague, of Aiken, in whose hands was left the disposition of the fund of $1,000 provided by the stated legislature for the purpose of paying the railroad fare of veterans to the Gettysburg Reunion, has been severely criticized by the old soldiers and others for the manner in which the fund was distributed. It appears as if Gen. Teague distributed the money to properly accredited old soldiers in order of their application, late applicants getting nothing. The following letter addressed to Gen. Teague and published in the State, shows the tenor of the criticisms heaped upon him:

"Your post card of the 11th inst., stating that you had given checks to 64 applicants and had exhausted the appropriation by the State, etc., etc., received.

"I do not understand by what authority you did this. For you know at the State reunion, the matter was taken up and there was motion, which prevailed giving each soldier who participated in the battle of Gettysburg, and desired to go to the reunion there $10. Afterwards this action on the part of our State reunion was reconsidered, because at $10 each the appropriation might be exhausted before it went around, and some good and worthy soldiers would be cut out; and that one soldier who fought in the battle of Gettysburg was just as much entitled to his proportionate share of the State appropriation as another, which he was. Therefore, the understanding, as I understand it, was for you to get in the names of all who intended to go to the Gettysburg reunion and apportion said appropriation to them.

"I sent in some names to you who fought in the battle of Gettysburg and made affidavit to this effect, certified to by a comrade. They were justly entitled to their share of the State appropriation because they are citizens of South Carolina.

"It would have been better for the first resolution adopted by the State reunion, giving each soldier $10 as long as it lasted to have remained, rather than the way you divided it."

When it became known that enough funds had not been provided for all the veterans who were unable to pay their expenses, the Columbia State came forward and proceeded to raise a fund by public subscription and generously started the list by a contribution of $100. About $800 had been raised in this way when Gov. Blease made an offer to Gen. Teague to go on a note with him to supply enough money to pay the railroad fare of all soldiers not provided for out of the $1,000, trusting that the legislature will make return of the money when it meets. The latest reports stated that Gen. Teague had agreed to the suggestion of Gov. Blease and that the money would be provided.

The following letter from W. A. Clarke, of Columbia, is expressive of the other side of the controversy:

To the Editor of the State:

Enclosed you will find check for $5, my contribution toward the fund you are raising to aid in transporting the needy Confederate veterans visiting Gettysburg. Your suggestion is a happy one, and the liberality of your subscription should meet with a quick response from other interested in this reunion.

I regret to see that the _____ of Gen. Teague in the distribution of the fund appropriated by this State has called forth some criticism. I am of the opinion that Gen. Teague has carried out the sentiment there expressed. For him to have made a longer division of the fund at his disposal would have given to each so small an amount as would have defeated the purpose for which the fund was intended. His application of the fund will prove to the best advantage and I trust that your liberal and timely effort will supply the deficiency.

W. A. Clarke

Columbia, June 19—Gen. Teague, besides issuing a complete list of the old soldiers who were provided with railroad fare out of the fund of $1,000, has issued the following statement:

"Comrade: The act of the legislature appropriating the $1,000 reads: 'Expenses to Gettysburg, reunion of Confederate soldiers who participated in battle fought at that place. Money to be expended under the direction of B. H. Teague, major general commanding S. C. division, United Confederate veterans.' I voluntarily brought the subject up before the convention of veterans at the Aiken reunion, that I might be guided by the opinions of comrades as to the disbursement of this fund. It was suggested by a comrade that $15 be given to each applicant, then by another $10 was suggested, then another thought it should be prorated by the amount required for each applicant's railroad fare. Finally, as no definite amount was agreed upon, by resolution, the whole matter was left in the hands of the commander. This resolution is recorded in the minutes of the convention 'to do as he thought best with it' now in possession of the adjutant general.

"For two weeks after the reunion the applicants came in slowly. In this time I issued a circular letter to my comrades, saying they must send in their names by June 15. This was done simply to hurry them up; nothing was said, or intended, that any one would be debarred after that time.

"After much thought, I concluded that it would be best to adopt the last suggestion offered at the reunion, especially since it looked as if there would not be many applicants. I did not know any more than the legislature, how many there would be and there was no means for finding it out, so I began to send out checks, in rotation, the amount of each applicant's railroad fare, as each application came in and continued this, until the $1,000 was paid out.

"The number of checks was 64. Since then, the number of applicants has run up to 200 or more in all. Now, had I waited until the last day possible, and divided the money equally among the over 200 who applied, there would not have been $5 apiece—not enough to take one hardly 100 miles and back. Then suppose on the other hand, that having been done, an applicant had said that was not the intent of the act—that it was intended each one's way should have been paid in full. You see I could not satisfy all. The trouble has not been with your commander—it has been with the legislature—it did not instruct me definitely and did not appropriate enough money to go around. I have done my best for you, comrades, giving my time, labor and expenses in this unsolicited and bothersome task.

"My heart goes out to the disappointed ones. I wish I had it within my gift to pay the way to Gettysburg of every comrade in the State—you would all be there. I have called on the people of the State to help you and have listed your names and if any money comes into my hands, I will send check to you as I have done to the others—first on the list, first served.

Yours truly,

B. H. Teague,

Commander.

* * *

LAURENS ADVERTISER
JUNE 25, 1913

GETTYSBURG HILLS FLECKED WITH TENTS

Old Soldiers to Meet on Famous Battleground.

THE BLUE AND GRAY IN CAMP TOGETHER
Fifty Thousand Visitors Expected in the Little Town of Gettysburg near where the Decisive Battle of the War was Fought Fifty Years Ago.

Gettysburg, Pa., June 22—The hills of Gettysburg, where the armies of Meade and Lee pitched their tents fifty years ago, are flecked today with canvass, harbingers of the tented city which will soon arise on the battlefield. The army of Civil War veterans from the north and the south—40,000 of them—are coming, some few in thread worn uniforms and all without their muskets, to hold a jubilee reunion on the fiftieth anniversary of the battle. Some of the scouts are already here; the advance guard will bivouac on the field within a week; the rank file will follow them not more than forty-eight hours later.

Veterans encampment, Gettysburg Reunion, 1913
(Library of Congress)

Every star of the forty-eight in the American flag is expected to have here its own quota of veterans. They will come as the guests of the National government, and of their respective states and territories, which jointly will spend more than a million dollars for their entertainment and comfort. To receive them the government and the State of Pennsylvania have made elaborate plans. One detail alone provides for furnishing the veterans more than 800,000 meals.

Pennsylvania has been planning for the celebration of the battle for more than four years. She has appropriated $415,000 as her share of the expense. Congress has appropriated $150,000 to defray the expense of the government's participation, and named a commission to help carry out the plans. Every State and Territory also accepted the general invitation to participate and nearly all of them appropriated money to transport veterans and commissioners.

The big camp is pitched on that part of the battlefield which lies southwest of Gettysburg. On nearly 300 acres of contiguous ground, 7,000 tents and more are going up under the supervision of the War Department. The camp lies partly on the scene of the first day's fighting and is not far from High Water Mark, where Pickett's famous charge shattered against the Union lines.

Five thousand tents have been erected for the exclusive use of the veterans. The camp has been laid out like a city. Each street and each tent has a number, so it will be easy for any veteran to look up a former comrade or foe. In the center of the camp will be the headquarters of the chief quartermaster. The veterans will be encamped according to States.

Although each tent is designed to accommodate twelve men, it has been planned to assign only eight veterans to each, so as to make them as comfortable as possible. Each veteran will have a separate cot, blankets and a mess kit, which will contain a plate, cup, knife, fork and spoon and will become his personal property when he breaks camp. Each tent also will have two hand basins, a water bucket, candles and two lanterns. With the preparation of meals the veterans will have nothing to do. These will be wholesome and substantial and will be served at the ends of the company streets.

"Only veterans of the Civil War may be provided food, shelter and entertainment within the great camp around the battlefield," reads the announcement of the commission. "Therefore, no woman or child or any man not a veteran will be given any food, shelter or entertainment. No veteran should bring to Gettysburg any member of his family or other person for whom he will have to obtain food and quarters outside the camp unless all arrangements therefore have first been made for them before he or they come to Gettysburg."

No veteran will be permitted to bring a trunk into camp, his baggage being restricted to that which he can easily carry himself. The care of it will rest with him.

The principle events of the celebration will be held on July 1,2,3 and 4, but in order to avoid congestion of traffic on the railroads and confusion at Gettysburg, the camp will be opened on Sunday evening, June 29, the first meal to be served at supper time. Twenty meals will be served to each veteran during the week if he is in camp that long and the camp will come to an end after breakfast on Sunday, July 6.

Veterans have planned to visit historic places in and about the great area where the battle was fought and where skirmishes occurred that led up to it, and to hold reunions. The great celebration will be in full swing on the morning of July 1, exactly fifty years to the day from the time the battle opened to the west of the town.

The program for the four big days is briefly as follows:

July 1—Veterans Day.   Appropriate exercises under the joint direction of the Pennsylvania Commission and the Commanders-in-chief of the Grand Army of the Republic and the United Confederate Veterans.

July 2—Military Day.   Under the direction of the Chief of Staff of the United States Army.

July 3—Civic Day.   Under the direction of the Governor of Pennsylvania, presiding and participated in by the Governors of the States, if they so desire. Addresses and music.

July 4—National Day.   Patriotic exercises, orations, with fireworks in the evening.

The exercises will be held in a great tent, one of the largest in the United States, capable of accommodating about 15,000 persons. This tent is at the southern end of the camp, beside the Emmitsburg road, down which Lee's army went after the close if the three day's battle.

Except for the time the main exercises are being held, the big tent will be given over to the veterans to hold such reunions as they may arrange. The tent is so constructed that it can be sub-divided into many sections for these reunions. For the identification of old soldiers who may not be easily recognized by former comrades because of the changes wrought by the hand of Time, each veteran is expected to wear his army, corps, division, brigade, regimental and society badges.

After the principal exercises on July 4, there is no schedule of events except such as may be arranged by the veterans themselves in the way of reunions and short excursions about the field and to neighboring places.

United States troops, whose camp will adjoin that of the veterans, will do constant police duty. Boy scouts will act as guides. Pennsylvania's State police also will be on duty.

The United States government has erected a mammoth field hospital close to the camp, fully equipped. The state also will have its hospital tents and the State Commissioner of Health will keep deputies in camp for constant inspection work. The State fire marshal, in addition, has assigned men to the camp and steps have been taken to prevent fires and to extinguish them promptly should any occur.

The commissary department will be under the direct charge of regular army officers and will be one of the most complete ever organized for a camp. There will be nearly 800 cooks; 125 bakers will furnish fresh bread every day for the big army.

The greatest care has been taken in arranging for the twenty meals that will be served during the week. The menu was written with due regard for the age of the men. It will be quite different from the hard tack and coffee and the occasional portion of bean soup or "sow belly" given the soldiers in the historic days of fifty years ago. This part of the camp arrangements is in the care of Major William R. Grove.

The town of Gettysburg, which has a population of a little more than 4,000, will be unable to care for the influx of visitors and thousands of them will be cared for in neighboring towns and cities as far away as Harrisburg and York. Practically every private house in Gettysburg will be turned into a boarding house. Many veterans who desire to attend the reunion and want to bring members of their families have been unable to obtain accommodations and must leave them behind.

Specially invited guests of the State and National Governments will be given quarters in the Seminary west of Gettysburg and in the building of Pennsylvania College north of the town.

* * *

SUMTER WATCHMAN AND SOUTHRON
JUNE 25, 1913

Three Gettysburg Veterans

Ex-Sheriff W[illiam] H[enry] Epperson [23rd South Carolina, Co. I] and Mr. Benjamin M. Powell [12th South Carolina, Co. I] will probably be the representatives of Sumter County's contingent of Confederate Veterans at Gettysburg. Both of these have received checks from General B. H. Teague to pay the railroad fare to and from Gettysburg.

Ex-Sheriff Epperson stated several days ago that he would certainly take the trip. He will visit his daughter, Mrs. Dawes for some time, while on the trip and later will go to see another daughter in Philadelphia. Mr. Powell has been sick recently and it is doubtful if he is able to stand the trip, but he stated that he was anxious to go and hoped to recover sufficiently before the time came to visit the famous battleground.

In Sumter there are three veterans of the battle, Mr. Powell, who was in McGowan's Brigade; and Messrs. W. P. Smith and Tom Burkett [1st South Carolina Rifles, Co. D], who lost a leg in the battle, who were in Kershaw's Brigade.

***

SUMTER WATCHMAN AND SOUTHRON
JUNE 25, 1913

MORE MONEY NEEDED

Garrison Asks for a Larger Appropriation

Washington, June 19—Secretary Garrison today asked the congressional military committee to guarantee an additional appropriation to take care of the Union and Confederate veterans at the 50th anniversary of the battle of Gettysburg next month.

Those in charge of the celebration notified the secretary that 50,000 veterans would be there instead of 40,000 as at first anticipated.

To provide tentage, subsistence, medicines and general care of the increased number about $25,000 more than the $150,000 appropriated will be needed. Assistant Secretary Breckenridge has gone to Gettysburg to canvass the situation.

***

NEWBERRY HERALD AND NEWS
JULY 1, 1913

A GREAT UNDERTAKING.
Caring For Veterans is a Tremendous Task

Gettysburg, Pa. June 29.--Army officers, crowds of visitors and veterans who are to participate in the exercises commemorating the 50th anniversary of the battle of Gettysburg said today the event would go down in history as one of the greatest of its kind ever witnessed. The officers said the magnitude of the undertaking would be difficult to grasp even if the encampment were for the entertainment of 50,000 men in the prime of life but when one considered that the average age of the veterans is 72 years, the task before those in charge of the camp must be released.

The real invasion of the quaint little border town began early this morning. It is expected to reach its height by tomorrow night and the little borough of 4,000 has tackled the proposition of caring for its guests.

To add to the difficulties and dangers of a situation hazardous under any circumstances, the weather is almost unbearable.

With a sun blazing savagely the humidity is so high that the least movement is productive of exhaustion. Thus far the veterans already here have contented themselves very largely with sitting about in shady places talking. Already there have been several cases of heat exhaustion.

By the telephone system in the camp, the construction of which involved the stringing of 120 miles of wire, it will be possible to telephone from any point in the camp to any part of the country reached by the telephone system.

* * *

EDGEFIELD ADVERTISER
JULY 2, 1913

The Battle-Flag of the 7th Regiment Goes Back to Gettysburg

Editor Advertiser: We leave today for the Reunion of the Gray and the Blue at Gettysburg, and I will carry with me the Battle-Flag of the 7th S. C. Regt. and let it float once more over the same ground it did so proudly, just 50 years ago. This flag received its baptism of fire and blood for the first time at the battle of Fredericksburg, December the 13th, 1862. Our first flag being torn to pieces with shot and shell, from Richmond to Sharpsburg, I can't recall just how many men were killed and wounded under its pure folds. John Clark was our color-bearer at Gettysburg, and wounded at that battle, and killed at Chickamauga, with this precious emblem in his hands. Miss Mary Poppenheim of Charleston S. C., is the custodian of our flag, and she has sent it to me to be displayed at Gettysburg one time more. I love this flag as a mother loves her first born, while I stand ready to strike down to the death any foe, who upholds insult in any way to the United States flag, but there never was, nor will be a flag that floats on land or sea that I can love as I do this. Three of my brothers were killed under it and three were wounded twice, hence I love it. Yes, I love it. So I am going to take it back and let the boys see what they run from so hurriedly across the meadow, and the wheat field. But then our breasts were full of daggers, now the white dove of peace will spread her silver wings over that once bloody plain, and united we will stand, the blue and the gray.

At the re-union at Chickamauga, I was in conversation with a beautiful little woman from "Ohio." She said to me, Mr. Wright, when I tell you what I am you won't like it, I'm a Yankee! Why I said, bless your little soul. I never in all my life had one thing against a yankee-woman, it was the yankee boys that I had the scrap with, and not the girls, so we were good friends thereafter. So it will be at Gettysburg, I am going to have a better time now than I did when I was there last, and expect to come back a better man. It was there that I had my closest call, as I saw it, and will tell it later, but I sure did do some clean running.

While at Chickamauga at the re-union I met a man by the name of Ben Benson, who said, in speaking of the little battle of Fort Sumter, April 1861: He said that Wigfall fired the first gun at the Fort. I told him that I would have to take issue with him there, for it was Pickett's daughter that did that, about which I will speak later. It was Wigfall who carried the dispatch to Maj. Anderson demanding the surrender of the Fort to the Confederate States of America.

J. Russell Wright [7th South Carolina Infantry, Co. G]

* * *

KEOWEE COURIER

JULY 2, 1913

MANY GO EARLY, AVOID RUSH.

Southerners Welcomed--Citizens Seek Hand-Shaking; Privilege.

Gettysburg, Pa.; June 26.-Gathering from North and South for the 50th anniversary of the battle of Gettysburg, several hundred veterans arrived here to-day, coming early, they said, in order to avoid the great rush of the early part of next week.

Mingling with the blue uniforms were some in gray, and the men from the South were given a hearty welcome. With their uniforms of gray topped by campaign hats, the Southerners soon became central figures on the streets, and scarcely a person they passed failed to stop and ask the privilege of a hand-shake. Warmer than all other was the welcome extended them by the Union veterans, many of whom are here for the opening of the State encampment tomorrow.

To-night the historic old Adams County Court House witnessed a repetition of the war-time campfire with its stirring, patriotic songs of the days of '61-65, and many speeches in which reminiscences of days gone by were mingled with suggestions and plans for the observance of the coming week.

Commander-in-Chief Alfred Beers, of Bridgeport, Conn., one of the first arrivals for the battle anniversary celebration, was one of the speakers to-night.

Final arrangements at the big camp wore completed to-day. Practically everything is in readiness to receive the first arrivals on Sunday, and to-day many veterans visited the place, inspecting the tents and furnishings, together with the arrangements for mess and sanitation.

The first squadron, Fifteenth United States Cavalry, Major Rhodes commanding, arrived during the day in a heavy downpour of rain after having been in march from Fort-Myers since Monday. The cavalry will be used in patrolling the battlefield, regulating traffic there and guarding the monuments from vandalism.

***

THE LAURENS ADVERTISER

LAURENS, S. C.

JULY 2, 1913

VETERANS GATHER ON GETTYSBURG FIELD

Soldiers of the Blue and Gray Fraternize Together where Once They Met in Deadly Conflict. Every Provision Made for Convenience and Comfort.

Gettysburg, Pa. , June 28—Army officers watching the crowds of visitors and veterans arriving to participate in the exercises commemorating the fiftieth anniversary of the battle of Gettysburg, said to-day that the event would go down in history as one of the greatest Reunions of its kind ever witnessed. The officers said the magnitude of the undertaking would be difficult to grasp, even if the encampment were for the entertainment of 50,000 men in the prime of life, but when one considered that the average age of the veteran is 72 years the task before those in charge of the camp must be realized.

The real invasion of the quaint border town began early this morning. It is expected to reach its height by tomorrow night, and gallantly the little borough of 4,000 has tackled the proposition of caring for its guests.

Weather Extremely Hot

To add to the difficulties and dangers of a situation hazardous under any circumstances, the weather is almost unbearable. With a sun blazing savagely the humidity is so high that the least movement is productive of exhaustion. Thus far the veterans already here contented themselves very largely with sitting about in shady places talking. Already there have been several cases of heat exhaustion.

By the telephone system in the camp, the construction of which involved the stringing of 120 miles of wire, it will be possible to telephone from any point in the camp to any part of the country reached by the telephone system.

The Fraternal Spirit

From shortly after sunrise until late at night the streets of Gettysburg were crowded with the veterans, North and South. Some of them paraded, cheering and singing in fraternizing exuberance with former foes, while others gathered in groups and recalled the stirring times of fifty years ago. Those overcome by the heat were treated at the emergency hospital of the State department of health and all are out of danger.

Veterans are arriving on every train and they are in town but a short time before a start is made for the big camp, the scene of which many have not visited since the stirring days of the Gettysburg campaign. In spite of the heat yesterday the maximum temperature being 98 degrees, many of them walked over the entire area and officials in charge said that the small number of prostrations demonstrated that the physical condition of the old soldiers was of the best.

Two Hospitals Ready

Elaborate preparations have been made to protect the health of the veterans while here. There are two large hospitals with a capacity of 1,800 designed only for seriously persons. These are supplemented by three regimental hospitals, 14 Red Cross stations and 20 first aid stations. A complete ambulance battalion of the United States army with 15 horse ambulances and two automobile ambulances will take care of any who fall sick. The provisional hospitals, besides wards and diet kitchens, have a complete operating room and the arrangements include everything down to a shower bath.

"We hope the elaborate arrangements we have made will not be needed," said Major Huntington at the provisional hospital. "It will be largely a question of weather. If it is cloudy we may not be needed at all. As it is, we do not expect any serious cases."

Representation by States.

Lieut. Simon Bolivar Buckner, son of the ranking surviving officer of the Confederate army, who is assisting Major. Normoyle, in command at the camp, to-day made public the number of old soldiers that each State expects to send to the Reunion.

Pennsylvania heads the list with 17,820; New York is second with 9,693, and New Jersey third with 1,989. Massachusetts will send 1, 836; Virginia 1,827; North Carolina 1,245; Michigan, 900; East Virginia, 810; Indiana, 666, and Illinois 513. Other States range from Connecticut's 450 to 81 from Oregon and 35 from Idaho.

Pennsylvania and New York will occupy the entire Northern section of the camp on both sides of Long Lane. Federal veterans from other States will be encamped between Seminary Ridge and Long Lane, while the wearers of the grey will occupy the site west of Long Lane at the base of the monument to Gen. Lee, now in course of erection at the point where Pickett's charge started.

Manassas Peace Banner

Manassas, Va., June 28—Probably one of the most unique banners that will appear at the Gettysburg Reunion has been dispatched from here to be placed before the quarters of the Manassas Pickett Post, G. A. R., and Ewell Camp, U.C.V. The banner, which is commemorative of the peace jubilee on the battlefield of Bull Run in July, 1911, at which celebration President Taft delivered the principal address, displays the "Stars and Bars" on one side and the "Stars and Stripes" on the other. In addition there appears the inscriptions, "Let us have peace—Grant," and "Duty is the sublimest word in any language—Lee". A special guard of honor, composed of veterans from both sides, will care for the flag.

President Wilson also on Scene.

Washington, June 28—President Wilson to-night decided to attend the 50th anniversary celebration of the battle of Gettysburg on the Fourth of July. He telegraphed Governor Tenor that he had reconsidered his previous declination and would make a brief speech to the veterans.

The President's decision followed a conference with Representative A. Mitchell Palmer, of Pennsylvania. The President had taken the position previously in declining to go, that he would be breaking his rules, established months ago, not to leave Washington for any speech-making occasion while Congress was in session.

Mr. Palmer pointed out, however, the importance of the Gettysburg celebration, its nation-wide significance, and particularly the spirit of sectional sympathy that would result from a speech by a Southern-born President at the Reunion of the North and the South.

The President had intended to leave Tuesday for New Hampshire to spend a few days with his family, but the trip will necessitate a rearrangement of plans. Mr. Wilson probably will be at Gettysburg only a few hours, and it has not yet been decided whether he will go by motor or by train. His plans probably will be announced on Monday.

Secretary Tumulty gave out this statement for the President:

"The President has felt constrained to forego his chance for a few days of much needed rest in New Hampshire this week because he feels it is his duty to attend the celebration at Gettysburg on Friday, the Fourth of July."

* * *

THE NEWS
FREDERICK, MARYLAND
JULY 3, 1913

RAIN COOLS GETTYSBURG

Veterans of Blue and Gray Are Enjoying Themselves

ONLY SEVEN DEATHS IN CAMP

Military Day Exercises Were Celebrated In Big Tent Before Slim Crowds; Many Reunions Were Held.

Gettysburg, Pa., July 3—An electrical storm swept over the encampment here and brought relief from the extreme heat to thousands of veterans, and with the temperature lowered they were able to really enjoy themselves.

Quite the most delightful feature of the encampment from any point of view is the disposition of Federals and Confederates to go arm in arm as they revisit those parts of the battlefield they have reason to know best or worse. Just as soon as mess was over the comrades sallied out eagerly to trace for themselves the movements of the great second day of Gettysburg, July 2, 1863.

All things considered, the veterans have stood up wonderfully against hardship, heat, excitement and unusual hours.

There have been only seven deaths and the prostrations and other cases of illness have been actually below the number reasonably to be expected under normal circumstances. One great danger to these old men who are enjoying themselves with the zest of children lies in the gin mills and saloons of Gettysburg town, at least half of the cases of prostrations and illness (about 200 altogether) have been caused by whisky.

There is, on the whole, very little drinking, because the veterans are having too much good, clean, wholesome fun.

It would be hard to count to keep tab on the many, many gentlemen who are entitled to be called "the Hon. Mr. So and So." There are governors by the half dozen, representatives and occasionally a senator.

These notables are rather lost sight of in this camp. The comrades apparently agree with Lincoln, who said in the Gettysburg speech: "The world will little note nor long remember what we say here, but it can never forget what they did here."

There were numerous regimental, brigade and division reunions, fore-gatherings held on the spot where the commands struggled on the second day of the battle.

One of our southerners at this reunion was William Moultrie Reed, C. S. A., a great grandson of General Moultrie. He had come from Lee county, S. C. to find the spot where he worked one gun of the Palmetto light battery for three minutes against all of General Hunt's guns that were thundering from Cemetery Hill. Moreover, he found the very spring, at least it was in the same place where he had quenched his thirst after the battle.

Exercises were held on Little Roundtop, near General Warren's statue, by Warren Post, of Brooklyn.

In the big tent which holds perhaps 10,000, military day was celebrated. Colonel Cowan, of Kentucky, who commanded a Federal battery, opened the meeting before 6000 veterans and visitors. The world had never witnessed such a gathering as this, the colonel said.

"All of us," he continued, "are proud of our army and navy, but we ought to build two ships for every one that Japan constructs. We ought not to let our coast/ states [be] exposed to risk." Major General John R. Brooke spoke for the Union veterans and J. C. Scarborough, of South Carolina, for the Confederates.

"For three years after the war I hated you," said Scarborough. "But now I love you, every bluecoat of you."

* * *

The News
Frederick, Maryland
July 3, 1913

SEVEN STABBED OVER SLUR

Veteran Resents Insult and Fight Begins

Gettysburg, Pa., July 3—Seven men were stabbed in a fight in the dining room of a Gettysburg hotel as a result of a fight which started when several men aroused the anger of an old veteran in blue by abusing Lincoln.

Several of the wounded men are in serious condition at the Pennsylvania State Hospital.

The state police are making desperate efforts to find the men who did the stabbing.

The wounded men are: Edward J. Carroll, sergeant of the quartermaster's corps, U. S. A.; David Farber, of Butler, Pa., a member of the state police; John D. Maugin, 434 South street, Harrisburg; Malcolm Griffin, of Bedford City, Pa.; Charles Susler, of West Fairview, Pa.; Hayder Reinsbecker, 341 York street, Gettysburg, Pa., and Harry A. Root, Jr., of Harrisburg.

Farber, Maugin and Griffin are in the most serious condition. Their wounds were in the left breast and the surgeons at the Pennsylvania hospital would not venture predictions as to their chance of recovery.

According to all the information the authorities could gather the fight began suddenly and was over in a few minutes. It began when the dining room was full of people and caused a panic among the scores of guests.

The old veteran, who was unhurt and disappeared in the melee, was sitting near Farber and Carroll, when he heard the slighting remarks about Lincoln. He jumped to his feet and began to defend the martyred president and berated his detractors.

The men who were stabbed, according to the information the surgeons gathered, jumped to the defense of the veteran when the others closed in. One man was arrested, W. B. Henry, of Camden, N.J.

* * *

NEWBERRY HERALD AND NEWS
JULY 11, 1913

AT GETTYSBUBG.

Gen. B. H. Teague, Commander of S. C. Division. U. C. V., Writes of the Gathering of Veterans on Historic Field.

To the Editor of the State:

By this time the South Carolinians who attended the Gettysburg reunion have no doubt returned and are at home again after experiencing one of the most remarkable and wonderful trips of their lives. The majority went on the Southern railway's special train, which started from Augusta last Sunday afternoon and which landed s at Gettysburg six hours late, our delay in the beginning being caused by the proverbial "hot box." Just here it may be well to draw conclusions as to which is to be preferred, the delays of a special train or the bother of change of cars on a regular schedule, which will get you there in time. Our special landed us at night in the grand camp and we were soon in our quarters, but to our dismay found our tents pretty generally depleted of cots and bedding—a raid having been made on them by others who wanted to double their share. It was not long, though, before those were replaced and tired veterans lay upon the battlefield. Supper had been missed so that all were ready for the ample breakfast that was given them in the morning. The part of the camp allotted the

Confederate veterans was along Confederate avenue of the now beautifully laid out battlefield and fortunately a grove of trees between it and the tents proved a source of great comfort, for the weather the whole week was fearfully hot. Our State flag was planted at the head of the street of the South Carolina camp as was also a genuine palmetto tree, the gift of your liberal and spirited townsman, Col. W. A. Clark. The camp was also designated by the streamers which adorned our special train and which bore the device "South Carolina Veterans for Gettysburg." These emblems attracted immediate attention and caused a visitation to us of many hundreds of the boys in blue.

Soon after breakfast on Tuesday morning the men scattered, each one anxious to find the spot where 50 years ago he had shot his foe, captured his flag, lay wounded or attained his nearest approach to the enemy's line of battle. Many attended the meetings in the "big tent," which had a capacity for 15,000 people and which at any meeting was no less than two-thirds full. The numerous historic points of the battlefield, the camps of the different States, the monuments on the field, the special reunions, the exercises of each day, and the magnificent display of fireworks all contributed towards filling every moment of our stay full of interest and pleasure. The magnitude of that great camp was astounding and illuminated at night by myriads of electric lights. A survey of it was a most beautiful and brilliant sight. The systematic management of this great gathering of people was a wonder of itself and it was its efficient employment of a small army of United States soldiers, State constabulary and civilians that protected the crowds from harm and perfected the details which abounded in such pleasure, comfort and satisfaction for them. It was the most successfully stupendous undertaking in a semi-civil and military way ever undertaken in any age, and fortunate and blessed was the individual who was there as a guest of the great and grand State of Pennsylvania. The spirit of friendliness and amity that pervaded the meeting of this multitude of people was beyond comprehension and comparison. The "glad hand" was offered continually and continually grasped and shaken, so that thousands of arms are sore from the muscular demonstration of good will. The speeches at all the meetings had never even a semi-note of discord, but breathed and proclaimed for the hereafter a spirit of American brotherhood, comradeship and peace. Never again on earth do we believe there will be gathered together such an audience of gray haired and bald headed men whose ages ranged between 65 and 80 years of age, as was seen at the meetings in the auditorium during the four days of this Gettysburg semi-centennial celebration. Such was its magnitude; such was the impress of its spirit and such was its pleasure, that in the language of a veteran one will cease dating every happening as occurring "since the war," but as "since the Gettysburg reunion." The only parade that took place of veterans was that of the Virginians, who marched from camp to the headquarters of the of governor of their State and were reviewed by him and then received a Confederate battleflag, captured during the war and now returned by their commander, Col. Mann, of Wisconsin, and accepted by Gov. Mann, of Virginia. Both of these whole-souled and patriotic veterans made appropriate speeches, fitting the occasion. Another most pleasing incident was the presentation by members of the Gettysburg commission of a gold medal and silver loving cup to the general secretary, Col. Lewis E. Beitler, under whose remarkable ability the celebration was so successfully managed.

B. H. Teague.

Aiken, July 7.

* * *

KEOWEE COURIER
JULY 16, 1913

THE GETTYSBURG REUNION

An Interesting Account of That Great Event by One Who Took an Active Part in the Famous Battle.

(D. H. Russell [1st South Carolina Cavalry, Co. F] in Anderson Mail.)

Gettysburg! What a flood of memories crowded upon me as I crawled out of my tent on the morning of July 1st, having reached there the night previous, and stood gazing in the morning light of the rising sun over the most famous battlefield in all civilized history, and found that the camp of the South Carolina division was on the slope of Seminary Ridge and not far from the point where Pickett's Division made its start on that most famous charge in all military annals—the charge that has been the theme of military men the world over since then, and the problem that they are still studying and will be studying for generations yet to come. And as I gazed about me and began to take in the surroundings, I found that I was evidently very near the spot where I had stood on that fateful July 3rd, 1863, a half century before. Here was Seminary Ridge, where the Confederate artillery shook the earth with its belching fire, and over yonder a half mile in front was Cemetery Ridge, where the Federal artillery united in the chorus, and the two made "a little hell on earth," such as had never been witnessed on this continent before and probably never will be again. While over yonder on the right, a mile and a half or more away, stood Little Round Top and Big Round Top, the first of which was the key of the position, and in between the famous Devil's Den, a place whose name fits it exactly, while over here to the left stood the little town of Gettysburg, a place destined to be forever afterwards famous in the annals of history.

Scene Floods the Memory.

Looking over this famous field the heart was thrilled with the memories of that day, big with events and pregnant with the fate of the Confederacy. Over yonder on the right stood Longstreet, a bronzed warrior—the "old war horse" of Lee; here in the center was A. P. Hill, who had learned war under Stonewall Jackson, and here on the left stood Ewell, the three corps commanders of an army that had never known defeat and that had shaken a continent with its mighty tread; and here in the plain, between the two ridges, lies the path traveled by Pickett's Division in that most famous charge of all history, the story of which will be read with eager interest by many generations yet unborn. And here I stood a half century after, near the spot where I stood on that fateful day, viewing the panorama spread out before me, in all its wide extent, of one of the world's greatest battles, if not the greatest.

"Fifty Years Agone."

Had I been told on that day that I would live to come back there fifty years later to witness the gathering of the survivors of two great armies which had made more history in three days than had been made in any three previous centuries, I would have mocked at it. And yet here it was an actual, living fact. And nowhere on all this green earth could such a scene have been enacted except in America. Here on this wide, extended plain was a tented city of more than 5,000 tents filled with the veterans from nearly every State in the Union, men who fifty years before were clutching at each other's throats in the death grapple of battle. It was wonderful, and the feeling of brotherhood exhibited by the men who wore the Blue and the Gray was something beautiful to witness; and especially was this noticeable on the part of the men who wore the Blue. It was "Hello, Yank," and "Hello, Johnny."

I spent the greater portion of one day in the Pennsylvania camp, and wherever I stopped a group of thirty or forty would gather around me, and it would be "Hello, Johnny, let's shake," and the reply would be "All right, Yank, come up," and they seemed loath to let me move on.

There was not a harsh word uttered anywhere so far as I heard, but we met as American soldiers who had illustrated American valor and manhood in the fiery ordeal of battle.

"We Believe You Johnny."

In talking over our "family fuss" I said to them that we fought from an honest conviction of what we believed to be right, for our homes and firesides and the right of self-government, and that we had no apologies to make for it, and numbers of them said, "We believe you, Johnny, for men could not fight as you did unless they thoroughly believed in what they were fighting for," and numbers of them said, "If we had been in the South we would have done just as you did."

As I came back in the afternoon toward my own quarters I passed through New York camp, and as I passed a tent full of Yanks they called out to me, "Come in here, Johnny; we want to talk to you," and they kept me there for two hours, and one of them, a glove manufacturer from Gloversville, N. Y., insisted on presenting me with a handsome pair of gloves of his own manufacture, and later he walked with me to the outside of his camp and talked of his Christian hope (he was a Methodist), and as we parted he said, "Johnny, let us answer at the roll-call up yonder," and on this we clasped hands and parted, perhaps forever here.

Their Heads Erect

One thing I specially noted, and was specially pleased with, and that was the bearing of our own men. They carried their heads up and moved about as men conscious that they had done their full duty and had nothing to be ashamed of, and could look the world in the face, and I believe it added to the respect and admiration with which the men from the North looked upon us, for it was self-evident from the beginning that these men had a high respect for us, and the mingling together and eating and sleeping with each other cemented the kindly feeling, and on all sides I heard the sentiment expressed, "You Johnnies have got to share in the pension fund, and we intend to make it hot for Congress until it is done."

A Touching Scene

I witnessed a touching scene just in front of our tent that will live in memory forever. We had with us the Rev. Mr. [J. E. L.] Amiker [1st South Carolina Infantry (State Troops, 6 Months)], a Baptist preacher from Orangeburg, and a veteran and a fine singer. Just after breakfast one morning he stopped under the shade of a tree near our tent and began to sing "When the Roll is Called Up Yonder," and, attracted by the full, salubrious tones of his voice as they rang out on the morning air, Johnnies and Yanks came pouring in, and some ladies from Pittsburg, Pa., gathered around, and all joined in the singing and carried all the parts and there wasn't a dry eye there when he closed, and all went up and shook hands with him. It was like a Methodist love feast.

"Uncle Sam" Provided

Just a word as to the provision for our comfort made by Uncle Sam. The streets were lighted by electric arc lamps, every tent had two lanterns with candles and eight to nine cots with two to three blankets and an abundance of straw to spread over the floor. The water was good, out of wells supplied with pumps, and at intervals the wells had coils placed in them and ice packed around them each morning. Our food was good enough for anybody. Here is what we had for breakfast: Bread and butter of the finest quality (I never saw better on a hotel table), either beef or mutton or breakfast strips, oat meal and milk, scrambled eggs in abundance, coffee, potatoes and either prunes or canned peaches. This is good enough for anybody, and will give an idea of our rations. Dinner and Supper were in keeping with this.

Good Feeling Everywhere

As showing the feeling between the Blue and the Gray, an incident occurred in our camp, when a few of us only were present, when we observed a whole column of New York blue coats file into our street under the command of an officer. They marched about half way up the street when we all stopped to see what it meant. The command was given, "Halt." "Front." "Right dress," and an officer stepped out and made a few remarks introducing Col. Tidball, who made a beautiful speech of welcome to the Carolinians. I looked all up and down the line for some one to respond, and there was no one came forward. I felt that South Carolina's reputation was at stake, and I doffed my hat and sailed in as best I could to do my best for my old mother State, and they gave me the "Hip, hip, hurra," so well known in the Yankee army.

6,000 Acres of Statues

The battlefield of Gettysburg is now owned by the government, about 6,000 acres having been purchased, and it is dotted all over with markers and monuments and statues. Cemetery Ridge is especially crowded with them in every direction. The equestrian statue of Gen. Meade overlooks the field on this side, while just below is the marker showing the high-water mark reached by Pickett's Division and also at the Bloody Angle. Just opposite Meade's statue Virginia is erecting one to Lee, and these two central figures of the great battle will stand for all time facing each other, the one on Cemetery Ridge, the other on Seminary Ridge, and each of them with artillery ranged along their respective ridges to-day, just as they were fifty years ago, on the day of the battle. No battlefield in the world is so well preserved as to show to the visitor in one great panorama all the salient points, the positions of the troops, the artillery, the cavalry and everything about it; and as I stood on Little Round Top and gazed over the wonderful sight it did not take a very great stretch of the imagination to feel that Lee and Meade and their phantom ghosts were charging and counter-charging over the field and re-enacting the scenes of fifty years ago. It saddens the heart of an old Confederate to realize how near we were to success that day—and yet so far. Military critics tell us that Lee's plans were perfect, and if his subordinates had carried them out Gettysburg would have been Lee's victory, and that by all the rules of military strategy he ought to have won. But his orders were not carried out, and he lost. "Of all sad words of tongue or pen, the saddest are, it might have been."

Yesterday—Today—Forever

Recognizing the fact that by the arbitrament of arms this is one great country—one and indivisible forever, and under one flag forever—still I was desperately in love with the Southland. She and her flag were my first love, and like a youthful lover who has buried his bride, I must be permitted to go to her grave once in a while and scatter a few flowers over it and shed a few tears on it, for I am the same old Johnny I was in the 60's, believe in the same principle, have the same convictions and expect to die with them and be buried in the old Confederate Gray.

* * *

Pickens Sentinel,
July 17, 1913

Pickens Man Enjoys Gettysburg Reunion

I have just returned from Gettysburg where the blue and the gray spent a most pleasant and enjoyable week together. We, I mean the South Carolina veterans, fared sumptuously, had an abundance of good things to eat and just as well cooked and served as we could expect at our table or in visiting our neighbors at our own home. They were extremely social and made us feel good all the while.

We had comfortable quarters and a number of ladies called to see us in the tents and invited us to their palatial homes, which was enjoyed by those who accepted the invitation.

I met and enjoyed a visit from Col. Wright, from Michigan, whom I found a pleasant caller in my tent. He confessed that we had them whipped at the second days fight at Gettysburg, but Gen. Hancock came just in time and rallied the men and overpowered us. He also acknowledged that we were fighters indeed and in truth hard to handle.

The ladies asked for a picture of a New York man who wore a suit he wore before the war when he was a member of the militia and he granted their request on condition that I stand by his side and hold his hand while it was taken, promising to send us a copy of the same.

Thus passed the fiftieth anniversary of the most noted and one of the most destructive battles, which will ever be fresh in the memory of many and so will the reunion at Gettysburg. It was a grand old time never to be forgotten.

---Liberty---

A. F. McCord [1st South Carolina Cavalry, Co. A]

* * *

NEWBERRY HERALD AND NEWS
JULY 18, 1913

High Water Mark of the Confederacy Gettsyburg of Today.

By Col. D[avid] A[ugustus] Dickert

The Gettysburg of fifty years ago was called "Lee's Waterloo," which was erroneous, for some of the Southern chieftain's hardest, fiercest and most successful battles were yet to come, Wilderness, Spottsylvania, Cold Harbor, Petersburg, etc. But no one, who was on the "fatal field" of a few days ago, would doubt for a moment that it was the Waterloo of sectionalism, bitterness and distress between the North and the South. Old scores of hatred, engendered by the war, seemed to have been entirely wiped from the slate and instead of "Yanks" and "Johnny Rebs" you heard on all sides, "Hail brother." "Ho comrade."

The general government and the State of Pennsylvania contributed near a half million dollars for the entertainment of the veterans, and fully that much was donated by the States, for the transportation of their individual troop, making the enormous total of one million dollars, for the peaceful meeting of the blue and the gray. Was the "game worth the candle?" Was the good effect equal to this prodigious expenditure of money? I for one, and I believe every one present, would say it was the best outlay possible, if we are to judge from good results in the future. We heard it talked on all sides, among the Federal soldiery, that the South's veterans should share equally with them, the nation's bounty, a part of the pensions, so lavishly bestowed upon those who wore the blue. I can't say that I seek any pension from the government, but if it should be granted and I am still living I dare say I would be patriotic enough to take it.

Speaking on general principles of the good cheer and love feast of the recent reunion, I went to that meeting with fifty years of bitterness and hatred pent up in my soul, more than the majority of the Southern veterans, for in my line of duty I had opportunity to see more of the wrongs done our women and country than most men, but I came away with ill feeling for none. Not that I have forgiven the North for everything they did to us, for fifty years is too short a time to forget and forgive all the South endured.

But since talking with any number of intelligent men from the North, and hearing their version of war I have become greatly mollified, enough at least, to keep me from cutting any of their throats. As a man said to me, from the old "Iron Brigade" from Michigan, "You men entered the army for a principle, we of the North, to get bread for our families; our mines, workshops and factories were all closed and we had to enlist for the bounty offered, or starve. All that talk you hear about the Northern men entering the army and fighting to save the union, is all stuff, gotten up by the newspapers, while as a fact, we didn't care a d___ whether you were in or out of the Union, so long as we had bread for ourselves and families." Well, I believe there is a lot of truth in this, but these sentiments were no reason why they should burn our houses.

The South Carolina contingent was hours late and got into camp some time after night. Col. Fair had preceded us, looked over the ground, lent us much aid in piloting us to our quarters and looking after our comfort for which every man from Newberry greatly appreciated. When we arose in the morning one vast sea of tents lay out before us and it was not until we saw old Round Top, silent, sullen, defiant, that we could get our bearing.

Gettysburg, the quaint old Dutch town of 17,000 inhabitants, was two miles to the north. The camp, or rather the "field of Mars," was traversed by two great thoroughfares, one in our rear, ran along a stone fence on Semitary [sic] Ridge, behind which "Tige" Anderson's Division of Hill's corps and McLaw's, of Longstreet, formed for the assault on the 2nd. This is called "Confederate Avenue," thus called I suppose, in honor of their visiting brethren. The other pike, on which runs the trolley cars, goes to "Devil's Pen" at the foot of Round Top, from this city. This was formerly called the Gettysburg road, on which Sickles Third Corp of Federals lay when McLaws' Mississippians, Georgians and South Carolinians so unmercifully assailed and shattered on the afternoon of fifty years ago.

The South Carolina veterans were tented between the Louisiana and Texas, while across the street, on which our quarters abutted were Federals of every hue, from Maine to the Dakotas. The camps were laid out on scientific principles by U. S. officers and everything pertaining to the ease, comfort and the health of the troop, was admirable attended to.

Did we have plenty to eat? Yes and spare. Beef, mutton, eggs, butter and every conceivable delicacy. Munrow Harris took a fright at a spread of dressed chickens, that I don't think he will forget during life. He led me to it. It was a table about five feet wide, more than two hundred feet long and piled as high as you could reach with the fattest chickens I ever saw. I was leaving for home, but "Mun" said he would stay to eat of those chickens "if it took all summer."

The thousand acres of the Gettysburg battlefield is one vast field of monuments and it would fill volumes to give descriptions of them and their inscriptions. Infantry monuments, with bronzed statues of soldiers on top, some loading their guns, others as if firing, while some were at rest. Wherever there had been a battery stationed you found massive monuments, some surrounded with condemned cannon and bronzed figures of cannoneers, surmounting the shafts. Every position occupied by troop, just before the deadly assault of four o'clock, has cast iron tablets, stating from what State and command these troops belonged to.

We were encamped somewhat to the left of where Pickett's assaulting columns were formed and here we came to the first monument on that part of the field. It was a monstrous piece of solid granite, fully ten feet square and perhaps ten or twelve feet high, with the simple inscription, "Virginia to her sons."

As you go down the pike just in rear of the memorable stone fence, you come upon the markers of Anderson's troop of Hills Corps who were on that day assigned to Longstreet, in lieu of Pickett. That general was then coming with all possible dispatch from Chambersburg, twenty miles away. The first of these was Posey's, then came Wright's, Perry's and Wilcox's. On a circular cast iron plate of about four feet in diameter, anchored to an iron post of a foot in diameter with the inscription, "Here fought on July the 3rd, 1863, the troop of ____ Brigade, composed the ____ regiment," marks every position. They were all alike, giving the simple fact, that such regiments fought there. Of McLaws' Division of which Kershaw's formed a part, are Barksdale's Mississippians, Wofford's Georgians, Kershaw's South Carolinians, and Simms' Georgians. To the right and front were Hood's four brigades.

Kershaw faced Ayers' regulars, the stubbornest and most determined troop in the Federal army, the brigade which saved the army from utter destruction on both fields of Manassas. These troops, as well as McCondless, who faced Simms, were posted in the wooded stretch of foothills of Round Top behind great boulders and piles of quarried rock. Barksdale and Wofford faced Willard and Robertson, in the lower part of the historic peach orchard. Before the fight was half over Weed's, Birmay's, Nevin's and Rogers' Brigades came to the aid of their hard pressed brethren. So you see on this part of the field the Confederates were outnumbered three to one. Round Top and Little round Top, just in our front, and the point at which all of Longstreet's forces were directing their efforts, were one blaze of cannon, which could reach and command every inch of our ground. Down near the foot of the ridge in the peach orchard Sickles had posted a battery of ten guns, with instructions to fire nothing but grape and cannister at the approaching infantry. Through this hail of shot we were forced to march against and forbidden to fire a gun. We walked over this battery with "hands down," but with a fearful loss, however, was forced to give it up, when night came on no horses to remove it. The loss among our own infantry horses was so great it was difficult of move even our own pieces.

The turnpike on which the Federal General Sickles had formed his columns, is a house near his left where his headquarters's flag floated fifty years ago. Now the old general, the only one of his rank on either side, sat receiving the homage of friend and foes. Thousands of Confederate stopped to pay their compliments, but I, somehow, had no such inclination. While he was no doubt a gallant foe, I have no such exalted opinion of a man who had ruined the lives of two innocent women, lording it over my State for two years in a "coach and four," then after having received and squandered near a half million dollars, the government has allowed him as pay, he within the present year begs the government for a pension. I would much rather doff my hat to the equestrian statue of General [Gouverneur K.] Warren, mounted on the cliffs of little Round Top.

The most casual student of the history of that battle well knows that this great engagement was the result of an accident and miscarriage of orders. Had the Federal cavalry general, Beaufort, received the orders to retire should his outpost be attacked, or had General Reynolds received the orders from Meade to fall back to Emmettsburg, should A. P. Hill move forward, no battle of the first day would have taken place. Had not General Warren, Meade's chief of ordnance, rode up on Round Top in the afternoon of the 2nd and put the army in position to meet the onrush of Longstreet, nothing could have saved Meade from total destruction.

After A. P. Hill had defeated the first and eleventh Corps, under Reynolds and Howard, the latter taking refuge on the bold and precipitous cliffs of Culp's Hill, half mile southeast of the town, Meade naturally concluded the battle would be renewed to the north of the town. He was rushing his whole army along Rock creek, just in rear of Cemetery Hill, where he had a light line formed. When Warren rode to the brow of Round Top, what he saw was enough to freeze his heart. Hood's division had already formed around the southern base of the mountain while McLaws' and Anderson's were preparing for the assault and not a Federal soldier in sight, save Weed's Brigade down in Devil's Den. Without waiting orders from his chief, he ordered all troops marching toward Gettysburg to turn to the left. The infantry came at a run and lined the slopes of the mountain behind boulders, stone fences, hedges and every conceivable place of vantage. The artillery came like mad and as the Confederates emerged from the groves in which they had formed, little and great Round Tops were one sheet of flame.

While General Warren was not killed here, his appreciative countrymen have erected an equestrian statue of heroic size on the very rock from which he saw first the Confederates forming. From here, after drinking a cool drink from the marble lined spring at Devil's Den, I proceeded to the rear of the Federal lines, along Cemetery Ridge. Near Meade's headquarters is the "city of the dead," in which ten thousand of the Confederates and Federal dead lie sleeping. A headstone is to each marked "unknown." They do not lie promiscuously but each in a plot to itself, and well might we say:

> "Under the sod, under the clay,
> Here lies the blue, there the gray."

Along the ridge and the valley of Rock Creek had stood Meade with the flower of the Federal army, 115,950 strong. Beyond lay Lee, with barely 70,000. Even with this disparagement between their forces one would ask why was Lee, with all his prestige, military training and transcendent genius of war, repulsed pitted as he was against a military mediocre, not long enough in command to have won the confidence and ardor of his troop? Look at the ground today and the answer is easy. It was a physical impossibility to drive any troop from this natural fortification. From the abrupt bluff, at Culps Mill to Round Top, runs several series of stone walls with cliffs in front, behind which troops lying down out of danger, making a double line of defense, perfectly shielded from the mass of bullets from the Confederates, the Southern army having to march to the assault, through an open and unbroken field of a mile in length. The best of this world's military critics, who have visited this field, pronounce it the best natural battlefield for defense on the Western continent and the wonder is, not that Lee was repulsed but that any of his men survived. As I left the field I thought of our Kentucky poet, when he sang:

> "On Fame's eternal camping ground,
> Their silent tents are spread
> And Glory guards, with solemn round
> The bivouac of the dead."

* * *

EDGEFIELD ADVERTISER
JULY 23, 1913

A Voice From Gettysburg.

Editor Advertiser: It is not my intention to write up this great gathering of the blue and gray. The big dailies will do that. We arrived at Gettysburg June 30, 9:30, with very few exceptions everybody is highly pleased, the air is laden with benedictions, the electric currents bid us welcome, but man and nature with one acclaim bid us truest welcome. This is a grand reunion, and will in the end prove a blessing to the whole country. There never was one like it in the history of the ages, nor there never will be the like again. Gettysburg stepped fifty years back in the halo of history and looked again upon an army of blue and an array of gray, meeting at her doorsteps to join in the semi-centennial celebration of the greatest battle of the war between the states, and to show to the world that bullet and saber scars are not so deep as the feeling of American brotherhood. Each day veterans in blue and gray trooped into the little town which lies so peacefully among the everlasting hills since Lee and Meade turned their legions southward so long ago.

The officials estimate the number of veterans up-to-date to be 45,000 probably the greatest array that ever assembled on Gettysburg field after Lee and Meade left it to glory, and to history. The central figures in a wonderful picture, are these veterans of "the greatest fighting force the sun ever shone on" shook off the weight of age and fought over again the battle that marked the high tide of the confederacy. They are here to honor the men who fought and died on both sides of the three days conflict of half a century ago, and to commemorate deeds of heroism unparalleled and unequalled. It is an army united in sentiment, and united in fact; for the blue linked arms with the gray. They marched the duty road together from the village; they sat down at the same mess tables and would tell to each other of their close calls; and if there was any ranker in any heart, any feeling of bitterness, it did not come to the surface.

There is a unique flag flying in the big camp tent which has been an object of almost adoration to all who have seen it, and it is agreed that it accurately represents the sentiments of every one. On one side is the stars and stripes, on the other a relic, the Confederate battle flag. Beneath in white letters are these historic declarations:

"Let us have peace.--Grant."

"Duty is the sublimest word in any language.--Lee."

I walked alone to-day to where Longstreet formed his line of battle, and through the wheat-field, and peach-orchard, down to the foot of Little Round Top a distance of about five hundred yards or more, which was made at double quick time, reaching the objective point it was then war to the knife. It was fifty years ago this morning since we made this charge, but I could in my imagination hear the roar of the cannon, the whistling bullets and the shouts of the men as across the meadow they flew sweeping the field with the bayonet. I stand today 3, where Pickett formed his grand division of Virginians to make the charge across Mission Ridge to Little Round Top, a charge that has gone down in history, story, and song, I can see his picture now as he draws his sword from its scabbard in the evening sunlight, with his long black hair waving in the evening breeze, and his eyes sparkling like the diamond, and as he cried with a loud voice first division, forward guide center, and as I followed his line of battle I could hear that same command echoing through the meadow and over the hills "guide center."

The battle flag of the 7th S. C. Regt, did go back with me to Gettysburg, and I unfolded it again on the same plat of ground that it floated just fifty years ago. It was very popular among the boys in blue. A number of ladies came over and took the picture of the flag, one lady told me that she had never seen a confederate flag, and had never talked with any person from the south before. This new meeting of the blue and gray, at this battlefield will do more in bringing about a better feeling between the north and south than anything that has ever taken place before in the history of the nation.

I have never enjoyed any gathering in my life more than this, and it is my opinion, after seeing and hearing what I did, that everybody was delighted while there, and went away with a broader mind, a higher idea of life, and a better man. Of course there are men who did not see it that way, and men who would find fault with everything, everywhere. But it was more like an old time Methodist love-feast, than anything else that I could think of, each was glad to see the other, every countenance was full of benign pleasure the whole time we were there. Why should it not be so, since we are a re-united country, we claim protection under the same flag, we are governed by the same laws, we read the same Bible and worship the same God, our future hopes, and future destinies are the same. "The strife is over!"

"Each fought for his own precious cause,

Each to his standard true,

Let them be praised, those gallant men--

What if in the gray or in the blue,

One cause was lost, the other won,

United now, they stand to-day,

A common brotherhood of men--

The grand old blue, the noble gray."

J. Russell Wright [7th South Carolina Infantry, Co. G].

* * *

EDGEFIELD ADVERTISER
JULY 30, 1913

The Gettysburg Meeting.

On the hallowed ground of Gettysburg, consecrated by the blood of the blue and the gray, after the lapse of half a century the North and the South meet with the East and the West under the American flag, to do honor to the soldiers still living, and to pay loving and respectful homage to those who are asleep in the stillest of all slumbers! Neither stress of time nor distance of home shall break or blur that friendship that our brothers sealed with their blood. And as we talk over together the wonderful and glorious events of those days of conflict; as we walk together over this great battlefield, we pause at the close of the day and clasp hands with each other and with hearts united we are constrained to breathe a silent prater that peace and fraternity may abide until the trumpet shall sound and life's shadows flee away forever. As we walked over this field of carnage, the Peach Orchard, the Wheatfield, and the "Devil's Den" where Kershaw fought and Barkesdale fell and so many brave men of the blue and the gray stained this soil with their blood, I uncovered my head and felt like plucking the shoes off my feet.

I could locate quite a number of places where we lost heavily. Whit Lott lost his leg at the foot of Mission Ridge near a large chestnut tree which is still standing, but it is dead. Only one apple tree is standing in the Peach Orchard, and it is also dead. I followed the line of Pickett's charge up to the very brow of Little Round Top, (the Yankees call it the "High water mark of the Confederacy") which has gone down in story and song as the grandest charge that has ever been recorded in the history of any war. It seemed to me that I could hear Pickett as he led the charge say, "Come on boys; press the battle to the gates--forward, guide center." That was fifty years ago. A large number has been spared to come back, bearing the olive branch, and the white dove of peace has spread her silver wings about the blue and the gray, saying, "How good and how pleasant it is for brethren to dwell together in unity."

This peace conference at Gettysburg has already done more to establish brotherly feeling than anything that has ever taken place, anywhere or in any country. A petition was gotten up in this camp asking Congress to pay back to the South the tax we paid on our cotton for three or four years after the war and I believe every man in blue signed it.

I was in company with three men in blue, two from Pittsburg, Pa., and the other from the state of N. Y., who, speaking of this meeting said: "I have seen and felt more since I have been here than I ever expected to see or feel this side of heaven. Not only the United States, but the whole world is looking at this meeting with wonder and admiration." And they went on to say with the tenderest feeling. "You Southern soldiers must have a pension as the Federals have."

I took the old battle flag back and let it float once more on that historic plain, and it was very popular, the ladies flocking to see it and to get a picture of a Confederate battle flag. A lady from Pittsburg came up and asked if she could see the flag. With pleasure I showed it to her. "I see from your badge that you are from South Carolina," said the lady. "Yes, madam, born and reared there, and a Rebel died in the wool." "Give me your hand then" said the lady, "when I get back home I can tell my people that I met and shook hands with a man from South Carolina-and a Rebel at that. You are the first Southern man that I have ever talked with." In a pleasant manner I asked her what kind of a thing she thought a South Carolinian looked like. "Why of course a body of noble, patriotic men."

It is my honest opinion that if such a meeting as this at Gettysburg could have been possible with the rank and file of the blue and the gray in the 60's peace could have been made at any time. But the fellows that fanned the war clouds most did the least. I shall never forget what Col. J. C. Smyley said to my father in April 1861. He said that he would be willing to drink all the blood that would be shed that the South could whip the fight and be back home in three months, and turning to myself and two brothers who were about ready to go to the front said, "Boys, when you get to Virginia, if the Yankees cross the Potomac give them h---. And we did. But the Colonel never did go, never did see or drink any blood. There were legions of that kind.

The men and women at Gettysburg were loud in their praise and admiration of the Southern soldier. Let me quote again this beautiful little Pittsburg girl. She said to me while looking at the flag, "You Southern people fought with a patriotic fury unequaled, and you have written your history in blood from Gettysburg to the Rio Grande. And perhaps you do not know it, but the Southern soldiers who followed Lee and Jackson are the admiration of the world to-day." I told her that I knew what she said was true, and had known it all these fifty years. I said to her, that is a grand eulogy, and that alone is worth coming to Gettysburg to hear from one of Pennsylvania's noble women. And she is good authority for she backed up what she said with history. I told her I was glad that I was in the struggle of the sixties, that I believed then as I do now that the South was right, but the negro was not in my thought, and while I live I shall believe that the South was right.

I want no greater heritage to leave my children than that I was a Confederate soldier. My bullet scars are letters of nobility.

J. Russell Wright [7th South Carolina Infantry, Co. G].

* * *

EDGEFIELD ADVERTISER
AUGUST 6, 1913

More About Gettysburg.

Editor The Advertiser:--It may be that I will give your readers skimmed milk in this letter, but that will be good for the nerves. After this letter the curtain will fall, and I will let the little city, quietly sleep midst the everlasting hills that once shook with the roar of conflict between two great armies. The third day of the greatest reunion the world has ever known, sixty thousand old soldiers, brave and true in a fraternal grasp, in embrace, in a God bless you! the picture of the greatest artist, the pen of the greatest writer, the tongue of the most gifted orator, would be as powerless to describe it as it would be to paint the rainbow or add fragrance to the flower. The fraternal feeling was so great that the soldiers cared for but little oratory or parade. Two things were apparent: the North came down to mingle with the, South and to hear this universal expression: "Look at their camps, their splendid uniforms, their military bearing, their love for the American flag." The two armies had a love feast that was real and grand.

We are citizens of the greatest country on earth, united as never before in the history of the republic. The South is better, the North is better, the nation is stronger.

I stood on Cemetery Ridge and saw the survivors of Pickett's old command search over the same valley of death, where they once left so many of their comrades just fifty years ago that day. The fated hour was 3 p. m. The same starting point, the same objective point, --a clump of trees where they broke through the lines only to perish or surrender, where it is said a captain of a battery commanded his men to give them grape and cannister without fuse. Spartans of America, steel clashing steel, and at last the victor tires at the gore where victory was so nearly won, and says grape and cannister without fuse. On the 4th of July President Wilson spoke to an immense throng, just fifteen minutes. He has a voice to charm, a face to inspire, a smile to appease. He is a great president of a great people.

Think of a government feeding 10,000 old veterans on chicken, ice cream and various other tempting good things.

I went over the field where General Reynolds was killed, and then to the battle lines from Cemetery Ridge to Spangler's Spring. This was on the Confederates' left where the wounded and famishing of both armies crawled together and drank water, thence along Culp's Hill where whole trees were shot down with cannon and musket balls. There is hardly a tree between the battle lines that is not scarred and knotty from being shot. The statue of John Burns, a citizen of Gettysburg, stands on the field. He gathered his rifle and asked permission to fight in the ranks, and was klled, which showed the spirit of the American citizen.

The Bloody Angle, the objective point of Pickett's charge, Little Round Top, Big Round Top, the Devil's Den, the Peach Orchard, the Valley of Death, where the markers indicating the position of the Confederate forces, make the field of wonderful importance. The statue of Miss Jennie Wade stands in the front yard of her home. She was killed by a Confederate soldier while working up dough. She was in a small brick house, the front door was closed, and the federals were in the cellar shooting at the Confederates 255 yards off in the open. The sharpshooters were shooting at the house, a ball passed through two large doors, striking the lady below the hips coming out at the throat. I notice a paper of West Virginia that made it read, 'Miss Jennie Wade was killed by a Confederate", saying nothing about a lot of federals in the Cellar shooting through a porthole, and the other fellow in the open.

J. Russell Wright [7th South Carolina Infantry, Co. G]

* * *

Laurens Advertiser
August 6, 1913

THE RE-UNION AT GETTYSBURG

Capt. J. T. Duckett, of Clinton, has sent to The Advertiser a copy of the Western Democrat, published at Hendersonville, N. C, containing an account of the reunion of the Blue and the Gray at Gettysburg, written by Capt. J. W. Wofford, who is remembered by many of the old soldiers of this county. The Advertiser takes pleasure in publishing this account of the re-union so that many of the old soldiers who did not attend may have the pleasure of joining with the younger people in getting a glimpse of the scene from a distance. The account is as follows:

To the Margret Hayes Chapter, U. D. C.

Having manifested so much interest in aiding veterans to attend the great Reunion recently held at Gettysburg, it was thought that this report of the trip should be made to your Chapter.

The delegation from this county, a jolly good humored and congenial crowd, consisted of the following veterans: J. P. Johnson, J. H. West, J. T. Williams, J. Harper Johnson and J. W. Wofford. Tickets were furnished a majority of them by your chapter. We left here on Sunday preceding the Reunion, and passed in Virginia several towns that were familiar to us during the war, viz: Orange, Culpepper Court House. Brandy station, Manasses near where the two battles, first and second Manasses, were fought. In one or the other we each participated. In a few miles we cross the historic Bull Run, we see Arlington in the distance, the house of General Lee. We soon reach Washington and after a short stay we take a special for Gettysburg and ride most of the way on the great Pennsylvania Railroad. It surpasses in speed and comfort any road that we had ever rode on. About 4 p. m. on Sunday we arrived at Gettysburg. We come to a halt in the town, (the road runs through the town.) Instantly two or more boy scouts enter the coach. "Keep your seats, gentlemen, don't move from your seats until we come for you." Slowly the train moves out on a spur about 1 1-12 miles to the camp. We alight and get together by States and march about one half mile, guided by the scouts, to that part of the camp assigned to North Carolina, and take possession of a large, commodious tent sufficient for eight persons, equipped with a cot, two blankets, two sheets, and two wash pans. This the tent equipment. We look around: 'tis a city of tents and covers about thirty acres; at night lit up by large electric lights, it is a sight to behold. The Boy Scouts, of which there are two thousand, are in evidence everywhere to look after the welfare of veterans and are kind and courteous in imparting information concerning the camp and appurtenances. Half past six, the supper bell clangs and we repair to the kitchen at the head of the street, and are furnished with a half gallon tin cup, a large tin plate, knife, fork and spoon, and pass by the large receptacles for the food, and are dished out the prepared meal in abundance. Falling back a few paces to the dining table, you take your seat.

The next day a regular stream of veterans from every section of the country pour out from the trains like bees from a hive, until It Is estimated that 50,000 veterans are in camp. They told us that 4,000 of the very best cooks and waiters were employed in the camp. They certainly knew how to cook as no complaint was heard about ill-prepared food. The arrangements were so complete that the whole army of veterans could be served in one hour. The sanitary arrangements are perfect, no foul smells, no flies; kitchen and streets neat; medical arrangements could not be better; a veteran prostrated by heat or taken suddenly sick. In less than ten minutes, he is on a comfortable cot in a hospital and receives treatment. Three artesian wells are in the camp affording over a million gallons daily, and piped along every street in camp, double faucets about 50 yards apart, and too water fountains bubbling up about the same distance. The kitchen or meal kits were given to all veterans and highly prized by them as souvenirs. The tents are of the very best and did not leak a particle. So much for the camp.

Now, how did we put in our time? Early in the morning we scattered, some to the ground fought over the first day, some to the second and some to the third. Of course, that part where a man fought was the place he wanted to see first. Markers were placed and it was an easy matter to identify and trace the movements made by the different commands, to visit the springs and branches where we got our water just fifty years ago today. How it brought up old recollections, the places where the fight was hottest, and where brave comrades fell. Then after tramping in the hot sun, a return to camp is made and much said about what was seen through the day, telling tales, cracking jokes and being boys again, visiting the big tent and smaller ones, listening to speeches and music. While resting in the shade on a grassy mound where Sickles had formed his advance line, in conversation with a very intelligent Federal soldier who had fought there, he was asked this question, "This seems to be a good line, why did you leave it?"

"Just simply to keep from being annihilated. They got about two thirds of us anyway," he replied, with a grim smile.

The next day we visited the more important points of the field, such as High Water Mark, National Cemetery, Pennsylvania Monument that cost $150,000, the headquarters of Lee and Meade and many others. The third day was spent very much like the other two in the meantime visiting other camps, hunting up old comrades, some of whom we had not seen since the close of the war. The fourth was Wilson Day, and of course, we all who could, went, and at night the great fire works on top of little Round Top was visible to all parts of the field and witnessed by thousands and thousands who came by railroad, auto and carriage.

I met two who fought Kershaw's line of battle on the second, when the following conversation took place:

"Comrade, did you fight here"

"Yes."

"Where?"

"Just where we are standing. By jingo, we fought right there," pointing to a monument about thirty yards distant. Another gripping of hands and on we go. Such scenes as these were taking place constantly, I verily believe this Reunion will clinch the sentiment that has been prevailing to a more or less extent for some time, to give from the National Treasury a pension to Confederate soldiers. When sounded, I believe that 49 out of 50 of the old Federal soldiers would endorse it.

By the way, Judge Clark, whom many of us wanted to go to the United States Senate on this platform in the last election, visited our tent twice while in camp and stated that he was still fighting for the measure and that he would stop off in Washington and shake them up a little. I think in a short time the matter will be tested and pensions granted, some wiseacres to the contrary notwithstanding. There are some among us well to do, who are too proud to accept it, and it hurts our cause forgetting the many poor old fellows and their wives who would be glad to get it.

Not a word was said in all the speeches or conversations that was in the least offensive or jarring to the most sensitive persons. Surely harmony prevailed.

It is useless for me to attempt to describe this great battlefield. Suffice It to say, it is ground beyond conception, the beauty of its natural scenery, enhanced now by upward of 500 tasteful and elegant monuments marking the positions occupied by troops. There is no spot in the world connected with more memorable events than the thirty-five square miles of ground which witnessed the terrible conflict between the Federal and Confederate troops on the first, second and third of July, 1863. There is but one Gettysburg and it is without doubt the most picturesque and interesting point in America for either the soldier or citizen to visit. Thousands from the old world visit it annually. Quite a number of hotels and boarding houses have sprung up to entertain them.

Gettysburg, during the battle, contained about 1200 Inhabitants. Now it numbers upward of 5,000. The lines of battle are marked by fine macadam roads and where a battery of artillery stood during the battle, there now stands two cannon pointing as they did then. All the woods and open fields are kept as they were then.

What I have written contains but a brief outline of a description of the present camp and battlefield. What good results are to follow this great gathering of the Blue and Gay, as I see it--it wipes out the last vestige of sectionalism and cements the North and South as nothing else could do, If you could have heard their great bands amid the Confederate camps play Dixie and other old war time pieces and listen to some of their host orators and feel the vise-like grip of their hands, and listen to their hearty greetings, "How are you, old comrade, so glad to see you so glad you accepted our invitation to come up here so we could see you. You thought you were right and like true Americans as you are, you fought and fought valiantly for that right, and gave us enough. We wanted no more. God bless you, old comrade."

All of this endorsing the sentiment expressed by President Lincoln, (as he stood upon the rock wall when he went to Gettysburg on the occasion of, laying the corner stone at the Federal cemetery.) "There were no slouches out there, (pointing towards the Confederate position,) and I am glad to be the countryman of those soldiers who assailed these heights."

Wherever you went upon the field you were met by old Federal soldiers and upon seeing your "Cross of Honor," you had to stop and talk with them. Close to 50,000 soldiers were killed and wounded in this battle, more than the combined losses in the American Revolution and Mexican war.

Almost all writers on Gettysburg have something to say about who was to blame on our side. I have always held to this that Longstreet was the cause of Lee's failure on the third day by not coming to time on the second day. If you believe Fitz. Lee, Pendleton, Early, Wilcox or Gen. Long, then Longstreet was ordered to open the battle very early in the day. This he did not do until about the middle of the afternoon and then as Hood's battalions of gray are moving down upon Little Round Top, Gen. Warren grasps the situation and rushes troops on the summit in sufficient numbers to hold It. How easy was it to take it in our possession any time in the forenoon and with it in our possession all the strongholds of Mead's lines would have been destroyed and he would have been forced to have waged the fight somewhere else, where positions would have been more favorable to our side. Any one standing upon Round Top can see this for himself.

Warren's statue is standing on a large boulder on top of Little Round Top, visible for a long distance. Many monuments are yet to be erected on the field. Arrangements are being made to erect an equestrian statue of Gen. Lee just across the road on Cemetery Ridge in front of where stands that of Gen. Meade.

Well, the war was finally ended. We did not win. I am glad we didn't. We are now a reunited country, strong in every respect that goes to make up a mighty nation, with no superior on the face of the earth, slavery abolished. Without the war, that would have been done any way; it was tottering on its last legs when the war came.

Was Lee's army whipped at Gettysburg? I do not believe now, neither did I then, that the army was a whipped army, but more of a drawn battle. The first day they were driven back through the town of Gettysburg with two corporals literally torn to pieces, to a position on Cemetery Ridge. On the second. Sickles with his command, takes a position way out in front of where Meade had told him. Greely says Sickles was spoiling for a fight and didn't believe Meade was. Sickles was driven hack by McLaws and Hood's divisions with heavy losses to the enemy. So in the first and second both sides agree that we got the best of it and on the third, that by the prestive of the day's fighting, Lee thought he could break, the centre and rout the whole army and the assault was made by Pickett's division and a few other brigades, about one-eighth or ninth of his forces, and failed to accomplish the desired result. Having pretty well exhausted his heavy ammunition, he thought it prudent to withdraw. The balance of the army was in splendid condition. The army remains there another day, no assault was made upon them, they surely did not consider then that our army was badly defeated. Our army quietly withdrew without baggage and ammunition back to and near the river and find it too swollen to cross and there formed our line of battle, threw down the gauntlet and awaited their coming for several days. They never came. I read recently an article from one close to Gen. Meade. In which he says there was about that time a council of war held. The corps commanders with but one exception Insisted on following up and renewing the battle while the river was high. Meade would not consent to give the order and pressed for his reasons said this: "I have just read a copy of a communication to President Davis from Gen. Lee in which he says that he has the situation well in hand and can repel any attack made upon him. Lee never makes any misrepresentations.' "

The morale of the army was good, the position was good, their spirits were high, they were hungry and mad and my impression then and now was that if Meade had given battle he would have got a licking long to be remembered. Lee crosses the river and; back In Virginia he soon sends his first corps, Longstreet, to reinforce Bragg at Chickamauga, and with the other part of his army he confronts and holds back the victorious Federal army, so-called, till the coming of Grant at Wilderness. This doesn't look like a much defeated army. The true reason for falling back after the third day was simply this: Want of heavy ammunition. It had been pretty well exhausted the last day and the risk was too great to stay there without it. Now, really is there not a little bit too much gush about the great turning point, the "high water mark," and the great victory at Gettysburg, the "back bone of the rebellion broken." etc.

Grant surely didn't believe all this talk after his conflict with Lee's army at Wilderness. Spottsylvania, Deep Bottom, Petersburg and other places. It was In the west, not In the east the sapping process began and the end came for the want of bread.

I have written this because it is history.

We return to our homes after the great Reunion glad that we went and those who did not go missed by far the greatest occasion of its kind that the world has ever seen since its creation.

* * *

Pickens Sentinel
August 14, 1913

Gettysburg Reunion

Dacusville, S. C., July 29, 1913

I thought it might be of interest to some of your many readers to hear of our trip to the great reunion at the famous battlefield of Gettysburg.

On Saturday afternoon at seven o'clock, June 30th, we boarded the north bound train at Greenville, S. C. and the next time we put foot on the ground we were at Gettysburg. It was night when we rolled in but it did not take long to find the row of tents marked for South Carolina, and were soon assigned to our tent where everything was arranged for our comfort during our stay.

The next morning we were up and dined on a most bountiful breakfast at seven o'clock, and then came to my tent with my old time friend and comrade, P[inckney] H. Williams [Capt. W. W. Fickling's Co., Brooks Light Artillery], of Spartanburg county, the only one of my company that I saw while there. He was a true-blue soldier and was in the awful fight at Gettysburg, getting severely wounded there and had to lie in that condition a day and a half on the battlefield. As we were walking over the grounds, he was pointing out the place he was when shot. A tall, stern looking Yankee was listening to Mr. Williams tell of his being so nearly killed there, when he interrupted him by saying: "Well, Sir, I am the man who was doing the shooting that day," when Mr. Williams answered, "Yes, and you're the very man that shot me, Sir."

We got a hack for one dollar each, with a guide who drove us all over the battleground and showed us many famous points. We went to Big Round Top and Little Round Top, the Devil's Den, and the spring where after the fight, the soldiers of the North and South mingled together and drank of the water there, it being the only water available. The spring and surroundings are well kept and beautiful.

There are many handsome and beautiful monuments erected in memory of the heroes of that day. The house where Jennie Wade was killed, the only woman killed during the battle, is still preserved. She was in the house making bread when a bullet came through and killed her at work. Among the many monuments there is one to be seen to her memory. There is also a handsome monument, the figure cast in bronze standing on a pedestal of native rock, called the "Hero of Gettysburg," in memory of John Burns, who at the advanced age of seventy years, shouldered his musket and entered the fray on the very opening day of this most awful conflict.

We went to a point called the "Bloody Angle," where in the midst of the fight ammunition gave out, and the battle continued, the men of both sides fighting with gun-rods, sticks, rocks and anything that could be had. The blood flowed freely there, and this noted spot is marked by a big slab to tell the passers-by of the awful conflict held there.

The grave-yard is one vast space where all the slain men were afterwards taken up and buried with a marker and flag at each grave. The government bought the land, said to comprise 6,000 acres, and keeps up the battle grounds, grave-yard, etc., by men paid to attend to this famous spot.

As to our treatment while there, it was royal, fit for a king. I never saw as much to eat, and it was prepared to the queen's taste. There was immense rock-walled pits built in the ground, where the remnants from every meal were thrown in and burned up—enough to have fed an army—thus keeping down flies and filth. Everything was kept clean and sanitary and Uncle Sam is to be congratulated upon being host to the largest number of persons ever reunited at one time, and in the most bountiful and kingly treatment. The quarter-master, who was a young man from Walhalla, S. C., and who issued all the provisions, told me that the coffee alone, that was consumed, was one thousand dollars worth daily.

Such mutton and beef I have never seen in all my life, with everything else in keeping.

The old Veterans were all jolly, having a gay time in spite of their gray hairs and advanced years.

One old fellow seventy-two years old, had his violin and struck up some of the old war tunes, and such dancing I never saw in Dixie, or by any one before.

Bar rooms were plentiful and the most men I ever saw in a bar room at one time was there, the most of them being Yankees. To the honor of the South I never saw a single old Southerner drunk, but saw plenty of old Yankees sitting around asleep, drunk.

On the battlefield is an old barn that was there during the war, it is still standing, though getting very frail, and the cannon just as they were left, still stand, and the old rock fences over which our men ran the Yankees, still stand, just as they were that day.

On Friday, I left Gettysburg, came down to Washington and spent two days sight-seeing in our beautiful capitol city. We left there Sunday and reached Greenville Monday, having had the grandest trip of my life, the memory of which will never fade.

-----W. J. Ponder-----

＊＊＊

LAURENS ADVERTISER
SEPTEMBER 24, 1913

Uncle John at Gettysburg.

By Wm. D. S.

I spent three of the happiest days of my life at the reunion at Gettysburg. I was the guest of the 21st Indiana Regiment and they entertained me in royal style. An incident of the fight 50 years ago came into my mind as I stood in front of the Round Top.

Nine of us Confederates were sent out on a scout, and we met eleven mounted men of the Union army. We went right at one another, and soon I was the only one left on our side, and two calvary [sic] men on the Union side. One of them made at me and was snapping his pistol right at my head, when I charged him with the bayonet. As I made a thrust his horse reared up and the bayonet went right through his heart, over went horse and rider. With the man pinned under the dead horse. Two of our Confederates, passing near, heard the row and rushed in and captured the other man, and helped me roll the horse off my man. They wanted to take the watch and pocket book of my prisoner, but I told them they could not rob my man when he had surrendered. I carried my prisoner to headquarters where I was told to take him to a certain officer, who was parolling the prisoners. We could not be incumbered [sic] with a lot of captured men being in the enemy's country and we needed every man in the ranks to fight our way out.

A woman was relating the capture of her husband to a crowd, who stood around her on Round Top. Standing below her, was an attentive listener to her story. When she finished I asked her permission to complete her tale. I am the man that captured your husband and parolled him in the Gettysburg fight. His son rushed down and threw his arms around me and hugged me. His wife and about a thousand Yankee women ran down the hill, and laid hold of me, shook hands and patted me nearly to death. I sure did have a big time! -Uncle John.

* * *

NEWBERRY HERALD AND NEWS
JANUARY 13, 1914

Gettysburg Reunion Note.

After the adjournment of the general assembly last year, General B. H. Teague, commander of the South Carolina division, United Confederate Veterans, and others very much interested in the Gettysburg reunion, found that the amount of money appropriated by you to give the deserving survivors from the State a trip to that reunion would not be sufficient. Some effort was made to attempt to raise the money by popular subscription. I took the position that this was very wrong; that I did not think the ex-Confederate soldiers of this State wanted to be held up as beggars or paupers, and even if some few did want to be so held up, I made up my mind that none of them should be. I, therefore, sent the following communication to General Teague and received from him the following reply:

June 21, 1913

General B. H. Teague, Commander South Carolina Division, United Confederate Veterans, Aiken, S. C.

Dear Sir: I have noted with regret though it was to be expected, that the appropriation by the legislature for the survivors from this State of the Battle of Gettysburg to defray their traveling expenses to anniversary soon to be held, is greatly deficient, providing for considerably less than one-half the number applying. South Carolina ought to give all her survivors of this great battle an opportunity to attend this reunion, and it has seemed to me nothing more than just that it should be done. I am satisfied the money can be secured through one of the banks, and that the legislature at its next session will be only too glad to make good the deficiency. It has seemed to me proper, however, that the matter should be taken up with you first, you being the direct representative of this State in charge of the distribution of the fund appropriated by the Legislature and the State's representative upon the Battle of Gettysburg commission, and I suggest to you that we give a joint official note for an amount necessary to make up the deficiency in the appropriation. I have no doubt the money could be secured upon such a note, and all the survivors from this State given an equal opportunity to take advantage of this reunion.

As time is pressing, I shall be glad to hear from you immediately.

Very respectfully,

Cole L. Blease,

Governor.

Aiken, S. C., June 23, 1913

Hon. Cole L. Blease, Columbia, S. C.

Am willing to sign official note as you suggest. Wire me if I can issue checks immediately and on what bank.

B. H. Teague,

Maj. Gen. Comdg., S. C. Div., U. C. V.

Columbia, S. C., June 23, 1913

Gen. B. H. Teague, Aiken, S. C.

Your wire. Make estimate of amount needed, sign note for that amount and forward to me, or come over to Columbia tonight.

Cole L. Blease,

Governor.

In the meantime I received the following very kind offer from Col. W. A. Clark, himself a Confederate veteran:

The Carolina National Bank of Columbia.

Columbia, S. C. June 24, 1913.

His Excellency, Cole L. Blease, Governor of South Carolina, Columbia, S. C.

Dear Sir: Referring to our conversation had yesterday over the phone, I desire now to confirm the same and to say that if desired the Carolina National Bank will be pleased to discount the paper referred to in order to enable the veterans who participated in the battle of Gettysburg to join in the semi-centennial celebration of the same.

Just 50 years ago the sons of Carolina offered their lives, a willing sacrifice in defense of what we understood to be our constitutional rights and liberties. It is, therefore, meet and proper that the present generation should furnish the means for these veteran soldiers to participate in the celebration of that battle, which afforded the highest test of American patriotism and heroism.

Yours truly,

W. A. Clark,

President.

I replied to Col. Clark as follows:

June 24, 1913

Col. W. A. Clark, President Carolina National Bank, Columbia, S. C.

My Dear Sir: Yours of June 24, confirming our conversation over the telephone has been received, and you have my sincere thanks, personally and as governor, for the same, and I desire to thank you on behalf not only of the veterans of South Carolina, but on behalf of the entire people of our State, for this very prompt and generous action on your part. A friend of mine very kindly volunteered to let us have this amount of money for this purpose, and will do so—in fact he has it in hand. However, if it is an inconvenience to your bank _____ _____ ,or if you prefer, as matter of course to do business with a banking institution along this line, especially in view of your voluntary kindness, I will therefore, accept your offer. I assure you, however, that there will be no loss in the matter, and that if the legislature does not make this note good your bank will be saved perfectly harmless in another way.

Very respectfully,

Cole L. Blease

Governor.

Gen. Teague and I thereupon made the joint note, copy of which is as follows:

$1,700

Columbia, S. C., June 24, 1913

On demand for the value received, we or either of us promise to pay to the order of The Carolina National Bank of Com., Seventeen Hundred and no 100 Dollars. With interest at the rate of 7 per cent, per annum.

(Signed) Cole L. Blease

Gov., South Carolina

(Signed) B. H. Teague

Maj. Gen. Com. S. C. Div., U. C. V.

This note is now in the Carolina National Bank. I ask you gentlemen to be kind enough to include in your appropriation bill the necessary amount to meet this obligation. I could say a great deal in praise of the confederate soldier, and what we owe him but I think we have all heard a great deal of that, and realize our obligation in these matters, and I am satisfied it is only necessary for me to bring this matter to your attention in order for it to receive favorable consideration. I shall, therefore, take up no more of your time in regard to it.

* * *

LAURENS ADVERTISER
JULY 2, 1915

OFF TO GETTYSBURG.

A number of Old Soldiers Who Fought at Gettysburg Off for the Reunion of the Blue and the Gray

Between fifteen and twenty old soldiers, who were in the great battle at Gettysburg when Meade checked Lee's march into Pennsylvania, are in Gettysburg attending the reunion of the Blue and Gray survivors of that great conflict. The old soldiers left Monday morning and by now they are camping on the battlefields over which they charged fifty years ago recounting the events of that great battle and fraternizing with those whom they fought years ago. The "boys" will remain there over the Fourty and will begin to return the later part of the week.

All of those going from this county were provided with railroad fare from the funds in the hands of Gen. Teague. Those from Cross Hill whose names are found elsewhere were provided with additional sum by the ladies of that place. Those going from Laurens and vicinity were: John T. Langston [3rd South Carolina, Co. I], W. A. McClintock [3rd South Carolina, Co. K], J. P. Caldwell, James Workman [3rd South Carolina, Co.

G], L. Nelson, R[obert] P. Adair [13th South Carolina, Co. F], T[homas] D. Duckett [3rd South Carolina, Co. I], J. R. Anderson, G[eorge] W. Hanna [15th South Carolina, Co. H], T. G. Anderson, B. F. Hollingsworth [3rd South Carolina, Co. I] and probably others went from Clinton and John S. Wilbanks [3rd South Carolina, Co. A], an inmate of the old soldiers home at Columbia from this county was also among this contingent.

* * *

STANDARD AND REVIEW, AIKEN, S. C.
JULY 15, 1938

THE OPEN FORUM
GETTYSBURG

Editor of Standard and Review:

On the morning of June 29th, at 2 A. M., we boarded a train of fourteen Pullman cars over the Seaboard to Gettysburg. This train was carrying the Veterans of South Carolina, Georgia, Florida, Alabama, Mississippi, Louisiana and Texas, said to have 1509 Veterans. After traveling through a large portion of South Carolina, all of North Carolina, all of Virginia, also Maryland, and well up into the northern portion of Pennsylvania, we arrived at Gettysburg at 6 p. m. the same day.

I wish to say Mr. Editor, our hearts and minds were filled with much anxiety (and I must say with nervous anticipation as to how we would be received.) The South Carolina Veterans occupied the front coach, as it was in 60's, South Carolina was the first to appear before that immense crowd that thronged the depot, I being the only one in full Gray uniform in our coach, as I passed from the door I heard a sweet voice sing out, "There's a Confederate uniform, isn't it lovely." I immediately raised my hat and made as graceful bow, as a boy of 90 knew how to make, instantly there was such hand clapping and smiling faces, that all questions as to our reception was completely banished.

We were under the discipline of the War Department, we were placed in busses (48 of which had been sent up from Washington) for our pleasure and carried to our camping quarters (tents) which were as comfortable as a plastered room, with two single beds with springs, mattresses, two sheets, two blankets, and two large pillows, also two chairs, pitchers and basin, and two cakes of castile soap. It was real cold up there at night, the next morning everyone was begging for another blanket, which was readily supplied. Our dining department was as nicely and conveniently planned as our tents. Each Veteran was required to have an attendant, whose duty it was to look at all times for the interest of his Veteran. I wish to say I was remarkably fortunate in securing a gentleman from Columbia (Clarence Richards). I will say just here anyone contemplating such a trip, I will gladly recommend Mr. Richards, there is none better. The next morning after a fine breakfast, I suggested to my attendant, that we visit the Blue Camp, as we were entirely separate, but not too far apart.

Mr. Editor, I really can't describe that visit, the scene was, I imagine, something like it will be when we reach the Heavenly Gate and our loved ones greet us. The first one we met on entering the Camp was the National Chaplain of the War Department, being familiar with all the ranks, he at once recognized my rank by my stars, he clasped my hand and threw his arm around my neck and pressed me to his bosom as if I had been his father, with the expression "God bless you my brother, my prayer is being answered, we are all one in Christ, no swords and bayonets to be tearing us asunder, now nothing but love and peace in all our hearts." By this time we were surrounded by a large group of Veterans in Blue, and every one gave me the same hand clasp and pressed me to their bosom with a "God bless you."

Mr. Editor, that was the spirit that pervaded the entire gathering. Everything was done for the Confederate Veteran, he was Pennsylvania's special guest. We were finely entertained by the best of music, forty-two bands were present, one from South Carolina, I was proud of it. I found whenever South Carolina was mentioned everyone present was all attention. They were perfectly ignorant as to the destruction of Sherman's march through the South, I told them as plainly, and truthfully as I could, they were shocked to hear it. Every lady I met was as sociable as if she was my sister, I am afraid to say how many times I faced a Kodak, at last I told them I would not face one unless they (the girls) would stand with me, in every instance they gladly consented. Later Mr. Editor I will be glad to furnish one or more of the cuts, so my friends can see how near together we got.

I met Gen. Longstreet's widow, she was gathering all those she could find who belonged to his corps, I was one of the number, wanted to have a moving picture made, which she did. Those who attend the movies may have a chance to see me chatting with Mrs. Longstreet. I also had the honor of having my picture with a widow who husband was a Major General in the Union Army, just at the base of Lincoln's monument, that is one I will send you when I receive it for your paper.

We were carried all over the Battle Ground accompanied by an expert guide, showing us the movement of each army during the three days battle. Cannons are there that are in the same position as when used. The Monuments are just grand. General Lee stands out as the greatest general in that battle. The North does not hesitate to honor him.

My story is now too long, but I will have to tell about the everlasting peace light. It's a magnificent piece of marble, about 50 feet in height. What emphasis was given by everyone to the everlasting peace when it was dedicated by the President. A beautiful soft light, yet so bright there to stand forever.

We left Gettysburg Wednesday afternoon at 7 o'clock, not without a hand clasp from everyone that could get near enough, with a hearty wish for a safe journey home. Truly Southern hospitality was completely overcome by Northern hospitality.

D[empsey] W[ardlaw] SEIGLER[98] [20th South Carolina, Co. B]

---

98. D. W. Seigler was the last surviving Confederate Veteran living at the Confederate Home in Columbia, SC. "Col. Seigler, Last Veteran At Home, Dies." The State [Columbia, SC] 12 Aug. 1944: 1. Print.

Appendix A

Confederate Order of Battle at Gettysburg for South Carolina Troops

Army of Northern Virginia - General Robert E. Lee

First Corps - Lt. Gen. James Longstreet

McLaws' Division – Maj. Gen. Lafayette McLaws

Kershaw's Brigade – Brig. Gen. Joseph B. Kershaw

2nd South Carolina Infantry –
Col. John D. Kennedy,
Ltc. Franklin Gaillard,
Maj. William Wallace

3rd South Carolina Infantry –
Ltc. David Langston,
Maj. Robert C. Maffett,
Col. James D. Nance

7th South Carolina Infantry –
Col. David W. Aiken,
Ltc. Elbert Bland

8th South Carolina Infantry –
Col. John W. Henagan,
Maj. D. M. McCleod

15th South Carolina Infantry –
Col. William D. de Saussure,
Maj. William M. Gist

3rd South Carolina Battalion –
Ltc. William G. Rice, Maj. D. B. Miller

Hood's Division – Maj. Gen. John Bell Hood
    Henry's Artillery Battalion –
       Maj. Mathias W. Henry,
       Maj. John C. Haskell
     Charleston German Artillery –
       Cpt. William K. Bachman
     Palmetto Light Artillery – Cpt. Hugh R. Garden
Artillery Reserve – Col. James B. Walton
     Alexander's Artillery Battalion – Col. Edward P.
     Alexander
     Brooks Artillery – Cpt. William W. Fickling
Third Corps – Lt. Gen. Ambrose P. Hill
    Pender's Division –
       Maj. Gen William Dorsey Pender,
       Brig. Gen. James H. Lane,
       Maj. Gen. Isaac R. Trimble
      McGowan's Brigade – Col. Abner M. Perrin
       1st South Carolina Infantry (Provisional Army) –
       Maj. Charles W. McCreary
       1st South Carolina Rifles –
       Cpt. William M. Hadden
       12th South Carolina Infantry –
       Col. John L. Miller,
       Maj. E. F. Bookter
       13th South Carolina Infantry –
       Ltc. Benjamin T. Brockman,
       Maj. Isaac F. Hunt
       14th South Carolina Infantry –
       Ltc. Joseph N. Brown,
       Maj. Edward Croft,
       Cpt James Boatwright
    Artillery Reserve – Col. Reuben L. Walker
     Pee Dee Artillery –
       Lt. William E. Zimmerman

Cavalry Units

Stuart's Division – Maj. Gen. J. E. B. Stuart
    Hampton's Brigade – Brig. Gen. Wade Hampton
        1st South Carolina Cavalry – Col. John L. Black
        2nd South Carolina Cavalry – Maj. T. J. Lipscomb
        Stuart's Horse Artillery – Maj. Robert F. Beckham
        Hart's Battery – Cpt. James F. Hart

Bibliography

Newspapers:

The Sumter Watchman and Southron; Sumter, S.C.

Fairfield News Herald; Winnsboro, S.C.

Atlanta Journal; Atlanta, Ga.

Manning Times; Manning, S.C.

Confederate Veteran Magazine

Newberry Herald and News; Newberry, S.C.

Laurens Advertiser; Laurens, S.C.

Edgefield Advertiser; Edgefield, S.C.

Aiken Standard; Aiken, S.C.

National Tribune; Washington, D.C.

News and Courier; Anderson, S.C.

Laurens County Advertiser; Laurens, S.C.

The Anderson Intelligencer; Anderson, S.C.

Keowee Courier; Walhalla, S.C.

Winnsboro News and Herald; Winnsboro, S.C.

The Charleston Daily News; Charleston, S.C.

The News; Frederick, Md.

Pickens Sentinel; Pickens, S.C.

Standard and Review; Aiken, S.C.

Published Primary Sources

Brooks, U. R. Butler and His Cavalry in the War of Secession, 1861-1865. Columbia, SC: State, 1909.

Brooks, U. R. and D. B. Rea. Stories of the Confederacy. Columbia, SC: State, 1912.

Caldwell, J. F. J. The History of a Brigade of South Carolinians, Known First as "Gregg's" and Subsequently as "McGowan's Brigade." King & Baird, Printers, 1866.

Dawes, "Service with the Sixth Wisconsin Volunteers", (Marietta, Ohio: E. R. Alderman and Sons, 1890.

Dickert, D. Augustus. History of Kershaw's Brigade. Newberry, SC: Elbert H. Aull, 1899.

Haskell, John Cheves, Gilbert E. Govan, and James Weston. Livingood. The Haskell Memoirs. New York: G.P. Putnam's Sons, 1960.

Perrin to Bonham, "Mississippi Valley Historical Review," 522.

Reports of Brig. Gen. Wade Hampton, C. S. Army, commanding brigade, with congratulatory orders JUNE 3-AUGUST 1, 1863.--The Gettysburg Campaign O.R.-- SERIES I--VOLUME XXVII/2 [S# 44].

Report of Brig. Gen. J. B. Kershaw, O.R.-- SERIES I--VOLUME XXVII/2 [S# 44].

Shooter, Washington, Captain Shooter letter, Drumbeat, newsletter of the Charleston Civil War Round Table, June 1989.

Welch, Spencer Glasgow. A Confederate Surgeon's Letters to His Wife. New York: Neale Pub., 1911.

Published Secondary Sources

Cisco, Walter Brian. Wade Hampton: Confederate Warrior, Conservative Statesman. Washington, D.C.: Brassey's, 2004.

Daly, Louisa Haskell. Alexander Cheves Haskell; the Portrait of a Man. Norwood, MA: Priv. Print. at the Plimpton, 1934.

De Leon T. C., Belles, Beaux, and Brains of the 60's. New York: G.W. Dillingham, 1909.

Gottfried, Bradley M., Brigades of Gettysburg: The Union and Confederate Brigades at the Battle of Gettysburg. Cambridge, MA: Da Capo, 2002.

Harman, Troy. "Hunterstown 1863, Battle History." Hunterstown 1863., 2008. Web. 14 Nov. 2015.

Hemphill, James Calvin. "James Ezra Tindal." Men of Mark in South Carolina: Ideals of American Life: A Collection of Biographies of Leading Men of the State, Vols1-3. Washington: Men of Mark Pub, 1907.

Johnson, Robert Underwood, and Clarence Clough Buel. "The Struggle for Round Top." Battles and Leaders of the Civil War. Being for the Most Part Contributions by Union and Confederate Officers. New Introd. by Roy F. Nichols. Vol. 3. New York: T. Yoseloff, 1956.

Jones, J. Keith. "The Boys of Diamond Hill: The Lives and Civil War Letters of the Boyd Family of Abbeville County, South Carolina". Jefferson, NC: McFarland, 2011.

Miller, J. Michael. "Perrin's Brigade on July 1, 1863." Gettysburg Magazine 13 (1995).

Pfanz, Harry W. Gettysburg, the Second Day. Chapel Hill: U of North Carolina, 1987.

Shevchuk, Paul M. "The Cavalry Fight at Fairfield, Pennsylvania, July 3, 1863." Gettysburg Magazine 1 (1989).

Tagg, Larry. The Generals of Gettysburg: The Leaders of America's Greatest Battle. Campbell, CA: Savas Pub., 1998.

Wise, Jennings C. The Long Arm of Lee ; Or, The History of the Artillery of the Army of Northern Virginia: With a Brief Account of the Confederate Bureau of Ordnance. Lynchburg, VA: J.P. Bell and, 1915.

Wittenberg, Eric J. Gettysburg's Forgotten Cavalry Actions: Farnsworth's Charge, South Cavalry Field, and the Battle of Fairfield, July 3, 1863. New York: Savas Beatie, 2011.

Wyckoff, Mac. "Kershaw's Brigade at Gettysburg." Gettysburg Magazine 5 (1991).

List of Images

Index

About the Author

J. Keith Jones is a two-time winner of the Gold Medal for History from the Military Writers Society of America for "The Boys of Diamond Hill: The Lives and Civil War Letters of the Boyd Family of Abbeville County, South Carolina" and "Georgia Remembers Gettysburg." A graduate of the University of South Carolina, he is a veteran of the information technology industry.

Keith has authored articles that have appeared in Gettysburg Magazine and Georgia Magazine as well as other publications. In addition to history, he also writes fiction. Keith lives in North Carolina with his wife Melissa and two rambunctious cats.

Photograph Credits

The photographs in this book are reproduced by permission and courtesy of the following:

Archivo Fotográfico de Montevideo (Photographic Archives of Montevideo):
  pages 76 (top), 81, 106, 107, 157 (left and right), 169, 202
Archives of the Asociación Granados-Marshall (Barcelona): pages 63, 64, 65, 73
Vani Leal de Carlevaro: pages 167, 239
Alfredo Escande: pages xiv, 2, 12, 20, 21, 68, 69, 76 (bottom), 77, 87, 95, 96, 163, 168, 191,
  192, 193, 207, 219, 241, 243, 289, 305 (bottom), 332 (left and right), 347
Ramón Ávila: page 339
Archives of the Fundación Andrés Segovia (Linares, Spain): pages 8, 71 (right)
Hemeroteca Digital de la Biblioteca Nacional de España (Digitalized Periodical Files
  of the National Library of Spain): page 84
International Guitar Research Archive (Music Department, California State
  University at Northridge): pages 50, 86, 260
The Puig Madriguera family: pages 23, 36, 39, 45, 47, 55, 62, 71 (left), 93, 103, 105, 108,
  110, 123, 125, 128, 129, 137, 141, 147, 151, 153, 170, 174, 177, 186, 187 (left and right), 199,
  200, 209, 225, 231, 235, 263, 267, 279, 281, 287, 293, 295, 296, 297, 298, 303, 305 (top),
  306, 308, 315, 322, 324, 325, 327 (left and right), 333, 335 (top and bottom), 336
Corazón Otero: page 217
Frédéric Zigante: pages 85, 139